Women in Islam

'It is the most detailed, carefully written book on this subject.'
Ursula King, *University of Bristol*

'. . . its major strength is to take women's issues seriously but in a way that takes traditional authority within Islam equally seriously and enables a fruitful debate between Muslim men, Muslim women, traditional Islamic learning and western academic discourse.'
Martin Forward, *Academic Dean*, *Wesley House*, *Cambridge*

The position of women in Islam is the subject of ongoing debate in both the Muslim world and the West. To a large extent, it is a debate triggered by the cultural encounter between Islam and the West. *Women in Islam: the western experience* investigates and illustrates those ways in which Islamic perceptions of women and gender relations tend to undergo significant change in western Muslim communities. Western notions of gender equality and individual freedom are shown to be a major influence upon Islamic discourse in the West. On the one hand this engenders a defensive Islamic response, entailing a tightening of the social constraints upon Islamic women. On the other hand, a progressive view sees rapprochement between Islamic and western ideas. Anne Sofie Roald shows how the cultural encounter between Islam and the West gives rise to fresh interpretations of Islamic texts, promoting new Islamic understandings in relation to issues of gender. Islamic attitudes towards such social concerns as gender relations in both micro and macro society, female circumcision and Islamic female dress emerge as responsive to culture and context, rather than rigid and inflexible, as is often perceived.

Anne Sofie Roald is Associate Professor at IMER (International Migration and Ethnic Relations), Malmö University, Sweden. A converted Muslim of Norwegian origin, she is the author of numerous articles on women in Islam.

Women in Islam

The western experience

Anne Sofie Roald

London and New York

First published 2001
by Routledge
11 New Fetter Lane, London EC4P 4EE

Simultaneously published in the USA and Canada
by Routledge
29 West 35th Street, New York, NY 10001

Reprinted 2002

Routledge is an imprint of the Taylor & Francis Group

Typeset in Times by
Florence Production Ltd, Stoodleigh, Devon
Printed and bound in Great Britain by
MPG Books Ltd, Bodmin

British Library Cataloguing in Publication Data
A catalogue record for this book is available from the British Library

Library of Congress Cataloging in Publication Data
Roald, Anne Sofie.
Women in Islam: the Western experience/Anne Sofie Roald
p.cm
Includes bibliographical references and index.
1. Muslim women–Europe. 2. Women in Islam–Europe. I. Title

HQ1170.R63 2001
305.48′697104–dc21 2001020407

ISBN 0–415–24895–7 (hbk)
ISBN 0–415–24896–5 (pbk)

To Adly without whose love, help, and encouragement this book would never have been written

To my children Hamza, Yaaser and Sondos

Contents

Preface

The present study is about the cultural encounter between 'Islam' and 'the West' with respect to gender attitudes among Arabic-speaking Islamists in Europe. The gender issue has been a hot potato in the debate about Islam among non-Muslims as well as in the discussion within the Muslim group. On the one hand, I have experienced constant accusations from non-Muslims that Islam is a religion hostile towards women. On the other hand, Muslims have expressed the belief to me that there was never a gender issue in Islam until 'the West' began to interfere in Muslim matters, suggesting that in their view an ideal gender pattern already exists in Islam and is present in Muslim society. It seems that cultural behaviour might be perceived from different perspectives from both sides in the cultural encounter between Muslims and non-Muslims. I write 'cultural behaviour' as I believe that what many from both sides judge to be Islamic very often turns out to be the Islamic sources interpreted through cultural experiences. The question of what are cultural and what are Islamic practices is the subject of ongoing discussion. Some researchers would, for instance, according to a contextual definition of religion claim that what Muslims believe is Islamic is part of Islam,[1] whereas many Muslims would define Islam as that which is written in the sources. With regard to the standpoint of these researchers, they regard 'Islam' as a discourse and have difficulties in distinguishing between 'high' and low' Islam. On the other hand, Muslims who claim that 'Islam' is what is written in the sources fail to observe the close link between religious manifestations and their surroundings. The historical development of Islamic law is an indication of how interpretations of the social issues in the Islamic sources are the result of dynamic interactions between Islamic scholars and society. There are probably some who would argue against the influence of culture on Islamic faith and practices by saying that the differences between the law schools rest on different levels of access to hadiths (narratives relating deeds and utterances of the Prophet). However, during my research into Islamic jurisprudence I have discovered that various scholars have different criteria in judging the authenticity of hadiths. In my view this might to a great extent be a result of cultural influences: the question of which hadiths are accepted as authentic becomes a matter of their compatibility with the particular scholar's social environment.

As cultural developments influenced the process of interpretation of social issues during the formative period of Islamic thought, likewise European cultural attitudes might influence the constitution of Islamic social ideas and practices in Europe. Cultural and religious customs which are not harmonious with the new context may be altered or modified on a conscious or an unconscious level.

What has come to dominate in the contemporary debate on gender and religion in general is what June O'Connor terms 'the three Rs of rereading, reconceiving, and reconstructing tradition' (O'Connor in King 1995: 45; see also O'Connor 1989). In O'Connor's terminology, 'rereading' means to review the religious sources according to 'women's presence and absence, women's words and women's silence, recognition given and denied women' (O'Connor 1989: 102). 'Reconceiving women' means in O'Connor's terminology to recover 'lost sources and suppressed visions' (O'Connor 1989: 103). 'Reconstruction' is explained first as a reconstructing of the past 'on the basis of new information and the use of historical imagination', and second as 'employing new paradigms for thinking, seeing, understanding, and valuing' (O'Connor 1989: 104). In an Islamic context the three Rs may be reduced to two Rs, namely the reselection or the rehierarchisation of source material, and the reinterpretation of the same. I identify these two categories since they are more relevant to the sphere of Islam. As the source material on social issues exists and is well known, questions revolve around what material to select (reselection) and which perspective to choose in the interpretation (reinterpretation) of the material.

Similarly to other world religions, the traditional interpretation of the social issues in the Islamic sources is androcentric.[2] As many Muslim women pursue higher education, they tend to look at the traditional Islamic gender pattern as an androcentric social construct, rather than as reflecting a divine order in terms of gender. Thus on a conscious level, Muslim and Islamic feminists are engaged in reselecting and reinterpreting the Islamic sources. Moreover, in the cultural encounter with western society, Muslims in general, male and female, may also rethink tradition in the pattern of the two Rs, but on an unconscious rather than on a conscious level.

Eric Winkel, an American convert to Islam, speaks of the reinterpretation of Islamic sources in terms of the establishment of 'an Islamic legal discourse'. He describes this as 'the discursive arena in which issues of societal importance get worked out. The legal discourse of Islam may be conceived of as a more or less flexible superstructure erected over the shari'a' (Winkel 1995: 3). In my view, Winkel's concept of 'the Islamic legal discourse' offers an adequate description of the recent process of change within Islamic legislation. According to Winkel, traditional Muslim practices such as clitoridectomy, which in a modern world has become a symbol of backwardness and female oppression, should be addressed within the framework of Islamic legal discourse. The objective of such a discourse is to look at the Islamic message as a whole and interpret ideas and practices from various angles in order to find solutions which are compatible with a broader understanding of Islam. The various shades of interpretation indicate a multiplicity of perspectives within the broad framework of Islamic creed that enable one to find perspectives suitable to one's time and place. The development of the Islamic concept of *shūrā* is an indicator of how other concepts might change in the future. In the 1970s and the beginning of the 1980s, many Muslims regarded *shūrā* as being different to a greater or lesser extent from western democracy, whereas in the mid-1980s and 1990s their understanding of the concept has changed to include western democracy as well as alternative democratic models (Roald 1994: 198).

The introduction by women of a female perspective into the interpretation of social issues in the sources has been a significant trend of the 1980s and 1990s. As female education increases, more women are coming into a position whereby they can take an active part in the discourse of Islamic legislation. Although there are certain requirements which must be fulfilled in order to be an Islamic scholar and few women today have the particular education demanded for this task, female influence in changing norms of Islamic behaviour is likely to increase as more and more women attain positions of social influence. As some Islamist movements have also opened up ways for women to participate in administrative bodies, female influence seems set to increase.

I am a Norwegian by birth and I converted[3] to Islam in 1982. At the time of my conversion I was a student at the Institute of Religious Studies at Oslo University. During my university courses I was faced with literature on Islam written by non-Muslims, and during my visits to the local mosques I was invited to read Muslims' own writings. There was a great discrepancy between the two camps and I discovered that authors from both sides had problems with distinguishing between 'Islam' and 'culture'. In 1985 I married a Muslim of Palestinian origin and we moved to Sweden, where I eventually became a lecturer and researcher at Lund University. As I pursued my Ph.D. I set aside the issue of gender, although I continued to feel great concern for women's issues in all areas of life. When I completed my Ph.D. dissertation I decided the time had come to look more deeply into the role of women and gender relations in Islam. As a converted Muslim of Norwegian origin, I regard myself to be in a middle position between European majority society and immigrant Muslim communities, with the possibility of making myself heard in both camps. I am therefore engaged in dialogue both between religious groups and between majority society and immigrants in general. Moreover, I always seem to come back to gender, first and foremost because it is a specific interest of mine but also because it appears to be *the* issue in all dialogue and discussion. The image of the suppressed Muslim woman is ubiquitous, and as I find it difficult to identify with such an image I think there is an urgent need to investigate the matter of gender in Islam.

The present study is not, however, a feminist study of gender in Islam. I do not regard myself as a feminist, but I consider the empowerment of Muslim women to be an important issue. In my view, many of the gender studies conducted by Muslim or Islamic[4] feminists tend to exclude the male perspective in favour of the female, while I consider it important to include both men and women in the process of interpreting Islamic sources. I understand the argument of Muslim and Islamic feminists that women have been oppressed for so long that women's rights can only be obtained by a radical change of perspective. However, contrary to many Muslim and Islamic feminists who do not take contemporary Islamic male scholars' views into consideration in their studies, I have observed a shift in these scholars' perceptions of women which I think it is important to nurture. One should not disregard the fact that men are still the ones who are listened to in Muslim society and Muslim communities in Europe, and by entering into fruitful cooperation with these scholars Muslim women might achieve greater influence in religious issues as well as in wider society. The importance for men and women of staying together is rooted in my conviction that in much research and thought about 'male' versus 'female', there is a tendency to forget the third party which is the child. In order to build a sound family and a sound society all parts have to fulfil their duties and thereby obtain their rights.

The prominent position of family life in Islam is reflected in the Islamic sources and in Islamic law. Many Muslims regard the family as the fundamental unit of society and the family's role is considered central in raising and educating children. The educational slogan of the founder of the Muslim Brotherhood, Ḥasan al-Bannāʾ – the individual Muslim (*al-fard al-muslim*), the Muslim home (*al-bait al-muslim*), and the Muslim Umma (*al-umma al-muslima*) (al-Bannāʾ 1984: 235) – points to the importance of the family in the establishment of Islamic society. Moreover, as the Muslim woman has been regarded as the most essential member of the family, the protection of women's traditional role has been one of the main topics of Islamist literature, particularly from the early nineteenth century. The maintenance of the family's spiritual status seems to be regarded in terms of the role of women in Muslim society.

Like Islamic feminists such as Amina Wadud-Muhsin and Riffat Hassan (Wadud-Muhsin 1992; Hassan 1990), I have discovered during research into the Islamic sources, Islamist literature and Islamic scholars' opinions, that the sources have often been interpreted both by historical and contemporary scholars from a male perspective. In addition, it seems that hadiths with weak narrator chains have been used to reinforce androcentric attitudes. The Egyptian Islamic scholar, ʿAbd al-Ḥalim Abū Shaqqa, has drawn attention to this fact in his investigation into the status of women in the time of the Prophet (Abū Shaqqa 1990).

When I started the research I saw my first task to be that of coming to terms with what is 'Islam' and what is 'culture', and I decided to investigate what is written in the Islamic sources. However, at an early stage I realised that what is written is not always what matters. This principle became evident during discussions with my colleague and former supervisor, Jan Hjärpe, and during the seminar of Islamology at University of Lund directed by him. One of Professor Hjärpe's recurring themes is that the function of a text is more important than the text itself, which implies that although something is written down, the written text does not always influence practice in actuality or as debated among various factions of Muslims. At the end of the day, it is the function of the text or how this particular text is perceived, which counts. When I understood this, I decided to look into the contemporary debate, both written and oral, in order to identify which ideas are prominent.

The contemporary Muslim debate is dominated by Islamists. By Islamist I mean a Muslim who regards Islam as a body of ideas, values, beliefs and practices encompassing all spheres of life, including personal and social relationships, economics and politics. As Islamists, particularly Arab Islamists, are often leaders within Muslim communities in Europe and thus in a position to influence these communities, I found it appropriate to limit the research to the intellectual Arab Islamist debate. In order to analyse the contemporary Islamic debate in Europe it has been necessary to turn to classical commentaries on the Koran as these still play a role in Arab Islamists' life, and to Arab Islamist writings in both European and non-European societies. It is important to link the European Islamic debate with the non-European debate, since although the all-encompassing globalisation process tends to be a 'globalisation of Western localism', the globalisation of ideas has also resulted in certain Islamic ideas becoming widespread on various continents. Islamic scholars in Muslim societies might therefore influence the thought of Islamic scholars and Muslims in Europe, and vice versa.

Changes in attitudes towards and perceptions of women might appear threatening for many Muslims who believe that Islam has a static foundation that, if disturbed, would cause any social and moral order built upon it to decline. This is an attitude I have often encountered during my fieldwork. I often heard the opinion expressed that lack of restrictions for women and childhood education would eventually undermine Islamic practice. In contrast to this, I also met the opposite attitude where change and openness to the cultural traits of others were regarded as being the only possibility for the survival of Islam both in the European context and in the Muslim world. These contrasting points of view reflect the breadth of ideas in the contemporary Islamic debate. In the following chapters I represent various points of view, since I consider it important to demonstrate the diversity of ideas rather than presenting one point of view as 'the only truth'.

In my early years of conversion to Islam, a journalist invited myself and three other Scandinavian converts to explain our reasons for converting. All four of us started with the standard formula that the main reason for our conversion was the security Islam represented with its clear and well-defined rules in all matters of life. The journalist asked us questions such as, is abortion acceptable in Islam? and, are men expected to follow a strict dress-code as women are? etc. To every question we had to respond that among Muslims there are differences in interpretation. Finally, the journalist asked how we could say that there are strict and fixed rules for everything in Islam, if in most cases there are differences in interpretation. At that stage I realised that he was right. When I later came to participate in various Islamic conferences in Europe, it was my experience that scholars would differ in points of view but that they would all present their particular ideas as 'the only truth'. I realised that this was a challenge which I could not resist. From then on I decided that, instead of accepting the views of others, I would investigate matters for myself and find out what the sources say, as well as looking into how scholars have interpreted these issues through history.

I became aware of the benefit of looking into the classical commentaries on the Koran and the Islamic sources when I read the American convert Amina Wadud-Muhsin's book, *Qur'an and Woman* (1992). Her approach to the study of women in Islam opened up the possibility of not only evaluating changes from one cultural setting to another, but also of understanding the immense breadth of interpretations of the social issues in the Islamic sources. The present study is therefore a result of an investigation into interpretations of social issues in the Islamic sources from various time-periods and different cultural settings with an emphasis on the contemporary European context.

In the cultural encounter between Arabic-speaking Muslims and the European cultural pattern, traditional notions of gender and gender relations are challenged. In order to evaluate whether western cultural attitudes play a part in immigrants' reconception of the Islamic family pattern, I applied a model with two poles which might be understood in terms of opposing ideals – 'Arab culture' and 'western culture'.[5] It is of interest to investigate how the Islamic texts relate to these two cultural patterns in the immigration situation in Europe.

Previous research

Studies on women in Islam have been many and of varying quality. Islamic scholars have written on different subjects within the field of gender issues. These scholars have, however, first and foremost been concerned with the area of female covering and the social segregation of the sexes. The issues they have raised revolve around questions such as whether women should cover their faces and hands or whether they should only wear a headscarf, and the degree to which men and women should be segregated in society: should girls and boys attend the same classes? Is it possible for men and women to work together? etc. From the late 1980s Muslim women have become active in the debate and have thus introduced a female perspective. Many of the Islamic books on women deal with questions which arise out of the antagonism between non-Muslims and Muslims. Some of them are apologetic reactions to this antagonism, whereas others are scholarly works of high quality such as Wadud-Muhsin's book (Wadud-Muhsin 1992).

The difference between my study and previous studies on the same topic is the notion of change and the particular forms of expression which Islam has assumed in Europe. I believe that this cross-cultural study might identify changes as well as contributing to such changes, since I am both an observer and, as most observers also are, a participant in the debate. Moreover, the work is inter-disciplinary, since it looks at texts from various angles and at empirical evidence.

I have been careful to cite the source material in a proper way, as I have often been upset by the way serious Islamic scholars and Islamists tend to deal with this. Hadiths tend to be mentioned without any reference to precise sources where they can be located. As I discovered during the process of this study, some scholars even appeal to hadiths with weak narrator chains in arguing for their particular points of view. The importance of accurate referencing cannot be over-emphasised, and the example of the Islamic scholar, Naṣir ad-Dīn al-Albānī (d. 1999), is outstanding in this respect, as he tends to give accurate references for every single hadith he quotes. It is interesting to note that the use of proper references was more common in past Islamic history than it has been recently. For instance, in Ibn Jawzī's (d. 1201) book on women, he not only gives accurate references but he also mentions the strength of the narrator chains.

Organisation of the book

Chapter 1 presents a theoretical discussion of how Muslims have been perceived in a western context. I then give an account of Islamic self-definition in terms of how Muslims perceive and identify themselves.

Chapter 2 discusses Islam and Arab Islamist movements in Europe. Although I refer to various groups I have chosen to investigate only the four main movements and trends: the Muslim Brotherhood, the Islamic Liberation Party, the *salafī* trend, and a more independent Islamist trend which I have label the *post-ikhwān* trend.

Chapter 3 gives the criteria for the selection of informants and interviewees[6] for this study. I also discuss issues related to fieldwork in consideration of my own roles as both a researcher and a Muslim.

Chapter 4 offers a theoretical discussion of the processes of change. The concepts referred to in this chapter are applied in the fieldwork material and the literary analysis in Part II.

Part II deals with various theological issues concerning women. In Chapter 5 I discuss sharia, and I indicate ideas of change in sharia as well as looking into some legal concepts. Chapter 6 deals with Islamic attitudes towards women in general and discusses attitudes encountered in the Islamic debate. After looking into the written material, historical as well as contemporary, I offer a presentation of attitudes which I found among Islamists in Europe. This pattern is repeated in all subsequent chapters where gender relations, polygyny, divorce and child custody, women's political participation, female circumcision and last but not least the issue of female 'veiling', are discussed.

With regard to transliteration, I have used the system of the *Encyclopaedia of Islam* with the exception of two letters: instead of *k* with a dot under it, I have used *q*; and instead of a *dj* I have used *j*. Although the *Encyclopaedia of Islam* recommends the use of *al-* and *'l-* for the definite article, I have chosen to use *al-* and *l-* only. Furthermore, the *Encyclopaedia of Islam* applies the diphthong *ay*, whereas I use *ai*. I have chosen not to transliterate some words, such as for instance hadith, sharia and jihad, as they have acquired common usage even in European languages.

Concerning the transliteration of proper names, I have transliterated Arabic names according to the method described above. However, for those writers who have written books in a European language, such as for instance Jamal Badawi, Fatima Mernissi and Nawwal Essadawi, I have retained the spelling of their names as they appear, since they are known by these spellings in the European context.

In the bibliography, authors with Arabic names that begin with definite articles such as 'al-' and 'at-' are listed according to their main surnames. For example, al-Hibri is included under 'H'.

As for the translation of the Koran, I mainly make use of Muhammad Asad's and Muhammad Pickthall's translations, but also do my own translations based on theirs. The hadiths in the study are my own translations.

I have conducted interviews with Islamists in Arabic, English and Scandinavian. Where the interviews are conducted in Arabic or Scandinavian, I have indicated this by adding [translation mine] to quotations.

The following study anticipates change in gender issues in Islam, but it is also a demonstration of the strength of continuity in the Islamic message. In the Islamic debate, the hermeneutic approach seems to work as a conserving factor, creating an understanding of Islam which might be suitable in changing circumstances. As will be demonstrated, Islamic ideas continue to flourish within new contexts, and as patriarchal attitudes give way, female perspectives are strengthened within these new contexts.

Acknowledgements

This study would not have been accomplished without the much-appreciated help of friends and colleagues and the financial support of The Swedish Research Council for Humanities and Social Research. During my research I was also given a travel grant by Zonta association in Lund.

First and foremost, my thanks go to my husband, Adly Abu Hajar, without whose assistance this study would never have come into being. His contribution in discussions with those I interviewed increased the effectiveness of the interviews. Furthermore, his support and our frequent discussions about the issue of women in Islam helped me to develop my ideas more fully throughout the study.

My six-month stay at the University of Wales in Lampeter as a research fellow in 1995–6 gave me a base for my fieldwork. I thank the staff and students at this university for their helpful contributions to my work.

I offer my special thanks to all my informants and interviewees in Great Britain, France, Holland, Belgium and the Scandinavian countries, and I also thank the Islamic scholars such as Rāshid al-Ghannūshi, Sheikh Aḥmad ʿAlī al-Imām and Sheikh Muḥammad Darsh, who willingly answered all my questions no matter how provocative these questions were. It was with great regret that I learned about the death of Sheikh Darsh during the course of this study. His wisdom and his humorous commentaries will be sorely missed by the Muslim Umma in Europe.

During the course of writing, I attended the Seminar of Islamology at the University of Lund and I thank the participants in this seminar, in particular Professor Jan Hjärpe, Jonas Otterbeck, Jonas Svensson, Torsten Jansson, Philip Halldén, Per Ryding, Ahmad Gholam and Armin Dannenberger. I presented parts of this manuscript at the Immigrant Seminar at Lund University, led by Professor Eva Hamberg, and I thank the seminar participants for their helpful remarks. I also attended the interdisciplinary seminar, *Purgatorium*, where parts of the study were presented. I am grateful to the anthropologists, Sara Johnsdotter, Aje Carlbom and Peter Parker who participated in this seminar and offered me their insightful comments during our discussions.

Some parts of the study were discussed at a conference held by the International Muslim Women's Union (IMWU) in Copenhagen, where Sheikh Aḥmad Abū Laban also participated in the debate. I thank the IMWU's members and the other participants who contributed to the discussion.

Special thanks go to the human ecologist, Pernilla Ouis, with whom I have had many discussions that gave birth to new ideas. I also want to express my gratitude to my colleague, Ylva Vramming, who has always encouraged and supported my work.

I am grateful to Sheikh Sayyid ʿAzzām who has helped me with works on Islamic jurisprudence and has patiently answered my questions on ancient Islamic scholars. Sheikh Aḥmad ʿAlī al-Imām, Doctor ʿAbd ar-Raḥim ʿAlī and Nora Eggen have read through parts of the manuscript and Amina Lombard has critically read and corrected the style and language of the manuscript.

I also express my thanks to Professor Ursula King and Doctor Martin Forward, both of whom read and commented on my manuscript and suggested helpful improvements. Doctor Tina Beattie undertook the work of revising and editing the text for publication, for which I am very grateful.

For the second time, I have to ask my children, Hamza, Yaaser and Sondos, to forgive me for not giving them enough time. There is, however, some solace in the thought that the present study might help to make life a little easier for them in the future.

I have to be thankful to my parents. Without their support and their way of raising me to accept responsibility in my early years, I would never have managed to complete this study.

Finally, I would like to state that, although people have helped and supported me, I am the only one responsible for any imperfections in this study. I pray to God the Almighty to forgive the errors and mistakes I have made.

Malmö, March 2000
Anne Sofie Roald

Part I

Theoretical and methodological reflections

Introduction

Interpretations of social issues in the Islamic sources have always been affected by interaction with surrounding social structures. However, there has in the past been little awareness that this is the case, and as a result Islamic social life has been presented as an absolute divine system. The recent recognition among Muslims of alternative possibilities with regard to the structuring of society, even within the framework of Islam, can be attributed to the fact that the last half of the twentieth century has been an era of widespread migration. In Part I, I identify changes in attitude which might be anticipated as a result of the Muslim experience of migration, asking how Muslims have been perceived by non-Muslims and how Muslims perceive themselves. This leads me to reflect on a number of theoretical and methodological issues relating to the question of continuity and change in Muslim communities in Europe. In Part II I present empirical material which demonstrates the extent to which such changes have in fact taken place among Muslims.

In research into Islam, misunderstandings and misconceptions arise both from the side of researchers and from the side of those being researched. This leads me to explore the reasons why Muslims agree to be objects of research, and to ask if researchers sufficiently understand these reasons. What happens when the researchers are themselves Muslims? Does this influence their research findings? These questions are addressed in Chapter 1.

The Islamic presence in Europe is perceived as a homogenous mass. However, even within national groups there are wide variations in terms of class, education and ideological standpoints. Arabic-speaking Muslims are influenced by many organisations active in Europe and based in the Arab world, and their different approaches to the Islamic message mean that Muslims sometimes come to divergent answers in response to the same questions. In Chapter 2 I address some of the research implications of this.

Any research project such as this must define its boundaries, since the potential area of research is too vast to encompass within one study. This means recognising the partiality and limitations of the research, while identifying those groups and perspectives which are most significant in terms of the questions being asked. In Chapter 3 I explain the process of selection and I say why I chose to focus on particular groups and movements in the course of my research.

Chapter 4 discusses ways in which widespread migration initiates processes of change in Muslims' understanding of the Islamic message, with the introduction of new cultural paradigms challenging traditional solutions to problems. Patriarchal values and social structures, which are a common feature in many Arabic-speaking countries, have affected Islamic interpretations and legislation in social issues. In their encounter with European society with its notion of equality between the sexes,

Muslims tend to be influenced by the views of the dominant culture in their reinterpretation of social issues in the Islamic source material. Such changes are hard to evaluate in a scientific study so I have chosen a bi-polar model, with two cultural patterns on either end of a scale, in order to illustrate how they might take place in the Muslim diaspora.

1 Research on Muslims

Introduction

I begin this study with a discussion of how Islam and Muslims are perceived in a western context and how Muslims' search for identity in a new cultural context tends to create misconceptions between various groups in society. During the course of this study I have been asked why I have chosen to study Arab Islamists and not, for instance, Bosnians (who are the original European Muslims), South Asians or Turks. I have even been confronted by one researcher who compared my study of well-educated Arab Islamists to a study of groups of illiterate Turkish women in European suburbs. These questions point to the huge problem researchers on Muslims and Islam face in a European context which brings together diverse Muslim groups from different classes with different cultural, educational, ethnic and national backgrounds. On the one hand, the problem of the distinction, or rather the 'non-distinction', between various kinds of Muslims is a result of the widespread model of thinking in terms of 'us and them' such that unacceptable characteristics are projected onto 'them'. On the other hand, Muslims themselves also contribute to the confusion. As Islam is the feature which apparently distinguishes Muslims from non-Muslims, many who in their home countries would not identify themselves in terms of Islam, will regard themselves first and foremost as Muslims in the cultural encounter with 'the West'.

Muslims in contemporary research

I want to draw attention to how Islam and Muslims have often been perceived in the public arena, or more specifically in official debate, as well as in the academic world in non-Muslim societies. In a multi-cultural context there tends to be dissonance between the ways in which various cultural groups perceive each other. This might be true for whole societies as well. Psychologically speaking, a person would judge her/himself by her/his ideals whereas one tends to judge others by their practices, and this is also true of interaction between different cultural groups (Elias and

Scotson 1994). Muslims living in Britain, for instance, would judge the majority group, the British, as a homogeneous group, referring to it as 'the other', thus emphasising characteristics and behaviour which are most *apparently* different from their own. Moreover, they will judge, not in view of their own praxis, but in view of their Islamic ideal. The same is true for the British, who will judge the *apparent* characteristics of Muslims in view of their own ideal based upon a conception of what is typically British. As interaction between Muslims and the majority population in most of the western European countries seems to be limited, the *apparent*, i.e. the outstanding, characteristics of the other cultural group become those which are highlighted in comparison with one's own ideological stance. Apart from judging one's own group according to an ideal standard and judging outsider groups according to their actual practice or behaviour, individuals belonging both to the majority and the minority group tend to 'stereotype *themselves* as well as others in terms of their common attributes as group members' (Turner and Giles 1981: 39). Moreover, I have observed that there is a tendency on both sides to perceive the other group in terms of that which is regarded as most 'extreme' in relation to one's own stance or practice.

Kenneth Ritzén, a Swedish historian of religions, in his numerous lectures[1] on the relationship between Muslims and majority societies uses the following model to illustrate the relationship:

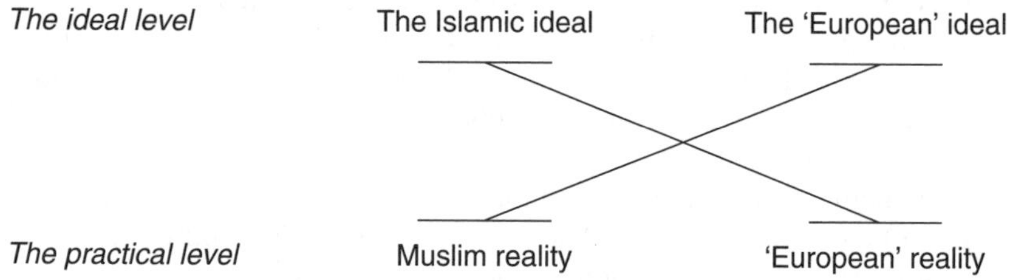

Figure 1

With regard to the majority society, those who have contact with Muslim immigrants and transmit their impressions to the rest of society are often social workers, teachers, etc. and they might focus on particularities of the group, such as identifying only problematic cases, rather than offering generalised descriptions. Moreover, the media has the potential to function as a mediator between various social groups but it is to a very large extent governed by the economic demands of promoting news, and news tends to be that which diverges from social norms. For instance, in Norway the Rushdie case had a powerful impact upon the ways in which the majority society perceived the Muslim minority. This was due to the fact that some Muslims of Pakistani origin who openly professed their support for the death sentence[2] were quoted in almost all newspapers and on radio and television programmes due to an assassination attempt on Rushdie's Norwegian publisher. Many Muslims in Norway publicly rejected the validity of the death sentence but they were not usually quoted in the media. The result was that Norwegians formed the impression that Muslims living in Norway supported the death sentence. The consequence of such mutual misconceptions, which arise as a result of the two levels of comparison described above, is increasing inter-group hostility.

In the academic sphere, similar dissonances in the perceptions of various cultural groups can be observed. According to two researchers, Fatme Göçek and Shiva Balaghi, studies of the Third World 'often contain Orientalist elements that treat social processes in cultures and societies other than [their own] as static or, at best, derivative' (Göçek and Balaghi 1994: 5). They claim that these studies tend to emphasise tradition in a way that establishes the idea of the tradition's immutability, since 'in order to justify its own hegemony, the western gaze needed to portray tradition in the Middle East as an immutable force' (Göçek and Balaghi 1994: 5). The Swedish researcher, Aleksandra Ålund, also points out how in the official debate in Sweden, 'the immigrant culture' is looked upon in terms of 'traditionalisms' in contrast to 'the detraditionalised Swedish culture' (Ålund 1991: 19). She further claims that in this picture 'stereotyped generalisations' about immigrant youths or immigrant women have made them become 'cases', and thus they have been exposed to 'negative fame', to use Michel Foucault's terminology (Ålund 1991: 19).

Edward Said's criticism of the occidental way of depicting Islam and Muslims has been regarded as polemic or provocative, but his arguments have created repercussions in the academic world. Said, in his book *Orientalism* (1979), calls attention to the close link between knowledge and power in the relationship between 'the West' and 'the Orient' (Said 1979).[3] Although as a scholar of contemporary literature Said has taken his material mostly from the literary sphere, one can read his analysis in political terms. He shows that knowledge is power since 'the Orient' could be ruled by 'the West' because 'the West' came to know 'the Orient'. However, at the same time Said also points out that the particular knowledge which 'the West' came to obtain about 'the Orient' was not always the same knowledge as 'the Orient' had about itself. A parallel argument which might also be interpreted in terms of this insider/outsider perspective is that of the French anthropologist, Louis Dumont, who suggests that social scientists tend to project their own prejudices onto the phenomena they are studying (Dumont 1977).[4]

In a later work, *Covering Islam* (1981), Said further discusses how Islam has been represented in western academia and in society at large. He points to the struggle which has gone on for centuries between Islam and 'the West', and he sees a connection between the contemporary stereotyping of Islam in western countries and the Middle East's oil supplies. He observes that there are huge generalisations on both sides, but the distinction between them lies in how the two entities have been presented. He writes:

> At present, 'Islam' and 'the West' have taken on a powerful new urgency everywhere. And we must note immediately that it is always the West, and not Christianity, that seems pitted against Islam. Why? Because the assumption is that whereas 'the West' is greater than and has surpassed the stage of Christianity, its principal religion, the world of Islam – its varied societies, histories, and languages notwithstanding – is still mired in religion, primitivity, and backwardness. Therefore, the West is modern, greater than the sum of its parts, full of enriching contradictions and yet always 'Western' in its cultural identity; the world of Islam, on the other hand, is no more than 'Islam', reducible to a small number of unchanging characteristics despite the appearance of contradictions and experiences of variety that seem on the surface to be as plentiful as those of the West.
>
> (Said 1981: 9–10)

It is interesting to note how Said uses the word 'Islam' in a geographical sense, which leads me to suggest that the opposition between 'Islam' and 'the West' might be perceived as a geographical opposition by a non-Muslim Palestinian such as Said. Since media stereotyping tends to equate Arabs with Islam, for example, or in many cases the Third World with Islam, a non-Muslim coming from a Muslim 'cultural sphere' might perceive such an opposition in geographical rather than in ideological terms.

Said further claims that 'the term "Islam" as it is used today seems to mean one simple thing but in fact is part fiction, part ideological label, part minimal designation of a religion called Islam' (Said 1981: x). He observes that 'there is a consensus on "Islam" as a kind of scapegoat for everything we do not happen to like about the world's new political, social, and economic patterns' (Said 1981: xv).

Said's discussion of the tension between 'the West' and 'Islam' is I believe grounded in the common debate in society in which the media is the main actor. When it comes to academic research on Islam and Muslims his analysis is not always applicable (cf. Rodinson 1991; Kepel 1985). What is apparent, though, is that there is a view of Islam in western countries which is different from the view of Islam that Muslims have. On the other hand, it is important to remember, as Said has rightly pointed out, that Muslims likewise tend to have distorted pictures of 'the West'. There is therefore a pattern of mutual misconceptions, and it is interesting to note how this pattern is very much a factor in the interaction between 'Islam' and 'the West', particularly on a general level.

In the academic sphere, I would argue that despite much excellent research, there are still researchers who, when dealing with Muslims or Islamists, tend to treat them as a homogeneous group (cf. Kepel 1993;

Zubaida 1989; Moghadam 1990). Although many researchers agree that Muslims in different countries follow various patterns of behaviour, this comprehension of Muslim heterogeneity has not always been extended to include the variety of Muslim immigrant communities in western European countries. For example, there has been great interest in the study of Muslim immigrant women but many of these studies – from undergraduate to post-doctoral level – represent Muslim women as a single entity (cf. Moghadam 1990).[5] Although efforts have been made to distinguish between Muslims of different nationalities, less importance has been attached to class and cultural backgrounds within one and the same national group. Furthermore, there has been insufficient awareness of the Muslim woman's relation to Islam. For a Muslim woman to emphasise her identity as a Muslim does not necessarily have to do with religious stances or religious feelings. Separation from their native countries and feeling that they are aliens in a foreign culture might push many Muslims to define themselves first and foremost as Muslims, whereas in different surroundings they would operate with other self-definitions. In such a situation 'Islam' tends to become a term of contrast which a Muslim woman might use to designate a traditional structure, history and society. Religious and ethnic identity cannot be isolated from other social influences. Claims to ethnicity, religiosity and gender might become means of expressing frustrations with prevailing cultural norms, which are then conceptualised by researchers who formulate theories and create social concepts.

Solh and Mabro have observed that some studies tend to be *theologo-centred* (El-Solh and Mabro 1994: 1), so that researchers interpret phenomena mainly from a religious point of view (cf. Huntington 1996; Pryce-Jones 1992; Sivan 1992). Other researchers take the opposite stance by omitting religion as an instrument of analysis in modern societies (cf. Mutalib 1990; Muzaffar 1987; Nagata 1984). I have observed that in the former approach, for example, researchers tend to talk in terms of *Islamic* politics when analysing the politics of *Muslim* states which often follow a secular political scheme (cf. Huntington 1996; Sivan 1992). With regard to the latter approach, my observations suggest that there is a one-dimensional horizontal analysis with no regard to the religious sphere, which in reality has a firm grasp on a great part of the world's population. Many Muslims view worldly and religious concerns as closely interwoven, yet researchers could miss the religious dimension which is important to take into account in the analysis of Muslim societies. This applies particularly to researchers who come from those parts of the world where the mainstream ideology demands a separation of church and state. An example of such horizontal analysis concerns discussion about Muslim women's veiling which has tended to be reduced to a socio-political phenomenon, since researchers do not consider the religious significance of the head-scarf/veil (*khimār*). However, although I am critical of studies which leave out some of these 'realities', I am also aware that all studies have to be selective. Given that the various fields of science have different methods and fields of interest, it is difficult for any one researcher to grasp the whole picture. Thus one must opt for a variable study which identifies one variable and presupposes other variables as constants.

The aim of this present study is in contrast to the two approaches to research outlined above, since I approach Islamic ideas as they are perceived by Islamists. I offer an 'insider's' perspective primarily due to my own relationship to Islam, but also because I give Islamists the opportunity to speak for themselves, thus presenting an 'inside' rationale for Islamist ideas and practices.

The political aspect of Islam

Many researchers on the recent Islamic resurgence concentrate on the political side of Islam while neglecting other aspects, which may be a consequence of the Islamist emphasis on political matters. With the nineteenth century's *salafīya* movement under the leadership of the anti-colonialist Jamāl ad-Dīn al-Afghānī, political issues came to the forefront of the intellectual debate. With the development of political ideologies in western society, Muslims began to define politics in an Islamic framework. Furthermore, Islamist political thought may have intensified as a direct result of the abolishment of the caliphate in 1924.

For centuries Islamic literature focused on rituals and matters related to micro society. Although most aspects of human life had been dealt with thoroughly, political life had to a large extent been separated from personal religiosity, and the development of Islamic political ideas suffered as a result. With the spread of *salafīya* ideas to the intellectual strata of society and with the increase in Muslim higher education from the 1960s onwards, these political ideas were adapted to twentieth century politics and the Islamic message was strengthened. Personal religiosity continued to exist side by side with the politicisation of Islam but it became less clearly recognisable. The traditional literature on matters of personal religiosity continued to be widely read and was regarded as applicable to Muslims of all times and places, but its influence was not perceptible to the observation of researchers. More obvious to them was the wide distribution of contemporary Islamic political literature and palpable social phenomena signifying religiosity such as 'veiling' and 'bearding'. Thus, researchers began to form the impression that Islam is mainly a political religion.

The emphasis on political Islamic thought in contemporary research on Muslims might also be attributable to the fact that religion in a western context tends to be considered as belonging to the personal sphere, which might make it difficult for researchers reared in such a tradition to wholly grasp the idea of Islam as 'a comprehensive system' (Roald 1994). In addition, Muslims themselves and particularly Islamists tend to speak in 'worldly' terms in their discussions with non-Muslims, thus conforming to non-Muslim perceptions. An example would be the way in which Islamists usually discuss women's veiling with non-Muslims. Veiling, which in an Islamic context is regarded as a religious phenomenon, is likely to be explained in worldly terms in discussion with non-Muslims. Muslims often explain to non-Muslim researchers that Muslim women cover their hair due to the importance of securing the family system or because of the need to see women in terms of their intellect and behaviour rather than their appearance. In such a discussion it is important to be aware of the various levels of argument that a respondent to a question might decide to use. It might be difficult to distinguish between the motive, the legitimation and what might simply be apologetic arguments in a respondent's statements. I will deal in more detail with such methodological problems later, but for now I would conclude that researchers' over-emphasis on particular issues might have to do with the nature of the cultural encounter which leads Muslims to appeal to worldly reasoning and hesitate to offer religious arguments.

Researchers of Islam and Muslims

It is important to ask *who* researchers of Islam and Muslims are, and what kind of educational backgrounds they have. Many studies of Muslims are conducted within the field of social sciences: anthropology, sociology, political science and international relations. Within these fields there is a tendency to emphasise theoretical and methodological matters, and social phenomena are often used to illustrate theories (cf. Turner 1994). Other researchers of Islam and Muslims come from the field of religious studies and particularly from the discipline of Islamology. As Jan Hjärpe has observed, in religious studies researchers' emphasis tends to be on material and religious phenomena. He has defined the two approaches, the social sciences' approach versus the religious studies' approach, as 'theory defined subjects' versus 'material defined subjects'.[6] It is significant that within the field of religious studies, particularly in Islamology, the method of focusing primarily on the interpretation of religious texts is decreasing and many researchers are relying more on methodologies associated with the social sciences. Religious studies encompasses methodologies drawn from a range of scientific disciplines such as sociology, anthropology and psychology. The different approaches within these various fields influence the outcome of the research.

Identity, role and role playing

I have already argued that the cultural encounter between non-Muslim researchers and Muslims might lead to misunderstandings or misconceptions. I believe this has as much to do with the tendency by Muslims to 'role play' in this cultural encounter as it has to do with some researchers representing Muslims in terms of 'western' standards. I would therefore like to draw attention to the problem of identity in a Muslim context. How do Muslims identify themselves and how can researchers identify and define Muslim identities – or role playing?

Identity might comprise the whole gamut of psychological, spiritual and material influences. At certain times or places particular issues are at stake which crystallise around the question of identity. Current controversies involve questions of ethnicity, gender, sexuality and religion. The question of identity becomes a question of *distinctiveness* or *oppositionality*, i.e. that which makes a person or a group *distinctive* from other persons or groups or that which makes them *oppositional* to others. Rapoport argues that ultimately

> all forms of identity, whether ethnic, religious, individual or whatever, depend on setting up a contrast with those who are different, i.e. have a different identity. These differences both separate and distinguish these social units and also lead to various forms of interaction or communication.
>
> (Rapoport 1981: 12)

In dictionaries a multitude of different meanings are attached to the term 'identity'. One of the suggestions is that 'identity' is the nature of something which remains unalterable under different conditions and different times. This definition leads into a philosophical discussion of the relation between *identity* and *continuity*, a philosophical concern since Heraclitus famously opined that we cannot step into *the same* river twice. Another common definition of 'identity' is 'the condition of being one thing and not another' (Rapoport 1981: 10). This definition depends upon the claim that 'the unit in question sees itself, and is seen by others, as being different to other units' (Rapoport 1981: 10). Kenneth Jones, on the other hand, explains identity as referring to the fact 'that one is *situated* within a series of social relations and *placed* as a social subject' (Jones 1978: 60). He goes on:

> The sustaining and modification of identity, established by social relationship and processes, is to a large extent a determinant of the social structure but, as Berger has said, this is a dialectical process in the sense that such identity does itself act upon the social structure.
>
> (Jones 1978: 60)

Jones concludes that identity is 'firmly rooted in social interaction and manifested in role performance' (Jones 1978: 74).

The understanding of identity involves both identity at an individual level and identity at a group level. Identity on an individual level comprises distinctive characteristics such as personality, physical and intellectual traits, and identity on a group level comprises social categories such as group-belonging, class, nationality and sex (Turner and Giles 1981: 38). Göçek and Balaghi have observed a tension between 'the social definition and the individual meaning of identity' (Göçek and Balaghi 1994: 7). They refer to Carolyn Steedman who explains that

> a modern identity, constructed through the process of identification, is at once a claim for absolute sameness, a coincidence and matching with the desired object, group, or person (perhaps a historical identity located on the historical past) and, at the same time, in the enclosed circuit of meaning, it is a process of individuation, the modern making of individuality and a unique personality.
>
> (Steedman 1991: 49, quoted in Göçek and Balaghi 1994: 7)

Steedman's description indicates the dilemma of female Islamists in Europe. On the one hand, there is the traditional identity of being a Muslim woman. This traditional identity is linked both to the home country and to the sacred text through the mediators of the text (the interpreters of the Koran and the hadiths, and the Islamic scholars). On the other hand, the Muslim woman is faced with a modern construction of female individuality that is independent of traditional biological and social roles. This process requires the individual to define her values and to choose the social model, whether Islamic or western or a blend of the two, that she wishes to conform to according to her needs and priorities.

The role of religion in the formation of identity

In Geertz's hermeneutic research model, religious systems are regarded as models *of* and *for* society (Geertz 1973). Religion, in this model, has to be regarded as part of identity at a group level. However, if religion is considered in transcendent terms, religious identity would be outside the realm of group identity and would apply at an individual level. Religious identity can therefore be said to manifest itself in different ways – at the level of group identity, individual identity or both – depending on how religion and religious sentiments are defined. Depending on such definitions, religious identity might provide material for a researcher's analysis on various levels.

At group level, religion gives people a tool to cope with the environment not only in a metaphysical sense, i.e. religion explains the inexplicable, but it is also perceived as a practical guide to behaviour in the material world and in this sense it becomes part of the social system. On an individual level, Hjärpe has observed that religion 'provides patterns of interpretation for what happens in one's personal life' (Hjärpe 1997: 267). Moreover, I have observed that religion gives the individual a way of expressing intense and fervent emotions. Many Muslim women of different nationalities have expressed their relations with the Divine in terms of love and intense feelings.[7] Several women have told me that sometimes during prayer or when they have their own personal 'conversation with God' they experience emotions similar to those one might encounter in a love relationship between a man and a woman. One Islamist woman suggested that the contemporary emphasis on relationships between men and women might be a substitute for people's lack of a personal relationship to God. 'The feeling of longing *thʿishq*) for God is a universal human instinct which has to be satisfied in one way or another,' she claimed.

I would define identity as those factors of a person's or a group's belief-system, nationality, ethnicity and class, educational background, rural or urban background, gender or sexuality which are highlighted at certain periods of time and in certain places in such a way that the various levels of identity are negotiable depending on circumstances. So, for example, a Syrian Muslim woman living in an urban area in Syria would probably emphasise neither her nationality nor her religion. She might be aware of her class background which would be a problem only if she belonged to the lower classes. It might also be that she would regard her gender as a matter of controversy, particularly if she were highly educated. For the same woman to live in Britain, however, her 'Muslimness', her nationality, her class and probably her gender would be matters of concern, and she would identify herself in these terms. In Muslims' encounter with non-Muslims, Islam therefore tends to become the identity marker no matter what relation the person has to Islamic rules and regulations. As long as one is part of the mainstream culture or belongs to the majority in society there is no need for an urgent quest for identity, but in minority situations these matters tend to be contrasted with mainstream opinions or characteristics and are rendered problematic.[8]

The search for identity

During my fieldwork on Islamic education in Malaysia and Pakistan in 1991–2, I discovered that there was an emphasis on both Muslim identity and Malay identity in Malaysia, where only slightly more than 50 per cent of the population are Muslims. Most Muslims are Malays, whereas the Chinese, who constitute approximately 35 per cent of the Malaysian population, mainly follow various Christian sects, Confucianism or Buddhism. The Hindu group constitutes approximately 10 per cent of the Malaysian population. As researchers on Malaysia such as Judith Nagata, Hussein Mutalib and Chandra Muzaffar (Mutalib 1990; Muzaffar 1987; Nagata 1984) are social scientists, they tend to regard Muslim religious identity in social terms. In their work there is a suggestion that Islamists' emphasis on Islamic identity is a mask for 'the real issue', which according to them is the ethnic identity of being a Malay. The consequence is that they omit the religious perspective from their analysis. Their main argument for reaching such a conclusion is that 'becoming Muslim' in the Malay language is equivalent to 'becoming Malay' (Nagata 1984; Muzaffar 1987). I think that the common conclusion of these researchers is due to the fact that their observation focused on only part of the search for identity of Malay Muslims. In my own research on Islamists in Malaysia I found that Malay Muslims tend to express their quest for identity in Islamic terms, which is most clearly manifest in their concern for alternative education (Roald 1994). Their efforts in the field of Islamic education have resulted in the establishment of Islamic schools and institutions with new curricula emphasising teaching from an Islamic viewpoint. In these schools there is an emphasis on children wearing Islamic dress which in Malaysia means that girls wear the traditional Malay dress, *Baju Kurong* and *Mini-telekong* (head-scarf). In the Malaysian Muslim Youth Movement's (ABIM) schools, boys were obliged to wear the traditional Malay ceremonial dress (*Baju Melaya*) on Fridays, due to the congregational Friday Prayer. I, in contrast to many other social scientists, do not interpret this as a particularistic approach but as evidence that Islamists express their 'Islamness' in various forms. In general I found that in the Islamic schools in Malaysia the emphasis in teaching and the curricula was not particularly focused on Malay or Malayness.

With regard to the Islamists' view on the education system as the basis for the formation of new generations, it was interesting to observe the lack of emphasis on ethnic sentiments in the theories and praxis of Islamic education (Roald 1994). In Malaysia, the highlighted identities are ethnic identity as opposed to the large Chinese ethnic group; Malay culture as opposed to both Chinese and Hindu culture and to the trend of 'westernisation', and lastly Muslim religious identity as opposed to the wide range of different religions which are flourishing in Malaysia. Thus, Islam and Muslimness become tools for the expression of distinctiveness from other groups. However, this does not mean that Islam and Muslimness are new phenomena for this ethnic group, neither does it mean that Islam and Muslimness are only 'tools', as suggested by Nagata and Mutalib. Islam was an important force in Malay society even before the 1969 revolt in Malaysia when it came into the forefront of the social struggle. It was, however, acting on a subliminal level rather than being a conscious tool for change (al-Attas 1978). In 1969 the political discourse changed. In Foucaultian terms one could say that Islamic terminology came to be 'within the discourse' (Foucault 1993) and it was well-suited to express distinctiveness from other groups in society. However, conflicts and struggles remained the same as before, with Islam as a substantial part of the conflicting pattern (Roald 1994).

The Malaysian example indicates how researchers have understood the politicisation of Islam in secular terms. I have suggested that on the one hand this might be due to the fact that Islamists' own discourse is expressed in worldly terms in the debate with secularised society. On the other hand, some social researchers have a tendency to over-emphasise the social aspect in their analysis of Islamic phenomena, thus disregarding ideas of religiosity within Islamism (see Nagata 1984; Muzaffar 1987; Kepel 1993).

Moving from Malaysia to Pakistan, I expected to find a much broader approach towards Islamic education with respect to the study of Islamic sources and the integration of worldly and religious matters in the educational system. Pakistan is often depicted as an Islamic state as the great majority of the population are Muslims with only a few per cent belonging to other religions. However, it became apparent to me that the Pakistan I encountered could hardly be characterised as an 'Islamic' state, but merely as a 'Muslim' state, as few phenomena or activities were actually referred to in terms of Islam. Islam as the dominant religion seems to have no function in the creation of identity, since identity is a matter of *distinctiveness* or *oppositionality*.

It is interesting to note that Muḥammad Iqbāl (d. 1938) and Abū al-Aʿlā al-Mawdūdī (d. 1979) from the Indian subcontinent were among the first scholars to raise the question of Islamic education (Roald 1994: 57–60). However, it is just as interesting to note that this occurred at a time when they were living in multi-cultural and multi-religious India. As al-Mawdūdī came to Pakistan after the partition of the subcontinent and established his Islamic movement (*Jama'at-i-Islami*) there, one could assume that this movement would be at the forefront of the campaign for Islamic education. However, when I met many of his followers in 1992 I came to realise that little effort or research was attached to this field in Pakistan. It also became apparent that those few schools which *had* an Islamic profile were careful not to announce this profile publicly. One headmaster of such a school explained:

> I try to have an Islamic direction in my school. However, I have to take care of not pronouncing this loudly. Pakistanis are not afraid of Islam as Islam is their beloved religion, but as it comes to education they seem to trust the secular schools more than the Islamic ones. Probably this is a result of the British colonialism, where we came to regard everything British as superior. If I told the parents that I want to have a focus on Islam in my school they would take their children out of school.

As the Koranic afternoon classes in mosques were well attended, it was obvious that it was not hostility towards Islam which made parents prefer secular schools. Rather it seems that parents had an understanding of Islamic education as consisting of exclusively 'religious studies'. In view of this, parents regarded the *official* Islamic education system as not socially 'useful' in comparison with the secular education system in terms of their children's career prospects.

The situation in Malaysia and Pakistan can be linked to the above discussion of identity. Whereas Islamic identity in Malaysia is a matter of *distinctiveness* and *antagonism* between groups in society in a way that provokes action, Islamic identity in Pakistan functions only to a limited extent as a sign of *distinctiveness* between groups. Most conflicts inside Pakistan are fought in ethnic or intra-Islamic (i.e. Shīʿī and Sunnī) terms.[9]

In Bernard Lewis' study *The Jews of Islam* (1984), he illustrates how *distinctiveness* or *oppositionality* has been a dominant factor in the sustained development of the Jewish people through history:

> A reading of medieval and modern Jewish history would seem to suggest that Jews in the Diaspora can only flourish, perhaps even only survive in any meaningful sense, under the aegis of one or the other of the two successor religions of Judaism–Christianity and Islam. Virtually the whole panorama of Jewish history, or rather that part of it which is of any significance between the destruction of the ancient Jewish centres and the creation of the new Jewish state, is enacted either in the lands of Islam or in the lands of Christendom.
>
> (Lewis 1984: ix)

Harold J. Abramson, a scholar on ethnicity and religion, expresses the same idea when he argues that 'it is only in contact between cultures, as in the classical role of migration, that ethnicity and religion assume a dynamic and social reality of their own' (Abramson 1979: 8). In the European context the cultural encounter between 'Islam' and 'the West' provokes an active response. Many Muslims turn to a Muslim identity and, as in Malaysia, the highlighted issue becomes, how can Muslims prosper? Moreover, for many Muslims in Europe as in Malaysia, Islam becomes a symbol of progress – Islam, not in a traditional sense, but in a new formulation where modern Islamic institutions are based on reselections or reinterpretations, both on an unconscious and on a deliberate level, of the Islamic sources.

Muslim self-definitions

Identity can be divided into smaller components. It has as much do with how one views oneself, i.e. one's *self-definition*, as it has to do with how one is perceived by others. In certain situations, *self-definition* might concur with others' perceptions. In minority/majority conflicts, however, others' perceptions tend to be expressed in stereotypical terms. Self-definitions also tend to change according to circumstances. For an Arabic-speaking Muslim woman living in a western European country, her self-awareness of being a Muslim would be pronounced in an environment of non-Muslims, whereas her nationality would be conspicuous in an environment of Muslims from other countries. In her own home, her identity as a woman would define her role, behaviour and work. A Muslim immigrant woman would often stress her Muslim identity in her meeting with western researchers. Sociologically speaking she is defined as a Muslim, and according to sharia she would be defined as a Muslim, since those who utter the *shahādatayn* (the two witnesses of faith) are regarded as belonging to the realm of Islam.[10] On the etic[11] level, Åke Sanders from the Institute of Ethnic Relations in Gothenburg, Sweden, has identified four categories of Muslims. A Muslim can either be an *ethnic*, a *cultural*, a *religious* or a *political* Muslim. An *ethnic* Muslim in this definition denotes a person who belongs to an ethnic group in which the majority of the population belongs to Islam; a *cultural* Muslim refers to a person who is socialised into a Muslim culture; a *religious* Muslim refers to a person who is performing the Islamic commands and a *political* Muslim refers to a person who 'claims that Islam in its essence primarily is (or ought to be) a political and social phenomenon' (Sanders 1997: 184–5). Sanders uses these categories in order to determine the number of Muslims in Europe, and his definition of an *ethnic* Muslim is particularly helpful in this respect. To arrive at an accurate figure is a difficult task as few European countries register religious affiliation. By regarding the whole Iranian group in Sweden as Muslims, for instance, it is possible to determine approximately the Muslim population of Sweden since the majority of Iran's population is Muslim. The use of Sander's categorisation in this sense is therefore acceptable.

While Sander's definitions might be relevant for researchers, particularly for quantitative research, I see it as essential for this particular study to turn to an emic definition, Islamists' own self-definition, in order to illustrate an Islamic manner of classification. In my fieldwork I have observed that the most common way for Muslims who adhere to the pillars of Islam such as praying, fasting, etc., to express their own identity in relation to other Muslims is to refer to the hadith which says that 'between a man and unbelief (*kufr*) is the leaving of prayer' (Sunan at-Tirmidhī, Book of Faith, no. 2543; 2544; Sunan an-Nisā'ī, Book of Prayer, no. 460: Sunan Abū Dāwud, Book of Sunna, no. 4058; Sunan Abū Mājah, Book of Performance of Prayer and Sunna, no. 1068; Musnad Aḥmad, *bāqi musnad al-anṣār*, no. 14451; Sunan ad-Dāramī, Book of Prayer, no. 1205),[12] and 'The contract between us [the Prophet] and them [the people] is the prayer. Those who turn away from it have made unbelief (*kufr*).' (Tirmidhī, Book of Faith, no. 2545 (in a slightly different wording also in Book of Faith, no. 2546); Ibn Mājah, Book of Performance of Prayer and Sunna, no. 1069; Sunan an-Nisā'ī, Book of Prayer, no. 459; Musnad Aḥmad, *bāqi musnad al-anṣār*, no. 21859 (in a slightly different version no. 21929).) In a literal reading of these hadiths a person can only be regarded as a Muslim if s/he prays, a concept which I have met many times. If we turn to the Islamic law there are different interpretations of these hadiths. According to Sayyid Sābiq in the Ḥanbalī law school, for instance, the most common notion is that a person who does not pray may be considered a non-Muslim (*kāfir*).[13] In the Ḥanafī law school, on the other hand, Sābiq has observed that a person who does not pray would not become a non-Muslim (Sābiq 1985 vol. I: 92–6). Islamic scholars often employ a scale of various different commitments to Islam based mainly on Ibn Taimīya's (d. 1328) categorisations (Ibn Taimīya 1972). I have attended many lectures and Friday sermons over the years and three main stages of belief are often referred to, deduced from a well-known hadith saying:

> One day while we were sitting with the Messenger of God (may the blessing and peace of God be upon him) there appeared before us a man whose clothes were exceedingly white and whose hair was exceedingly black: no signs of journeying were to be seen on him and none of us knew him. He walked up and sat down by the Prophet (may the blessing and peace of God be upon him). Resting his knees against his and placing the palms of his hands on his thighs, he said: O Muhammad, tell me about Islam. The Messenger of God (may the blessing and peace of God be upon him) said: Islam is to testify that there is no god but God and Muhammad is the Messenger of God, to perform the prayers, to pay the alms-tax, to fast in Ramadan, and to make the pilgrimage to the House (Mecca) if you are able to do so. He said: You have spoken rightly, and we were amazed at him asking the Prophet; saying that he had spoken rightly. He said: Then tell me about *imān* (faith, conviction). He said: It is to believe in God, His angels, His books, His messengers, and the Last Day, and to believe in divine destiny, both the good and the evil thereof. He said: You have spoken rightly. He said: Then tell me about *iḥsān* (perfection of faith). The Prophet said: It is to worship God as though you are seeing Him, and while you see Him not yet truly He sees you. . . . Then he took himself off and I [Umar] stayed for a time. Then the Prophet said: O Umar, do you know who the questioner was? I said: God and His Messenger know best. He said: It was Gabriel, who came to you to teach you your religion.
>
> (an-Nawawī 1976: 28–32)[14]

According to the explanations which are given to this hadith, a person is a *Muslim* in the first stage, which indicates that a person commits him/herself at least to the five *arkān* (the five pillars of Islam).

The second stage is that of being a *believer* (*muʾmin*). This is the stage which one leading Islamist I interviewed referred to as 'the stage of God's control'. He continued: 'Whatever one does, God accounts for to the minute detail.' This stage is also related to Islam's *ʿaqīda* (creed) as it is expressed in the hadith: the belief in God, His angels, His books, His messengers and the Last Day, and belief in divine destiny, both the good and the evil thereof. From an emic perspective we can see that the procession from the first to the second stage, as it is explained by Islamists, starts with the practical Islamic obligations (orthopraxis) and ascends to the level of belief. One Islamist explained that if one is a *believer* one is also a *Muslim*, whereas to be a *Muslim* does not necessarily mean that one is also a *believer*.

The last stage is considered to be that of being a *muḥsin*, i.e. one who has perfected the faith and 'one should worship God as if one saw him and if one does not see Him one has to know that God sees everything'. In discussions with many preachers and Islamists in general they expressed the idea that with persistent excellence of performance of worship, a Muslim may attain awareness of God. However, it was explained that this stage of *iḥsān* is allowed only to a few, and in sharia-oriented sufism only the Prophets or the saints (*awlīyāʾ*) are regarded as having any possibility of reaching this stage.[15] I was further told that it is difficult even to reach the stage of being a *believer*. A Koranic verse which I often heard recited in my discussions with Muslims of various affiliations about the categorisation of Muslims is regarded as referring to the different stages related to the Islamic message. It goes: 'They [the Bedouins] said: We believe (*ʾāmannā*). Say [Oh, Muhammad] you have not believed, say rather that you have surrendered (*aslamnā*) [to God]. Faith (*imān*) has not entered your hearts' (K.49: 14).[16]

Furthermore, Islamists I have met in Europe or in the Arab world often say that faith is in the heart, and practice is that which confirms faith. They link this saying directly to the importance of action. At the same time they emphasise that action is interwoven with intentions and neither actions nor intentions can be regarded separately.

If I have understood the Islamists properly, that leaves most Muslims at the stage of being *Muslim* only. In my discussions with Islamists I observed that they do distinguish between the various kinds of Muslims. Islamists in Europe are faced with a negative image of Islam, which they regard as resulting from the fact that many Muslims in Europe neither adhere to the Islamic commandments nor have much knowledge of the Islamic sources. This negative image is, in their view, built on observation of the common group of Muslims, which makes it important to distance themselves from this group in terms of the degree and quality of 'Muslimness'. The problem has been how to distinguish between differences in praxis among Muslims and how to judge the 'quality of Muslimness'. In ancient times Islamic scholars such as Ibn Taimīya and Ibn Qayyim al-Jawzīya (d. 1350) have deduced categories from the Koran which pertain to the level of 'Muslimness'. These categorisations are frequently referred to by contemporary Islamists, particularly the *salafīs*,[17] and they include *ʿāṣi* (the disobedient), *fāsiq* (the trespasser) and *munāfiq* (the hypocrite). In my discussions with Islamic scholars and Islamists, the distinction between *ʿāṣi* and *fāsiq* was explained as follows: whereas the former refers to shortcomings associated with failing to fulfil the basic Islamic obligations such as prayer and fasting, the latter refers to practices which actually commit violence to the Islamic law, such as drinking alcohol or committing adultery. As for the *munāfiq*, in the definition of the Islamists and Islamic preachers this is a person whose outward appearance or identity does not correspond to his/her inward attitudes, or his/her words and deeds.[18] I find it interesting that the categorisation of Muslims by these classical scholars has a place in the contemporary debate. Whereas in ancient times identifying who was and was not Muslim had to do with practical issues such as the payment of taxes, a person's social status, etc., contemporary discussion of the same topic has more to do with ideology and the promotion of a certain interpretation of the Islamic sources.[19]

Islamists refer to the fact that the Koran and the hadith literature deal with how to define hypocrites. In discussions and lectures Islamists and Islamic preachers referred to hypocrites in an historical context. According to them, the hypocrites represented a great danger for the newly established community of believers as the constant situation of war and unrest made every element of uncertainty a threat to the community's stability. They further listed four characteristics of hypocrisy, referring to hadiths in which the Prophet Muhammad was observed to have said: 'four characteristics make anyone who possesses them, a sheer hypocrite; anyone who possesses one of them possesses a characteristic of hypocrisy till he abandons it' (Bukhārī, Book of Faith, no. 33; Muslim, Book of Faith, no. 88; Sunan an-Nisā'ī, Book of Faith and Law, no. 4934; Musnad Aḥmad, *musnad al-Mukthārīn*, no. 6479).

The four signs of being a hypocrite were listed as follows:

1 Whenever one speaks, one tells a lie.
2 Whenever one promises, one breaks the promise.
3 Whenever one is entrusted, one betrays.
4 Whenever one quarrels, one behaves in an imprudent, evil and insulting manner (or whenever one quarrels, one deviates from the truth).

In Muslim's hadith collection it is explicitly stated that these characteristics make a person a hypocrite even though this person observes fasting and prayer and professes to be a Muslim (Muslim 1971 vol. I: 41). I have understood from my discussions with Islamists that hypocrisy and unbelief, although comparable, are not identical in Islam, although the difference is explained as being only one of degree. I believe this might be the reason for the difficulty Islamists seem to have in explaining the distinction between the states of hypocrisy and unfaith (*nifāq/kufr*).

The above categorisations are all mentioned in the Islamic sources. It is interesting to note that the Koran distinguishes between different groups, between Muslims of different categories and between non-Muslims, such as the differentiation between the People of the Book (*ahl al-kitāb*), which includes Jews and Christians, and people belonging to other religions. These categorisations might, however, have different definitions within the various Islamic movements and trends.

How then is it possible to distinguish between those Muslims who are culturally or ethnically defined with Islam and those who are motivated by the pillars and the creed of Islam (*arkān* and *ʿaqīda*)? In contemporary times there is no official control of Muslims' Islamic practices. The individual is responsible for her/his own Islamic performance. But even though one might assume that this lack of control from above would make it more easy to separate practising from non-practising Muslims, this is not always the case. For instance, how does one define those Muslim intellectuals who write about Islamic issues but are not motivated by the pillars and the creed of Islam, their interest in Islamic issues having more to do with the fact that they are what Sanders would call 'ethnic' Muslims? What about Muslims living in Europe who define themselves as Muslims but do not adhere to the pillars and the creed of Islam? To what extent do researchers' difficulties in distinguishing between the multitude of variations in Muslim practice and belief influence research results? Just as today one can hardly determine what is specifically 'English', 'American', 'French' or 'Swedish', I believe that, due to these different perspectives, one similarly cannot specify what is typically 'Muslim' or 'Islamic'. This might be compared to the statement by the Norwegian anthropologist, Thomas Hylland Eriksen, in the Swedish newspaper *Sydsvenska Dagbladet*, that the only thing which is typically Norwegian is to say that something is typically Norwegian (Hylland Eriksen 1994).

Bearing in mind the diversity and complexity of Muslim identities and affiliations, I now offer a general survey of modern Islamic trends and movements, focusing particularly on those which are relevant for my area of research. In Chapter 3 I shall explain in more detail my criteria and methods in the selection and interviewing of participants for the research.

2 Arab Muslims in Europe

Introduction

There are various Arab Islamist movements, organisations, associations and trends in Europe. Most of these consist of a small elite with varying degrees of support among Muslims in general. It is mostly members and sympathisers of these organisations or associations who are involved in Islamic activities in European countries;[1] some of them even have a strong influence on the development of Islamic thought in general. The movements fall into two main groupings, the one being Islamist movements with their base in Muslim countries, such as the Muslim Brotherhood (*al-ikhwān al-muslimūn*), the Islamic Liberation Party (*al-ḥizb at-taḥrīr*), Sufi orders (*ṭarīqāt*), and the *salafī* trend. These are less affected by change since they are to a large extent controlled by their mother organisations. The other grouping is made up of what might be described as independent organisations, insofar as these movements originate in Europe as a Muslim response to European influence. The issues which concern many Islamic organisations in Europe are those which arise out of the Muslim encounter with European culture, and they include questions such as how to live as a Muslim in a new cultural context, and how to make Islam compatible with the modern world. Such questions have prompted a variety of responses among Islamic movements. In what follows I give details of the ways in which the Arab Islamist presence is manifest in contemporary Europe, and I explain the main differences and similarities in their various approaches. Since many Muslims as well as non-Muslims tend to regard most Islamic trends in terms of 'fundamentalist' or 'Islamist' movements, in the interests of clarity I will begin by defining 'fundamentalism' and 'Islamism'.

'Fundamentalism'

There has been a tendency by the western media and some academic researchers to describe Islamic activism in terms of 'fundamentalism' (Moghadam 1990; Zubaida 1989). However, the discussion of 'fundamentalism' has been over-simplified in the western context in a way that has generated religious stereotypes. When such terminology is translated from one cultural context to another it tends to acquire different meanings, and the term 'fundamentalism' does not mean the same in the Islamic cultural sphere as it does in western usage. Many researchers overlook this difference and persist in using the word in its western sense, and this creates misunderstanding when the issue of 'fundamentalism' is discussed between the two cultures.

In the media, 'fundamentalism' has come to denote the activities of religious groups, and it is particularly associated with violent or aggressive practices. The 'Fundamentalist Project', launched by R. S. Appleby and M. E. Marty, is one example of the word being used in this sense (Appleby and Marty 1995). However, while some researchers perpetuate this generalised concept of Islamic activism, others have tried to find more appropriate terms to describe the multiplicity of religious activities being referred to. The Swedish researchers David Westerlund and Carl Fredrik Hallencreutz have observed that

> this broad use of the term [fundamentalism] has become increasingly irrelevant. As a derogatory concept, tied to Western stereotypes and Christian presuppositions, it easily causes misunderstandings and prevents the understanding of the dynamics and characteristics of different religious groups with explicit political objectives.
>
> (Westerlund and Hallencreutz 1996: 4)

This observation is particularly true when it comes to the representation of Islam. For instance, the Muslim Brotherhood is often depicted in the media as a 'fundamentalist' organisation, suggesting an association between this organisation and violent activities. This distorts public perceptions of the Muslim Brotherhood, which is in fact a moderate organisation advocating change through education (*tarbiya*) of the masses rather than violent revolution, and its significance for society is thus not fully appreciated (Roald 1994).

Hjärpe is also sceptical about the concept 'fundamentalism'. In his book *Araber och Arabism* (*Arabs and Arabism*), he argues that it would be better to avoid the word 'fundamentalism' when referring to Islam (Hjärpe 1994: 160), explaining that the term was first used in the early twentieth century by conservative Christians within American Protestant Evangelicalism who were reacting against the growing influence of the historical-critical method of biblical interpretation. Between 1909 and 1915 a series of twelve paperback tracts entitled *The Fundamentals* were distributed. According to Hjärpe, 'the tracts represented an evangelical, conservative Protestantism which claimed the inerrancy of the Bible . . . as a historical and "scientific" document' (Hjärpe 1994: 160). Implied in the idea of the inerrancy of the Bible, Hjärpe explains, was a literal understanding of the story of the seven days of creation in Genesis 1–2 so that this was regarded as an historical account (Hjärpe 1994: 160–1). Hjärpe's argument is supported by the work of Hallencreutz and Westerlund, who reject the common notion that 'fundamentalism' involves a literal reading of the religious text. They argue that 'it is important to stress that the point of conflict between [Christian] fundamentalists and others was not literalness but *inerrancy*' (Westerlund and Hallencreutz 1996: 4).

According to Hjärpe, the term 'fundamentalism' came to be applied to Islamic movements as a result of comparisons between Christian 'fundamentalists' and politically engaged Muslims, based on the claim that both groups had political aims which they pursued through political and juridical means. He writes:

> This implies that when one compared [Christian fundamentalism] with movements in the Muslim world, it was not the hermeneutics, the interpretation of the text, or the degree of 'literalism' which was the issue. It was rather the similarity in view of the *function* of religion, the view that religion is an instrument for the legislation and administration of the state, the objectification of religion as a societal system, separated from the individual's belief and understanding.
>
> (Hjärpe 1994: 161 [translation mine])

Hjärpe also points to the use of the word 'intégrism' in the French debate on Islam. In a similar fashion to the use of the word 'fundamentalism', 'intégrism' was taken from a Christian historical phenomenon. 'Les intégristes' were those who refused the reforms of the Catholic Church. To compare this movement to revolutionary movements in the Muslim world is thus, in Hjärpe's view, somewhat inaccurate (Hjärpe 1994: 161).

According to Hjärpe, the word 'fundamentalism' entered the debate on Muslim religio-political movements at an early stage. Islamists living in Europe suggest that 'fundamentalism' came to be translated into Arabic as *uṣūlī* in the 1980s, either through French or English literature. In an Islamic context the term acquired positive connotations, since it came to be associated with 'a return to the fundamentals, i.e. the Koran and the Sunna of the Prophet'. The positive content of the term is linked to the word *aṣl*, derived from the root *ʾ-ṣ-l*, the meaning of which has to do with 'source' or 'noble origin'. In the ancient madrasa system and even in the present sharia-institutions, two of the basic subjects are *uṣūl ad-dīn* (the fundamentals of Islam) and *uṣūl al-fiqh* (the fundamentals of jurisprudence). *Uṣūl ad-daʿwa* (fundamentals of the call to Islam) has been incorporated in the studies of sharia more recently (Roald 1994).

Thus, the word 'fundamentalist' has different connotations depending on whether it is being used in an Islamic or a western context. A 'fundamentalist' is a Muslim who 'returns to the pure sources', i.e. to the Koran and the Sunna. This excludes Muslim traditionalists who adhere strictly to the four orthodox Islamic law schools, and it might also exclude followers of Shīʿī Islam except the Ayatollahs who are the exclusive interpreters of the Islamic sources. Sunnī Muslims who would be 'fundamentalists' in this meaning of the word are those who adhere to a *salaf* ideology of Islam, which means that instead of accepting the established scholarship represented by the four Islamic law schools, Islamic sources have to be interpreted directly or indirectly according to the beliefs of the first three generations of Muslims. The *salafī* movement which builds on this ideology adheres to the *salaf* ideology both in creed (*ʿaqīda*) and in jurisprudence (*fiqh*), and it has a tendency to understand or to follow the Islamic sources in a literal manner. Without denying that the interpretative process always contains elements of the interpreter's biography and is therefore perhaps never entirely literal, one can say that as far as Muslims are concerned, those closest to interpreting the sacred text literally are the followers of the *salafī* movement who tend to accept the text with less concern for a hermeneutic understanding than other groups. In addition, the *salafī* movement refutes the Islamic law school system *in toto* and seeks to establish rules and regulations which are applicable to all Muslims. By disregarding the Islamic law schools' jurisprudence with their tolerance for different points of view (*ikhtilāf*), and instead looking for the strongest proof (*dalīl*) in every case, the *salafīs* claim to search for 'one single truth'.

However, if the expression 'fundamentalist' is understood in terms of what Westerlund and Hallencreutz consider to be its original meaning, i.e., a person who regards the sacred scripture as inerrant, the term 'fundamentalist' would, as Hallencreutz and Westerlund have observed, apply to nearly all Muslims (Westerlund and Hallencreutz 1996: 6). In contrast to inter-Christian debates about the authority and meaning of the Bible, the Koran has not been subject to the historical-critical method of study in an intra-Islamic context. Islamists and nearly all Muslims tend therefore to believe in the inerrancy of the Koran – the Koran *is*, by definition, the words of God. Thus, depending on how the word 'fundamentalist' is defined, it might refer to only a small section of Islamic activists, or it might encompass nearly all Muslims.[2]

One could also argue that the term 'fundamentalism' has been transformed from its original meaning to become a label of religious political activism, but this definition is inaccurate in an Islamic context. Islamists have various attitudes towards political activism. For instance, most followers of the *salafī* movement, which I have suggested is the closest to being a 'fundamentalist' movement according to one of the original meanings of the word, do not have any expressed political aim, although politics are implicitly incorporated within the *salafī* ideology. The Muslim Brotherhood on the other hand has political aims, but its methods are peaceful rather than violent (Roald 1994). As 'fundamentalism' often tends to suggest violent activities, I would argue that even the Muslim

Brotherhood cannot be regarded as a 'fundamentalist' movement in the contemporary meaning of the word.

To use 'fundamentalism' to describe religious activism in *all* religions is misleading since the various religions have different aims and dogmas and undertake different activities. With regard to Islam, the term cannot possibly convey the whole spectrum of Islamic activism, since this varies in the different movements and includes both those who advocate violence and those who are committed to peaceful means. Nor do I think that the word can be used to indicate any particular attitude which might be identified as Islamic, since the various Islamic movements have disparate views with regard to dogmatic as well as political issues. Therefore, it is questionable whether the term 'fundamentalism' can be applied to Islam in any sense, whether in terms of religious interpretation, actions or attitudes.

'Islamism'

Another term which has entered the scene is 'Islamism' or 'Islamist'. The term *islāmī* (Islamist) is a self-denotation used by Islamic activists from the late sixties onwards. A Palestinian Islamic activist who studied in Algeria in the early seventies explained:

> At the universities in Algeria in the seventies, we – the students who regarded Islam as a system of life, as an ideology – used the term 'Islamists' (*islāmīūn*) in order to contrast ourselves to the other students with other world-views. At my university there were us, the Islamists, there were the communists (*ash-shuyūʿīūn*), and there were those students who were only concerned about worldly matters. The latter we labelled *breadists* (*khubzists*).
>
> [translation mine]

This would suggest that the term 'Islamist' was coined by Muslims in response to the modern labelling of world-views in terms of '-isms' and '-ists', such as communism, socialism and capitalism.

Hjärpe believes that *islāmī* is an arabisation of the French 'Islamists' adopted by the newspaper *Le Monde* as a substitute for the term 'les intégristes' (Hjärpe 1994: 162). The term 'Islamism' generally denotes activities identified with Islam. In this study I define an 'Islamist' as a Muslim with an Islamic world-view or a Muslim who regards Islam as a way of life. According to this definition, an 'Islamist' regards Islam as a body of ideas, values, beliefs and practices which explicitly or implicitly encompasses all spheres of life including personal and social relations, economics and politics. Furthermore, 'Islamism' includes a multitude of Islamic perspectives ranging from traditional Islam, for example when referring to certain Sufi-groups, to more modern approaches such as contemporary Islamic movements. Given that this is a broad definition, I have decided to identify various subgroups within Islamism. What becomes apparent is the heterogeneity of the Islamic movements as well as of Islamists. As my study deals exclusively with Arabic-speaking Sunnī Islamists, the wide variations even in this area indicate even greater diversity with respect to the whole Muslim Umma.

'Modernity/modernism'

There is a common misconception that defines 'fundamentalism' in opposition to 'modernism'. Westerlund and Hallencreutz challenge this dichotomy, arguing that

> Within . . . religious contexts modernism is associated with the philosophical values of the Enlightenment, which are regarded as anti-religious and are thus naturally refuted by Muslim 'fundamentalists'. However, they are clearly not against modern technological and scientific achievements. They do not see an opposition between reason and religion – Many Muslim 'fundamentalists' are students at or alumni of faculties of science and medicine. They do not aim to re-establish some form of medieval society, although the earliest period of Islamic history is an important source of their inspiration. Their goal is to 'Islamize' the modern world, not to reject it. . . . Hence one should be careful not to over-emphasise the issue of 'fundamentalism v. modernism'.
>
> (Westerlund and Hallencreutz 1996: 6–7)

The question which arises is whether Islamic movements are opponents or promoters of modernity. While many researchers regard 'fundamentalism' as opposed to modernity, Hallencreutz and Westerlund suggest that 'fundamentalism' is not necessarily in opposition to modernity but rather to modernism, and in particular to that aspect of modernism defined as 'the idea that consensual norms and ultimate values can be located in a secular or non-religious source' (Westerlund and Hallencreutz 1996: 6). In arguing this they build upon Bruce Lawrence's study, *The Defenders of God*, which deals at length with the ideology of religious movements and their relationship to modernity and modernism. Lawrence distinguishes between the two, defining 'modernity' in terms of modern technology and communications, and 'modernism' in terms of an ideology to do with belief in the infallibility of science and human reason. According to these definitions, one could argue that many Islamic movements have a positive attitude towards 'modernity' given that they use modern technology to spread their message. 'Modernism', on the other hand, is less compatible with their ideologies as these are, to a greater or lesser extent, based on belief in an 'absolute truth' deduced from the sacred texts (Lawrence 1989).

Another aspect of modernism, however, might be belief in the evolution of social structures in terms of the progressive development of society. In this sense, Islamists who refute traditionalism, i.e. the strict adherence to one of the law schools, would be the modernists of Islam, both in terms of 'modernity' and 'modernism' in Lawrence's terminology. The International Institute of Islamic Thought (IIIT) in Herndon in Washington DC is a unique example of this because it sees progress in Islamic knowledge in terms of its being 'updated' by modern developments.

Bryan Turner, a sociologist of religion, claims that Islamists defend modernism against the pluralism and fragmentation of postmodernism. He argues, 'Islamization is an attempt to create at the global level a new *Gemeinschaft*, a new version of the traditional household which would close off the threat of postmodernity by re-establishing a communal ideology'(Turner 1994: 93). Turner does not offer an explanation of what this 'communal ideology' might amount to since he discusses 'Islamic fundamentalism' and 'Islamisation' only in general terms. One could however extrapolate from his argument to suggest that the idea of a 'communal ideology' might be related to the idea of one homogeneous 'truth'. This is consistent with the views of many Islamists whose goal is a homogeneous understanding of Islam. However, the nature of 'truth' which might be implied in Turner's idea of a communal ideology depends just as much on how one defines 'Islamism' as on how one defines 'modernism' and 'postmodernism'. If 'Islamism' is understood in terms of 'fundamentalism', i.e. as involving a *literal* reading or belief in the *inerrancy* of the religious texts, and 'modernism' entails the claim that there is one truth in contrast to 'postmodernism' which implies a multiplicity of truths, then Turner's 'communal ideology' might involve the idea of an absolute truth. On the other hand, if 'Islamism' includes Muslims with a hermeneutic approach to religious texts, then it might be difficult to talk about a communal ideology in terms of an absolute understanding of truth. The hermeneutic approach might allow for discrepancies in interpretation and tolerate variations in meaning, which would suggest a postmodern multiplication of 'truths'. For example, if one takes the Islamist movement as a whole, the *salafī* trend at one extreme might entail claims to an 'absolute truth', while the *ikhwān* trend to a certain extent would accept the idea that differences in time and place give rise to a variety of interpretations of Islamic social issues.

Furthermore, I would argue that rather than seeing Islamists as offering a defence of modernism against the threat of postmodernism, the postmodern era might be regarded as a triumph for Islamists. Particularly for Muslims living in western countries, the postmodern idea that there is not one truth but many allows them to assert their Islamic ideas with confidence. In the modernist understanding of truth, not only Islam but all religions suffered, since this concept of truth was based on agnosticism and a secular world-view. With the fragmentation of the modernist view, Muslims along with the followers of other religions have been able to express their religious beliefs publicly. The New Age movement with all its various shadings is a symptom of the same phenomenon.

The ideology of the Islamist movements might be opposed to a modernist ideological paradigm, but the means adopted by such movements are those of modernity. In a Muslim context, the opposition between modernity and modernism might be better described as 'modernisation'[3] versus 'westernisation', since Islamism is a reaction to the globalisation of western localism.[4] Many Islamists claim that they believe in modernisation, i.e. they accept the benefits of modern technology, whereas they resist the westernisation, or western localism, that goes with it (Hjärpe 1994: 163–4). The issue at stake is this: how is it possible to preserve an Islamic ideology in the western atmosphere which is created by modern technology, particularly information technology? This issue is important in the Muslim world, but it is more important for Islamist movements in Europe and the United States. The constant flux of modern ideas necessarily has an impact on Muslim thought and behaviour, and changing frames of reference might persuade Muslims to import new ideas into Islamic sources.

Cooperative versus competitive inter-groups

I have argued that there is a tendency for non-Muslims in Europe to perceive Muslims as belonging to a homogeneous group. However, within the group 'Muslims in Europe' there are many subgroups such as Bengali Muslims, Pakistani Muslims, Arab Muslims, African Muslims and converted Muslims. We can also identify cross-groups divided according to social status and educational background. These last characteristics play an important role in establishing divisions within the subgroups. John C. Turner, a social psychologist, has on the basis of test results deduced that '*competitive* inter-group interaction increases in-group/out-group biases', whereas '*cooperative* inter-group interaction tends to decrease social distance and in-group/out-group biases' (John Turner in Turner and Giles 1981: 74). Although Turner's results are based on laboratory research, his idea of *competitive* versus *cooperative* inter-group interaction is of value for the present study. I would suggest that it is more likely for Arab Islamist intellectuals who are active participants in European society to belong to the model of *cooperative* inter-group interaction, in which the outcome is supposed to be a decrease in in-group/out-group biases. Arab Islamists with little formal education living on state or unemployment benefit, on the other hand, would probably belong to a model of *competitive* inter-group interaction, as they would have little or no contact with the society at large. An example of the latter is the situation of Arab Islamists living in Sweden. As Sweden has had relatively open borders, many refugees came to Sweden in the 1980s and in the beginning of the 1990s. Many Arab Islamists are refugees with little formal education living on state benefits. They are marginalised in Swedish society, and I have observed that the term 'Muslim' in Sweden, in the negative sense of the word, has become almost synonymous with being an Arab. At the same time there is tension between majority society and Muslims due to a number of factors, including the strained economic situation of the 1990s after years of the economy being burdened with an extensive social welfare programme. Arab Muslims in Sweden tend to live in segregated suburb areas. In the large towns there are suburbs in which a considerable proportion of the population is Muslim, particularly Arab Muslims. The interaction between Arab Muslims and Swedish society at large is thus marked by structural in-group/out-group biases.

In contrast to this pattern of *competitive* inter-group interaction is the model of *cooperative* inter-group interaction found among Arab Islamist intellectuals in Britain. Many Arab Islamists came to Britain to pursue postgraduate degrees then decided to stay there after completing their studies. Many Iraqi students who came at the end of the 1970s and in the beginning of the 1980s remained in Britain due to the Iraq–Iran war and the strained political situation in Iraq. Syrian Islamist students did not return to their homeland due to the acute situation between the authorities and the Syrian branch of the organisation of the Muslim Brotherhood from the early 1980s. Egyptian Islamist students remained in Britain due to their insecure position in Egyptian society. Moreover, in Britain there are Islamist intellectuals from other Arab countries such as Palestine, Libya, Sudan and the Maghreb-countries: Tunisia, Algeria and Morocco. Some of these well-educated Arab Islamists hold high positions in British society, such as university teachers, medical doctors and engineers.[5] As they play an active part in British society it is likely that these people are in constant contact with individuals from the majority group. Since this is not an artificially manufactured form of contact, which was the case in the past when social policy decisions promoted racial and migrant integration, but a contact situation in which the individual from the minority group plays an actual role in society, there is the potential for individuals in such interaction to exert a mutual influence over one another's attitudes and ideas.

It is also important to consider the leading role played by Arabs in the past, and I would argue that Arab Muslims still fill this leadership role. It is in the Arab world that *salafī* ideology, with its rationale of going back to the 'pure' sources, the Koran and the Hadiths, is most widespread. The more extreme *salafīs* omit the rulings of the four traditional Islamic Law schools (*madhāhib*, sing. *madhhab*), whereas the more moderate ones relax the strict law school system and freely choose between the rulings of the four schools. According to my observations, Muslims and Islamists think that in order to be able to search for their own rulings in the Koran and Sunna, individuals must have an extensive knowledge of the Arabic language and the Islamic texts and commentaries written in Arabic. This idea is also expressed by many scholars in the past, such as Jalāl ad-Din aṣ-Ṣuyūtī, an Egyptian commentator on the Koran from the fifteenth century, who lists the qualification of being an authority on the sciences of the Arabic language as one of three essential conditions for being able to interpret the Koran (aṣ-Ṣuyūṭī n.d. vol. II: 75). I have further observed that non-Arabic speaking Muslims, such as Turks, Indo-Pakistanis, Malays and Indonesians, tend to adhere to the law school system to a greater extent than do Arabic-speaking Muslims. The widespread idea of the importance of the Arabic language might be one reason why non-Arabic speaking individuals adhere to law schools rather than searching for their own rulings.

In my fieldwork I discovered that the importance of the Arabic language as the language of the Koran and the hadiths leads many Arab Islamists to feel that they understand Islam 'in the correct way'. This notion is linked to the idea of responsibility and leadership of the Muslim Umma, an idea which is particularly expressed in European and North-American Islamism. It is interesting to note that non-Arabs in Europe are concerned with the Arab language and many non-Arabic speaking Muslims try to learn Arabic as the language of the Koran.

Arab Islamist intellectuals in Europe operate on different levels which are instrumental in shaping their self-esteem. On the *personal* level, the individual sees himself or herself as having a high status within the larger society, which might promote a cooperative attitude towards the social majority. In the Muslim community, his/her self-esteem is that of a leader in terms of both social status and Arabness. However, on the *social* level, as part of a minority group his/her self-esteem is low in relation to the majority society, and inter-group interaction on this level will be marked by a competitive attitude towards members of the out-group.

If one considers how these variables affect changes of attitude on a personal and a social level, one can assume that, on the one hand, as part of a minority group Islamists would reinforce the traditional attitudes they brought with them from their homeland. This is probably true in the group situation and at the level of inter-group interaction. So, while acting in a group and when the focus is on the individual's group identity, influences and attitudes regarded as coming from the majority group would be refuted. However, changes in attitude among well-educated Islamists would occur at the personal level through interaction with the broader society, while the less educated sector of the Muslim group and those who do not take an active part in society would remain at the level of reinforcing traditional attitudes. An assimilation process is less likely to take place in interaction with secondary contacts, i.e. contacts outside intimate circles such as the family or close friends. However, interaction with secondary contacts still promotes the exchange of ideas and attitudes which will eventually bring about changes and changing processes in personal attitudes. These changes will then be introduced into the social level during group interaction and in-group intellectual work, and slowly the attitudes of the whole group will move more into line with those of the majority society.

The media also has a role to play in the process of change. However, with the introduction of satellite television channels, the local media tend to play a less significant role than they used to do. In many Swedish suburbs where the majority of the population are immigrants, for instance, satellite dishes can be seen on nearly every balcony and a Swedish journalist has commented on the tendency of immigrants to reach beyond the Swedish reality towards their home countries (referred to in Carlbom 1998). Aje Carlbom, a Swedish anthropologist whose main research is on one of the suburbs with a large Arab community, has observed that in its local context the satellite dish might be an obstruction with regard to integration in Swedish society. He writes:

> The satellite dish is one of the instruments in the Muslim enclave of Rosengård [a suburb in southern Sweden] which give the inhabitants the possibility of living in a non-Swedish context. It is . . . easier to get hold of Arabic, Turkish, Bosnian, German etc. daily newspapers in Rosengård and its near environment than it is to get hold of the biggest morning newspaper in Sweden, *Dagens Nyheter*.
>
> (Carlbom 1998: 7, footnote 9 [translation mine])

Islamic directions

In my research into Islamic movements I have distinguished nine different categories. As this study is concerned with Arab Sunnī intellectual Muslims I deal at length only with those groups which are relevant. The nine categories are as follows:

1 Shīʿī Islamic movements.
2 National Islamic organisations.
3 Sufi orders.
4 The *tablīgh* movement.
5 The Jihad movement.
6 The *salafī* trend.
7 The Islamic Liberation Party (*al-ḥizb at-taḥrīr*).
8 The Muslim Brotherhood (*al-ikhwān al-muslimūn*).
9 The *post-ikhwān* trend.

Shīʿī groups

The Arab Shīʿī Islamic movements consist mainly of Lebanese and Iraqi Muslims. Among Lebanese refugees in Europe there are people belonging to Hizbullah (*ḥizb allāh*) and Amal. Among the Iraqi Shīʿī Muslims, the most active groups are the Daʿwa Party (*ḥizb ad-daʿwa*), the Islamic Activity Organisation (*munaẓẓama l-ʿamal al-islāmī*) and the Highest Council for the Islamic Revolution (*al-majlis al-aʿlā li th-thawra l-islāmīya*), all of which are religio-political opposition groups. I do not take the Shīʿī groups into account as it would make this study too broad. I would however suggest that within the different Shīʿī Islamic movements there are equally broad variations in perceptions of women as in the Sunnī Islamic movements.

National Islamic organisations

By national Islamic organisations I refer to organisations in different European countries which work nationally with close links to their countries of origin. In particular, Muslims from Morocco and Algeria tend to be organised in such groups, for instance in Belgium, France and Scandinavia.

Sufi orders

The Arab Sufi orders in Europe are mainly of the *qādirīya* and *shādhilīya* groups, both of which came to Europe from Morocco and Algeria. These are introvert orders which are active mostly within Moroccan communities in Belgium and France. Their main activities are *dhikr* sections and spiritual lectures in local mosques. However, there is a third Sufi order which is quite different from these two, and this is the *ḥabashī* group which has a strong foothold in Europe, particularly in Scandinavian countries.

The *ḥabashī* movement differs from other Sufi orders in its approach towards Muslims outside its own ranks and in its methodology. At the risk of over-simplifying, one could say that the *ḥabashī* movement, which has its headquarters in Lebanon, is the Sufi group which is most actively involved in socio-political work in Europe. Its founder, Sheikh ʿAbdullāh al-Ḥabashī, travelled from Ethiopia (*ḥabash* is the Arabic word for Ethiopia) to Syria where he came into conflict with other Islamic scholars, before settling in Lebanon. During the civil war in the 1970s he attracted many followers, mostly from Beirut, and the *ḥabashī* movement spread to western countries with the wave of Lebanese refugees. The movement is most active in Switzerland, Canada and in the Scandinavian countries, where among other activities they have established kindergartens and schools.

The *ḥabashī* movement has certain characteristics in common with the Egyptian Islamic movement *at-takfīr wa al-hijra* (Excommunication and Migration) (cf. Kepel 1985). In matters of creed (*ʿaqīda*) they would accuse some Muslims of being non-Muslims (*kuffār*, sing. *kāfir*).[6] For instance, they depict revered Islamic thinkers such as Ibn Taimīya (d. 1328) and Sayyid Quṭb (d. 1966) as non-Muslims due to their adherence to the *salaf* creed (see below). According to the *ḥabashī* movement, those who adhere to a *salaf* creed are anthropomorphists since they believe in a literal interpretation of God's attributes and deny any other explanation or interpretation of these attributes.[7] In matters of jurisprudence (*fiqh*) the *ḥabashī* movement has a more lenient interpretation of Islamic rulings than the *salafī* movement, which adheres to a strict understanding of Islamic law. Furthermore, the *ḥabashīs* believe that supplication can be directed to the Prophet Muḥammad or to the saints so that they in turn might supplicate to God on the Muslim's behalf, a belief which they claim is supported by the hadith literature. The *salafīs*, on the other hand, claim that supplication to the Prophet was only possible during the Prophet's lifetime, and to accept the possibility of an intermediary between God and man is unbelief (*kufr*) as it violates their concept of the unity of God (*tawḥīd*). So whereas the *ḥabashīs* believe that it is part of the Islamic creed to regard the Prophet Muhammad and the saints as intermediaries between man and God, the *salafīs* regard this as unbelief (*kufr*) due to the stress they lay on 'the true creed' which is *tawḥīd*. These two movements, the *salafī* and the *ḥabashī*, represent the two poles of the Arab Islamist movement in Europe. They are also the movements which are in greatest opposition to each other since they both accuse the other of being non-Muslims, as a result of the conflict which arises out of their different understandings of *ʿaqīda* (e.g. the intermediary role of the Prophet Muḥammad and the saints).

Another Sufi group which is active in the European context is the *shādhilīya* order, which originates mainly in Syria and Jordan. This order advocates adherence to the rules of the Shāfiʿī law school. Its Jordanian Sheikh is Sheikh Nuah Ha Mim Keller, an American convert to Islam. With his English translation of *The Reliance of the Traveller*, Shāfiʿī legislation became known to an English-speaking public. Sheikh Nuah travels widely in the western world and has many followers among converts and among second and third generation Muslims. One of his main objectives has been to establish educational programs in sharia legislation for Muslims living in western countries. Many scholars of Islam living in the West come from Muslim countries and therefore they have little understanding of western society. Sheikh Nuah regards the Islamic education of western Muslims as essential for addressing the problems faced by Muslims as minority groups in western countries.[8] A follower of Sheikh Nuah suggests that renewal tends to come from within the Islamic law schools, which I believe is the response of the adherents of these schools to a changing society with changing social roles and attitudes.

The tablīgh movement

The *tablīgh* movement (*Jama'at-i-Tabligh*) came into being on the Indian subcontinent in the 1920s, founded by Mawlāna Muḥammad Ilyās, a pious Muslim teacher (Roald 1994: 271–9). His main aim was to educate illiterate Indian Muslims in Islamic beliefs and practices. After establishing Islamic schools in the Merwat area, Ilyās decided that the only way to ensure permanent change among the students was to withdraw them from their home environment. He devised programmes which required that students gathered together in mosques or in Islamic schools for days and weeks away from external influences. Because the organisational structure of the *tablīgh* movement is loose in comparison with many other Islamic movements, it never became an organisation but remained an association. It is a movement devoted to group *daʿwa* (call to Islam), activities and *tablīgh* (preaching).

The ideas of the *tablīgh* movement spread to all parts of the world by way of travelling groups of *tablīgh* missionaries, and through *tablīgh* activities in Indo-Pakistani communities in various countries.[9] According to Mawlāna Waḥīd ad-Dīn Khān, a follower of the *tablīgh* movement, the mission tends to be more acceptable to a low-educated Muslim audience.[10] The preaching is often on a very basic level, with the Islamic message being promulgated in an engaging manner with legendary miracle stories along with Koranic verses and hadiths on ritual and spiritual subjects. Its political neutrality has allowed the movement to carry out its *daʿwa* work without interference from political authorities, in contrast to many other Islamic groups. Another feature is that the mission of the *tablīgh* movement is directed primarily towards Muslim males (Nagata 1984: 117). Although wives of *tablīgh* missionaries sometimes travel with the male group they are generally urged to remain at home, and most Islamic activities among women are performed in private houses.[11] The movement regards women as the main educators of the children, and women's place is considered to be in the home at the service of their husbands and children.

The *tablīgh* movement has had ramifications in the Arab world, particularly in Morocco and lately in Egypt as well.[12] The Indo-Pakistani population has an extensive *daʿwa* programme in Europe, but large Moroccan groups are also active in this form of *daʿwa* work, particularly in Great Britain, Belgium, France, Norway and Denmark. As the mission of the *tablīgh* movement is addressed directly to the Muslim community, the *Jama'at-i-Tabligh* can be described as an introverted *daʿwa* group. Few attempts have been made to convey the Islamic message to the non-Muslim population.

The Islamic Jihad

The Islamic Jihad has its roots in the Muslim Brotherhood.[13] The Jihad is not one single group but a collective term for a number of underground groups with different aims and methods. The common objective, however, is to fight with military means as far as is considered necessary. The Islamic Jihad can be regarded as a consequence of first the Islamic Revolution in Iran, and second the Afghan war. In the Afghan war many Arabs fought side by side with the Afghan *mujāhidīn* (here: freedom-fighters), and the fighting revolutionised many Islamists. One of the Jihad groups consists of disaffected members and sympathisers of the Muslim

Brotherhood who perceived the movement's education of the masses as slow and ineffectual in comparison with militant action. The main initiator of this group was the Muslim Brotherhood member, ʿAbdullāh ʿAzzām, a former lecturer in sharia at Jordan University in Amman. His view was that, as long as any Muslim country was under attack by non-Muslims, fighting was obligatory. His great example was Sayyid Quṭb, in whose footsteps he followed and whose ideas he developed, particularly with regard to the concept of *jāhilīya* (pre-Islamic time/time of ignorance).[14]

The *salafī* trend (see p. 50) also has a Jihad branch which has strongly established groups in the Algerian civil war, known as the Armed Islamic Groups. Members of these groups are often known as 'the Afghans' as many of them have been *mujāhidīn* in the Afghan war. 'The Afghans' are also active in other Arab countries, where their main aim is to fight foreign powers 'trespassing' on Muslim land. Women in this group are less visible in the wider society, as the sole domain of women is considered to be the home.

A third group which also belongs to the Jihad movement is that which the media have named *at-takfīr wa al-hijra* (Excommunication and Migration). This group tends to regard itself as the only rightly guided one, and as a result its members regard Muslims who disagree with them as non-Muslims. They also tend to withdraw from the rest of society as, in their view, Muslim and non-Muslim societies alike are non-Islamic. In a similar fashion to the Jihad group within the *salafī* trend, the role of women in this group is regarded as primarily domestic.

In Europe, members of and sympathisers with the Jihad groups mostly come from Algeria and Egypt. However, these groups are often marginalised both as a result of the rejection of their idea of Jihad by other Muslims, and because of their own withdrawal from the rest of society.

As my interviews have been mainly conducted with members of the Muslim Brotherhood, the Islamic Liberation Party, *salafīs* and people within the *post-ikhwān* trend, I will describe these groups in more detail, and I will also say something about the representation and role of women in each.

The Muslim Brotherhood

I have written elsewhere about my investigation of the Muslim Brotherhood (*al-ikhwān al-muslimūn*) in Jordan in connection with the movement's educational programme.[15] In this study I offer a brief introduction to the movement's history and present some of its ideas. In the 1920s, Egypt was marked by burgeoning Arab nationalism (Hourani 1962; Raḥmān 1970: 643; Hitti 1961: 751). A growing political consciousness in the colonised Muslim countries and the widely-held view that Muslims had failed in the struggle against the western powers paved the way for the continuation and elaboration of Jamāl ad-Dīn al-Afghānī's (d. 1897) political interpretation of the Islamic sources. The establishment of the Society of the Muslim Brothers in 1928 became a milestone for the Islamic revival of the twentieth century.[16] Although Ḥasan al-Bannā᾽ (d. 1949), the founder of the Muslim Brotherhood, cannot be regarded as a direct successor to the two reformers of the *salafīya* movement, al-Afghāni and Muḥammad ʿAbduh, he was nevertheless influenced by their ideas. But in contrast to the ideas of the intellectual *salafīya* movement which never really succeeded in gaining a significant foothold in society, al-Bannā᾽ attracted a wider public audience owing to his insistence on education (*tarbiya*) for the whole community. Many of the Brotherhood's members regard al-Bannā᾽ as the Islamic reformer of the twentieth century Hijra according to the hadith which says that 'Verily, at the beginning of every century, God sends to this Umma, one who renews its [the Umma's] religion'. The writings of the Muslim Brotherhood, and in particular those of al-Bannā᾽, have influenced many of the contemporary Islamic movements throughout the world. al-Bannā᾽ was a charismatic leader, and during his lifetime the movement spread to other Muslim countries. The first Palestinian branch was established in Jerusalem in 1946 (Cohen 1982: 144; al-ʿUbaidī 1991: 48) and in Jordan the movement was established in 1945. Today it has spread throughout the Arab world and there is even a branch in Malaysia called JIM (Pertubuhan Jama'ah Islah Malaysia).

The general organisation of the Muslim Brotherhood is headed by *al-murshid al-ʿāmm* (the General Guide) who is at the time of writing (2001) Muṣṭafā Manshūr. Together with the two general bodies, the General Guidance Board and the General Council, he leads the world organisation of the Muslim Brotherhood. According to the rules of the organisation this leading authority is based in Egypt (The Muslim Brothers 1989: 402). Every country has a General Supervisor, an Executive Office and a Council.

An applicant for membership must serve a probationary period of a minimum of six months but more usually a year. When he is inducted as a working brother, he has to swear an oath to the organisation (The Muslim Brothers 1989: 404). These strict regulations make the Muslim Brotherhood a cadre organisation. The members are expected to work hard in *daʿwa* work, which carries with it great personal sacrifices. Inside the organisation, members must show obedience (*ṭāʿa*) to the leader. This emphasis on obedience has had a negative effect, as indicated by the the criticism by members and Islamists outside of the organisation, which has been directed at its organisational structure (an-Nafīsī 1989).

Due to its high level of political activities the organisation of the Muslim Brotherhood has been perceived by outsiders as a predominantly political group, although its grassroots activities have focused on education. A broad training network for the general public has been built up as part of its *daʿwa* activities. Even although *daʿwa* work is performed openly, the procedures and forms of the organisation and the names of its members are in principle secret.[17]

Most of al-Bannāʾ's publications have an overtly political thrust. His most important treatises have been collected in *Collected Treatises of the Martyred Ḥasan al-Bannāʾ* and they tend to present Islam from a political angle, although in keeping with his Islamic aims, politics are interwoven with Islamic spirituality to form a unity. al-Bannāʾ wrote:

> The Muslim Brotherhood is:
>
> 1 The call of *salafīya:* because they [the Brothers] call for the return of Islam to its pure sources – God's book and His Prophet's Sunna.[18]
> 2 The path of the *sunnīya*: because they take upon themselves to act according to the pure Sunna [the Prophet's example] in all activities of life, particularly in creed (*ʿaqīda*) and worship as far as is possible.
> 3 The truth of *sūfīya:* because they know that the foundation of all good (*khayr*) is the purification of the soul, the cleaning of the heart, persistence in action, the respect for all creation, the love of God and commitment to the good.
> 4 A political society: because they demand the reform of authority inside [the Muslim territory] and a change in the view of the relationship between the Islamic Umma and the nations outside [of Muslim territory]. They train the masses in strength and nobility, and strive for their nationality (*qawmīya*) to the ultimate extent.
> 5 An athletic community: because the Brothers are concerned with their bodies and they know that a strong believer is better than a weak believer.
> 6 Intellectually learned union: because Islam makes searching for knowledge a duty for every Muslim, man and woman. And because the clubs of the Brothers are in reality schools for learning and training, and institutes for training (*tarbiya*) the body, the intellect and the spirit.
> 7 An economic enterprise: because Islam is concerned with organisation of capital and its gain. . . . 'Verily God loves the gainfully employed believer.'
> 8 Social thought: because they are concerned with the disease in Islamic society and they seek ways of treating it and curing the Umma from it.
>
> (al-Bannāʾ 1984: 122–3 [translation mine])

In this statement a central innovation of the Muslim Brotherhood is apparent. It views Islam as a comprehensive system (*an-niẓām ash-shāmil*) which includes all aspects of human life. The *ikhwān* (Muslim Brothers) see their view as contrary both to that of secular political groups, which tend to ignore any religious reality, and to mystical groups which they see as holding themselves aloof from political life. They regard the comprehensive system of life as representative of 'the natural religion' (*ad-dīn al-fiṭra*) (cf. Hedin 1988). The *ikhwān* consider their approach to Islam to be 'contemporary' (*muʿāṣir*). Islam has to be interpreted according to a particular time and place within an Islamic framework. al-Bannāʾ's stress on the need to educate the masses and thereby to bring about a change in society has penetrated much of the work within the movement. This emphasis on mass education is clear in his slogan for development: The individual Muslim (*al-fard al-muslim*), the Muslim home (*al-bayt al-muslim*) and the Muslim Umma (*al-umma l-muslima*) (al-Bannāʾ 1984: 235). al-Bannāʾ and his followers regard gradual change in society as the best method, in contrast to the Islamic Liberation Party which has a revolutionary ideology. The Muslim Brotherhood can thus be regarded as moderate, and not 'fundamentalist' in the sense of using violence to achieve its goals. Its profile as a 'fundamentalist' movement is due to the idea of 'returning to the pure sources' and the Koran as the Word of God.

In the following description of perceptions and practices with regard to women in the organisation, I refer to the results of my fieldwork in Jordan which I conducted from January to July 1992 and from June to August 1993.[19] The experience of the Muslim Brotherhood in Jordan might be a good indicator of gender policies in the movement as a whole. In order to give some indication of changes within the organisation in the Arab world, I also refer to my later visits to both Jordan and Egypt since 1994.

Family relations and gender relations in Muslim society are important issues in the social training of the Muslim Brotherhood.[20] The Muslim Brothers, as well as many other Muslims, regard the family as the fundamental unit of society. The family's role is central in raising and educating children, and each member of the unit has a role to play. Local practices, which vary from one place to another, have influenced the regional development of *fiqh*. The Muslim Brothers share the traditional Muslim interpretation of women's and men's roles in society, which can be summarised as follows: the man's duty is to support the family, while the woman should mainly stay at home and attend to the children's upbringing.

Islamist theory and practice tend to differ when it comes to women's issues. Literature on the position of women in Islam, as well as lectures given by male Islamist scholars to women, convey the message that a large measure of respect and reverence should be the lot of a practising Muslim woman in the family and in Muslim society. Women are portrayed as equal to men in matters of worship and divine reward, and differ from men only in their specific social responsibilities, i.e. women and men have the same value as human beings, but have different social roles (M. Quṭb 1985: 195; see also Mernissi 1987). However, many Islamist women hold the view that their reality is in practice significantly different from the theoretical position. Nevertheless, the picture is not entirely unambiguous since, as one of my informants pointed out, the Muslim Brotherhood's policy is in fact to encourage women to study at colleges and universities, although she added that they prefer women to study sharia since their main task is to educate children in an Islamic spirit.

The Muslim Brotherhood in Jordan admitted women into the organisation in the late 1970s and it has an active women's branch.[21] There are usually no mixed meetings or congregations, with the exception of lectures for women given by male scholars and some cultural gatherings. There are no women either in the Muslim Brotherhood's Council nor in their parliamentary group. However, students have nominated female Islamists in student union elections, and in the student election at the Jordanian University in Amman in the spring of 1993, there were thirteen Islamists out of seventeen elected females (*ar-Ribāṭ* 17/3–93, issue 108: 2).[22] While this election result is interesting, it is difficult to judge whether it indicates a new trend in women's issues among Islamists or if it pertains only to the university milieu.

In women's *usra* (study groups) or in external women's education groups, the focus is often on *fiqh* pertaining to femininity rather than on woman's active participation in society. The emphasis is on the twenty-fourth Sura of the Koran, *Light*, which deals with women's dress and chastity in general. The woman's role as a wife and mother has thus been given preference over her potential contribution in intellectual fields or social activities outside the home. The great gap between theory and practice on the question of women in the Muslim Brotherhood is described by Samīra Fayyāḍ, a leading female Islamist in Jordan: 'Nevertheless, when it comes to practice and application we find Islamists reluctant to acknowledge that Islam allows women to move in a circle much wider than they themselves [the Islamists] admit' (Fayyāḍ 1992: 10).

From my fieldwork I discovered that the Muslim Brotherhood promotes an idea of male hegemony in the Islamic family system. This is reinforced by Fatḥī Yakan, who is an official of the Muslim Brotherhood's branch in Lebanon. His book, *What does Membership in Islam Mean?*, is basic reading in the *ikhwān*'s training programme (Yakan 1992). In the chapter 'To be a Muslim with his family and in his home', he states how important it is for a Muslim man to treat his family in a civil manner according to the example of the Prophet who is reported to have said, 'The best of you is those who are best with his family. And I am the best of you with my family' (Yakan 1992: 54). However, Yakan continues:

> My relationship with my wife is . . . within the limits of sharia. And it [the relationship] should not be at the expense of Islam or that which God has forbidden. It has been said by the Prophet (peace be upon him): 'Nobody obeys a woman in what she desires,[23] without God putting him in the fire.' 'God does not find anybody with a greater sin than one whose wife is ignorant (*jahāla*)' and 'Misery on the servant of his wife'.
>
> (Yakan 1992: 55)

These three sayings of the Prophet referred to by Yakan lend themselves to a variety of interpretations depending on the attitudes of the reader. They can be read as implying disrespect for women in general, or one might argue that the scope of such statements was limited to non-practising Muslim women. Using hadiths in this manner, citing them without reference to their context, leads to misunderstandings and differences of opinion. The important issue here is not so much which hadiths exist, but rather which hadiths have actually been selected for use.

Isḥāq Farḥān, a leading Islamist in Jordan, stated in 1992 that he promoted the idea of official female participation in the organisation of the Muslim Brothers, but he thought that at the time the movement was 'not mature enough' in either its male or female branches (Roald 1994: 155). It is interesting to note that Farḥān and a few others who expressed similar ideas obtained their higher degrees in the United States or Europe. Many female Islamists said that they think attitudes towards women are changing. The 1993 student union elections with women nominees were referred to as an indication of such change. The Islamic Action Front, which was established by members of the Muslim Brotherhood, initially did not accept women as members. Women were first acknowledged as having an official role to play in political life in 1994, and in 1994–5 Nawwāl Faʿūrī became the first woman to be a member of the governing council (*majlis ash-shūrā*) of the party.

In 1994, the central office of the Muslim Brotherhood in Egypt issued a report called *The Role of Muslim Women in Islamic Society according to the Muslim Brotherhood*. Although this report originated in Egypt, it is also important in a European context as the movement's policies are to some extent centralised. The report refers to women's rights to vote, to be elected, to occupy public and government posts and to work outside the home in general. The Muslim Brotherhood approaches these issues in terms of the Koran and Sunna, thus using theological arguments to determine the role of women in modern society.

Women are portrayed first and foremost as mothers and then as wives. The report further states that 'women make up half of society and they are responsible for the nurturing, guidance and formation of subsequent generations of men and women' (The Muslim Brotherhood 1994: 3). One important clause states that 'it is the female who imbues principles and faith into the souls of [the] nation' (The Muslim Brotherhood 1994: 3). This statement conveys a common idea within the movement: 'The mother is a school' (*al-umm madrasa*). It also communicates the idea of women as bearers of cultural and social traditions and even of the patriarchal system. In most parts of the world women are responsible for the informal education of children, so that one could argue that the maintenance of a global system of patriarchy lies in the hands of women. This idea is implicitly suggested by Fatima Mernissi in her book, *Beyond the Veil*, in which she draws attention to the fact that male superiority is fostered from a very young age by mothers and female relatives (Mernissi 1975).

In the Muslim Brotherhood, the notion of women as educators of future generations has resulted in a view of the role of women as primarily mothers and organisers of the domestic sphere (The Muslim Brotherhood 1994: 10). This idea is upheld in books written by members and sympathisers of the movement, although these writers also mention that in Islam it is not wrong for a woman to work outside the home (Sābiq 1985; M. Quṭb 1985).

The common non-Muslim notion that Muslim women do not have the same value as Muslim men is refuted by the Muslim Brotherhood's report. It clearly states that 'the general rule is equality between men and women' (The Muslim Brotherhood 1994: 9). As for the distinctions between them, the report asserts:

> These differences (those specific characteristics that distinguish the female from the male) are due to the separate functions that have been accorded to the male and the female. It is because of these complementary and necessary distinctions that a man becomes attracted to a woman and a woman becomes attracted to a man and a marriage can be a happy, constructive and healthy one.
>
> (The Muslim Brotherhood 1994: 9)

Implicit in this is an affirmation of equality between men and women as far as worship and the relationship between human beings and God are concerned. Similarly, in criminal cases as well as in matters of impropriety in society, men and women are liable to the same punishment and both have social responsibilities (The Muslim Brotherhood 1994: 5). However, in the view of the Muslim Brotherhood, these responsibilities are different for each sex.

Zainab al-Ghazzālī al-Jubailī

Although female activities inside the Muslim Brotherhood are generally segregated from male activities, some strong female personalities have influenced the work of the movement. The most influential is the Egyptian 'Hagga' Zainab al-Ghazzālī al-Jubailī, whom I met and interviewed in Cairo in March 1997. She is the first woman who has written a complete commentary of the Koran (*tafsīr*), or as she expressed to me: 'I am the only woman who has an *existing* commentary as I am sure that other Muslim women in Islamic history have written documents which have been lost.' Zainab al-Ghazzālī was born in January 1917, and at the age of 18 she became involved in women's issues through Hūdā Shaʿrāwī's feminist organisation. However, she left in 1936 after a year with this group and established her own organisation, the Centre for Muslim Ladies (*al-markaz al-ʿāmm li s-sayyidāt al-muslimāt*).[24] This group was established 'for the promotion of Islamic *daʿwa* and the return of Muslims to their Lord's Book and the Sunna of His Messenger' (Z. al-Ghazzālī 1987: 13). In 1937, Zainab al-Ghazzālī met with Ḥasan al-Bannā'. At the time, he wanted to form a women's branch of the Muslim Brotherhood and he tried to persuade her to merge the Centre for Muslim Ladies into his organisation. Although she was sympathetic to his Islamic work she refused, and it was not until 1948 that she pledged allegiance to al-Bannā'. She has been a devoted member of the Muslim Brotherhood ever since.

In her personal life Zainab al-Ghazzālī has shown strong determination in her Islamic activities. When her first husband reneged on an oral agreement that they had made before marrying that she would be free to continue her Islamic work and expected her to stay at home instead, she divorced him. When she married her second husband she asked the same condition of him, and this time she was able to continue her work. In her book about her imprisonment, *The Return of the Pharaoh*, she recounts how she had meetings with men from the Muslim Brotherhood not only during the day but also in the middle of the night, and how her husband accepted this without participating in these meetings himself.

Zainab al-Ghazzālī was arrested and severely tortured during the reign of ʿAbd an-Nāṣir. She was imprisoned from 1965 to 1971, and was released through the intervention of the Saudi Arabian king.[25] When I met her in Cairo in 1997 she had recently turned 80 years old, but she was still giving lessons on Islam to young girls. I was present during one of her lessons where she spoke for more than an hour without notes. She is a charismatic personality and I observed how every person in the room was affected by her. Zainab al-Ghazzālī is a living legend among Arab-speaking Islamists. She deserves much of the credit for how women are perceived on an ideological level inside the Muslim Brotherhood with its openness towards female education. At the same time it is important to be aware of the cultural context that she lives in. Her view of women's role in society and gender relations in Islam is marked by her Egyptian cultural surroundings.

Zainab al-Ghazzālī's book *The Return of the Pharaoh* was first published in Arabic during the seventies and was reissued in its fourteenth edition in 1995. In 1994 an English translation was published by the Islamic Foundation. With her commentary on the Koran, *naẓarāt fī kitāb allāh* (*Reflections of the Book of God*), she has entered Islamic official debate not only in the Muslim world but also in the western world. I refer to her commentary on the Koran, first in view of the fact that it is the only existing complete Koranic commentary by a female, and second because her commentary is also read by Muslims living in Europe. It is interesting to look into whether her commentary is different from commentaries by males, and to consider if the shift from male to female perspectives entails a change in interpretation.

The Muslim Brotherhood allows for the possibility of diversity and change in its understanding of Islam, both in its acceptance of regional differences and in its *salaf* creed with the idea of 'returning to the Koran and Sunna'. Moreover, as many members of the Muslim Brotherhood are highly educated, they often follow a pattern of *cooperative* inter-group interaction within mainstream society. In spite of these factors, however, the institutional pattern of control within the Muslim Brotherhood might obstruct change to a greater extent than within independent movements.

In Part II I offer a more detailed discussion of the Muslim Brotherhood's perceptions of women, as many of my informants in Europe belong to this organisation. As indicated above, the movement has a liberal view with regard to female higher education. In addition, many women who are married to members of the Muslim Brotherhood or are themselves part of the women's branch are educated at universities or colleges in the Arab world. The women from the Muslim Brotherhood therefore qualified to participate in my study, by fulfilling my requirement that participants should have completed secondary education.

The Islamic Liberation Party

The Islamic Liberation Party (*ḥizb at-taḥrīr al-islāmī*) was established in Jerusalem in 1948 by Sheikh Taqī d-Dīn an-Nabhānī (d. 1977) from Haifa, who had an Islamic education from al-Azhar (Roald 1994: 101–4). In 1952 the party applied to be registered as a political party in Jordan, but the request was refused on the grounds that political parties were prohibited in Jordan. Sayyid Quṭb of the Muslim Brotherhood was in contact with the Islamic Liberation Party and negotiated with them with a view to sharing a common platform, but this endeavour ultimately failed (Amīn 1982: 77).

The party regards the establishment of the caliphate as essential. The founder's view was that all contemporary Islamic and nationalist movements and parties failed to achieve this goal after the fall of the caliphate in Turkey because they had not succeeded in raising the intellectual, political and social achievements of Muslim society.[26] It is a matter of controversy whether or not an-Nabhānī used to be a member of the Muslim Brotherhood. Suha Taji-Farouki, an academician who has investigated the party, argues that he never was a member (Taji-Farouki 1996: 2; 1996: 6). It is obvious that there are similarities between the Islamic Liberation Party and the Muslim Brotherhood in various fields, particularly in the political field. Although an-Nabhānī never explicitly defined Islam as a political system (Taji-Farouki 1996: 5), his followers today have adopted the Muslim Brotherhood's notion of Islam as a complete system (*an-niẓām ash-shāmil*). an-Nabhānī's view of Islam as a doctrine which 'is in harmony with human nature' is similar to the Muslim Brotherhood's notion of Islam as 'the natural religion' (Roald 1994: 124, cf. also Hedin 1988). On the other hand, I have identified many dissimilarities between the two organisations. Even in the sphere of politics, the approach of the Islamic

Liberation Party is different from that of the Muslim Brotherhood, particularly when it comes to actual methods. Whereas the Muslim Brotherhood promotes a gradual change of society (*tarbiya*), the Islamic Liberation Party has a revolutionary approach – the establishment of the caliphate. The greatest differences can be located within their approach to the Islamic jurisprudence (*fiqh)*, where the Islamic Liberation Party tends to take a more traditional view in gender issues than the Muslim Brotherhood. In summary, I would say that Taji-Farouki is probably right in concluding from evidence she has gathered from internal sources in the Party that an-Nabhānī never was a member of the Muslim Brotherhood. The importance of this claim is that it fosters greater awareness of the differences between the two groups, instead of identifying them within the same framework.

an-Nabhānī wrote many books which delineate the ideology of the party. Politically speaking, he saw the establishment of the caliphate as the central idea of the party's platform. This is reflected by the party's organisation under a centralised power which promulgates for all members, wherever they live, the same political and ideological stance to which all must give their assent.[27] Such unanimity implies that all members will promote similar ideas and have similar positions on religious and socio-political matters (*ḥizb at-taḥrīr* 1963: 88; 1953: 71). This notion of unanimity is in contrast to the approach of many other Islamic movements and in particular to that of the Muslim Brotherhood, which stresses the importance of local circumstances in its political analysis. On a practical level, however, it seems that members of the Islamic Liberation Party do adapt to the environment, particularly with regard to social issues.

In 1992 during my fieldwork in Jordan, I met the leader of the Islamic Liberation Party in Jordan, Abū ar-Rashta. According to him, commanding what is right and forbidding what is wrong (*al-amr bi l-maʿrūf wa n-nahy ʿan al-munkar*) is an obligation for which the Islamic state and its leadership alone are responsible. This view appears to have led the members of the Islamic Liberation Party not to engage in work associated with social institutions such as education, welfare, economic enterprises or the building of mosques (*ḥizb at-taḥrīr* 1985: 40; 1953: 25).

al-ʿAbdālāt, a Jordanian researcher on Islamic movements, has observed that the Islamic Liberation Party seeks to achieve its goals in three stages. The first stage in which the members receive their ideological education is conducted in secret. The second stage consists of practical participation in society and public dissemination of the party's ideas. The third stage is the re-establishment of the caliphate (al-ʿAbdālāt 1992: 106).

an-Nabhānī's view on legal matters was that 'true Islam' can only be achieved by returning to the Prophet's and his Companions' approach to the Koran (Taji-Farouki 1996: 51), and this led him to repudiate the traditional institution of Islamic scholars (*ʿulamāʾ*) (Taji-Farouki 1996: 37). He criticised traditional scholars for 'violating the Islamic legal rule by shying away from politics' (quoted in Taji-Farouki 1996: 87),[28] and he was also critical of the famous Islamic philosophers of the Golden Age of Islam, claiming that they had not evaluated Greek philosophy in the light of Islamic doctrine and had thus introduced non-Islamic traits into their understanding of Islam (Taji-Farouki 1996: 51). In order to avoid modern interpretations of the Islamic sources being corrupted by modern ideologies such as capitalism, socialism etc., an-Nabhānī argued 'that all foreign ideas must be evaluated on the basis of the Islamic doctrine, and rejected outright if they contradict any aspect of it' (Taji-Farouki 1996: 52).[29] In a similar fashion an-Nabhānī accords primacy to revelation, in contrast to the 'rational' trend in Islam both in historical and contemporary times which either subordinates revelation to reason or puts revelation and reason side by side. In spite of his rejection of the methods of traditional Islamic scholars and his promotion of the independent non-madhhab approach, it seems that an-Nabhānī still adhered to traditional legislation. His ideas in matters of sharia indicate that he accepted some of the methods of traditional sharia, such as analogy (*qiyās*) and consensus (*ijmāʾ*), whereas he rejected others, such as public interest (*maṣlaḥa*) and local customs (*ʿurf* or *ʿadāt*). Taji-Farouki has analysed his approach to Islamic law, and she concludes that in some matters he tends to follow the methods of the Shāfiʿī school, whereas in others his position resembles the historical example of the strict Ẓāhirī school of thought (Taji-Farouki 1996: 57–63).

In my opinion, the Islamic Liberation Party's ideas sometimes correspond with those of the *salafī* trend. an-Nabhānī, like the *salafīs*, believes that the Prophet's example should be imitated *in toto* (Taji-Farouki 1996: 58–9). This is in contrast with, for instance, the Muslim Brotherhood and many other Islamists who see the Prophet's example as divided into three different categories: first, the Prophet's sayings, actions and decisions which are the basis of sharia regulations; second, the Prophet's actions that are linked to his special status as a Prophet, for instance his marrying more than four wives, and third, the Prophet's sayings, actions and decisions that are associated with his human status or his cultural background and traditions particular to the Arabia of his time, such as those concerning clothing or food (Abū Zahra n.d.: b:89). Another similarity with the *salafī* trend lies in an-Nabhānī's belief that consensus in Islamic legislation corresponds to consensus among the Prophet's companions only. I would claim that these matters are of importance for matters of gender relations. As some Koranic verses and hadiths restrict the movements of the wives of the Prophet, as shown below in the section on the *salafī* trend, the same texts might indicate probable models of gender relations within the Islamic Liberation Party.

Although an-Nabhānī tends to interpret Islamic law in a strict manner, he shows a 'modern' approach to the issue of *who* should interpret the Islamic sources (the question of authority). He claims that not only is *ijtihād* an obligation for those who have the necessary competence, but he also calls for unrestricted *ijtihād*. It is important to draw attention to the fact that, although he demands competence for performing *ijtihād*, he also believes that all Muslims are 'potentially capable at least of deducing legal rules in relation to individual issues, and could consult the numerous reference works available in the fields of Arabic language, jurisprudence and legal evidences for advice in this respect' (Taji-Farouki 1996: 55). In this matter too his stand might be likened to that of the *salafī* trend. I refer to an-Nabhānī's approach to *ijtihād* as 'modern' because such an approach suggests a modern individualistic understanding of Islam. However, this is limited by an-Nabhānī's view that Muslims should strictly follow *all* the hadiths.

As for women within the Party, Taji-Farouki has observed that although women's membership is permitted, it is also regulated (Taji-Farouki 1996: 144). There is strict gender segregation in all party activities and, in Taji-Farouki's view, women are marginalised within the movement. She claims that women usually have their own study-circles, but my observation in Jordan did not support this claim. In my interview with Abū ar-Rashta, he stated that since the main task of women is keeping house and bringing up children, women's training is mainly the concern of their husbands. This might be a consequence of the political situation in Jordan where the Islamic Liberation Party is under surveillance and where the party's leaders are frequently jailed (Roald 1994: 101–4).

The Islamic Liberation Party is also present in western countries, where it has been increasingly active since the 1980s. Members are settled all over western Europe, but it is in Great Britain that they have the strongest presence. The party's greatest strength is on university campuses, but with the International Muslim Khilafa Conference at Wembley Arena, London, in August 1994 it manifested its presence nationally in Britain. One faction broke with the party in Britain and established a new group called *al-muhājirūn* (the migrants). This group consists to a great degree of non-Arab Muslims, whereas in the mother party the majority are Arab-speaking.

The relationship of the Islamic Liberation Party to other Islamic groups in Europe and particularly in Britain is not harmonious. Instead of cooperation with other movements, members of the party tend to take a competitive and oppositional attitude towards them, and their attitude towards western society in general is one of confrontation. There have been confrontations not only between party members and non-Muslims, but also between party members and members of other Islamist movements. Jewish groups have opposed the party's intensive anti-Zionist propaganda. At times their activities are banned. All this makes other Islamist movements with a more cooperative attitude towards their host societies feel that the Islamic Liberation Party is undermining their activities. One independent Islamist living in Britain explained:

> We have worked for many years in order to establish a relationship with the authorities as well as with the non-Muslim society in general.

> In just one second this work becomes void because of their [the Islamic Liberation Party's members] activities and attitudes.

As for women, party members in Jordan have a more traditional understanding of women's roles than do other Islamists in the region. Taji-Farouki, whose research on the Islamic Liberation Party was carried out both in the Arab world and in Britain, concludes that women are marginalised within the party. However, she does not distinguish between the role of women in the party's branches in the Arab world and in Britain. The question therefore arises as to whether the view on gender relations presented by party members in Jordan is representative for the Arab world only, or whether the party's understanding of women's role in society, like its political ideas, is centralised and part of the party programme.

In the Islamic Liberation Party's Proposed Constitution for an Islamic State from 1979, one section is entitled 'The social system'. This section deals with women in the Islamic state and its main message is gender segregation in all fields of society. Article 109 states: 'Segregation of the sexes is fundamental. They should meet only for some concern that is acknowledged by the Law, such as trading, or for the sake of which the Law permits such mixing, such as the pilgrimage' (in Taji-Farouki 1996: 206).[30]

A woman's primary duty is regarded to be mother and housewife, but at the same time the Constitution states that 'a woman is granted the same rights as a man, and the same duties are enjoined on her as on him, apart from those which Islam, through its legal evidences, has prescribed specifically for women or specifically for men' (Article 110). The same article grants women the right of pursuing professional work, although I would argue that the segregation of the sexes imposes a restriction on women's professional work. This apparent contradiction between strict sex-segregation on the one hand and women pursuing professional work on the other is not necessarily a contradiction as the Constitution pertains to an ideal Islamic state. Understood in the context of the Saudi experiment with its total gender segregation in all fields of society, one realises that such a segregated system actually demands female professionals. The important issue is thus to look at the actual practice in Europe where Muslims are in a minority position, in order to ask how the European situation challenges common Muslim perceptions.

In political matters, the Islamic Liberation Party maintains that a woman can vote, she can be appointed as an employee of the state and be a member of the Umma Council, but she can never be in a governing position:

> It is not permitted for a woman to assume responsibility for government. She thus can be neither a Caliph, an aide, a provincial governor or a district governor, and she cannot undertake any task that is considered to be an aspect of government
>
> (Article 112)

It is interesting to note that there has been a change between the 1953 version for which an-Nabhānī was responsible, and the 1979 version which was published after his death in 1977. In Article 111 in the 1953 version, it is explicitly stated that women can be appointed to positions within the judicial system (with the exception of the Court of Complaint), whereas this point is omitted in the 1979 version. As the issue of female judges is one of differences of opinion (*ikhtilāf ar-ra'i*) among Islamic scholars, it might have been considered wise to omit it in order to avoid disparity among party members.

As for the personal relationship between the sexes within the bond of marriage, the party's Constitution explicitly claims this to be one of trust and tranquillity. 'A husband's guardianship (*qiwāma*) of his wife is to be executed in the spirit of protecting her and taking care of her, and not in the spirit of command and control' (Article 116).

The potential for change within the Islamic Liberation Party seems to be less than within the Muslim Brotherhood. In contrast to the Muslim Brotherhood's allowing for regional differences within the party's ideology, the Islamic Liberation Party has a more rigid and centralised structure. However, many of the party's members are highly educated and are active in wider society, or they are students enrolled within a western educational system. Many members are thus potentially in a pattern of *cooperative* inter-group interaction with mainstream society, although previous experience suggests that students belonging to the Islamic Liberation Party, particularly in Britain, tend rather to be in a *competitive* inter-group interaction pattern with the rest of society.

The salafī *trend*

I have dealt with the *salafī* trend elsewhere (Roald 1994: 104–8), but I will briefly summarise its history before I investigate its ideas and activities in Europe. *Salafī* ideas are rooted in the *wahhābī* school of thought which originated on the Arab Peninsula at the time of Muḥammad ʿAbd al-Wahhāb (d. 1787) in the eighteenth century. It is important to note that this movement is not the same as the reform movement *salafīya* of Jamāl ad-Din al-Afghānī and Muḥammad ʿAbduh in the nineteenth century. Although one could argue that the nineteenth century *salafīya* movement and the Muslim Brotherhood of the twentieth century were built on many of the same ideas as those of the *wahhābī* movement, there are major distinctions between them owing to the fact that they developed in very different ways. The *wahhābī* movement developed in a closed, non-colonised atmosphere, and it therefore evolved trends particular to such a society. The other two movements developed in an atmosphere of western colonisation of Muslim countries, so that their understanding of Islam was a result of the encounter between the traditional and the modern. It is interesting to note that although ʿAbd al-Wahhāb advocated 'the return to the Koran and the Sunna', the practice of Wahhabism on the Arab Peninsula was to adhere firmly to the Ḥanbalī school of thought. The novel aspect of ʿAbd al-Wahhāb's approach was that it followed the Ḥanbalī law school strictly and rejected practices permitted in traditional Islam, such as wearing amulets with Koranic verses or visiting the graves of the Prophet's companions or saints, which was forbidden on the grounds of *shirk* (associating partners with God).

Even though the *salafī* trend varies slightly in its professed views between various Arab countries, it is united in its commitment to the direct interpretation of the Koran and the Sunna of the Prophet. The conflict between the *salafīs* and the more 'rationalistic' Islamic trend represented by the Muslim Brotherhood is not a new one (Abū Zahra n.d.; al-Ashqar 1982). Some scholars, such as Muḥammad al-Ghazzālī (d. 1996), have compared the conflict between these two movements to the differences between the historical stand of the people who adhered to the hadiths and the people who believed in scholars' opinions (M. al-Ghazzālī 1989).[31] However, the question arises as to whether this is an adequate comparison, since these early Muslim movements were mainly concerned with looking to base adjudications upon methodological principles, whereas the contemporary Islamic movements are reform movements.

The ideas of the *wahhābī* movement did not expand from the Arab Peninsula until oil wealth facilitated their spread to other parts of the world. In Saudi Arabia some Islamic universities have been established and they are concerned with exclusively Islamic teaching. A generous scholarship system makes these universities easily accessible even to students from impoverished countries. *Salafī* ideas have been disseminated by the graduates of these universities, who work as Imams or teachers in other countries.

Sheikh Naṣr ad-Dīn al-Albānī (d. 1999) lived in Jordan, and he is regarded as one of the prominent Sheikhs of the movement even outside of Jordan. He has revised many of the great hadith-collections with the purpose of validating the hadiths. First, he authenticates their *isnād* (chain of narrators). Thereafter, he scrutinises their content, searching out any possible contradiction with the Koran or other more reliable hadiths. Followers of other Islamic movements often accept parts of his validation of hadith-collections, but they criticise his many *fatwās* (formal legal opinions) based on these validations. He is therefore accepted outside the *salafī* trend as a *muḥaddith* (hadith scholar), but not as a *mufti* (one who delivers formal legal opinions) or a *mujtahid* (one who performs *ijtihād* (independent judgement in a legal or theological question)).

The *salafī* trend is loosely organised. According to Sādiq Amīn, a researcher on Islamic movements, the *salafīs* consider allegiance to a leader as a religious innovation (*bidʿa*) (Amīn 1982: 72), so they have no authorised leader or hierarchy. Their educational activities are restricted to lessons in mosques or in private homes. In the spring and summer of 1991, I attended lessons for women in a mosque. When I returned to

Jordan in the beginning of 1992 I discovered that these lessons had been moved to private homes. It was explained to me that al-Albānī had proclaimed a *fatwā* that women should not have meetings in the mosques as there is no evidence that women had Islamic meetings in the mosques during the time of the Prophet. Thus women meeting in the mosque is in al-Albānī 's view a religious innovation.

The term '*salaf*' refers to *al-aslāf* (the three first generations of Muslims): *aṣ-ṣaḥāba* (first generation: the companions of the Prophet), *at-tābiʿīn* (second generation: followers of the companions) and *tābiʿī at-tābiʿīn* (third generation: the followers of the followers). The *salafīs* regard the example of these Muslims as normative both in terms of *ʿaqīda* (creed or doctrine) and *fiqh* (jurisprudence).

The central idea is to interpret the Koran and the Prophet's Sunna in accordance with the understanding of the three first generations of Muslims. Although this is also an issue in the Muslim Brotherhood, the *salafīs* go further in this regard. The *salafīs* consider the problems of the Muslim Umma to be a result of diverse understandings of Islam which stem in part from Muslims' adherence to particular *madhhabs* (orthodox schools of Islamic law) (Amīn 1982:71; cf. al-Albānī 1993). In interviews and discussions with *salafīs* I observed that they reject the *madhhab* system entirely, and on every single *fiqh* question they look for the strongest evidence (*dalīl*) in the Koran and the Sunna, thus searching for 'one single truth'. They emphasise the idea of innovation (*biḍʿa*), which refers to that which is not explicitly mentioned in the hadiths or was not practised by the three first generations of Muslims, for example in the foregoing example of outlawing lessons for women in mosques.[32] They make a distinction between innovations in religious matters (*al-biḍʿa ad-dīnīya*) and innovations in worldly matters (*al-biḍʿa ad-dunyawīya*), while other Islamic groups or movements usually mention five degrees of innovation: *ḥalāl* (permissible), *mustaḥabb* (recommended), *mubāḥ* (indifferent), *makrūh* (detested), and *ḥarām* (prohibited or banned). The *salafīs* reject every manner of *al-biḍʿa ad-dīnīya*, but certain *al-biḍʿa ad-dunyawīya* are deemed acceptable.[33]

The strict *salafī* approach to *fiqh* is unique to the movement. The *salafī* view of *ʿaqīda* is to some extent shared by the Muslim Brotherhood, but the latter is more tolerant of a multiplicity of views in jurisprudence as they are not *salafī* in *fiqh*. Due to doctrinal conflicts between the Muslim Brotherhood and the *salafīs*, Islamic debate, particularly in the Arab world and among Arabs living in western countries, is characterised by detailed and abstract discussions on the Islamic creed, such as detailed discussions of how to understand God's attributes, and *fiqh*, such as whether or not wearing a gold necklace is *ḥarām* for women.

The *salafī* view of women and their role in society is strict. Women are encouraged to stay in their homes, a view which is criticised even by some of the *salafī* women themselves. Many women wear face veils. In this issue they follow the Saudi grand *muftī* ʿAbd al-ʿAzīz Ibn Bāz (d. 1999). Generally speaking, the *salafī* trend tends to take the strictest legal position. This has estranged many Muslims from their ideas and attracted many others.

In Europe the *salafī* trend has some strong footholds, for instance in France, Great Britain and Holland. Even in the Scandinavian countries there are large groups of *salafīs*, particularly among Arab and Somali groups. Strong material and financial support has enabled *salafī* thought to spread through Europe, and some of the Arab oil states in the Muslim Gulf have established some European centres where *salafīs* actively propagate Islam. This interpretation of Islam tends to attract Muslims with little formal education who become more religious in the cultural encounter with 'the West'. However, although the *salafī* understanding of Islam is non-integrationist with regard to European society, some *salafīs* become more moderate in this respect as time goes on. Conversely, with the increasing marginalisation of immigrants in European society due to unemployment and poverty, many *salafīs* become more strict in their interpretation of Islam, as can be seen from the following example from Sweden, where many Arab *salafīs* have little education.

In 1996 an imam who belongs to the *salafī* movement gave a Friday sermon in which he posed a question as to whether or not Muslim women in Sweden should go to the mosque. He explained that according to Islam nothing prevents a woman from visiting a mosque, but in his view the social environment demands that a woman should stay at home as the streets in Sweden are not secure for women. He went on to explain that on the one hand women represent a temptation (*fitna*) to Muslims as few Muslim women in Sweden wear a face-veil, and on the other hand he saw a danger of women being raped if they went out of their houses. This preacher represents some sectors of the *salafī* trend, although there are also *salafīs* with a much more open approach both to European society and to the issue of women in Islam.

After the Gulf War in 1992, the movement split into various factions. In Europe three approaches can be identified within the *salafī* trend. One approach includes those *salafīs* who continue to support the Saudi system, both politically and religiously. This implies that they still have substantial material support from the Saudi Arabian government. The other faction has rejected the Saudi political system due mainly to its support of the western alliance during the Gulf War, although it continues to support the Saudis' religious understanding and practice of Islam. The largest *salafī* group is the third, which rejects the Saudi system *in toto*. This group also gives women the greatest freedom in wider society. Whereas the two former groups see female activities as restricted to domestic affairs, particularly in Europe where there is no gender-segregation in society, the latter gives women a broader range of female activities although segregated from male activities. Inside the *salafī* trend as a whole, the role of women is understood in terms of the Koranic verse: 'And stay in your houses. Adorn not yourselves with the adornment of the Time of Ignorance (*jāhilīya*)' (K.33: 33). This verse is regarded by many non-*salafī* Islamists, however, as directed to the wives of the Prophet only, due to their special status as 'mothers of the believers'. To support this claim they refer to the immediately preceding verse which says: 'O, you wives of the Prophet! You are not like any other women. If you keep your duty [to God], then be not soft of speech, lest he in whose heart is a disease aspire [to you] but utter customary speech' (K.33: 32).

There is a notion within the *salafī* trend that it is the husband's duty to teach his wife Islamic knowledge, and this tends to restrict *salafī* women's movements outside the home. There are, however, some *salafī* women who gather weekly to study Islamic sources. These gatherings are mostly led by women, although men might occasionally give lectures. All in all then, *salafī* ideology is directed towards gender segregation. This is strongly reinforced in the European context where *salafī* women rarely play any part in wider society, despite the stress on female activities in these societies.

Although the *salafī* trend is undergoing a process of change due to its rejection of the four Islamic law schools and its attempt to establish a new 'law school' based on 'one single truth', this change does not seem to be oriented towards a rapprochement with mainstream culture in Europe. Rather, it seems to constitute a shift away from traditional Islam towards a more Wahhābī-based ideology. As few of those belonging to this trend in Europe have higher education, they tend to follow a *movement intellectual* (Eyerman and Jamison 1991: 98)[34] rather than investigating religious issues for themselves. Although this trend is not as strictly organised as the Muslim Brotherhood and the Islamic Liberation Party, the aspect of social control is strong due mainly to the role of the *movement intellectuals* whose ideas are reflected in the trend. There are strong indications that many followers of the *salafī* trend are in a *competitive* inter-group interaction pattern with the social majority in Europe. This is particularly true of Sweden where most followers live in suburbs inhabited mainly by immigrants and are dependent on state benefit, but in other European countries there are also indications that followers of the *salafī* trend are less socially integrated than for instance members of the Muslim Brotherhood and the Islamic Liberation Party.

The post-ikhwān *trend*

To understand the nature of the *post-ikhwān* trend of Arab Muslims (which might also be referred to as the 'independent Islamist trend'), it is necessary to return to the beginning of the contemporary Islamic resurgence movement in the 1970s and 1980s. Many of the Islamist organisations which mushroomed in the Muslim world as well as in Europe and the

United States were implicitly or explicitly under the direction of the Muslim Brotherhood. One of these organisations was the International Islamic Federation of Student Organisations (IIFSO) with headquarters in Kuwait. Although this organisation is small, it had a vast influence on the religious and political development of Muslims living in Europe. IIFSO's primary aim was *daʿwa* and its main task came to be the translation of books from Arabic into most of the world languages. IIFSO's brochure makes available translations of books in more than seventy languages. These cover works by most of the well-known Islamists associated with an *ikhwān* trend of thought, such as al-Bannāʾ, Sayyid and Muḥammad Quṭb, Yūsuf al-Qaraḍāwī, Muḥammad al-Ghazzālī, Abū al-Aʿlā Mawdūdī, Abū al-Ḥasan an-Nadawī and even the eighteenth century Islamic scholar in the Arab peninsula, ʿAbd al-Wahhābī (d. 1787). Gulf businessmen often paid publication costs, and as the translated books were free of charge they were widely distributed. Turks, Indo-Pakistanis, Bosnians and Albanians, the largest Muslim foreign communities in western Europe, would have IIFSO books translated into their languages.

Pernilla Ouis, a researcher in Human Ecology in Sweden, has investigated how a certain understanding of Islam became pervasive in Europe due to the influence of these IIFSO books. She claims that oil wealth enabled the spread of this interpretation of Islam so that it came to be regarded by many as the only true version (Ouis 1997). Ouis does not portray this particular understanding of Islam in terms of the *ikhwān* ideology, but it is obvious that this trend is over-represented when one considers the authors of the IIFSO books. The *ikhwān* notion of a 'rational' understanding of Islam is prominent in most of the books and the idea of 'the return to the Koran and Sunna' is promoted. Furthermore, the political interpretation of Islam, which describes Islam as a complete system of life, is a distinctive feature of this literature.

I believe that Ouis's account of the spread of a particular understanding of Islam is correct for the 1970s and 1980s, but in the 1990s this *ikhwān* ideology has diversified into various trends from rigid formalism to Euro-Islam. Prominent among these is the *post-ikhwān* trend which, although scattered and heterogeneous, builds upon the *ikhwān* ideology spread by the IIFSO books.

While many of the books manifest the *ikhwān* ideology, many have also gone beyond it. Muḥammad al-Ghazzālī, Muḥammad Quṭb and Sayyid Quṭb are regarded by a number of Muslims as having developed their ideas beyond the ideology of the Muslim Brotherhood. Although they were former members, both al-Ghazzālī and Muḥammad Quṭb left the Muslim Brotherhood. According to Kepel, Sayyid Quṭb's last book, *Milestones*, and also parts of his commentary on the Koran, *In the Shade of the Koran*, are far ahead of the Muslim Brotherhood's ideology (Kepel 1985). But while Sayyid Quṭb became revolutionary due to his specific circumstances, Muḥammad al-Ghazzālī developed in another direction. In his book written in 1989, one can observe his independent way of thinking with regard to *fiqh* questions (M. al-Ghazzālī 1989). al-Ghazzālī epitomises the development of thought beyond *ikhwān* ideology which I describe as the *post-ikhwān* trend.

I would further claim that many European converts to Islam belong to this category, mainly because they were among those targetted by the literature published by IIFSO. As most traditional Islamic literature is only available in Muslim languages such as Arabic, Turkish, Urdu and Malay, IFSO literature became by definition the 'convert literature'. Many converts thus came to adhere to this specific *ikhwān* form of Islamic discourse. However, many converts also tend to develop away from the controlled *ikhwān* trend to a more independent view where *ikhwān* ideas still predominate within a more free-thinking atmosphere. Although I have not dealt specifically with converts in my discussion, I would point out the great influence converts have had on Islamic ideas in Europe. One such example is the American convert to Islam, Nuah Ha Mim Keller, who translates classic Islamic texts into English. Another is the Jamaican convert, Bilal Philips, who writes *salafī* literature adapted for western converts. Converts have generally been active in groups working side by side with 'born-Muslims', and there has been an intensive exchange of ideas between them.

The *post-ikhwān* trend is not a group but rather a composite of various individuals from different backgrounds but with some traits in common. Many of these people do not even know each other and would probably not recognise the designation, '*post-ikhwān* trend', when confronted with it. However, I use this term to suggest that there are many people who are born out of the *ikhwān* tradition with its *salaf* direction, but who have turned away from organised Islamic activities within either the Muslim Brotherhood or organisations linked to it. Many of them are now active Islamic workers in various Islamic European organisations.

Common to Muslims within this trend is that they uphold the *ikhwān* and the *salaf* notion of 'returning to the Koran and the Sunna', the *ikhwān* idea of Islam as a 'rational' religion and the understanding of Islam as a complete way of life. In this sense I would label these Muslims as subscribing to *ikhwān* ideas (i.e. *ikhwānī fikrī*). On the other hand, many of them would refuse the Muslim Brotherhood's political actions in many Muslim countries, and they would resist the organised control of life within the movement (i.e. *ikhwāni niẓāmī*; organised *ikhwān*). As for educational standards, many of these Muslims belong to a highly-educated elite of Arabs living in western countries.

This *post-ikhwān* trend seems to be the most susceptible to change as people belonging to this group are highly educated and often have influential positions in European society. Thus, they tend to be in a *cooperative* inter-group interaction pattern with mainstream society. Furthermore, they are neither dependent on *movement intellectuals* for religious judgements, nor do they belong to an organisational structure with social control which might obstruct ideas of change.

Conclusion

In my fieldwork I have concentrated on four main Islamic directions: the Muslim Brotherhood, the Islamic Liberation Party, the *salafī* movement and the *post-ikhwān* trend. My experience with Arabic-speaking Muslims in Europe is that community leaders and active *daʿwa*-workers often belong to these movements and trends. Islamic conferences and seminars in which Muslims of various directions participate are frequently arranged by organisations such as the Muslim Brotherhood, the Islamic Liberation Party and the *salafī* movement. It is interesting to note that lecturers who are invited to such events usually belong to mother organisations in the Arab world. This might suggest that first-generation Arabic-speaking Muslims in particular tend to be more concerned with mother organisations and general policies in their countries of origin than they are with the actual migrant situation or with politics and official policies in the host society.

In the next chapter I explain the various criteria for my selection of informants and interviewees in this study.

3 Defining the area of research

Introduction

Taking into account the difficulties of demarcating the various types of Muslims, I have decided to focus on a limited group of people, namely Arabic-speaking, Sunnī Islamists who are first- or second-generation immigrants from Arab countries. In the following I will name them Arab(s). I would like to make clear that many Islamists whom I have interviewed in this study do not necessarily have explicit political commitments, rather their political ideas are latent within their system of thought. Furthermore, I have concentrated on educated Islamists who, although a small group, often have leading positions among European Muslims. They would frequently be involved in institutional work, and in many countries they are the link between the non-Muslim authorities and common Muslims. As the Islamic presence in northern Europe in particular is a new phenomenon, Muslims are faced with daily challenges to their faith and traditional practices. Often it is the intellectual elite who respond to these challenges, attempting to find solutions in the new context.

The present study is an investigation into the greatest challenge which faces the Muslim community in Europe, namely the reconstruction of gender roles in the new society. It is not an anthropological study but aims to have a religio-scientific approach. However, in order to investigate Islamist ideas and attitudes to gender I have used a variety of different methodological approaches in the collection of data, including some drawn from the field of social sciences. My research methodology includes questionnaires, discussions, interviews, group discussions, participant observation, and participant description.[1] I attended various meetings and conferences arranged by different Islamic groups, particularly the Muslim Brotherhood and the *salafī* movement. I visited the headquarters of different organisations and spoke with their leaders and members. I have collected field data in the Scandinavian countries, Great Britain, the Netherlands, Belgium, France and Switzerland, with an emphasis on Great Britain, France and Scandinavia.

Criteria for the selection of informants and interviewees

At the beginning of the fieldwork, I listed eight criteria for the selection of informants, interview objects, and other members of the Muslim community:

1 They should be Arabic-speaking, Sunnī Islamists, belonging to the group of first- or second-generation immigrants from an Arab country.
2 They should be well educated, preferably with a university degree.
3 They should have a certain amount of Islamic knowledge.
4 They should observe the Islamic commandments (at least adhere to the five pillars (*arqān*) of faith).
5 They should have an expressed Islamic world-view.
6 The female informants and interviewees should use a head-cover with or without a face-veil.
7 They should be active in Islamic information work (*daʿwa*).
8 They should have lived in Europe for more than ten years.

The first criterion: nationality

Informants and interviewees in the study were required to belong to the Arabic-speaking community. Those who have Arabic as their first language have the advantage of being the bearers of the language of the Koran and the hadiths. Although the Koran and some of the hadith literature are translated into many other languages, the Arabic language with its Islamic terminology conveys many connotations which demand a profound mastery of the Arabic language to be adequately understood. In the Arab world the *salaf*-ideology, with its notion of turning back to the 'pure sources', the Koran and the Hadiths, is more prevalent than in other Muslim countries. This is probably due to the ability of Arab speakers to search the Islamic sources for evidence (*dalīl*), instead of accepting ready-made judgements from one of the four law schools (*madhāhib*, sing. *madhhab*) or from contemporary Islamic scholars. I have observed that there is a tendency among non-Arabic-speaking Muslims to be more dependent on Sheikhs or Islamic scholars for judgements in Islamic matters. I would not deny that this tendency also exists among Arabic-speaking Muslims, but I believe that Arabic-speakers, particularly the well-educated ones, are those who hypothetically speaking have the best resources for reinterpreting the Islamic sources in a new environment due first and foremost to their mastery of the Arabic language.

I have chosen to deal with the Sunnī direction of Islam as I believe that the differences between the two directions, Sunnī and Shīʿī, when it comes to hadith literature and interpretations of the Koran, demand more time and space than I can possibly devote to such a study. However, by investigating changes and modifications in gender attitudes within the Arab

Sunnī direction in Europe, I believe that it is also possible to anticipate changes within the Arab Shīʿī direction. In the Muslim diaspora I have observed a trend towards conformity between these two directions. This might have to do, on the one hand, with increased contact between the two in the immigrant situation, and, on the other, with the exposure of persons of both directions to television programmes of the same Arab satellite channels. I have met many Arab Shīʿī Muslims who follow Yūsuf al-Qaraḍāwī's weekly Islamic programs on the Qatarian Satellite program *al-Jazeera*, as well as the numerous Islamic debate programmes on other Satellite channels, programmes which to a great extent are promoted within a Sunnī context.

The second criterion: educational standard

Initially, my criterion was that my informants and interviewees should have tertiary education. Whereas many Arab men in Europe, particularly Arabs living in Great Britain, have university degrees, many Arab women have only completed secondary education. This applies primarily to first generation immigrants. (It is interesting to note, though, that many of the Iraqi immigrant women who came to Great Britain in the 1970s and 1980s were graduates from universities in their home country.) Due to the fact that many Arab women living in Europe do not have university degrees, I decided to extend my survey to include female informants who had secondary level education.

The American convert to Islam, Nuah ha Mim Keller, states that there are certain conditions listed for being a *mujtahid* (a legalist formulating independent decisions in legal or theological matters) in the classical sources (N. Keller 1991: 15–26; 625–32). Some Muslims, particularly *madhhabists* (those adhering to one of the four law schools) consider there to be no or possibly only a few *mujtahids* at the present time, in the sense that there are few Muslims who have the amount of Islamic knowledge required for such a task. Others however, particularly Islamists, would agree that scholars might conduct *ijtihād* in a small scale. The Tunisian Islamist, Sheikh Rāshid al-Ghannūshī, who is the leader of the prohibited Tunisian Islamist party *al-ḥaraka an-nahḍa* (The Renaissance Movement) explained in the interview I conducted with him that it is possible to have partial *ijtihāds*, meaning that although there might not be a *mujtahid* who can rule in all fields of Islamic knowledge, there might be scholars who are capable of making *ijtihāds* within their own fields of speciality. It is interesting to note that al-Ghannūshī is not an Islamic scholar in the sense of having a degree in sharia, as his academic speciality is philosophy. He tends, however, to make *ijtihāds*, particularly in political matters, as a leader of a political party.

The third criterion: Islamic knowledge

I decided that my informants and interviewees should have a certain amount of Islamic knowledge. University degrees are not necessarily sufficient for the individual Arabic-speaking Muslim to be able to apply the Islamic sources to European reality, since the process of reinterpretation or reselection of legal decisions demands an extensive knowledge of Islam. Broadly speaking, a person's knowledge might traditionally have been understood as equivalent to how much of the Koran and the hadith literature s/he had memorised. This notion has changed however, since particularly educated Muslims tend to regard understanding, problem-solving and the ability to apply knowledge as more valuable than memorising (Roald 1994). Thus, in defining one of my criteria for informants as Islamic knowledge, I am looking for persons with a broad awareness of the Islamic sources rather than Muslims who have memorised great parts of the same.

During my fieldwork on Islamic education in Malaysia, Jordan and Pakistan in the early nineties, I came across a notion in the Islamist debate that in the past families would send their most intelligent male child to study Islamic law. In the present time, however, the most intelligent child would be sent to study engineering or medicine, whereas the child with poor school results would be sent to study Islam. This is part of a model of explanation as to why the Muslim Umma has degenerated both intellectually and socially. It is interesting to note that of the persons I have referred to in this present study, only a handful have an Islamic educational background, and very few of my informants and interviewees were educated within the human sciences. Most of the highly educated Islamists living in Europe are educated within the fields of medicine or engineering. Hjärpe has coined the phrase 'engineer-Islam' to describe the form of Islam promoted by such people. This raises a question which is outside the scope of my research, as to whether this form of Islam has incorporated values related to this field of science, such as 'rationality', 'progress', etc.

The fourth criterion: Islamic commandments

Informants' and interviewees' observance of Islamic commandments is essential to this study. However, this is a delicate issue since to question Muslims about their Islamic practice is not regarded as appropriate. I have observed that many highly educated Muslims living in western countries have a purely cultural involvement in Islam. Islam for them signifies a culture with which they identify in contrast to the majority society in a pattern of 'them and us', but they would not be committed to follow the Islamic obligations such as praying and fasting. This group of people is not of interest for the present study, since I see it as essential to the research that the informants are committed to Islamic commandments. I thus introduced a question on Islamic practice in the questionnaire. For the unstructured interviews, I selected candidates through referrals and through personal knowledge of their commitment to Islam.

The fifth criterion: Islamic world-view

I stipulated that informants and interviewees should have an Islamic world-view, by which I mean Islamists and Muslims who regard Islam as a way of life in one form or another. To avoid conceptual confusion I would prefer to speak in terms of 'Islamic-minded' Muslims, thus indicating Muslims with an Islamic world-view who try to live up to an Islamic ideal, with the understanding of Islam as a comprehensive religion with the political aspect either explicitly or implicitly stated. However, as I have incorporated various groups of 'Islamic-minded' persons into my research, and as the term 'Islamic-minded' is a 'loaded' term, I have decided to use the collective term 'Islamist' and 'Islamism' in order to cover various forms of the understanding of Islam.

The sixth criterion: female covering

The female informants were required to wear a head-cover in one form or another. In an Arab Islamist context, I have observed that female covering is of the utmost importance. In the various Sunnī law schools there is agreement that the head-scarf is regarded as obligatory (*farḍ*) attire for women from the age of puberty (Sābiq 1985; az-Zuḥailī 1989). Shīʿī Muslims, on the other hand, require that girls should cover from the age of 9. As many Islamists have explained to me, one of the verses which deal with the covering of women is in the Koranic Sura *Light*, which starts with the words: 'This is a Sura which We have bestowed on you and made it obligatory (*faraḍnāhā*)' (K.24: 1). In their view the stipulation that this particular Koranic Sura is obligatory reinforces the idea of female covering as obligatory for Muslim women.

I want to stress that I do not believe that the Islamic covering necessarily indicates 'religiosity' or 'non-religiosity'. I assume that there are uncovered religiously devoted Muslim women, as well as non-committed Muslim women who wear head-scarves due to external pressures. Nevertheless, I consider the wearing of a head-scarf to be an indicator of commitment to Islam.

The seventh criterion: Islamic information work

This criterion specified that informants and interviewees should be active in Islamic information work (*daʿwa*). This condition is essential for the goal of the present research. The data should not only say something about the limited group of people represented in such research, it should also indicate broader developments. All over Europe there are many groups active in spreading Islam.[2] Members and sympathisers of Islamic movements are particularly active in this work. Arabic-speaking men and women who master the host country's language also teach Islam to groups of non-Arabic speaking Muslims. The men and women I have selected for this research, therefore, have a widespread influence on Islamic development in Europe, as their attitudes and their understanding of Islam are transmitted to a wider audience and not necessarily only to Islamists. Furthermore, many of the informants and interviewees are intellectuals within their traditions who have written books and pamphlets which are distributed to various members of the Muslim communities in Europe. Many of them are also, due to their *daʿwa* work, leading members of their community and that makes them even more valuable as informants and interviewees.

As for those Islamists with whom I had unstructured interviews, I selected those who were regarded by other Muslims as having an extensive knowledge of Islam and were giving lectures about Islam on various levels. I have been careful to quote only those who have extensive Islamic knowledge and are active in *daʿwa* work.

The eighth criterion: length of stay in Europe

At the beginning of the fieldwork, I established the criterion that informants and interviewees should have been living in Europe for more than ten years. An extended period of residence is important because of changes in personal values and beliefs which one could assume would occur over a period of time in a new cultural environment which is substantially different from the culture of origin. As my fieldwork progressed, however, I quickly realised that this criterion was impeding the research, and that by distributing questionnaires to those who had been in Europe for more than ten years I would gather only a limited number of responses. I therefore changed the criterion to five years for the questionnaires. With regard to unstructured interviews with persons who frequently give lectures at meetings and conferences, I accepted some who had lived in Europe for less than five years. I found that the amount of time spent in Europe is significant when it comes to issues of personal change, but other factors such as knowledge of the language of the host country, educational background, direction, outlook and personality are factors which are just as important.

Interviews, participant observation and discussions

The questionnaire consisted of thirty questions, including both open-ended questions and multiple choice answers. Apart from questions on personal data such as age, gender, civil status and educational background, most questions were open-ended. The open-ended questions consisted of texts from the Koran and hadith literature concerning women or gender relations. Most questions were formulated along lines such as: how do you understand the Islamic concept of 'a wife's obedience to her husband'? Other questions related to polygyny, the equivalence of two female witnesses to one male witness, inheritance, men's management of/responsibility for women, divorce, Islamic veiling, statements on female nature in the hadith literature, Muslim women's position in society, the role of the Muslim woman, and attitudes on gender and gender relations in general.

I distributed 250 questionnaires to educated Arab Muslims, men and women (the men needing to have a university degree or equivalent, and the women needing at least to have finished secondary school and preferably with a university education). The questionnaires were given selectively to those who met the criteria outlined above. I also handed out twenty questionnaires to Arab Muslim youths between 17 and 25 years of age, who were born in Europe or had at least gone through the formal education system in Europe. I handed out the questionnaires at conferences held by the Muslim Brotherhood and in mosques with members belonging to the *salafī* trend, the Islamic Liberation party (*ḥizb at-taḥrīr*) and independent associations. I also handed out questionnaires to individuals whom I knew either from referrals or from personal contact.

I received eighty-two responses (nine from the youth), of which forty-seven were from men (four from the youth) and thirty-five were from women (five from the youth). Of the questionnaires which I handed out personally almost all were returned, whereas the questionnaires I left in mosques and at conferences generated fewer responses, presumably because people were not motivated to answer due to the lack of personal contact. Members of the Muslim Brotherhood and independent Islamists adhering to the *ikhwān* way of thinking represented more than 80 per cent of the returned questionnaires. The other 20 per cent of respondents adhered to the *salafī* trend and the Islamic Liberation Party.

I asked fifteen people, men and women, whom I wanted to approach for unstructured interviews to write their names on the questionnaires. In the unstructured interviews, I used their answers to the questionnaires as my starting point in order to penetrate more deeply into the topic of gender relations in Islam. Some of the interviewees tended to have a formalised attitude towards Islamic issues in their answers to the questionnaires, i.e. they wrote what they *thought* was expected of them or what they regarded as 'the true Islamic view'. Some even skipped certain questions as they thought they did not have the proper knowledge to answer them. However, in the unstructured interviews they became more personal and offered more individual opinions. I also stayed in four families for four to twenty days to observe gender roles and gender relations within the families. In order to evaluate changing ideas in the cultural encounter between 'Islam' and 'the West', I used the method of 'life-stories' by which a person is invited to tell her/his life-story.

In addition to the interviews conducted with questionnaire respondents and within families, I had unstructured interviews with male and female scholars in leading positions such as Sheikhs, leaders, guides, advisers, teachers or mentors in the Arab Muslim communities in Europe. I tried to make a broad selection in order to present a variety of views. I also had semi-structured interviews with leading individuals such as Sheikh Rāshid al-Ghannūshī, who is the leader of a Tunisian Islamic political party and thus belongs to the *ikhwān*[3] stream of thought, and Sheikh Darsh who, up until his death in the autumn of 1997, was a member of the Sharia-council in Europe. Sheikh Darsh described himself as belonging to an *ʿĀsharī* creed[4] as he explained that this was how he was educated at al-Azhar. Thus, unlike many modern Islamists he did not have a *salaf* creed. However, he said that he fully sympathised with *ikhwān* ideas as he found 'the establishment of the Muslim Brotherhood and its development in Muslim society as a great experience in the life of the Muslim Umma in recent history'. I also interviewed Fu'ād Ḥussain, one of the leaders of the Islamic Liberation Party in Great Britain, and an imam from the *salafī* movement's headquarters, the Islamic Forum (*al-muntadā al-islāmī)* in London. Most Islamists in leadership positions are male. In order to present a woman's perspective, I interviewed Zainab al-Ghazzālī in Egypt who is regarded as the 'grand old lady' of Islamic leadership. She is a member of the Muslim Brotherhood and is the first woman who has written a (surviving) commentary of the Koran (see Chapter 2). I asked for further commentaries from some other scholars and famous persons, such as Muḥammad Fu'ād al-Barāzī who lives in Denmark, Sheikh Aḥmad ʿAlī al-Imām from Sudan, and Wiṣāl al-Maḥdī also from Sudan. I taped some of these interviews, and I made extensive notes during others. I give the full names of these Islamist leaders and scholars, but when quoting from questionnaires or interviews with common Islamists I have used pseudonyms to protect their identities.

In the conferences I was active in group discussions and I also had individual discussions with many of the participants. I made notes during most of these, and most of the unstructured interviews were taped. I also attended lectures in order to observe which ideas were emphasised. Apart from the conferences, I went to many group-meetings and attended lectures for women in different mosques in order to obtain a broad view on attitudes towards women. In the discussions I actively participated by posing questions and arguing points, and thus contributed to the further development of the discussions. Lastly, I had personal contacts with Muslims in different countries and during interaction with them I formed a good impression of the various streams of thought among Islamist Arabs.

From my extensive travels in the Muslim world I have had many discussions with Islamist leaders and common Muslims belonging to various groups, and I have thus obtained an understanding of the different approaches to Islam. I have also witnessed changes in attitude towards women and their roles in Muslim society, so that within the short span of five to ten years Islamist women have come to play a more active role in the development of modern Islamic understanding in various Muslim countries, such as Jordan, Egypt, Sudan, the Arab Emirates and the Maghreb countries (the North African countries).

Last but not least, in the years since I became a Muslim I have been in regular contact with Muslims of different ideologies and different approaches to Islam. I have thus lived within the Islamist 'environment' for a long time, and much of what I write about is informed by my own experiences even prior to becoming a professional researcher.

Written material

With regard to the written material I have selected for the research, I have attempted to choose literature relevant to a European context. Some scholars whom I have quoted are living and active in Muslim communities in Europe. Sheikh Darsh and Jamal Badawi are of this category, and both have written books directed to a 'western Muslim public'. Both have played a part in the understanding of Islam in Europe and both can be situated within a broader *ikhwān* interpretation of the Islamic sources. I have also quoted from Arab literature but I have selected those authors who have an audience in European countries. Sayyid Quṭb (d. 1966), Sheikh Muḥammad al-Ghazzālī (d. 1996), Sheikh Yūsuf al-Qaraḍāwī, ʿAbd al-Ḥalīm Abū Shaqqa (d. 1996), Sayyid Sābiq and Zainab al-Ghazzālī all belong to the *ikhwān* stream of thought. I have also looked into the work on female veiling by Muḥammad Fu'ād al-Barāzī, a Syrian scholar from the Muslim Brotherhood living in Denmark.

Of the scholars mentioned above, al-Qaraḍāwī is of particular interest in a European context. Many of his books are translated into other languages such as English and French. During my visit to Malaysia in 1991–2 I discovered that many of his books were translated into the Malay language and Malay Islamists often referred to his writings. I have referred above to his weekly television programme called *Sharia and Life* (*ash-sharīʿa wa l-ḥayā*) in which he answers questions from Muslims all over the world. It is interesting to note how often these questions come from Muslims living in western countries who are trying to adjust to Islam in the context of western life.

Other authors of interest to European Muslims include Sheikh Nāṣir ad-Dīn al-Albānī, Sheikh Wahba al-Zuḥailī, Ḥasan at-Turābī and Sheikh Nuah Ha Mim Keller. Sheikh al-Albānī comes from the *salafī* stream of thought, but his books are widely read by non-*salafīs*. Sheikh al-Zuḥailī has written a book on *fiqh* (jurisprudence) of the four Islamic law schools which is widely read in Europe. I have also chosen to look at books written by at-Turābī as some of them have been translated into English. Although at-Turābī is within the *ikhwān* stream of thought, he differs from the others by being more daring in his reinterpretation of social issues in the Islamic sources. Sheikh Keller represents the *madhhabist* point of view in his 1991 translation of the Shāfiʿī law school manual *Reliance of the Traveller* by Aḥmad ibn Naqīb al-Miṣrī (d. 1368). This work includes commentaries by traditional Islamic scholars on points on Islamic law requiring current interpretation as well as lengthy appendices on subjects which are problematic to Muslims, such as television, charging interest on loans and contraception. I have been unable to find any books specifically on gender and gender relations by members of the Islamic Liberation Party.

For commentaries on the Koran I have referred to those which are frequently used by Islamists of various persuasions. The commentary of ʿImād ad-Dīn Ibn Kathīr (d. 1373) is particularly important as it is widespread and is accepted by the whole spectrum of Arab Islamists. I refer to Muḥammad ibn Jarīr aṭ-Ṭabarī's (d. 923) commentary as his work is also acceptable to the great majority of Muslims in general and many later commentaries are built on his. I further refer to Fīrūz Ābādī's (d. 1416) Koranic commentary in which he builds on ʿAbdullāh Ibn ʿAbbās' (d. 687–8) commentaries. I turn to this commentary in an attempt to get some insight into the very early understanding of the Koran, as Ibn ʿAbbās was the Prophet Muḥammad's cousin and is regarded as the most knowledgeable of the Companions and the source of Koranic exegesis. However, as Ābādī's commentary was written more than 700 years after Ibn ʿAbbās, one can assume that Ābādī has selected, on an unconscious or on a deliberate level, those of Ibn ʿAbbās' commentaries which coincide with his own understanding. I also refer to Muḥammad ʿAbduh's (d. 1905) and Rashīd Riḍā's (d. 1935) commentary, *tafsīr al-manār* (*The Lighthouse Interpretation*), as many contemporary ideas about Islam have their origins in the eighteenth century's intellectual *salafīya* movement.

Methodological reflections

In the discussion which follows I refer to researchers such as Rosaldo, Marcus and Fischer, and Hastrup, who might be regarded as belonging to the scientific discipline known as 'Reflexive Anthropology'. In this approach the field of research tends to be regarded as less important than the researcher's development from 'uninitiated' to 'initiated' in a certain cultural context, so that the story of the field of study often becomes the story of the researcher's own experience. The researchers in question come from western universities and their fieldwork throws them into a totally different cultural sphere. After completing their fieldwork they return to their own cultural context and in all likelihood search for new areas of interest. Although I use these researchers as references, I have certain reservations about this approach. Their situation is different from my own, because although I also come from a western university I do not return 'home' with a new perspective after completing my fieldwork studies. Rather, I continue to be part of the reality that I am writing about.

Although I see aspects of these researchers' work as important, I do not go the full way in following their approach. The present work is not a story about me, it is a story about Arab Islamists in Europe. Although as a researcher I am present in the field and at times perform my own independent analysis and offer my own commentaries, the main object of this study is the development of Islamic understanding in the western context. So when I refer to research within the field of 'Reflexive Anthropology' I do not imply that I belong to this discipline. I have selected those aspects which I regard as valuable for my study and left out others, but I am also critical of some of its premises.

In the approach of 'Reflexive Anthropology' it has become important for the ethnographer to ask him/herself why one chooses to study a particular phenomenon. Initially, when I started to consider the present study, my object was to record Islamic attitudes to women held by Muslims with extensive knowledge of Islam. As Islam is a scriptural religion with a comprehensive canonical literature, I was of the opinion that what can be termed Islamic is that which can be linked to the text (*naṣṣ*). However, as the study developed and I discovered the great variety of interpretations of texts, I came to realise that it is not easy to state that one version is more Islamic than another. The same text might produce various readings depending on the interpreter's general understanding of Islam, his/her educational background, personality, and cultural and social affiliations. During the course of my study I experienced a shift from one concept of religion to another. My starting point was a normative understanding of Islam, which involved asking questions such as, 'what is Islam?', or 'what does Islam say?' By the end my perspective had changed and my questions were more along the lines of, 'what can be found in the Islamic texts?', and 'what is the outcome of various interpretations of the text?' This change in my approach can partly be explained by the influence of Hjärpe's emphasis on the *function* of religion. However, another important factor is my discovery of different points of view in Islam, and the realisation that Islamic texts tend to be interpreted according to the cultural context of the interpreter. The present study does not aim to define the effects of the various interpretations, but is rather intended to settle what Islamists define Islam to be in specific contexts. I have chosen to deal with educated Islamists with a certain amount of Islamic knowledge. Thus, this study will convey a first-hand account of Islamists' understanding of what Islam *is* according to the sources, the Koran and the hadiths, rather than according to traditional ideas and practices. That traditional ideas and practices are factors in the process of interpretation is unavoidable, but Islamists will at least claim that these are secondary influences.

In fieldwork studies it is important to be aware that some communities are easier to access than others. It is also important to be aware that it is difficult to get permission to study Muslims in general and committed Muslims in particular. This is partly a reaction to the way Muslims and Islam have been perceived by non-Muslims, both in an historical and a contemporary perspective. Particularly in the social sciences, research was and still is to a great extent used as a tool of western imperialism (Rosaldo 1989: 68–9; Marcus and Fischer 1986: 34). Muslims, particularly Islamists, believe that non-Muslims misunderstand Islamic ideas and practices either deliberately or as a result of a conflict of attitudes.

The problematic nature of the relationship between Muslims and western researchers is many-faceted. First, it arises out of the difference in aims between the researcher and the research object. A committed Muslim might agree to be studied or to be interviewed because s/he wants to give the 'real picture of Islam' in order to correct misunderstandings of Islam. The researcher, on the other hand, is looking for structures in order to explain the meaning of observed phenomena. As the perspective of the level of analysis, the etic level, rarely coincides with the perspective of the level of the social actors, the emic level, the social actors might be sceptical towards researchers and mistrustful of their intentions. It is always difficult to accept others' perception of oneself, and it has been suggested that this explains why people working in scientific institutions, for instance, are reluctant to be researched upon (Branté 1984; Gerholm and Gerholm 1992).

Second, the antagonism between Muslims and western researchers indicates differences in world-views and misunderstandings which might arise in the encounter between different 'cultural languages'. On the one hand, attitudes inherent in a certain concept or term can be lost in translation from one language to another. On the other hand, the translator's selection of words in the translation is influenced by her/his attitude and cultural background. Moreover, as cultural attitudes are often embedded in concepts these tend to change in the translation process and to acquire new cultural meanings.

The important issue in all this concerns the objectives of the researcher. I have mentioned the search for structure, which I take as a common reason for conducting a study of a particular group. However, in anthropological literature, one can observe other objectives implicitly expressed. Paul Stoller, an American anthropologist, states in his book, *In Sorcery's Shadow*:

> But the Songhay fascinated me. They were proud. They were stubborn. Like the warriors of their imperial past, they were hard and aggressive. These qualities drew me to the Songhay, for I wanted to be more like them. Attracted by the ethos of these people, I decided to let the Songhay lead me along their path.
>
> (Stoller and Olkes 1987: 11)

Stoller's work is as much a reflection on the methodology of his fieldwork as it is a study of the Songhay community in Nigeria. During his fieldwork, he became an apprentice of an influential Songhay sorcerer and the reader witnesses his journey from innocence to experience in the performance of magic, and his struggle to understand the magical incidents he experiences. This existential journey is the plot of the book, while on a meta-level the tension between ethnography and anthropology, which also becomes an issue of concern for Stoller, is its leitmotif. Stoller enquires into the issue of the subjectivity of research. His wife joined him at a time when he was absorbed in the magical sphere. For him she represented 'rationality', but despite her presence and her 'objectivity', inexplicable incidents occurred. Stoller's conclusion is summarised in his statement that 'The Songhay world challenged the basic premises of my scientific training. Living in Songhay forced me to confront the limitations of the Western philosophical tradition' (Stoller and Olkes 1987: 227). Ethnography thus becomes a question of belief. The researcher's distance and objectivity might be challenged in their epistemological foundations and the question of 'truth' is forced into the foreground.

Stoller's study is of significance for my research. He was an 'outsider' who became an 'insider' while I was an 'insider' from the beginning. The question which arises is to what extent my position influences the outcome of the research. I would claim that as Stoller became an 'insider', he came into contact with knowledge that he would never have obtained as an outsider. He learned how to bewitch other persons and he even performed such bewitchment. It is interesting to note that he makes a point of not transmitting the exact knowledge of this to the readers, thus adding to the mystery.

As an 'insider' I acquired knowledge which would perhaps never have been accessible to a non-Muslim researcher. Moreover, as an insider I have the same interest as other 'insiders', and my quest for knowledge often coincides with that of the research objects. I thus believe that the knowledge a Muslim researcher obtains in studies on Muslims is *different* from the knowledge a non-Muslim might obtain due to different approaches and due to the difference in 'cultural language', i.e. perceptions of objects or statements, between Muslim and non-Muslim researchers. I would also suggest, however, that differences in acquired knowledge and perceptions do not always have to do with being a Muslim or a non-Muslim. Although I can, as a Muslim, be regarded as an 'insider' in this study, I am also an 'outsider' since I am both a non-Arab and a convert to Islam. Thus I am neither an 'outsider' nor an 'insider', but rather someone 'in between'.

In a religious study it is not possible to clearly differentiate between 'insiders' and 'outsiders' in terms of secularity and religiosity. In some cases a secular Muslim might share attitudes and ideals with secular non-Muslims rather than with Islamists. Likewise, in some cases religious Christians might share attitudes and ideals with Islamists rather than with secular Christians in their own community. These are all important factors to take into consideration not only for researchers themselves in the context of their fieldwork, but also for those who read the research findings.

There is the obvious risk that an 'inside' researcher might miss some information. As the 'insider' knows the informant's world-view, the researcher might forget to ask follow-up questions to the informant's response to certain questions. Deviations from the common trend might therefore be overlooked. The 'insider' might take for granted ideas which an 'outsider' might investigate further in a way which sometimes elicits different answers.

A second issue raised by Stoller which is applicable to my own research concerns the identity of the researcher. Stoller goes through an identity crisis: is he the sorcerer's apprentice or is he the anthropologist? I have also sometimes faced a dilemma over my identity. Confronted with views which I would like to defend or reject I have had to ask myself: am I first and foremost a Muslim or am I first and foremost a researcher? When talking in terms of 'we and they' I frequently find myself switching from the one to the other. However, I do not think that there necessarily has to be a conflict between the two, and perhaps some of the conflict which I have experienced at times has been due to the way Islam has been studied in western countries. The critical and apparently disparaging attitudes which one finds in some literature on Islam written by non-Muslims creates a sense that the scientific approach necessarily involves excessive criticism which is not always apparent in scientific studies of other subjects. This attitude can probably be attributed to 'the West's' cultural heritage of Orientalism. Since this is a well-established attitude within the academic study of Islam, it might take time to change. Thus the problem for me is not to choose between two identities, but to come to terms with a specific scientific approach and maybe to try to offer alternative methodologies in this particular area.

Values in research

Louis Dumont has pointed at how, in the comparison between different societies, *hierarchisation* of values plays an important part in the outcome of the research. He writes:

> That our system of values determines our entire mental landscape can be readily realized from the simplest possible example. Let us suppose that our society and the society under study both show in their system of ideas the same two elements *A* and *B*. That one society should subordinate *A* to *B* and the other *B* to *A* is enough for considerable differences to occur in all their conceptions. In other words, the *hierarchy* present in a culture is essential for comparison.
>
> (Dumont 1986: 7)

Much social research is about comparison on an unconscious or on a deliberate level, as the researcher necessarily analyses the material in terms of differences in values. What seems to be implied in the above statement is that western scientific methodology has a hierarchy of values which is inherent in social research on other cultures or societies.

In Rosaldo's book, *Culture and Society*, he reflects on the nature of research and the methodology used in the social sciences, and he disputes Weber's idea of a value-free science. According to Rosaldo, previously science was 'masculine' and 'detached'. The aim of the researcher was to clarify the world rather than to change it (Rosaldo 1989: 168–73). He gives the example of Frank Hamilton Cushing's criticism of 'going native research' at the beginning of the twentieth century. Cushing asserted that this approach was non-scientific for by becoming a participant the researcher lost the ability to obtain true scientific knowledge (see Rosaldo 1989: 179–80).

Rosaldo is critical of the traditional model of research. He argues that the detached researcher would overlook the relation between daily life and rituals and would also fail to take into account the influence of powerful emotions by only observing the external manifestations of an event. He contends that one can only comprehend a phenomenon through one's personal experience, and he illustrates this by referring to his own experience of loss when his wife died during fieldwork among the Ilongots, a head-hunting people, in the Philippines. The Ilongots had explained that the rage they experienced in bereavement caused them to go out head-hunting. Rosaldo initially did not accept this explanation, but his own experience of loss led him to understand that grief *could* cause anger and rage (Rosaldo 1989: 2–12). He describes how before the death of his wife he tried to conform the Ilongot head-hunting system to western scientific models of reality, but afterwards he changed his perspective and came to recognise that ethnographers tend to transfer categories and classifications suitable for their own societies and apply them to societies with different social structures (Rosaldo 1989). He thus highlights various difficulties for researchers in the field, most of which are associated with a lack of comprehension of different cultural perspectives.

I question whether Rosaldo would have recognised the rage he experienced as grief if he had not had the Ilongot system as a frame of reference. I would suggest that a person who endured similar emotions in a context which did not identify rage as part of the grieving process would not necessarily be able to consciously comprehend these feelings of rage, and might instead harbour feelings of guilt on an unconscious level, leading to depression and anger if these feelings could not be acted out. As perspectives shift according to culture and society, so does the expression of emotions which are often culturally conditioned.

In my own fieldwork, I believe that it is easy for me to understand what informants or interviewees 'really' mean as we share a common worldview and a common 'cultural language'. The issue at stake thus becomes, is there any 'real truth'? Does it mean that because I am a Muslim I have easier access to another Muslim's inner reality, since to a great extent I share this 'reality'? My answer would be that as far as it is possible to enter another person's 'inner reality', people of the same world-view are closer to doing so than people of different world-views. Moreover, I would suggest that part of the recent debate on 'truth' which concerns anthropologists such as Rosaldo arises out of differences in 'cultural languages' and 'cultural perceptions' between researchers and researched.

Whose point of view?

The anthropologist, Victor Crapanzano, has attempted to mirror Moroccan society through the story of Tuhami, a Moroccan bachelor (Crapanzano 1980). Although I accept the case-study method as a good indicator of attitudes in certain societies, cultures, subcultures, etc., I am also aware of the many variables encountered in this method. The personal characteristics of the researcher are of great importance to the outcome of the study. Kirsten Hastrup, a Danish anthropologist, has referred to the researcher's *biography* in terms of his or her gender, age, class, personal experiences and mental state of mind (Hastrup 1992: 117–19). A person's outlook and attitudes result from individual features and characteristics, social circumstances and previous experiences. Since the researcher is the one who poses the questions and defines the field of interest, his or her conscious or unconscious reactions are likely to define the parameters of interest in any interaction between the researcher and the informant.

Moreover, the informant has expectations of the researcher. Crapanzano's book is full of sexual metaphors. These may have been introduced into the discussion by Tuhami, the Muslim research object, because he anticipated that the researcher would be interested in sexuality due to the Muslim conception of western man as being obsessed with sex. We cannot be sure whether Tuhami's constant talk about his sexual life, or rather the lack of it, is prompted by his image of the researcher or if it is a matter of genuine concern to Tuhami himself. As Crapanzano also used a translator in his conversations with Tuhami, it is hard to know how many of their exchanges were interpreted and conveyed in a certain way by the translator. Thus, we do not know whether it was Tuhami who had a particular interest which caught the attention of Crapanzano, or whether their discussions were influenced by the perspectives of the translator, or whether it was the researcher who asked leading questions which directed Tuhami to the topic of sex.

The risks involved in using a translator are also highlighted by Stoller in his reflections on fieldwork. Stoller stresses the importance of having a profound knowledge of the local language, since he believes that the translator adds an extra interpretation of the material. He likens an interpreter to 'a life jacket: it keeps one afloat – even saves one from drowning – but it inhibits immersion and prohibits deep exploration' (Stoller and Olkes 1987: 228). In my research I, like Stoller, had the benefit of being familiar with the language of the informants. As I speak a form of Arabic which is close to standard Arabic, I am able to communicate with Arabs of various nationalities. I believe that my understanding of Arabic and my knowledge of Islamic terminology made it easier for me to understand what was 'really' meant than if I had the interviews translated into English or one of the Scandinavian languages, given that the translation of Islamic terms affects their meaning as concepts change from one cultural sphere to another.

The New Zealand anthropologist, Michael Jackson, has dealt with the question of 'truth' in his book, *Path Toward a Clearing: Radical Empiricism and Ethnographic Inquiry*. Jackson once came across a man who claimed to have turned into an elephant. This was a well-known notion in this particular society, and such accounts were often associated with socially marginalised persons. The first time the man told Jackson the story he did not attach any importance to it. As his fieldwork progressed, however, he became aware of the significance of the man's experience, and he started to look for him. When he found him, the man had lost interest in the story and refused to talk about it. Reflecting on the incident, Jackson decided that the man probably had some incentive for telling the story the first time, whereas the second time his social circumstances had changed and he no longer needed to tell the story. In his assessment of the truth content of the story, Jackson concludes that researchers are unable to ascertain whether an informant's narrative is true or false, rational or irrational. The researcher has to regard the narrative as 'a sensible truth', for, as Jackson explains, 'if illusions have real and useful consequences then they are truths' (Jackson 1989: 115). He considers it important to take a pragmatic attitude towards inexplicable incidents experienced by informants, suggesting that:

> Like human beings everywhere, we often claim that what is true is that which corresponds to what is proven, given, or real, but in our quotidian lives we tend to act as pragmatics. In crisis we make do with whatever is available in order to cope, and we judge the truth of whatever beliefs we take up in terms of where they get us.
>
> (Jackson 1989: 118)

Jackson and Rosaldo have approached the problem of 'truth' in different ways, and their conclusions are marked by the problematic 'us and them' pattern. This pattern is described by the anthropologists Broch-Due and Rudie, who have observed that 'our emics govern the creation of our etics, by means of which we try to come to grips with the emics of others' (Broch-Due, Rudie and Bleie 1993: 7). I suggest that part of the problem of judging 'the truth' has arisen as a consequence of the difference in 'cultural spheres' between the researcher and the researched. I find it of great interest to note that Stoller does not emphasise the issue of 'truth', although after a while he realises that his informants have lied to him. As he enters the Songhay sphere, however, the informants take him more seriously. I believe the reason that he does not enter into a deep discussion of 'truth' is a result of his entering into the Songhay society in a way which is entirely marked by a 'going native' approach. Moreover, as he became an 'insider' he started to understand what was 'really' going on and the issue of 'truth' seems to have become less interesting.

As many anthropologists have pointed out, a researcher is part of his/her own cultural background with a private biography which colours the outcome of the research. Marcus and Fischer describes ethnography as 'conversation across cultural codes' (Marcus and Fischer 1986: 29), and they explain this with reference to Geertz, arguing that 'the anthropologist . . . chooses anything in a culture that strikes his attention and then fills in detail and descriptive elaboration so as to inform readers in his own culture about meanings in the culture being described' (Marcus and Fischer 1986: 29).

Hastrup recognises that the ethnographer becomes a subject, a he or a she, in the discourse of 'the others', but she argues that the ethnographer in the field is not her/his 'normal' 'I'. Due to the objectification of the ethnographer, s/he becomes a-historical and is thus freed from the bounds of her/his time so that the subject and the object concur. The ethnographer, according to Hastrup, is captured between two worlds – the world of the ethnographer and the culture s/he describes. However, the ethnographer is released in the third world, the world of the anthropologist (Hastrup 1992: 117–19). Hastrup regards the ethnographer's biography as decisive for the outcome of the research, since the reality experienced in the field 'is not the unmediated world of the "others", but the world *between* ourselves and the "others" (Hastrup 1992: 117). Thus in her view, ethnography as 'anthropology's distinctive *method* of research' (Hastrup 1992: 117) is the description of reality, whereas anthropology is the interpretation and the deciphering of reality.

Hastrup's conclusion is built on Geertz's research. Geertz is one of the major spokesmen for 'cognitive anthropology', i.e. that part of anthropology concerned with reflection on fieldwork methodology and the researcher's role in the outcome of the research. Geertz explores the tension between scientific understanding and moral perception. According to him, this tension is a result of the researcher seeing the society as an object, whereas he experiences it as a subject. The researcher lives in reality and becomes his own informant as he perceives and reflects, and the result is that the subject and the object become a unity (Geertz 1980).

Hastrup's and Geertz's discussion has made me question my own role as a Muslim and a researcher of gender in Islam. As I am both an activist in the Islamic debate on gender and a researcher on the same, it is natural that I am not only an observer of the debate but I am also active in forming the debate. In my discussions with Islamists I posed provocative questions which if they had been posed by a non-Muslim researcher might have been dismissed or brushed aside with the argument that 'this is a western concept' or 'these are feminist ideas'. However, since *I* was asking the questions it was necessary for them at least to consider them and try to give 'acceptable' answers. So I am not only a researcher but I am also a participant who is moving the debate forward. Thus Hastrup's idea that the world of the researcher is not the unmediated world of the 'others', but the world *between* ourselves and the 'others' does not apply to my own research. The fact that I am part of the debate *and* a researcher makes the two worlds fuse in a way I believe they do not do when the researcher and the researched come from different cultural spheres.

Gender in the field

Gender is another issue of concern with regard to the researcher's role in the field. It might be that a male researcher observes different events and structures from those a female researcher would observe in the same situation. Moreover, a male researcher will probably be given different answers from the interviewees, as they have different expectations of men and women. In Muslim communities, the distinction between male and female researchers is more pronounced than in other groups due to the segregation between the sexes in these communities. This segregation is not always visible, but even when men and women are present in the same room there will be an invisible barrier due to a strong *idea* of segregation inhibiting interaction between the sexes. The result is that men and women have access to different information. Male researchers have less access to Muslim female spheres than have female researchers to Muslim male spheres. A female researcher who wants to interview a male Muslim might find difficulties in communication due to invisible barriers. In my discussions with male Islamists I was accompanied by my husband who not only functioned as a bridge between the interviewees and myself, but who was also active in posing questions. I am convinced that without his help I would not penetrated the issues to the same extent and would probably not have been given such honest answers. Moreover, the fact that he personally knows many of the scholars and European Islamists facilitated my access to interviewees and avoided prejudices which they might otherwise have had towards me as a western researcher. For Islamists, my husband legitimated my research and because of him I was able to ask provocative questions which I am convinced I could not have asked without his presence. Given that the issue of gender is often problematic in a Muslim context, I think it is an acceptable solution for a female researcher to be accompanied by a male supporter or colleague in interviews with male scholars and other male Islamists.

Fieldwork as dialogue

Fieldwork is in the first place about dialogue and confrontation. All parties to this dialectic process have imaginative concepts about 'the self' and 'the other', and these influence the construction of reality in the encounter between the ethnographer and the 'other'. Marcus and Fischer speak in terms of 'the metaphor of dialogue' which has become the focus of anthropological discussion on writing. They claim that the 'metaphor of dialogue' has replaced the earlier 'metaphor of text', saying:

> Dialogue has become the imagery for expressing the way anthropologists (and by extension, their readers) must engage in an active communicative process with another culture. It is a two-way and two-dimensional exchange, interpretative processes being necessary both for communication internally within a cultural system and externally between systems of meaning
>
> (Marcus and Fischer 1986: 30)

Although I recognise the role of dialogue in ethnography, I approach it with a certain amount of scepticism since much depends on how one defines 'dialogue'. 'Dialogue' might be understood in a more abstract sense as something similar to 'interaction'. In this sense I would agree with Marcus and Fischer, as dialogue in this sense of the word points to an interaction between two parties, and the presence of the researcher creates new structures for informants. However, if 'dialogue' is defined as a mutual exchange of experiences, a definition which I prefer, I think that dialogue, at least in a Muslim context, is rarely a prominent characteristic of fieldwork. In my own experience as a research object, researchers do not always express their disagreement with or objection to an informant's statements and attitudes, even though the informant might convey values profoundly opposed by the researcher. Without any sign of opposition, the informant thinks the researcher agrees with his or her views and s/he might continue along the same track to develop new lines of thought which in another situation s/he would not arrive at. This is the nature of the dialectical process in verbal interaction. Particularly in a Muslim context, many researchers avoid expressing criticism or opposing views for fear of being excluded from the field, and this strongly affects research on Muslims and Islam. The researcher by her/his passivity is active in creating new structures due to the *lack* of dialogue rather than due to dialogue, structures which would probably be different if the researcher had been an active participant in the 'dialogue'.

Reflections

Studies on Islam and Muslims in western universities and even in universities in Muslim countries have mainly been carried out by either non-Muslims or Muslims who have adopted western world-views, which more often than not includes a scientific research methodology even when applied to non-western societies and non-secularised communities. As a result, much of the information on Islam and Muslims is disseminated by researchers with a commitment to other 'ideologies' or religions than Islam.

This raises the question as to what happens when Muslims themselves begin researching their own communities. Will there be a conflict between the 'inside'/'outside' approach? Can a study of Muslims by a Muslim be regarded as wholly scientific? Can a person who belongs to the same creed as the research-object be objective? I suspect that the answer is that it is impossible to be objective in *any* research as all research will necessarily be coloured by the researcher's world-view. The 'inside'/'outside' approach is a complex issue which will become increasingly important as more and more Muslims attain higher education in western countries. However, as I have pointed out above, it is important to be aware that even in a Muslim context, in the encounter between Muslims as researchers and Muslims as research-objects there will still be a conflict between the various levels and directions of 'Muslimness'.

The researcher's commitment is important for the outcome of the research. I believe that it has been of benefit to the present research that I am myself a Muslim. The question of gender relations in Islam and in Muslim society is loaded with cultural values both in a Muslim and in a non-Muslim context, and the debate has become over-heated so that the tension between the 'cultural language' of Muslims and that of non-Muslims is likely to cause antagonism. As I am a person 'in between' I believe I have the potential to transmit knowledge from one cultural sphere to another, while at least to a certain extent preserving the integrity of this knowledge.

Having thus established the parameters and methodology of my research, in the next chapter I will look at various patterns of change and changing processes in the migration situation.

4 Theoretical reflections on change and changing processes

The underlying issue which informs this study is that of change and changing processes in the interpretation of social issues in the Islamic sources, since I am looking at how attitudes to women and gender relations change in the cultural encounter between 'Islam' and 'the West'. Changes on the ideological level are difficult to evaluate, as Sven-Eric Liedman explains in his book, *I Skuggan av Framtiden* (*In the Shadow of the Future*): 'It is possible to calculate the course of the satellites around the world with tremendous exactitude, whereas no technical calculation can possibly decide whether Sweden is a more democratic country than Great Britain' (Liedman 1997: 37 [translation mine]). Changes and changing processes in Muslims' interpretation of social issues in the Islamic sources form the initial phase of the study, but it also anticipates further changes in the future. I outline below various models which I apply in order to better understand the mechanism of change from one cultural context to another.

For Muslims in Europe, it seems that Islam has two main functions which might be two sides of the same coin. In terms of its cultural understanding, Islam has a conserving effect in the preservation of identity in a new cultural context and, as interaction with social majorities increases, Islam offers Muslims an opportunity to distinguish themselves from the majority in the acquisition of identity. On the other hand, the flexibility of interpretation of social issues in the Islamic sources affords the possibility of developing new interpretations in the new cultural context. This reinterpretation of the Islamic sources is a process which might occur on several levels. On a conscious level a deliberate reinterpretation might occur, whereas on an unconscious level the fact that the sources are placed in new contexts might result in them being 'filled' with partly new content. The latter might be the case even among groups of Muslims who would categorically deny any reinterpretation of the sources or any renewal of Islam. It is important to note that such unconscious changes in understanding are more as a result of socio-economic changes in the new context than owing to any considered process of theological or philosophical reflection. The question is whether or not such changes have to occur in order to avoid an awkward discrepancy between social reality and an ideal model of reality.[1]

Change and changing processes

I would suggest that, as many Islamist immigrants hold high positions in society, they will be part of the social power-base and will thus have a certain influence on changes occurring at the level of the majority society. At the same time they are exposed to constant pressures from the majority society, particularly concerning matters of Islamic ideology. These pressures can work two ways, because they can either force immigrant groups into a more segregated existence or they can cause Muslims to reevaluate their ideas and attitudes. According to most Muslims, the Islamic sources, the Koran and the Sunna, cannot be changed. However, there is the possibility of reinterpretation or a reselection of interpretations of social issues in the Islamic sources which might lead to changes in the approach to Islam. It is important to be aware that these reinterpretations or reselections are often conducted on an unconscious level with non-verbalised changes of attitude as the driving force.

Kim Knott, in her study on religion and identity, emphasises that just as 'ethnic identity is not a static phenomenon . . . religion is not static either' (Knott 1986: 169). E. M. Pye, another researcher on religion, explains:

> Since religion is subject to the passage of time, religious leaders and believers are forced to respond to everlengthening perspectives. In particular the transmission of religion from one culture to another whether geographically or chronologically means that new cultural elements are introduced to the tradition and new demands are made upon it.
>
> (Pye 1979: 17, also quoted in Knott 1986: 170)

Knott points to how religious changes occur through immigration and settlement experiences. She maintains that 'no religion remains unchanged through such occurrences. Beliefs, practices, social organisations, and religious experiences adapt and develop as a result of the new geographical and social location' (Knott 1986: 171). She further states:

> They [the immigrants] have brought their own religious and cultural traditions. It is these, in interaction with the new environment, which produce consequent religious changes – new interpretations, new forms of religion and religiousness, and a new self-consciousness concerning religious matters. The precise nature of the changes which occur will stem partly from (I) the nature of the religion itself (e.g. its unity or diversity, its universality or its ethnic particularity) and

> (II) the nature of the other cultural factors such as language, customs, food and dress, etc.
>
> (Knott 1986: 172)

Whereas Knott focuses upon change in the immigration situation in general, the Norwegian anthropologist Fredrik Barth has penetrated the question of change more profoundly. Barth distinguishes between 'the cultural' and 'the social', but whereas he sees 'culture' being in a state of flux, he believes that 'social organisations' tend to have distinct boundaries (Barth 1995: 14). In the light of Barth's theory of 'social organisations', one can regard Muslim social organisations as containing social patterns of control which can prevent a rapprochement between ideologies or between individuals belonging to different social organisations. Furthermore, the strength of patterns of control within social organisations depends on the tension which exists between the various factions within society.

Within Arab Islamism in Europe, Barth's concept of social organisation can be applied to depict Islamist movements in particular. Social patterns of control which obstruct change can then, in Barth's terminology, be seen as being stronger within organised Islamist movements and trends than in the broader context of Islamism. Although there are changes of attitude within Islamic movements, the changes among individuals within movements are less than those outside movements. Changes of Islamic perceptions of women in a European context might therefore be more pronounced among independent Islamists than among Islamists belonging to the various Islamist movements.

Edward Said has also dealt with changes in the immigrant situation. He says:

> The exile knows that in a secular and contingent world, homes are always provisional. Borders and barriers which enclose us within the safety of familiar territory can also become prisons, and are often defended beyond reason or necessity. Exiles cross borders, break barriers of thought and experience.
>
> (Said 1990: 365)

Said's words convey a sense of rootlessness which might be a consequence of exile, while also suggesting how change comes about as a result of exile. There is an obvious tension between, on the one hand, the security and safety of a familiar situation and, on the other hand, the insecurity and changeability in the situation of the exile. The ideas and attitudes which determine a person's approach to the environment are bound to change in the transference from familiar to alien conditions.

There are many studies on immigrants' adjustments to new environments. Muhammad Anwar, a British sociologist of Pakistani origin, has in his study of Pakistanis in Britain dealt with concepts such as 'assimilation', 'acculturation', 'integration', 'absorption' and 'adaptation'. Anwar observes that these concepts have been used interchangeably, but he argues that they all contain a variety of subtle meanings (Anwar 1985: 7). Anwar presents a range of views, and he starts by demonstrating Parson's distinction between social and cultural assimilation which he explains as follows:

> Social assimilation emphasises the process of adaptation to the receiving society's system of interaction between individuals and collectivities. Cultural assimilation involves adopting the content and patterns of values, ideas and other symbolic systems that are essential in the 'shaping of human behaviour and the artefacts produced through behaviour'.
> (Anwar 1985: 8)

Anwar's conclusion is that all previous theories are based on a minority/majority approach where the majority ideology dominates. He suggests that 'there are different types and levels of accommodation and assimilation. Even if an immigrant is objectively assimilated, what about his subjective identity?' (Anwar 1985: 9). Anwar expresses a desire for a model of integration which he describes as 'a situation in which a group continues to be an integer or unit on its own, but one which as part of a greater whole is accepted by the majority' (Anwar 1985: 10). He understands this as a situation in which an immigrant is part of 'a primary community based on kinship-friendship networks among his fellow migrants' while at the same time having a contractual tie with the host society in the employment and education fields (Anwar 1985: 10).

Anwar argues that there are two ways of understanding 'integration' depending on one's point of view. He maintains that immigrants understand integration as 'acceptance by the majority of their separate ethnic and cultural identity', whereas from a majority point of view, integration reflects the 'ideology of the dominant group' (Anwar 1985: 110), which conveys the notion that 'any group unabsorbed, or not assimilated is considered to upset the equalisation of social relations in the society' (Anwar 1985: 9). This last stand reflects the situation of immigrant groups in a subordinate power position. It is interesting to note that the main immigration policy in Sweden is to assist immigrants in order for them to integrate into Swedish society. The 'Euro-Islam Conference' in Stockholm in June 1995 was an indicator of this policy. However, there is a subtlety in this notion of 'Euro-Islam' which Anwar identifies above. In the term 'Euro-Muslims' I sense a presupposition that some Muslims are more 'conformed' than other Muslims. There seems to be a hierarchy of norms implicit in the term 'Euro-Muslim' according to the level of conformity to the premises of the majority which might be refused by many Muslims. Conversely, there are factors impeding integration from the side of the host country. Most Muslims, even highly educated ones, meet obstacles in their search for employment in Sweden.

The process of assimilation or acculturation of an immigrant group can best be described as one whereby immigrants' behaviour, customs and lifestyles become indistinguishable from those of the majority society. C. A. Price, a researcher of immigration, has pointed out that the process of assimilation is not necessarily complete. While immigrants assimilate in some ways, they tend to keep up their own traditions in other ways (Price 1969: 215). In a Muslim context, this might mean that an immigrant might assimilate or adjust fairly well (i.e. perform his/her social duties) while at the same time maintaining an Islamic lifestyle in the primary environment.

Abramson describes a form of marginalisation which he calls *socio-cultural exile*. He explains this as a phenomenon experienced at the individual level in which the individual perceives himself/herself as a total alien in the present surroundings (Abramson 1979: 5–29). I believe that there is a tendency to regard *socio-cultural exiles* only in individual terms, since accounts of alienation are often conveyed to the broader society by intellectual individuals. Individual experiences of exile are communicated through fiction or intellectual reflections, such as in the literature of the American Jewish authors Bernard Malamud and Isaac Bashevis Singer, or in the academic literature of Edward Said and Gayatri Spivak, the American-Indian professor of literature, rather than by *movement intellectuals*. Thus, the experiences associated with exile tend to be perceived by readers on a purely individual level. However, it is important to be aware that such experiences are just as true of communities as of individuals, and they can be lived through both at the inter-personal and the inter-group level.

Kenneth Jones, in his article 'Paradigm shifts and identity theory: alternation as a form of identity management' explores how the notion of scientific objectivity was profoundly challenged in the 1950s and 1960s, primarily by Kuhn in *The Structure of Scientific Revolutions* (1962), but also less explicitly by Wittgenstein in his *Philosophical Investigations* from 1953. Jones writes that 'not only Kuhn but also Wittgenstein (d. 1953) has drawn attention to the process of being able to see both social and natural phenomena differently from the way they may previously have been viewed' (Jones 1978: 68). On reading this it struck me that this change in outlook is a process which occurs on different levels. The way a concept is transformed and modified in order for its content to be compatible with a changing world is part of a broader process of change. An example would be the translation of the Koran from Arabic into Swedish in 1917 by Zetterstéen. He translates the phrase '*qawwamūn ʿalā*' (from the Koranic verse: 'The men are *qawwamūn ʿalā* the women'; K.4: 34) as *föreståndare* which in English denotes 'manager of' or 'the one in charge of', terms with connotations of power and rulership. In the 1990s Muhammad Knut Bernström, a former Swedish diplomat and a convert to Islam, translates the same word as '*ha ansvar för och omsorg om*' (Bernström 1998: 104) which means to 'be responsible for and take care of', wording which has a slightly different connotation. What process has taken place in the interval between the two? Is it possible in a period of approximately eighty years for the content of a Koranic concept to change so fundamentally? I would argue that there are many variables to take into consideration in this matter. Although one can argue that Zetterstéen was not a Muslim and might therefore have shared the prejudices of Orientalist scholars towards the Islamic religion which were common in his time, it is important to note that Zetterstéen's translation of this specific Koranic verse carries the same connotations as we can find in Islamic literature in Islamic history.[2] We might presume that Bernström, as a late twentieth century Muslim, understands the relationship between men and women in contemporary Swedish terms. In this context it seems that European converted Muslims are very much part of their own cultural context. Although many converts tend to become 'cultural Muslims', i.e. to submit to a certain ethnic-cultural setting because of marriage to a born Muslim, this does not apply to everybody. However, as I will explain in a later chapter, the change of Koranic concepts is part of a process of change which is not only a feature of western countries but which has had repercussions in the Muslim world as well.

The basket metaphor

Hjärpe has discussed the question of change in the cultural encounter between 'Islam' and 'the West'. He proposes a metaphor which represents all religious traditions and all ideologies as baskets. 'The basket' is 'the set-up or area of traditions in a specific religion or ideology, as we can find it in its activities, i.e. all the rituals, narratives, historiography, categorisations, terminology and observances that constitute a group's heritage' (Hjärpe 1997: 267). His idea is that baskets leak from inside and absorb from outside, i.e. that old concepts might leak out and new ones might be absorbed. He suggests, 'that which has once been in use might be put back – or disappear for ever. Much has disappeared from the baskets in the course of centuries, other things have been added' (Hjärpe 1998: 34 [translation mine]). Moreover, the basket with its contents is there to choose from in times of need. The contents are latently present but there is not always a need for everything in it. Rather one selects from the basket what one is presently in need of and 'that which has relevance in a given situation' (Hjärpe 1997: 267). Hjärpe further links the basket to a person's perception. By referring to Hjalmar Sundén's Role Theory, he explains how

> the tradition, rituals, narratives, and vocabulary, and the 'roles' which they offer the individual, function as patterns for the very perception. Of all the stimuli, which reach our senses every instant, only a very few are chosen by our brains and interpreted as a perception. The contents of 'the basket' function as filters.
>
> (Hjärpe 1997: 269)

As for Islam, this metaphor might stand out as a blasphemy for many Muslims, I would suggest because of the widespread notion that there is only 'one truth'. However, in my view this picking and choosing or selection from 'the basket' is what actually happens. In the Islamic tradition of legislation a multitude of different rules and regulations have been established. On any particular issue many different interpretations have been promoted. These interpretations are based on particular circumstances and are influenced by factors of time and space. In the various regions of the Muslim world, Islamic law was established with an emphasis on one form of legislation rather than another due to the specific situation of each society and the preferences of scholars in the area. With the coming of western colonial powers to the Muslim world, the canonised Islamic law changed, at least to a certain extent, bringing into Islamic legislation new principles. One example is the Anglo-Muhammadan Law of the Indian subcontinent. According to Asma Khader, a Christian lawyer in Jordan, one example of how western colonialism brought oppressive elements into Islamic law is the 'honour killing' of women. 'Honour killing' became, in her view, part of many Middle Eastern countries' legislation due to the influence of the Napoleonic Code on Egyptian legislation in the nineteenth century. Khader sees 'honour killing' as a fusion between Egyptian tribal custom and the Napoleonic Code resulting from France's occupation of Egypt and the subsequent influence of French custom on Egyptian society. This law, she says, was later copied and canonised by Lebanon, Palestine and Jordan (*Guardian Weekly*, 16 November 1997: 23).[3]

With the development of the *salaf* ideology, the search for what 'really' happened began. Questions such as 'what did the Prophet really do or say?' might in their most extreme form culminate in the idea of 'one absolute truth'.[4] I will argue that if the principle of the search for 'one truth' is completely accomplished, one consequence might be that the idea of the Islamic universality will suffer. As 'one truth' emerges, the flexibility of religious injunctions according to time and place will fade away. In this case, Hjärpe's metaphor of Islam as a basket might have less validity. However, this particular consequence of the *salaf* ideology depends upon the extent to which one accepts this ideology with its rejection of the historical development of sharia. It is possible to accept the *salaf* ideology as an idea while at the same time considering factors of time and space, in which case Hjärpe's model becomes valid. In my view it is the latter form of the *salaf* ideology which is most common among Islamists in Europe, although in the *salafī* movement the *idea* of 'one truth' is prevalent and the time and space factor is rejected. I believe that for many Islamists to live in Europe is less a matter of reinterpretation of the social issues in the Islamic sources than it is a reselection (*ikhtiyār*) of relevant or compatible Islamic rules and regulations from a vast legal resource, i.e. it is a selection from 'the basket' according to need and relevance.

The idea of relevance or compatibility reflects the process which immigrants undergo in their interaction with their host society. In particular, immigrants who take an active part in society tend to exchange traditional concepts which cease to be functional with new ones which are more efficient or relevant in new surroundings, i.e. they are picking from 'the basket'. An example is the role of women in society. In traditional Islamic thought there is a notion that men are in charge of the economic maintenance of the family. This notion is also supported by the Koran: 'Men are responsible for [alternatively: in charge of, manager of] women, due to that which God has preferred some of them over others and due to what they spend of their property' (K.4: 34). Fatima Mernissi, a Moroccan sociologist, has observed that in Morocco, the idea of male support of the family is purely a traditional idea which has little to do with reality. According to her, Moroccan women have at all times played a substantial role in the maintenance of the family, particularly in rural areas (Mernissi 1987). This is probably true for most of the Muslim world as women have been agricultural labourers for centuries, but in the process of urbanisation it seems that they were given the role of housewives. However, in recent years female participation in wider Muslim society has increased.[5] There are a number of different reasons for this, including the fact that the market economy in most countries tends to regulate supply and demand in such a way that one salary is not enough for a household to sustain a decent standard of living. Other reasons might be the increase in educational opportunities for women and the influence of the feminist movement originating in western countries with its emphasis on economic independence for women.

As women start to perform more visible roles in society, attitudes towards women's roles tend to change on the ideological level. There is still a notion among Muslims that women are in charge of domestic affairs, but the emphasis has shifted from regarding the home as the *only* responsibility to regarding it as the *first* responsibility. Thus, it is acceptable for a Muslim woman to work outside the home, if she takes care to fulfil her primary task inside the home first. Interestingly, even among Muslim men, particularly those living in western countries, there is a tendency to draw attention to those Hadiths which portray the Prophet as performing domestic chores and those Hadiths which illustrate the father's role in the upbringing and education of children. So, as resources and conditions change, attitudes change in order to be relevant and compatible with contemporary life.

The issue of second-generation Muslims is much broader than that of first-generation migrants. As Anwar has observed, many of the Muslim immigrants looked upon themselves as 'immigrants' not as 'settlers', and among them there is a tendency to think in terms of temporariness. Anwar calls this 'the myth of return' (Anwar 1987: 112). In his study of attitudes among second-generation Pakistani Muslims in Britain, he remarks that those who are usually described as second-generation immigrants do not regard themselves as immigrants, but as first-generation British Muslims. Anwar's observation that these second-generation Pakistani Muslims belong to another category than their parents coincides with what I observed among Arab Islamists in Europe. Second-generation Muslims have gone through a completely different educational system than their parents. This makes them ask different questions from a different angle. The methodology in most educational systems in the Muslim world is built on memorisation of facts and acceptance of taught knowledge, whereas in the western world there is an emphasis on questioning taught knowledge and on problem-solving.[6] In addition, children of immigrants tend to live in two cultures: the host society and the home environment, which often differ fundamentally concerning values and moral issues. Anwar writes that 'their world is not the "old" or the "new", but both' (Anwar 1987: 112)

In his research into Muslim attitudes, Anwar asked questions such as, should marriages be arranged, should Muslim girls be allowed to wear western clothes, and how often does one pray? As he asked both parents and children, the answers serve as an indicator of change from first-generation to second-generation Muslims. It is interesting to note that his major finding was that, although second-generation Pakistani Muslims are changing their attitudes to a certain extent, this change is less marked than in non-Muslim immigrant groups. For instance, whereas 60 per cent of a group of approximately 400 first-generation Muslims pray once a day or more, the percentage for second-generation Muslims was as high as 48 per cent. Concerning the question of arranged marriage, 68 per cent of first-generation Muslims promoted such a practice, whereas 53 per cent of the second generation did.

Anwar found that to a great extent relationships in the family are governed by Islamic principles such as respect for elders, protection of the family and the duty of taking care of parents (Anwar 1987: 114). He also found, however, that it appears that a process of 'secularisation' has started among young Muslims. The second point in his conclusion is that he has seen some cases of return to the community by those who tried to break away under the influence of western ideas. He sees this return as a result of 'the rejection and hostility encountered by them as members of a minority group in an unsympathetic world' (Anwar 1987: 120). He believes that as a reaction to this experience, some young people tend to return to the community and some also become ardent Muslims.

Anwar does not mention which social group of immigrants formed the basis for his research, nor does he give any indication of Islamic commitment among the group. This makes his research results less reliable in terms of being able to predict future trends among Muslims in general. I think, however, that it was not Anwar's aim to make such a prediction, but rather to give an indication of a dawning process of change.

The normative field

Anna Christensen, a Professor of Law in Sweden, has developed a concept which she terms 'the normative field'. She builds her representation of this concept on Douglas Hofstadter's work, *Metamagical Themas*, from 1985, in which he develops the theme of the *human being's train of thought.* According to Christensen there is a parallel between Hofstadter's description of the human being's train of thought and 'the juridical thought as it actually functions'.[7] She points out that 'the legal regulations' effect on moral formation' is frequently referred to whereas little attention is given to 'the effect of moral on legal formation'. 'Much of the content of legal regulations, not least in the social dimension', she claims, 'is simply a juridical codification of the moral customs and basic attitudes which exist in society.' Christensen further argues that there are basic principles within jurisprudence which are of a purely technical character, but that actual legislation is most often based on moral principles which build on ideas of what is right and what is wrong in society. She sees a pattern in the content of legal regulations which she designates 'the normative base pattern'. She further argues that there are various forms of 'normative base patterns' which exist independently within the various legal fields. The various 'normative base patterns' 'are floating around influencing each other'. The 'normative field' is, she says 'the social field of jurisprudence. The various normative base patterns function as poles which attempt to attract the legal regulation.' Christensen's conclusion is that in most societies, legislation is based on general values and attitudes.

As Islam is regarded as a law-based religion, it is appropriate to apply Christensen's model of the 'normative field' to illustrate how different cultural influences pull in different directions in the Muslim immigrant situation. The model can portray how new attitudes originate in the tension between different cultural patterns, and it can also demonstrate how such changes of attitude influence the formation of Islamic law in a new context. The two poles, 'Arab culture' and 'western culture', might in Christensen's terminology be depicted as 'the Arab cultural base pattern' and 'the western cultural base pattern'. I define these two ideal cultural patterns broadly as a pattern of *patriarchal* gender structures versus a pattern of *equality* gender structures respectively. The latter pattern might also be regarded in the light of the post-World War II concern for human rights and resistance to the oppression of and discrimination against those in subordinate positions, a concern which culminated in the Universal Declaration of Human Rights.[8]

In the immigration situation, when an Arabic-speaking Muslim comes to a western European country, tension arises between these two poles. This field of tension is the 'normative field' in Christensen's terminology. Those ideas and attitudes that originate in the tension between the two cultural base patterns depend on which of the two dominates. If the person in question mostly mixes with 'one's own kind', i.e. persons coming from the same place of origin and more or less having the same basic attitudes towards life, the consequence will be that the 'Arab cultural base pattern' will dominate. The result is probably a reproduction of cultural and religious traditions. If the person, however, comes into more direct contact with the wider society, be it secondary as well as primary contact, the situation will in all probability be different. The result might then be either total assimilation, where the 'western cultural base pattern' dominates, or the two base patterns might pull from both sides and the result might be something in between. Within the two cultural base patterns there are various subpatterns linked to factors such as nationality, personal disposition and age. Included in the 'Arab cultural base pattern', for instance, are the various Arab nations with their diverse cultural expressions. Similarly, the 'western cultural base pattern' includes patterns of various countries, and even within countries subpatterns manifest themselves. I will therefore also refer to other cultural base patterns, such as the 'African cultural base pattern' and also local cultural base patterns within the Arab world. The cultural form of expression created by immigration can extend on a large scale from domination by one pole or the other to something in between. The 'normative field' where the process of interpretation takes place lies in between these two main poles. The various cultural base patterns play a role in the selection and the interpretation of the Islamic texts. In subsequent discussions, I will use the categories the 'Arab cultural base pattern' and the 'western cultural base pattern' as typologies in a Weberian sense.[9] If we link Christensen's concept of the 'normative field' to Hjärpe's basket metaphor, the basket comprises the two cultural patterns, the 'Arab cultural base pattern' and the 'western cultural base pattern', as opposite poles, together with the Islamic sources and the Islamic literature.

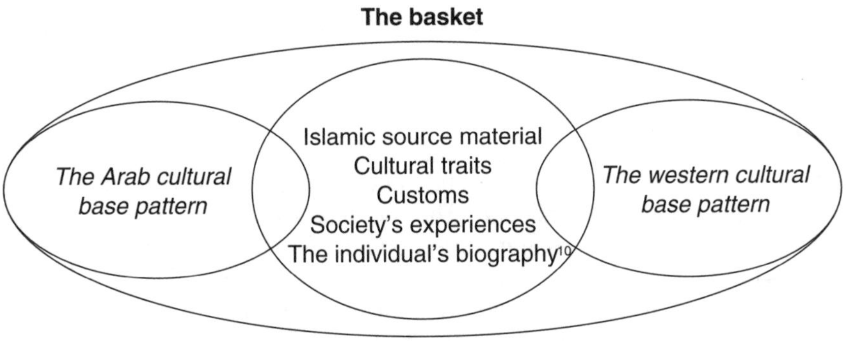

Figure 2 The basket. The centre circle will overlap with one or the other depending on the degree of contact with and perceptiveness to the influence of the host society.

The Islamic sources and the Islamic literature are interpreted through the two cultural base patterns, the 'Arab cultural base pattern' and the 'western cultural base pattern'. I believe that the result will vary according to the degree of contact with the host society. As Islamism is a reaction to modernism in Bruce Lawrence's terminology (Lawrence 1989),[11] as well as to westernisation which has influenced the Muslim region, the Arab Islamist who comes to Europe has as a starting point a certain idea of what I would call 'the ideological West', i.e. the secular world-view. The particular understanding of Islam held by Islamists is therefore based on the influence this secular world-view has had on the Muslim world. The Islamist world-view is dynamic as it is a world-view in change. I would suggest that the change which has already occurred from the traditional Islamic world-view to an Islamist world-view makes the latter more susceptible to further change than is the traditional understanding of Islam with its stress on the law school system. In Part II of this study, I will show how this change manifests itself in Arab Islamists' encounter with the western strain of thought. I will look into aspects of the problems of legislation in this encounter. How do the two poles influence the content of 'the basket' in the various matters of Islamic legislation in a world where traditional patterns are exchanged and attitudes towards social relations are different from their home countries?

To illustrate how the 'normative field' is operating in practice we can look at the writings of the Egyptian scholar Muḥammad Mutawallā ash-Shaʿrāwī (d. 1998). ash-Shaʿrāwī is a traditional scholar whose views on women and gender relations are built on a patriarchal system (ash-Shaʿrāwī n.d.). On the other hand if we look at the feminist theologians, consisting of female scholars educated in western countries, their debate is built on notions of equality between the sexes. One can assume that, for instance, Amina Wadud-Muhsin, an American convert to Islam, in her book *Qur'an and Woman* (1992) interprets Koranic notions in view of her own cultural background which is the 'western cultural base pattern'. As she has few influences from the 'Arab cultural base pattern', it will have a lesser impact in her Koranic interpretation.

The past in the present

The Islamist debate is a narrow and specific discourse which can appear incomprehensible to outsiders. The boundaries of the discourse are restricted and in transgressing these boundaries one risks being excluded from the process of change. This is particularly true in the discussion of the position of women in Islam. Taslima Nasreen has experienced such exclusion since, according to Islamists in her homeland of Bangladesh, she has claimed that the Koran has to change. If she had been understood as saying that *interpretations* of the Koran have to change, she would probably not have been excluded from the debate. Fatima Mernissi, on the other hand, is an example of the opposite effect. Because she dresses her battle for Muslim women's rights in Islamic garb, she gains a foothold for her particular form of feminism in the Islamic debate.

Islamism might be understood in terms of a reaction to 'the globalisation of western localism', where local western cultural ideas overflow to the rest of the world, particularly through the media but also through western influences in general. With the cultural encounter between Muslims and 'the West', which started as early as the seventeenth century and intensified in the nineteenth, the trend of 'turning back to the pure sources, the Koran and the Hadiths' manifested itself (Hourani 1962; Brown 1996). This trend has developed and it might be seen as implying that the modern Islamist discussion of the role of Muslim women in society becomes a discussion about the role of Muslim women in Arabia in the seventh century. However, I would claim that the present discussion is not about an *idea* of a past ideal female role, but a discussion of a female role relevant to or compatible with contemporary society in light of the Islamic sources. In the process of interpretation, contemporary socio-cultural influences play a part, and this results in a contemporary Islam. In a similar way, traditional Islamic law reflects the society and culture of the Islamic Middle Ages, rather than depicting society and culture as it 'really' was at the time of the Prophet.

Islamic History

Daniel Brown, a researcher on Islam, has noted that modern Islamic discussions 'are indeed new and a product of modern circumstances, but in other

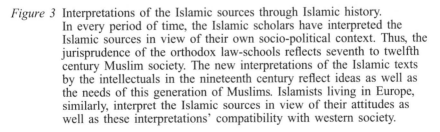

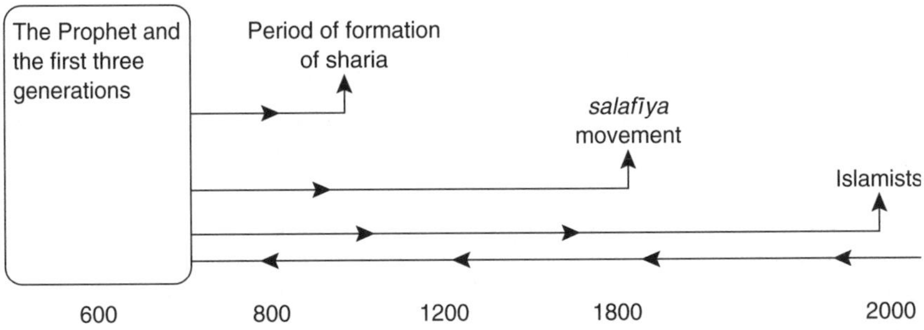

Figure 3 Interpretations of the Islamic sources through Islamic history.
In every period of time, the Islamic scholars have interpreted the Islamic sources in view of their own socio-political context. Thus, the jurisprudence of the orthodox law-schools reflects seventh to twelfth century Muslim society. The new interpretations of the Islamic texts by the intellectuals in the nineteenth century reflect ideas as well as the needs of this generation of Muslims. Islamists living in Europe, similarly, interpret the Islamic sources in view of their attitudes as well as these interpretations' compatibility with western society.

respects they look surprisingly like discussions that took place during the formative phase of Islamic legal thought' (Brown 1996: 6). Both the modern discussions and the discussions of the Islamic past can be described as 'the past reproduced in the present'.[12]

The theoretical framework

The theoretical framework of this study is a reflection upon various levels of change. The study is built on three main assumptions. The first assumption is that changes in Islamist minority groups in Europe are brought about first and foremost as a result of the groups' interaction with majority society. As competitive groups are less prone to change, groups which are in a cooperative position vis-à-vis majority society tend to be influenced by the socio-cultural traits and norms of this society. Competitive groups tend to have a hostile attitude towards majority society. However, even groups which manifest no explicit hostility towards majority society may also be in a competitive position as they will mainly act within their own groups. Thus the contact with the majority society is sparse.

The second assumption is that depending on the degree of contact with majority society, Arab Islamists oscillate between the 'Arab cultural base pattern' and the 'western cultural base pattern'. The selection from 'the basket' is dictated by the position which the individual maintains in relation to the normative field.

The third assumption is that changes within the minority Islamist group are affected by whether one belongs to an Islamic movement or not, and the rigidity of the Islamist movement one belongs to. Movements themselves are subject to transformation, but this transformation tends to be less conspicuous than are changes within groups of Islamists outside Islamic movements. Islamist movements are dominated by movement intellectuals formulating the ideology of the movement. Furthermore, the 'social organisation' within movements tends to obstruct change. Individuals belonging to movements are thus less prone to changes outside the scope of the movement's official ideology.

By applying these analytic methods I investigate how changes in attitudes towards and perceptions of women are manifested in an Arab Islamist context in Europe. In Part II, I look into various aspects of women's issues and gender relations. It is, however, important to understand the base of Islamic legislation and I will therefore start the next section with a brief introduction to Islamic law.

Part II

Reflections on the empirical material

Introduction

Sharia is a confusing concept for Muslims and non-Muslims alike. Is sharia a divine law or is it a law built on divine sources? Are these two really one and the same thing? Is there any possibility of change within the framework of sharia or is it an unchangeable law valid for everybody until the end of humankind? These are questions activated by the process of social change in general and the migration situation in particular. In the Muslim world, social change has altered traditional gender and family patterns. In the non-Muslim world, Muslims in the diaspora are faced with new social structures which are challenging the foundations of traditional faith and practices.

Part II of this study deals with various aspects of sharia and its practices. What images of women are conveyed by the Islamic sources and how have these images been understood by scholars in different times and places? More importantly, what are recent perceptions of women and how do these manifest themselves in the contemporary Islamic debate?

Another issue of the utmost importance concerns the question of whether or not God has destined an eternal divine gender pattern suitable for all humankind. How should hadiths, in which social behaviour in early Islamic history is portrayed, be understood in today's situation? Is this particular social pattern intended as eternal guidance, or is there any space for hermeneutical readings of these hadiths?

The discussion on gender roles becomes particularly conspicuous when we turn to the matter of women's political participation in Islam. In the Arab world, few women are elected Members of Parliament. In the Sudan for instance, which has a relatively high number of female MPs, most of the women are only indirectly elected as members of various women's organisations represented in Parliament. In the Gulf region, the Gulf war at the beginning of the 1990s sparked the discussion about women's political involvement. However, this did not result in any real empowerment for women in the Gulf until the late 1990s. Qatar paved the way for female suffrage and women's right to be elected in the spring of 1999. Kuwait's Emir followed this with a promise of female political participation a couple of months later, but his proposal has been voted against a number of times in parliamentary sessions. As a whole, women are a minority in political life in the Arab world, and the discussion of whether sharia allows women to activate themselves in the official sphere has to take account of this fact.

Muslims regard the family as the basic unit of society. The question is what kind of family this refers to. Is monogamy or polygyny the preference among Muslims? How should the Koranic passages about polygyny be understood? Do scholars living in western countries have different ideas about polygyny than scholars in the Arab world? What about divorce and child custody? How has social change influenced Islamic thought in family issues? Divorce in Islam has been one of the most controversial matters in the cultural encounter between Islam and 'the West'. The notion that Muslim women have no right to divorce their husbands except in extraordinary cases, such as male impotency and excessive abuse, has engaged Muslim feminists, as well as westerners in general. The question thus becomes, what is written in the Islamic texts and what is merely traditional practice in the various Muslim countries.

The issue of female circumcision has aroused powerful emotions in western countries. There are various attitudes towards this practice even within Muslim countries. Moreover, the confusion is extreme as there are also variations between the Islamic law schools in this matter. What did the Prophet say about female circumcision and how can his ideas be understood? Furthermore, are these hadiths reliable, and how is it that it is primarily in countries where female circumcision was common in pre-Islamic times that this practice is still followed? The most important question is how authorities in Muslim countries can put an end to such deep-rooted customs.

The last issue which I discuss is that of veiling by Muslim women. The veil's connotations of female oppression and total segregation between the sexes have dominated the discussion. Muslim feminists in particular have been negative towards veiling. Fatima Mernissi's book on veiling has influenced researchers on Islam to such an extent that they would proclaim that women's veiling is not a Koranic injunction (see Mernissi 1987). But it is important to ask how reliable Mernissi's argument is in scientific terms. More importantly, what does the Koran say about female clothing and what can be found in the hadiths?

All the issues dealt with in this empirical part of the study indicate the importance of women's active involvement in the interpretation of social issues in the Koran and the hadiths. As women in Islamic history have to a great extent been excluded from the process of interpretation and developing Islamic legislation, the new situation in which many women now pursue higher education might bring Muslim women into a more active position in matters of legislation. This is particularly true in the context of migration, since Islamic law functions as a law for the majority society, whereas Muslim immigrants in Europe live as minority communities.

Presentation

In the following exploration of various Islamic issues pertaining to gender in general and women in particular, I will look first at statements from the Islamic sources – the Koran and the hadiths which are used in the contemporary debate. Second, I will investigate what can be found in the classical literature, i.e. in the commentaries of the Koran, about the subject under discussion. Third, I will refer to contemporary written sources, and as a conclusion I will refer to the results from my fieldwork among Arab Islamists. I will mainly analyse the statements of a few persons within the four main Islamist directions in Europe: the Islamic Liberation Party, the *salafī* movement, the Muslim Brotherhood and the *post-ikhwān* trend. I have attempted to let the four directions be represented by at least one man and one woman, but sometimes when the two are very similar I present only one side, and sometimes I have not quoted anyone from a group as their statements coincided with those of other groups. Of the four main groups I have concentrated on individuals from the Muslim Brotherhood and from the *post-ikhwān* trend, because in these groups more ideas have been expressed and I have found more potential for change. I have chosen four people who primarily represent these two directions, namely Khadīja and Aḥmad from the Muslim Brotherhood, and Ziyād and Amal from the *post-ikhwān* trend (all four names are pseudonyms). All the *salafīs* I interviewed both in writing and orally continuously quoted the Koran and the hadiths, suggesting a more literal form of interpretation, whereas those from the two former groups were more open in their interpretation of social issues, bringing in their own views in light of the text. I had a similar experience during my fieldwork in Jordan at the beginning of the 1990s. When I went to Friday prayers in mosques with *salafī* preachers, I noted that their Friday sermons consisted mainly of quotations from the Koran and the hadiths, whereas preachers belonging to the *ikhwān* trend were using the quotations more as an approach to contemporary problems. Thus, the *salafīs* talked in more idealistic terms than the *ikhwān* preachers did. As for members of the Islamic Liberation Party, I refer less to them as their perceptions of women often coincide either with *ikhwān* or *salafī* thinking.

In some chapters below I do not follow any order in terms of referring to views from all four groups, but have rather selected those statements which I believe present a comprehensive view of contemporary Islamic images of women.

5 Reflections on sharia

To understand issues of gender and perceptions of women in Islam it is necessary to look into the matter of Islamic legislation. What is the nature of sharia and is there any potential for change in Islamic law? Traditionally, sharia was a matter for a small religious elite and ordinary Muslims were dependent on this elite's interpretations of the Islamic sources. Although this is still true, I have already explained that the Islamic arena is opening up to modern ideas in the cultural encounter between Muslims and the western world in both western and Muslim countries.

I will take as my starting point Sheikh Yūsuf al-Qaraḍāwī's view on sharia. al-Qaraḍāwī believes that Islamic law is built on both specific and general rules and regulations (al-Qaraḍāwī 1995: 104). Within specific rulings he includes family law and the law of inheritance and estate, whereas general rulings apply to those matters not specially mentioned in the Koran and Sunna. al-Qaraḍāwī specifies the latter as those 'issues which are conditioned by factors of specific time, environment, stage of development, political and military circumstances, etc.' (al-Qaraḍāwī 1995: 105). al-Qaraḍāwī's words indicate a certain flexibility in sharia matters. At first glance it seems that he regards Islamic legislation in family matters as belonging to the more specific rulings of sharia, but by looking more closely at his writings I discover that he actually insinuates that in certain circumstances even these matters can change. I believe we have to interpret his vagueness on this point as a result of the sacred character family law in Islam has acquired through the centuries. The Personal Status Law has been one of the few areas of Islamic legislation which has had the benefit of being implemented in court from early Islamic history to the present time. To suggest changes in this area might thus create a reaction from traditional Muslims.

In December 1998 I conducted an interview with al-Qaraḍāwī in Qatar. I discovered that to a certain extent he advocates consulting a female perspective with regard to gender issues. In his weekly religious programmes at the al-Jazeera Satellite channel he tends to do the same. To my surprise I realised that this female perspective must be due to the fact that in his research institute he employs female researchers who help him to look up Islamic texts relating to the issues he discusses. Furthermore, in our discussion about sharia he promoted a progressive view, saying that 'as for our standstill and stop [in development] in our position: the celestial bodies do not stop their movements and the earth does not stop its rotation'. al-Qaraḍāwī's reference to 'our standstill and stop [in development] in our position' points to what has commonly been called the closure of 'the gates of *ijtihād* [individual legal reasoning]'. The concept of the closure of 'the gates of *ijtihād*' is a forceful rhetorical device in the contemporary debate about change. Referring to such a closure to explain Muslim backwardness in recent history opens up a way for the acceptance of new interpretations particularly of social issues in the Islamic texts.

Aḥmad Ḥasan is a Sunnī scholar from the Indian subcontinent. Ḥasan has discussed the common notion of the closure of 'the gates of *ijtihād*'. He claims that after the death of the Prophet there was a trend among his companions and followers to try to unify Muslims through establishing ideas of conformity. *Ijmāʾ* (consensus) was in his view one of the means to bring together Muslims in the weak and unstable emerging Islamic Umma. Another means was the establishment of the concept of *jamāʿa* (community) (Ḥasan 1984: 9–17). Furthermore, conformity (in Ḥasan's terminology *taqlīd*),[1] was a result of the notion of 'bringing together', meaning that despite the major schism in early Islamic history, as early as the ninth century 'the Qu'ran and the *Sunnah* of the Prophet began to be interpreted in the light of the decisions of the masters (early jurists) and not independently' (Ḥasan 1984: 17). In Ḥasan's view, the gates of *ijtihād* closed as early as the ninth or tenth century.

I would argue, however, that 'the gates of *ijtihād*' were never closed, as social evolution meant that scholars were constantly faced with new situations to take into account. What I believe happened was that new *ijtihāds* stopped replacing old ones. However, even this is only partly true. Even although Ḥasan believes that there was a cessation in independent intellectual reasoning, his study refers to how some scholars from later Islamic history stressed the need for *ijtihād* and actually performed it. He specifically mentions prominent scholars such as Ibn Ḥazm (d. 1064), Ibn Taimīya (d. 1328), Ibn Qayyim al-Jawzīya (d. 1351) and ash-Shawkānī (d. 1834). These scholars, particularly the former three, have played an important role in the history and development of Islamic law. The fact that they performed *ijtihād* at a time when it is commonly believed that *ijtihād* had ceased to be performed, indicates that the 'gates of *ijtihād*' were never actually closed.[2] Furthermore, by looking at old law books within the different Islamic law schools one can observe that there was not always one specific rule covering any particular phenomenon. Rather, different scholars within the same law school reached different conclusions (az-Zuḥailī 1989 vols I–VIII). In general one can say that laws concerning any particular phenomenon tend to approach it from various angles, taking different circumstances into account. With the development of Islamic law within various regions, diverse situations were more or less catered for according to the society in which it developed.

In traditional societies few new phenomena were encountered, but with the coming of the colonial era there were social changes which violated many boundaries of traditional Muslim society. The impact of change and Muslim reactions towards this change are processes which have developed over a period of more than two centuries. One could argue that, since historically speaking Islamic law was flexible and developed differently in the various regions, modern changes could also influence the further development of sharia. It is of interest to note that many of the Islamists I have interviewed, even in the Muslim world, refer to how Shāfiʿī changed his way of ruling when he travelled from Iraq to Egypt (see also Philips 1988: 123).

Ḥasan argues that Islamic rules are moral rather than legal. He believes that the aim of the Koran is to build an Islamic society 'on the basis of morality and justice, and not strictly on legal foundations' (Ḥasan 1984: 23). 'Hence,' he writes, '[the Koran's] emphasis [is] on ethics and not on law.' He goes on to argue that 'the Qu'ran tends to bring about a community characterised by faith and morality' (Ḥasan 1984: 23). It is particularly interesting to note that Ḥasan's book, which was first published as early as 1978, explicitly advocates the idea of sharia as variable according to time and place. In works by most Arab Islamist authors from the same period, such as Muḥammad Quṭb, Sayyid Quṭb, Yūsuf al-Qaraḍāwī and Muḥammad al-Ghazzālī, the same idea is implicitly rather than explicitly stated. An exception to this is the Sudanese scholar, Ḥasan at-Turābī. In the early 1970s he wrote a manuscript, *al-marʾa bayna taʿālīm ad-dīn wa taqālīd al-mujtamaʿ? (The Woman Between Islamic Teachings and Traditions of Society*). Although it was read by Islamic scholars such as Muḥammad al-Ghazzālī, at-Turābī's ideas had not at that time spread throughout the Arab world. In 1993, the manuscript was translated into English and entitled *Women in Islam and Muslim Society*. The book is widely distributed, particularly in western countries. In this book at-Turābī analyses, with references to the present situation of Muslim women, various attitudes towards women in the light of the hadith literature. In addition, with regard to the present situation, he demands changes of the rules concerning women in Islamic legislation (at-Turābī 1993). Not until the end of the 1980s did other Arab Islamists, such as al-Ghazzālī and al-Qaraḍāwī, resume the call for changes in the *muʿāmalāt* (interhuman relationships) sphere of *fiqh* (jurisprudence) (al-Qaraḍāwī 1990; M. al-Ghazzālī 1989; 1990).

Asghar Ali Engineer is another scholar from the Indian subcontinent. He has written a book *The Rights of Women in Islam* (1992) which is read by Muslims living in the western world. It is important to know that he belongs to the Boharas group of Muslims (an Ismāʿīlī sect), as this influences his perceptions of the Islamic law. Engineer claims that the term 'sharia' was not in common use before the fifteenth to sixteenth century CE (Engineer 1992: 7). He constructs his argument on the fact that prominent scholars such as Abū Ḥamīd Muḥammad al-Ghazzālī (d. 1111) and Abū al-Fatḥ Muḥammad ash-Shahrastānī (d. 1153) hardly mention the term 'sharia'. However, I would counter this by pointing out that Ḥasan, in his study, shows that ash-Shahrastānī actually uses the word 'sharia' and in Ḥasan's view, he uses it synonymously with *minhaj* (method) and *sunna* (Ḥasan 1984: 13; cf. ash-Shahrastānī 1910 vol. I: 48). Furthermore, Ḥasan also indicates that ʿAbd al-Mālik al-Juwainī (d. 1085) uses the term 'sharia' in its technical sense. al-Juwainī argues that '*ijmāʾ* is the strap and support of the sharia and to it the sharia owes its authenticity' (al-Juwainī n.d., quoted in Ḥasan 1984: 18). In this particular matter, it seems that Engineer's Ismāʿīlī background influences his view on sharia, leading him to draw specific conclusions.

Engineer's purpose is to show that sharia has wrongly obtained divine status in spite of the fact that Islam is flexible by nature. As a demonstration of sharia's flexibility he refers to the case of slavery in Islam, which he regards as being equivalent to the issue of women. Slavery used to be acceptable in feudal and pre-feudal societies even to the slaves themselves (Engineer 1992: 2). However, with the coming of capitalism attitudes towards slavery changed and it was eventually abolished. Muslim theologians used to justify slavery as there is no explicit prohibition of slavery in Islamic sources, but today, with it no longer being generally acceptable, 'no one invokes the scripture to justify it [slavery] and insist upon that "divine right" vested in those who owned slaves' (Engineer 1992: 2).

As Engineer points out, the notion of sharia is often misunderstood by 'those not well versed in the origin and the development of sharia' (Engineer 1992: 6). However, given that he identifies the main problem as lying in the notion of its divinity and immutability, I would like to add that the idea of a uniform sharia also creates misunderstanding among non-Muslims and Muslims alike. In the case of non-Muslims, both in the media and in serious research one reads references to those such as fundamentalists (or Islamists) who want strictly to follow the sharia. The question is then which form of sharia is meant here? What does the researcher or journalist mean by the word 'sharia', and what do Islamists mean by the same? It seems that the notion of sharia has become stereotyped particularly in a western context, but also to some degree among Muslims. Most Muslims know that there are four main Sunnī Islamic law schools,[3] in addition to the Shīʿī Jaʿfarī Islamic law school prevalent within the Twelver Sect. However with the rise of *salaf* ideas, the notion of surpassing the Islamic law schools and returning to the Koran and the Sunna, i.e. the reproduction of the past in the present, has also become established. This quest to turn back to 'one truth' has created an idea of sharia as rigid and inflexible.

All this raises the question, 'what is sharia?'. In Hans Wehr's *A Dictionary of Modern Written Arabic*, the term sharia is explained as 'the revealed or the canonical law of Islam'. In view of this, I want to elucidate some of the concepts within the topic of Islamic law in order to avoid misunderstandings in the discussion that follows. Linguistically speaking, sharia comes from the root *sh-r-ʿ* which means *to go* or *to enter*. The word 'sharia' means literally 'the way to the watering place' which indicates the place where the animals gather for drinking water, and in a more general sense it means a path. In the Koran the word is mentioned once: 'Then We have set you [Muḥammad] on a path (*sharīʿa*) of [Our] commandment, so follow it, and do not follow the whims of those who do not know' (K.45: 18).

Four more derivations of the root *sh-r-ʿ* are mentioned in the Koran. Two of the derivations denote the act of ordaining rules: *sharaʿa* (third person singular refers to God) and *sharaʿū* (third person plural refers to partners to God), 42: 13; 42: 21. A third derivation has to do with being visible. The fourth derivation is *shirʿa* and the verse goes: 'For each one [people of the various divine Scriptures] We have made from you (*minkum*) a path (*shirʿa*) and a way (*minhāj*)' (K.5: 48). In both 45: 18 and 5: 48 the idea is that God has given a path (*sharīʿa* and *shirʿa*) which human beings should follow. In the latter verse there is an indication that the path (*shirʿa*) referred to is already staked out as the path is 'from you' [people of the various divine Scriptures]. It is important to note that searching through the hadith literature I found no mention of the word *sharīʿa*. The word *shirʿa*, however is mentioned in hadiths which explain the Koranic verse 5: 48.

In the lexicographic work *al-lisān al-ʿarab* (*The Arabic Tongue*) from the thirteenth century, the terms *sharīʿa* and *shirʿa* are explained as that which 'God established (*sanna*) of rules (*ad-dīn*) and commanded with it such as fasting, prayer, pilgrimage, *zakat*, and all benevolent actions derived from the coast of the sea (*shāṭiʾ al-baḥr*)' (Ibn Manẓūr 1955 vol. VIII: 176 [translation mine]). From my reading, I do not think that in *The Arabic Tongue* the term 'sharia' is used as a technical term such as it is in contemporary Islamic debate. This might lend some support to Engineer's claim that the term 'sharia' was not in common use until the fifteenth or the sixteenth century. Although Ḥasan has indicated that it was used earlier, it might be that it was used in a general sense rather than as a specific term denoting 'the Islamic Law'.

In contemporary Islamic literature, sharia is regarded as 'the divine Law' with God as 'the Law-giver' (Doi 1984: 2). I have already referred to Bilal Philips, a Jamaican convert who studied in Saudi Arabia for many years and whose writings show him to be influenced by the *salafī* trend of thought. Philips writes that sharia 'refers to the sum of Islamic laws which were revealed to the Prophet Muhammad (p.b.u.h.), and which are recorded in the Koran as well as deducible from the Prophet's divinely-guided lifestyle (called the *Sunnah*)' (Philips 1988: 1–2).

Philips further distinguishes between sharia and *fiqh*, giving three points of difference between the two. He says:

1 Sharia is the body of revealed laws found both in the Koran and in the Sunna, while *fiqh* is a body of laws deduced from sharia to cover specific situations not directly treated in sharia law.
2 Sharia is fixed and unchangeable, whereas *fiqh* changes according to the circumstances under which it is applied.
3 The laws of sharia are, for the most part, general: they lay down basic principles. In contrast, the laws of *fiqh* tend to be specific: they demonstrated how the basic principles of sharia should be applied in given circumstances.

(Philips 1988: 2)

Engineer and Philips have quite divergent ideas of what sharia *is* and how it developed. Engineer sees sharia as the end product of centuries of legal interpretation (*fiqh*). This was a developmental process that introduced changes into sharia according to time and place, thus interpreting sharia as flexible. Philips takes the opposite view, seeing sharia as static, as the solid foundation from which *fiqh* arose and as consisting of the revealed laws found in the Koran and Sunna. The task, in his view, is to determine the real words and true intentions of the Prophet, which can best be deduced from the rulings of the older scholars of note nearer in time to him. At the end of the process of study of the Koran, Sunna and the first three generations of Muslims, one seeks to find the legislation for each point of Islamic law. A further point of contrast is that Philips does not draw attention to the individual differences between those early scholars, whereas Engineer looks at the effects of time upon a scholar's perspective and rulings.

I would suggest that sharia can be regarded as an idea or an abstraction of a Divine Law with general laws or basic principles of prayer, fasting, social behaviour, etc. These basic principles are those which can be characterised by the legal evidence of certainty (*ad-dalīl al-qaṭʿī*). Jurisprudence (*fiqh*), on the other hand, is that which differs in the various regions. The various rulings of jurisprudence are built on legal evidence of uncertainty (*ad-dalīl aẓ-ẓannī*), and *fiqh* is the concrete legislation which gives detailed information on *how* to pray, *how* to fast, *how* to behave, etc.[4] *Fiqh* differs in the various regions and between scholars as there are different accesses to hadith, different ways of assessing a hadith's authenticity, different legal concepts such as *maṣlaḥa* (public interest), *ʿurf* (custom), *ʿamal ahl al-medīna* (the practice of the Medinian population), etc. *Fiqh* is considered to differ, however, only within the frames of evidence of uncertainty. I would claim, however, that even within the frames of 'certainty', i.e., in cases where the ruling is mentioned explicitly in the Koran and thus might be regarded as a God-given law, there might be various rulings according to circumstances. For instance in matters of theft, where the ruling is given in the Koran, there are elaborations of *how* much, *why*, etc. in *fiqh* and these factors might influence the punishment.

In addition to sharia and *fiqh* is the *qanūn*, the actual contemporary legislation in the various Muslim countries, legislation which builds partly upon *fiqh* but also on local customs and rules and regulations introduced by the western colonial powers. Muslims accept the variables of *fiqh* and *qanūn*, yet they reject the idea of change in sharia. I believe that it is mainly the notion of sharia's divinity which leads to the division between Muslims in this matter. The confusion in terminology creates misunderstandings which obstruct change. Some well-educated Muslims and Islamists within fields other than Islamic law tend to talk in terms of changes to sharia when what they really mean is changes to *fiqh* and *qanūn*, and Islamic scholars respond by refusing to contemplate change as sharia in their view is unchangeable. Had the former talked in terms of changes in actual legislation, i.e. *fiqh* and *qanūn*, there would probably not have been such misunderstanding between the two factions as there is a general consensus that *fiqh* and *qanūn* can change according to circumstances.

There is, however, another factor to take into account. Many Islamic scholars perceive their position as leaders of the Muslim Umma as threatened due first to the decline in their official authority, but also to their 'inability to deal with happenings in the real world'. The latter was explained to me by one leading Islamist living in Europe, and it was confirmed by many others. It was seen as a consequence of the nature of sharia institutions in the Muslim world, where emphasis on detailed theological and scholastic discussions preoccupied the students' time instead of them learning how to deal with 'the real world'.

Sources of Islamic legislation

Sharia, the Islamic law, switches between two dimensions: the horizontal and the vertical. The horizontal dimension covers legislation in the social sphere, where rights, responsibilities and obligations are drawn up in terms of inter-human relationships (*muʿāmalāt*). The vertical dimensions have to do with the human being's relationship with God (*ʿibādāt*). The latter is thus the overarching aspect of the law, as even social relations are regulated by belief in God as the Creator of all things. According to Joseph Schacht, there was a break between these two dimensions in early Islamic history, and the Personal Status Law was the only part of the *muʿāmalāt* legislation which the Islamic scholars were free to apply without interference from the Muslim political authorities (Schacht 1950). With the coming of colonialism the Personal Status Law is the only canonic law in various Muslim countries which might be regarded as being based on Islamic legislation in spite of the external influences of western legislation (*Guardian Weekly*, 16 November 1997).

The sources of Islamic law are in the first place the Koran, Sunna, *qiyās* (analogy) and *ijmāʾ* (consensus), which are called the Roots of Jurisprudence (*uṣūl al-fiqh*). In addition to these four basic categories, other legal principles can be referred to in certain cases: *istiḥsān* (legal preference), *istiṣlāḥ* (public interest), *istiṣḥāb* (continuity or permanence) and *ʿurf* (customs (which do not contradict any of the principles of Islamic Law)). The four accepted law schools (*madhāhib*), Ḥanafī, Mālikī, Shāfiʿī and Ḥanbalī, have different approaches to the various legal categories.

Legislation within the Ḥanafī law school, for instance, depends less on hadith than the Mālikī and the Ḥanbalī law schools. Abū Ḥanīfa (d. 767), the founder of the school, was born and lived in Kufa in Iraq. His disciples claimed that he had personally known some of the Prophet's Companions (Shalabī 1969: 171–2), but according to Waines, Ibn Khallikān (d. 1282) casts doubt on this claim (Waines 1995: 67–8). The relationship of the jurists to the Companions of the Prophet or their successors seems to have been important in shaping the legal view of the early Islamic legislators. Abū Ḥanīfa, for instance, lived far from Mecca and Medina, where most of the Companions and their successors lived. This might have influenced his view on the Prophet's example and the example of the 'people of Medina' (*ʿamal ahl al-medīna*), important legal principles for Mālik ibn Anas (d. 795), the founder of the Mālikī school. In contrast to Mālik's stress on these two legal principles, the Ḥanafī-school's main legal principle after the Koran and the Sunna is *raʾi* (decision based on one's individual judgement).

Muḥammad ibn Idrīs ash-Shāfiʿī (d. 820) had studied Mālikī law in Medina and during his studies in Baghdad he came into contact with Ḥanafī scholars (Waines 1995: 67). One of his concerns was to integrate the various approaches to the law. Waines describes his legal thought as being marked by a 'rigorous application of philosophical distinctions and linguistic arguments to his analysis of scripture and Traditions' (Waines 1995: 68). It was ash-Shāfiʿī who developed the concept of the Roots of Jurisprudence with its four categories. Although these principles were already common among Islamic scholars of the time, ash-Shāfiʿī was the one to crystallise and systematise legal thinking within the accepted approaches to Islamic law. In particular, he developed the concept of analogy based on the Koran and the Sunna, in order to 'eliminate or severely restrict the use of the jurists' discretionary opinion based on *raʾi* or *istiḥsān*' (Waines 1995: 69).

Although ash-Shāfiʿī's principles also partly penetrated the legal thought of the two former schools, the Ḥanafī and the Mālikī, Aḥmad Ibn Ḥanbal (d. 855), the founder of the last law school was not utterly convinced by ash-Shāfiʿī's theory of *qiyās* (analogy) and *ijmāʾ* (consensus). Ibn Ḥanbal was a staunch follower of the Prophet's Traditions. He was trained in Mecca and Medina but he also travelled widely within the Muslim empire, collecting a large number of hadiths. Ibn Ḥanbal's main principle was therefore to apply the Sunna of the Prophet as an explanation of the Koran. According to Waines, Ibn Ḥanbal considers the Koran to be understood in its literal sense, thus refusing allegorical interpretations of the text.

A third source of law for his legal thought came from the legal opinions of the Prophet's Companions. Interestingly enough, for Ibn Ḥanbal, *ijmāʾ* was linked primarily to the Companions and their immediate successors, although he rejected or was doubtful of the authority of the *ijmāʾ* of scholars in general. Furthermore, Ḥasan claims that Ibn Ḥanbal was among those scholars who believed that acceptance of the Companions' *ijmāʾ* was part of the creed (Ḥasan 1984: 96–7). According to Ḥasan, who paraphrases Ibn Taimīya, Ibn Ḥanbal's strong emphasis on the Companion's *ijmāʾ* was due to the fact that:

> There is no question on which the Companions had not given their opinion. With the territorial expansion and the spread of Islam they were confronted with a number of complex problems. But they sought their solution on the basis of the Qur'an and the *Sunnah*. . . . In their own day the Companions in general did not argue on the basis of *ijmāʾ*. The reason is that the Companions themselves were the people of *ijmāʾ* (*ahl al-ijmāʾ*).
>
> (Ḥasan 1984: 179)

Each of the four main law schools have their individual approaches which have influenced their legal thought and the actual formation of jurisprudence. However, all the schools had one thing in common, namely that the Koran and the Sunna of the Prophet early in history came to be interpreted in the light of the decisions of the masters (early jurists) and not independently. This has been regarded by some scholars as one of the reasons for the decrease in the use of *ijtihād* from the ninth century onwards (Ḥasan 1984).

For a long period in history there was a tendency to adhere to one particular law school. Although many scholarly institutions, such as for instance al-Azhar in Egypt, taught the approaches of various law schools, the notion of adherence to one particular school prevailed in the whole Muslim world with the exception of certain scholars such as Ibn Taimīya. Ibn Taimīya, although belonging to the Ḥanbalī law school, made *ijtihāds* which sometimes opposed the legislation of his own law school. He was thus a *mujtahid muṭlaq* (unrestricted or absolute *mujtahid*).

With the coming of the modern era, one of the first things to happen within Islamic law was the emergence of the idea of eclecticism. The notion of 'the return to the pure sources' which was implicitly stated in the thought of the *salafīya* movement of the nineteenth century and was later repeated in Ḥasan al-Bannāʾ's thought, was initially expressed in terms of eclecticism in that one could choose freely from the legal rules of the four Islamic law schools. This is apparent in a book by a member of the Muslim Brotherhood, as-Sayyid Sābiq, *fiqh as-sunna* (*The Jurisprudence of the Sunna*), written in the 1940s. Sābiq's book is arranged under legal topics. Koranic references and some hadiths are referred to in every topic, as well as the judgements of the law schools. As a conclusion he offers what is, according to him, the strongest legal judgement. Although there is a strong tendency to 'return to the pure sources, the Koran and Sunna', in Sābiq's book, the legal judgements of the law schools also play a great part. It seems that although the *idea* of 'the purification of the law' is present, Sābiq's conclusions are built more on a selection from judgements of the orthodox law schools.

Another legal work which was published in 1984 is a follow-up to Sābiq's book. This eight-volume work is written by Wahba az-Zuḥailī and it is called *al-fiqh al-islāmī wa adillatuhu* (*Islamic Jurisprudence and its Evidences)*. This work is much more detailed than Sābiq's. az-Zuḥailī is careful to bring in the Koranic verses and the hadiths which deal with the various legal matters, and he also gives the respective judgements of the four law schools. At the end of every chapter he gives details of actual legislation in some Arab countries.

It was not until the spread of the *salafī* movement's ideas from the 1970s onwards that the notion of 'the return to the pure sources' became systematised. The *salafī* scholar Naṣr ad-Dīn al-Albānī's 'purification' of the hadith literature, i.e. the scrutinisation of the authenticity of hadiths' narrator chains, influenced Islamists belonging to other directions of Islamic thought who to a certain extent used his books as references. In the *ikhwān* trend the consequence of the idea of 'returning to the Koran and the Sunna' is manifest in an hermeneutic approach to the hadith literature systematised by al-Ghazzālī and al-Qaraḍāwī (al-Qaraḍāwī 1990; M. al-Ghazzālī 1989; 1990).

This study is mainly concerned with legal evidence from the Koran and the Sunna. In my interviews with scholars and Islamists in Europe I discovered that law schools were rarely referred to. As a rule, the interviewees would state: 'According to the Koran and the Sunna, so and so . . .'. I turn now to a discussion of the Koran and Sunna, and the concept of *ʿurf* which I believe has played a part in the formation of Islamic law in early Islamic history as well as in contemporary Islamic thought.

Koran

The Koran is the main source of Islamic legislation. It is regarded as the word of God revealed to the Prophet Muḥammad. The Koran is addressed sometimes directly to Muḥammad, at other times to all the Muslims, to all believers (*muʾminūn*) or to the whole of humanity.

The origin of the Koran has been scrutinised by Muslims and non-Muslims alike. A common trend is that Orientalist scholars tend to be sceptical about Muslims' interpretation of history (cf. Wansbrough 1977; 1978; Rippin 1990; 1993), whereas other researchers tend to more or less accept 'the insider view' (cf. Burton 1977) or explicitly choose not to make any judgement on the issue (see Waines 1995: 278). According to Muslim sources, the Koran was written down in the lifetime of Muḥammad. Abū Bakr, the first caliph, started to collect the Koranic parts immediately after his take-over, and by the time of his death the Koran had been compiled (Ṣāliḥ 1979: 74).[5] At the time of the reign of Uthmān, Huḍaifa ibn al-Yamān discovered that Muslims from different parts of the empire had different readings of the Koran. At that time there were no dots and no vocalisations of the text. He drew Uthmān's attention to the danger of discrepancies in the reading of the text. Uthmān ordered Zaid ibn Thābit, who had also been involved in the collection of the Koran under Abū Bakr, to check the different pronunciations and correct them according to the dialect of the Quraish (Ṣāliḥ 1979: 78).[6] But it was not until the reign of ʿAbd al-Mālik (685–705), with the expansion of the Muslim Empire and the successive conversion of many non-Arabs, that the dots and the vocalisations became part of the text (Ṣāliḥ 1979: 90).

The Koran was revealed during two distinctive periods, the first being the time of Muḥammad's stay in Mecca, and the other the Medina period. The revelations from the Mecca period are marked by an emphasis on *tawḥīd* and belief in the Day of Judgement. Sayyid Quṭb, in his book, *Milestones*, talks about the thirteen Mecca years of constitution of the faith, before the actual legislation of Islam started (S. Quṭb 1983). Verses to do with legislation on social matters are mainly revealed in the Medina period, during which Muḥammad acted as a community leader. It is, however, important to be aware that the Koran is not a law book. Esposito has noted that only a very small part of the Koran contains explicit legal injunctions. He says:

> While the *Quran* does contain prescriptions about matters that would rank as legal in the strict, narrow sense of the term, these injunctions, in fact, comprise but eighty verses. The bulk of *Quranic* matter consists mainly of broad, general moral directives as to what the aims and aspirations of Muslims should be, the 'ought' of the Islamic religious ethic.
>
> (Esposito 1982: 3)

It can be argued that the Koran gives general guidance of conduct rather than legislative rules. In some areas, such as inheritance, divorce and diet, it is more explicit. As for the status of women in the Koran, there is disagreement among contemporary researchers and Islamic scholars as to whether the Koran came to improve the status of women or the opposite. The latter is the stand of Muslim feminists such as Leila Ahmad. Ahmad, in her book *Women and Gender in Islam*, claims that in pre-Islamic times, women held high positions and that matrilineality was widespread (Ahmad 1992: 41; 43; 44). In her view, Islam came to have both pragmatic and ethical perspectives. In the ethical field, she sees Islam as promoting an egalitarian vision. However, she believes that the egalitarian vision of Islam was 'in tension with . . . the hierarchical structure of marriage pragmatically instituted in the first Islamic society' (Ahmad 1992: 63). Thus the pragmatic aspect of Islam over-ruled the ethical aspect. The consequence was that Islam came to change a fairly egalitarian society into a society of purely male control. She builds her argument on the work of the early Orientalist, Robertson Smith, in which he suggests the existence of a matriarchal society in pre-Islamic times in the Muslim area (Ahmad 1992: 43).

Conversely, Islamic scholars argue that the Koran came to improve the status of women substantially. Gender relations in pre-Islamic Arabia, in their view, were based on male dominance and women had no rights whatsoever. For instance, they refer to how the Koran came to prohibit the pre-Islamic practice of girl infanticide, and how women's lack of economic and social security in cases of inheritance and divorce were changed for the better by Koranic injunctions (al-Mawdūdī 1972; M. Quṭb 1985).

Some western scholars are also of the opinion that the Koran improved the status of women. Esposito sees the Koranic injunctions in matters of marriage, divorce and inheritance as reforms: a woman came to be 'a legal partner to the marriage contract rather than an object for sale' as the dowry (*mahr*) was given to her instead of to her family. Unlimited polygamy became restricted with the additional requirement that the husband should be totally just to all his wives. A waiting period (*ʿidda*) was instituted in matters of divorce in order to provide an opportunity for reconciliation and to protect unborn children. Lastly, women were given the opportunity to inherit (Esposito 1982: 4–5).

Throughout history many Islamic scholars have written commentaries on the Koran and interpreted it in view of hadith literature and individual analysis. The various interpretations, particularly of social issues, are influenced by time, space, and the commentator's specific approach and biography. The commentaries could be based on lexicographic or syntactic references, or they could be of a philosophical nature with an emphasis on personal opinions. The hadith literature also had a prominent place in many commentaries, particularly in order to explain the background of certain Koranic verses.[7] The understanding of the Koran can thus differ according to which hadiths one accepts and the degree of emphasis one puts on the various other legal concepts of Islamic law.

Sunna

In literature and in discussions with Islamists, there is recurring reference to 'returning to the Koran and the Sunna'. Furthermore, 'Sunna' is often used synonymously with 'hadith'. In discussions I have noted that there is actually a confusion of these two concepts, and from the discussion and literature I have established that 'Sunna' usually refers specifically to 'the Prophet's Sunna', but it might also be used in a wider context to refer to the Prophet's Companions' and their immediate successors' behaviour in addition to that of the Prophet. The early Islamic judges believed that the Prophet's Companions followed the Prophet's 'Sunna', which then meant his example (Rahman 1996: 130–1), and the Companions' behaviour also became an example to follow. Sunna refers therefore to an established religious norm built in the first place on the Prophet's example, then on *ijmāʾ* (consensus) of the Companions, and, for the Mālikī Law school, even on the practice of the people of Medina. Hadith, on the other hand, refers more specifically to the Prophet's example, although there are some hadiths which refer to God (*ḥadīth al-qudsī*). Not all Sunna is reported through hadiths.

As for the Sunna of the Prophet, there are three categories: what the Prophet said, his deeds and his approval of certain deeds. The hadith literature underwent a process of strict scrutiny by the hadith collectors in the ninth century. In the science of criticism of hadith various categories were established. The hadiths were accepted or rejected according to two criteria: the content (*matn*) of the hadith and the chain of narrators (*isnād*). The collectors further established two types of classification of the hadith. First, the hadith was classified as *successive* or *multiple* (*mutawātir*) (more than three/alternatively nine narrator chains), and *isolated* (*aḥad*) (less than four/ten narrator chains) (N. Keller 1991: 626–7).[8] Second, every hadith was classified as authentic (*ṣaḥīḥ*),[9] good (*ḥasan*), weak (*ḍaʿīf*), or refused (*mawḍūʿ*) according to its narrator chain and its content. The *isolated* hadiths were again divided into three categories (Ṣāliḥ 1979):

1 Hadiths with between three and four (alternatively up to nine) narrator chains called *famous* (*mashhūr*).
2 Hadiths with two narrator chains called *respected* (*ʿazīz*).
3 Hadiths with one narrator chain called *strange* (*gharīb*).

It is important to note, however, that it is possible for a hadith to have multiple narrator chains even though there is only one 'first observer', i.e. only one of the Companions heard or saw the actual happenings, but as this 'first observer' told the story to many other people the hadith in question was spread through multiple narrator chains. As the Companions were regarded as reliable, their narratives were accepted *per definition*.

This categorisation of hadith plays a part in the present debate on gender relations. Hadiths which are classified as *isolated* have been used in legislation and in the formation of attitudes in Muslim society. The Egyptian scholar, Muḥammad al-Ghazzālī, has discussed this matter, as has the Islamic feminist, Riffat Hassan (Hassan 1990). In his book al-Ghazzālī rejects the widespread use of *isolated* hadiths in Islamic legislation (M. al-Ghazzālī 1989: 18). It is of particular interest that Islamic male scholars such as al-Ghazzālī with a wide audience, and thus with authority, are becoming more receptive to the idea of a profound scrutiny of existing Islamic rules and regulations.

The hadith literature is of a much more controversial nature than is the Koran. Muslims have not subjected the Koran to an historical-critical investigation such as Christian scholars have done with the Bible. Thus, Islamic scholars regard the Koran as *literally* the word of God. On the other hand, there are different views on the hadith literature. The hadith literature is different among Shīʿī and Sunnī Muslims as Shīʿī Muslims mainly accept only hadiths based on the authority of ʿAlī, the Imams and followers of the Shīʿī creed. In addition there are some Muslim intellectuals who are critical towards hadiths, such as the group called Pervezians in the Indian subcontinent who reject the hadith literature *per se* (Brown 1996). Western scholarship on Islam also tends to take a negative view of the authenticity of the hadith literature. Lammens, Marglíouth and Schacht see the concept 'Sunna of the Prophet' entirely as a formulation of Arabs, pre-Islamic and post-Islamic alike (Rahman 1996: 132). Islamic scholars such as al-ʿAẓamī and ʿAlī reject this claim (al-ʿAzamī 1978; M.ʿAlī 1996; see also Juynboll 1983; Motzki 1991), and a western scholar on Islamic law, Noel J. Coulson, attempts to reconcile the two opposing views by claiming that 'an alleged ruling of the Prophet should be tentatively accepted as such unless some reason can be adduced as to why it should be regarded as fictitious' (Coulson 1964: 64–5; also quoted in Waines 1995: 276).

Scholars from the Indian subcontinent seem to have a more flexible attitude towards Islamic law, including the hadith literature, than have Arab scholars. Fazlur Rahman (d. 1988) is a scholar with roots in the Indian subcontinent. He is controversial in an Islamic context and is regarded by many as too modernistic in his approach to Islam. However, at the same time he is respected for his encyclopaedic knowledge of classical Islamic scholarship (Koya 1996: x). Although Rahman is critical as to *how* hadiths have been used, he still approves of the hadith literature as an *idea*. He argues:

> And if all hadith is given up, what remains but a yawning chasm of fourteen centuries between us and the Prophet? And in the vacuity of this chasm not only must the Qur'an slip from our fingers under our subjective whims – for the only thing that anchors it is the Prophetic activity itself – but even the very existence and integrity of the Qur'an and, indeed, the existence of the Prophet himself become an unwarranted myth.
>
> (Rahman 1996: 177–8)

For Muslims, the hadith literature constitutes the explanation of the Koran. In the Koran it is said that one should pray, but there are no elucidations as to *how* one should pray or *how many times* one should pray. Likewise, Muslims should pay *zakāt* and give *ṣadaqa* but few details are given about *how* or *how much* one should give. Whereas the Koran gives the general guidelines, the hadith literature specifies these guidelines.

However, as shown in the section on Islamist directions in Europe, there are discrepancies between the different movements regarding how to interpret the hadiths. The *salafī* trend usually accepts all authentic hadiths on a similar footing, whereas the *ikhwān* trend tends to distinguish between the various hadiths. In my discussions with members of the Muslim Brotherhood they referred to the three categories of hadiths which Abū Zahra has defined in his book *uṣūl al-fiqh* (*Roots of Jurisprudence*): first, the Prophet's sayings, actions and decisions which are the basis of sharia regulations; second, the Prophet's actions that are linked to his special status as a prophet, for instance marrying more than four wives. Third, the Prophet's sayings, actions and decisions linked to his human status or his cultural background or traditions particular to the Arabia of his time, such as clothing or food (Abū Zahra n.d. b: 89).[10] Abū Zahra's classifications seem to give a clear approach to the hadith literature. However, on closer inspection it is obvious that it might be difficult to distinguish the various hadiths on the basis of these categories.

The problematic part of the hadith literature is that which concerns the socio-political field. How should for instance the hadiths on the Prophet's political example be understood? How can his example in general be relevant for contemporary society? Furthermore, many hadiths on women reflect the views of traditional society. How should these be understood today? What happens with the Islamic injunctions which are given at a time with specific social patterns, when these patterns no longer exist? Are these Islamic injunctions valid for every time and place or is it possible to interpret them in the light of changing circumstances? There are various approaches to these questions. Islamic feminists such as Riffat Hassan and Amina Wadud-Muhsin avoid any extensive consideration of the hadith literature in their discussion on gender relations in Islam. Engineer, on the other hand, tends to take a selective view of many hadiths dealing with women. This is an obvious consequence of his Ismāʿīlī background, with its different approach to the hadith literature. He states:

> We do not wish to attempt a critique of hadith literature, but suffice it to say that many hadiths (tradition) came into being later in keeping with the cultural and socio-religious prejudices of the 1st and 2nd centuries of the Islamic calendar. These traditions must be treated with great caution and one should not rush to draw conclusions from them. Unfortunately, many sharia formulations are based on such traditions and thus many of the rules reflect the cultural prejudices of the Arabs and the Persians rather than the greatness of the *Quran* and its just and liberal outlook.
>
> (Engineer 1992: 13–14)

I would argue that Engineer and some of the Islamic feminists, such as Hassan and Wadud-Muhsin, tend to be just as selective with the hadith literature as the traditional scholars they accuse of the same. Engineer, by indicating that most of the hadiths which are biased toward women are fabricated, cuts the ground away from under the hadith literature as such. Some Arab scholars, such as at-Turābī, al-Ghazzālī, and al-Qaraḍāwī, have taken an hermeneutic approach to these particular hadiths about gender relations, also taking into consideration the caution one has to exercise over this issue in a Muslim context. I predict that these latter scholars' hermeneutic approach to the hadith literature will have a more penetrating force among Muslims in the present wave of social change than the approach of Engineer and Islamic feminists.

ʿUrf (custom)

Local customs have influenced the development of Islamic legislation in the various regions of the Muslim empire. As Islam spread, verbalised and non-verbalised regional customs compatible with Islamic principles became part of legislation. With regard to verbalised local customs, two of the law schools, the Ḥanafī and the Mālikī, regarded them as possible sources of legislation so long as they did not contradict the letter or the spirit of the Islamic sources (Philips 1988: 67; 73). As for non-verbalised customs, local notions and practices became incorporated in the law as they influenced the way the Islamic texts were interpreted by scholars in various regions. As a consequence, female circumcision became part of local expressions of sharia in countries such as some African countries, which often coincide with 'the nomadic belt', where such practice was pervasive before the coming of Islam. However, in countries where this practice was not in common use, such as in most Arab countries, female circumcision was never practised. It is interesting to note that in some countries such as Syria which adhere to the Shāfiʿī law school which is one of the two law schools which promote female circumcision, the practice of female circumcision has never been in common use. This is probably because it was not a pre-Islamic custom in the region.

As for the role of custom in Islamic legislation, it is important to be aware that in the Southeast Asian countries the customary law, the *ʿadat* law, came to constitute a legal system side by side with sharia. I presume that this was because Islam came fairly late to this area. It was not established until the fifteenth century (al-Atas 1986), and at that time Islamic law was well established and was not amenable to development within a Southeast Asian framework. Sharia and the *adat* law thus came to exist as two irreconcilable systems of law, in contrast to those countries where customs were actually incorporated into Islamic law.

As late as the eleventh century, scholars discussed whether *ʿurf* should be regarded as another root of Islamic jurisprudence. According to Gibb and Kramers a general acceptance of *ʿurf* never did occur (Gibb and Kramers 1974: 615). It is, however, important to note as I have mentioned above, that *ʿurf* has played a part in the formation of the law, but it is the unwritten or rather non-verbalised customs and laws which survived religious change as these were deeply rooted in prevailing attitudes and consciousness of the people in society. The written or verbalised local customs which already existed with the advent of Islam were more easy to reject since Islam manifested itself as a 'new arrival' and the 'old' was something to dissociate oneself from. It is important to note that when I say that *ʿurf* became part of Islamic law, I mean the *moral* part of the prevailing customs in the various areas. In general one can say that the predominant moral standard often plays a part in legislation, as indicated by the Swedish Professor of Law, Anna Christensen (Christensen 1996).[11]

In the Koran, the term *ʿurf* is mentioned twice in this grammatical form (K.7: 199; 77: 1), and it refers to 'kindness'. In verse 7: 199, there is an explicit reference to '*ʿurf*' as 'goodness', and thus one may conclude that *ʿurf* in the Koranic sense of the word might be regarded as referring only to 'good and morally accepted' customs. The Koranic verse says: 'Keep to forgiveness and enjoin kindness (*ʿurf*), and turn away from the ignorant.' In the Koran another form of the root *ʿ-r-f*, '*maʿrūf*', is mentioned thirty-eight times. '*Maʿrūf*' is translated into English as 'known', 'generally accepted', 'that which is good' or 'equitableness'. The term is used for instance in matters of divorce: 'When you divorce women and they are about to reach the end of their waiting-term, then either retain them in a generally accepted manner (*maʿrūf*) or let them go in a generally accepted manner (*maʿrūf*)' (K.2: 231). The term *maʿrūf* is also used in another context in the Koran, in the commonly quoted statement: 'Enjoin what is right (*maʿrūf*), and forbid what is wrong (*munkar*)' (K.7: 157; *passim*). Looking at the basic meaning of the term *maʿrūf*, it has to do with generally acceptable customs in certain cultural contexts and particularly within an Islamic framework. The word *munkar*, on the other hand, basically means 'that which is *not* generally accepted' or that which is 'disavowed' in certain cultural contexts and particularly within an Islamic framework.

The question which then arises is what happens when what is 'generally accepted' and 'right' or what is 'not generally accepted' or 'wrong' changes from one period of time to another or from one society to another. Since the root *ʿ-r-f* with its derivation generally refers in the Koran to that which is good and moral, I believe this refers to that which is morally good at various times and in various places within the framework of Islamic principles. As Islam is regarded as a universal religion, there may be space within its framework for various interpretations of what is generally accepted and what is not generally accepted depending on the time and place.

It is important to draw attention to the fact that there might be various levels of legislation. In my fieldwork I have discovered that in the sphere of legislation Islamists refer to both moral and legal aspects in the actual legislation on women's issues. The moral aspects can be regarded as regional customs or attitudes which vary according to time and place. I would suggest that much actual Islamic legislation is built around the moral sphere of the seventh to ninth century. Thus in my fieldwork I have encountered the idea among many Islamists that, even when Islamic law gives one judgement, they would add upon further scrutiny that one also has to take into consideration human feelings and *ʿurf*. An example is in matters of polygyny, where many Islamist women have said that although a man has the *right* to marry a second wife even without telling the first wife, this is not the right behaviour according to *ʿurf*. The same view was expressed by an Islamist man when we discussed divorce, and he said that 'the Law says one thing whereas one also has to take into consideration human feelings'. I believe that it is in this tension between legal and moral considerations that new legislation will emerge and establish itself in a new context.

The return to the Koran and Sunna

I would like to draw attention to the notion of 'returning to the sources', i.e. the reproduction of the past in the present, which has tended to be interpreted as an attempt to go back to seventh century Arabia. Islamists who turn to the sources intend to search for the 'genuine understanding': what *actually* happened and what was the *genuine* intention behind a happening or a saying of the Prophet? This method can be understood as undiluted conservatism: Islamists wish to conserve traditions and attitudes prevailing in the time of the Prophet and his Companions. However, what actually happens is that the interpretation does not focus on how the historical event *actually* occurred but it becomes an unconscious process in which the most important consideration is: how can one possibly live according to this historical example today? What really takes place is that the reinterpretation becomes a reconstruction of historical events in which one's own biography and life situation play a large part. What becomes apparent is the unconscious or conscious change in that which is *maʿrūf* and that which is *munkar* within the framework of Islam, in relation to that which is perceived as 'generally accepted' or 'right' and that which is '*not* generally accepted' or 'wrong' in different social contexts.

at-Turābī represents an interesting approach to a new interpretation of social issues in the Islamic sources. In his book, *minhaj at-tashrīʿ al-islāmī* (*The Islamic Method of Legislation*), he argues that scholars in early Islamic history appealed to the Greek cultural heritage in the formation and understanding of Islam. Likewise, it is possible for the contemporary Muslim generation to apply modern scientific methods while hoping that Muslims will stay aloof from the wrongdoings inherent in these methods and fulfil the wisdom inherent in them (at-Turābī 1990: 12–13). at-Turābī is not only amenable to a reopening of *ijtihād*, which according to him is an individual interpretation of the sources which anybody with an adequate amount of Islamic knowledge can do, but it seems that he even pleads for a totally new form of legislation.

When I met Sheikh Darsh (d. 1997) in his home in London in December 1995, we discussed the question of changes in sharia and changes in perceptions of women in the cultural encounter with 'the West'. He explained:

> It is a matter of understanding the environment in which we live and a reflection of the changing positions and changing situations. We Muslims have to take these changes into consideration when we look into the life of the Muslim woman. Social changes are the reasons why Muslims today talk of *fiqh al-aqallīyāt*, the *fiqh* for Muslim minorities.[12] In the past, the scholars worked within the *fiqh* of the Muslim state. Now [in western countries] we Muslims are a minority. Thus, we have to consider these changes in order to be able to reflect the new situation and to clarify our attitude. We have to know what is cultural and what is Islamic to be able to make valued, mature judgements.

As Darsh was the leader of the Sharia Council in Britain, I asked him whether he was working in this way in order to find solutions to contemporary problems. Darsh firmly rejected the idea that he was involved in such work as it is only in its initial phase. 'What I do', he said, 'is only to relieve women who are strained in difficult relationships and in difficult situations of life.' He stressed that this 'minority *fiqh*' is not necessarily a matter of reinterpretation, since he explained that 'in the traditional books of Islam law we find every possible point of view. This shows the greatness of the law.'

Darsh was very careful to emphasise that he was not in a position to make *ijtihād*. He also stressed that there are limitations to being a *mujtahid*. 'Either one can be fully *mujtahid* or *mujtahid* within a particular school [i.e. *mujtahid juzī*],' he said.

> If you are *mujtahid* within a particular school, you must be aware of books by such and such and you have to stick to that particular school. What we can do is to look into what is recorded and the former points of view. What we do in the present situation is to find that which is the more appropriate to the Muslim community, and then we accept that particular point of view.

This attitude of denying that their legal judgements are *ijtihāds* is true of many recent Islamic scholars and is not particular to Darsh. I believe that it indicates the difficulties and challenges which modern scholars are faced with today, in Muslim society in general with its rapid social changes, and in western countries' Muslim communities in particular, with their diversity of nationalities, traditions and Islamic perceptions. The lack of a central authority and the variety of views among scholars have caused internal problems. The challenge of reinterpretation or revaluing of the Islamic sources has brought about conflicts over *whose* interpretations are valid and *who* has the right to interpret the sources. Although validity of an Islamic scholar's judgement to a great extent depends on his/her audience, e.g. whether judgements are accepted or not by the people, the problem of the scholar's particular knowledge and authenticity arises.

Reflections

The confusion in terminology when it comes to Islamic legislation seems to create misunderstandings between scholars of various movements. Whereas Ḥasan and, to a certain extent, al-Qaraḍāwī, see sharia in terms of change, more traditional scholars reject any changes in sharia. However, the same traditional scholars do not reject changes within the field of jurisprudence (*fiqh*). As long as this confusion is perpetuated, it might be difficult to harmonise the various positions. As shown above, Islamic legislation is to a great extent built on scholars' deductions from the Koran and Sunna. These deductions are a result of how scholars understand the Islamic texts and they are therefore rooted to a great extent in the various scholars' backgrounds and personal characteristics. Cultural patterns are variables in these scholars' backgrounds and personal characteristics. The issue thus becomes: how might Islamic legislation change when Islamic scholars either move to western countries or when Muslims born and raised in 'the West' become Islamic scholars? Moreover, the Islamic texts are now available to a wider audience due to the increase in educated Muslims on the one hand and technology on the other, since one computer can contain the whole hadith literature. These factors might be seen as the main reasons why even scholars in fields other than Islamic studies become active in the Islamic scholarly debate. In what follows I show how in the Muslim immigration situation in Europe, various variables such as the degree of integration into the majority society 'cultural base patterns', and directions in Islamic thought contribute to the process of change in attitudes towards women and gender relations.

I now turn to various women's issues within Islamic law and in each case I will discuss the sources and how the sources have been understood in different contexts. I begin with the overarching subject of general attitudes towards women in Islam.

6 Perceptions of women

Religious texts have been interpreted from an androcentric point of view for centuries (King 1995; Schüssler Fiorenza 1983). Islam has been accused of such a biased reading of the text more than the other two monotheistic world religions, leaving out the female perspective *in toto*. Below I will consider various perceptions of women in Islam and indicate diachronic as well as synchronic changes.

The understanding of religious texts in general and androcentric religious texts in particular depends on how 'literalist' one is in approach. Islamic texts, particularly the hadith literature which reflects early Islamic society, contain patriarchal attitudes as they came into being in patriarchal and male-dominated societies. Similarly, androcentric texts are found in Christian and Judaic scriptures, but many followers have chosen to divert attention away from statements which are not compatible with contemporary society. An outstanding example, which has its parallel in Judaism, is the issue of female priests in Lutheran Christianity. The Pauline injunction that women should keep quiet in congregations (1 Corinth. 14: 34–5) has particularly in the Scandinavian countries been used in the argument that no woman can be the spiritual leader of a Christian congregation. However, with the advent of feminist theology and hermeneutic approaches to such biblical passages, there is now a female priesthood in these countries (Schüssler Fiorenza 1983; 1994; Bird 1991; Hampson 1990).[1]

A prominent example of androcentric interpretations in the Islamic context is how *shūrā* has been interpreted mainly as a political concept, whereas in the Koran it is mentioned not only in a political context but also in the context of family matters.[2] For instance, on the question of whether the mother should breast-feed her child, the parents of the child are told to make counsel (*shūrā*) with each other (K.2: 233). It is true that the passage in question is linked to the matter of divorce and many scholars consider it only in that context, but other scholars claim that although this particular passage is linked to divorce, the content of the verse has to be seen as a general matter (ʿAbd al-ʿĀṭī 1977: 95).

I would like to draw attention to another example which does not necessarily have to do with a male versus female interpretation, but has more to do with levels of education and the specific *fiqh* approach a person has, whether traditional or a 'return to the Koran and Sunna'. In my discussions with Muslims in general, of various nationalities and various directions from the mid-1980s onwards, I have observed that the Koranic verse 4: 34, which indicates a power relation between men and women, was generally referred to more often than other verses which deal with the marital relationship in terms of mutual love and tenderness (K.9: 71; K.2: 228; K.4: 19; K.30: 21). In contrast to the general trend among Muslims, I discovered in my fieldwork among Islamists in Europe that the tendency was to include all aspects. The issue is thus not always so much which texts exist but which ones are selected, deliberately or undeliberately. This selection process might be based on verbalised or non-verbalised attitudes. As Hjärpe has observed and conceptualised in his basket metaphor, in any tradition, religious or secular, it is difficult to take the whole picture into account. It is therefore necessary to select aspects of the whole, whether or not this selection entails a process of conscious deliberation (Hjärpe 1997). Texts are present in their entirety in the body of religious literature, but one tends to choose and interpret texts, intentionally or unintentionally, according to what is compatible with one's own attitude. Thus out of a whole field of possible texts and their interpretations, one appeals to some in daily life while excluding others. This applies to androcentric interpretations as well as to feminist approaches to various religions. I have argued elsewhere that Muslim feminists tend to be selective in readings of religious texts in a similar manner to Muslims with an androcentric attitude. Muslim feminists favour hadiths which are in favour of women, whereas they criticise and refuse hadiths which portray women negatively (Roald 1998; Roald and Ouis 1997; see also note 7 below).

Below I consider various statements about women taken from the Koran or the hadith literature which have been referred to in my discussions with Muslims and Islamists. Many hadiths characterise the female Companions to the Prophet in a positive way. ʿĀ'isha, the wife of the Prophet, enjoys a particularly elevated status in the hadith literature. It is interesting to note that ʿĀ'isha is portrayed as a very strong personality who also took part in political disputes. ʿĀ'isha's status in the Islamic sources and in Islamic literature contradicts the image of timid and restrained Muslim women which has penetrated the non-Muslim world (Spellberg 1994; az-Zarkashī 1970). Moreover, the hadith found in al-Bukhārī which says that the best women of the tribe of Quraysh are those who ride camels (al-Bukhārī, Book of Marriage, no. 4692; Muslim, Book of Virtues of the Companions of the Prophet, no. 4589; Musnad Aḥmad, *musnad banī hāshim*, no. 2774) promotes the idealisation of active and energetic women. In this chapter, however, I concentrate on those statements which are controversial and which have been used to reinforce the notion of Islam as a religion oppressive to women among Muslims and non-Muslims alike.

Women in the Koran

In the Koran and in the hadith literature, there are various statements concerning human beings in general, and statements concerning women in particular. In the Koran, of particular interest is the verse which says that men and women have been created out of one single soul. Riffat Hassan, an Islamic feminist with Indo-Pakistani roots who lives in the United States, has dealt with this issue in a feminist context (Hassan 1990), and below it will be viewed in an Islamist context.

The Koran says:

> O Mankind! Be conscious of your sustainer, who has created you out of one living entity (*nafsin wāḥida*), and out of it created its mate, and out of the two spread abroad a multitude of men and women. And remain conscious of God, in whose name you demand [your rights] from one another, and of these ties of kinship. Verily God is ever watchful over you.
>
> (K.4: 1)

The passage 'created you from one single entity' is mentioned five more times in the Koran (K.6: 98; 7: 189; 30: 21; 31: 21 and 39: 6). The verse quoted above has a prominent position in contemporary Islam, as it is rendered in the hadith literature that the Prophet always recited it in the beginning of the Friday sermon. Thus particularly *salafī* preachers, who follow strictly the Sunna of the Prophet, would usually start their Friday sermon with this verse.

In a western context, Muhammad Asad (d. 1992), the Jewish convert to Islam, remarks in his commentary of this verse in his Koranic commentary, *The Message of the Qur'an*:

> Out of the many meanings attributable to the term *nafs* – soul, spirit, mind, animate being, living entity, human being, person, self (in the sense of a personal identity), humankind, life-essence, vital principle, and so forth – most of the classical commentators choose 'human being', and assume that it refers here to Adam. Muḥammad ʿAbduh, however, rejects this interpretation (*Manār* IV, 323 ff.) and gives, instead, his preference to 'humankind' inasmuch as this term stresses the common origin and brotherhood of the human race (which, undoubtedly, is the purport of the above verse), without, at the same time, unwarrantably tying it to the Biblical account of the creation of Adam and Eve. My rendering of *nafs*, in this context, as 'living entity' follows the same reasoning. – As regards the expression *zawjahā* ('its mate'), it is to be noted that, with reference to animate beings, the term *zawj* ('a pair', 'one of a pair' or 'a mate') applies to the male as well as to the female component of a pair or couple; hence, with reference to human beings, it

> signifies a woman's mate (husband) as well as a man's mate (wife). Abū Muslim – as quoted by Rāzī – interprets the phrase 'He created out of it (*minhā*) its mate' as meaning 'He created its mate [i.e. its sexual counterpart] out of its own kind (*min jinsihā*)', thus supporting the view of Muḥammad ʿAbduh referred to above. The literal translation of *minhā* as 'out of it' clearly alludes, in conformity with the text, to the biological fact that both sexes have originated from 'one living entity'.
>
> (Asad 1984: 100)

Asad is a typical example of the cultural encounter between Islam and 'the West'. He was of European origin, turned to Islam at an early age and acquired an extensive knowledge of the Arabic language. In the above passage the 'western cultural base pattern' is apparent, with its firm notion of equality between the sexes. As a European convert to Islam, Asad's writing is marked by a cross-fertilisation of various cultural ideas and patterns. The idea of 'the past reproduced in the present' is also an element in the text Asad refers to Rāzī, a well-established authority in Islamic literature. By linking Rāzī to the more controversial Muḥammad ʿAbduh, whose 'rational' style of argumentation is regarded with scepticism by many Muslims, ʿAbduh's (and Asad's) conclusion of equality between the sexes becomes acceptable. It is significant that Asad appeals to ʿAbduh, the nineteenth century Egyptian reformer who advocated the introduction of western ideas into a framework of Islamic principles. Asad's conclusion which links the term '*zawj*' to the male as well as to the female indicates a preference for sexual equality. The equality of the sexes in a spiritual sense (i.e. the relationship between the individual and God) is an established notion among Muslims in general, whereas in social matters Islamists in particular have viewed men as superior to women. It is, however, noticeable that Asad does not discuss the distinction between the social and the spiritual spheres, but discusses equality in general terms.

As Asad has noted, the traditional understanding of the passage 'We have created you out of one living entity' is that this 'living entity' is Adam, the first man (cf. Ibn Kathīr 1981: 355). The same idea can also be found in twentieth century commentaries (cf. S. Quṭb 1986; see also aṣ-Ṣabūnī 1981: 258). It is interesting to note that in Fīrūz Ābādī's commentary from the fifteenth century, which is based upon his understanding of Ibn ʿAbbās' interpretation of the Koran, he claims that the meaning of 'one living entity' is Adam, but at the same time Ābādī adds that Eve existed within this soul of Adam (Ābādī 1988: 77). Ibn ʿAbbās is known to be one of the earliest commentators on the Koran, but as his commentaries are not collected together as an entity many later scholars have selected parts from them to include in their own Koranic commentaries.

Zainab al-Ghazzālı has a similar understanding of this passage to that of Ibn ʿAbbās (according to Ābādī's interpretation). She explains:

> Verily, the man and the woman, they are together one living entity. The soul was the man but then it was divided into a second part; the woman. The significance of this is that the life of one of them without its other half, is a life which is not complete.
>
> (Z. al-Ghazzālī 1994a vol. I: 281 [translation mine])

An analysis of the various Koranic commentaries indicates that the female perspective represented by Zainab al-Ghazzālī in this particular case coincides with that of ʿAbduh and Asad, but is regarded by many Islamists as too 'rationalist'. It is also worth noting the similarity between this perspective and the interpretation of Ābādī.

In the questionnaire addressed to Arab Islamists in Europe, I quoted the Koranic passage: 'We have created you out of one living entity and out of it created its mate' and I asked: 'How do you understand this passage?' Amal is one of the respondents with whom I conducted an in-depth interview based on her answers in the questionnaire. She has a degree in natural sciences and came to Europe more than ten years ago in her early twenties. Amal is fluent in the language of the host country and although she does not work outside the home, she actively participates in the wider society, giving lectures to non-Muslims about Islam and taking part in social discussions. Amal does not belong to any group but during our discussions I came to understand her position as being within a *post-ikhwān* trend. Amal's response in the questionnaire resembled that of Islamic feminists such as Hassan and Wadud-Muhsin (Hassan 1990; Wadud-Muhsin 1992). She wrote: 'Man and woman were created from the same origin without specifying who was created first. – It may be that they were created at the same time, which indicates a spiritual equality of man and woman.'

Amal has drawn the conclusion that as there is no specific indication that the man was created first, it might be that men and women were created at the same time. However, although she suggests spiritual equality between men and women, which is an established notion, she does not go further to suggest social equality between the sexes.

Ziyād is a social scientist who has lived in Europe since the beginning of the 1980s. He is in his mid-forties and works in a non-Muslim environment. Ziyād can also be placed within the framework of a *post-ikhwān* perspective, having *ikhwān* ideas as a starting point but having developed ideas independent of any organisational ties. He remarks that 'out of it created its mate' means that 'the two, the man and the woman, are the same and that they are similar'. He says: 'It does *not* mean that the woman is created from a man.'

Khadīja is a leading Islamist who has lived in Europe for only a few years. She has studied sharia and is a well-known lecturer at Islamic conferences and meetings. As Khadīja mainly communicates in Arabic, she has few contacts outside the Muslim community. Although she represents the *ikhwān* view as a member of the Muslim Brotherhood, Khadīja also promotes a female perspective, saying:

> I understand by this text that the woman and the man are equal in their humanity, intellect, rights and obligations. Moreover, I understand that the 'entity' (*nafs*), in order to perfect its virtues, must necessarily unite its two sides, the woman and the man, in the frame of sharia [translation mine].

Khadīja reflects the idea, also promoted by Zainab al-Ghazzālī, that matrimony is the completion of life. The man and the woman together form an entity which from creation was destined to become a unity.

Aḥmad is also a representative of the Muslim Brotherhood. He has a scientific education from a European university and has lived in Europe for nearly twenty years. However, Aḥmad does not work in his professional field but is a *daʿwa*-worker inside the Muslim community. He asserts:

> The two spouses resemble one another because they are created from 'one living entity' (*nafsin wāḥida*), and they are different because they are two different personalities. But this resemblance and this difference (difference due to the difference in their role in their life) leads to a unification to a perfect whole, and to stability and peace for both of them [translation mine].

The above statements offer a lofty view of the relationship between man and woman in the bond of marriage. The idea of the ideal married status recurs often in discussions with Islamists. The emphasis that every Muslim should be married if possible reflects the notion that the ideal relationship between a man and a woman can only occur within marriage, a legal partnership. It is important to bear in mind that both Khadīja and Aḥmad belong to the Muslim Brotherhood and thus promote a typical *ikhwān* notion with an idealistic tendency, whereas Amal and Ziyād both belong to the *post-ikhwān* trend. Ziyād answered in the questionnaire 'a woman is not created from a man', an answer which suggests an awareness of problematic issues. When I asked him in discussion what he meant by this answer, he said:

> In my dealings with Muslims I have come across men who might use Koranic statements in order to claim male superiority. They have unfortunately read the Koran with cultural lenses. I therefore stressed [in the questionnaire] the point that a woman is not created *from* a man. Everyone with a mind can understand that God has not created one part of humanity with a greater value than the other. Spiritually speaking, from the viewpoint of God, we are all similar.

The above answers are representative of those of other respondents. It is significant that the interviewees stress the spiritual equality between men and women. The common Islamic notion of the spiritual equality between the sexes is drawn from this as well as other Koranic verses, whereas another Koranic passage, 4: 34 deals more specifically with what has been interpreted in terms of a social hierarchy between the sexes which I shall consider in a later chapter.

Khadīja's and Aḥmad's answers reflect Barth's idea of social organisation, whereby the social structure of the movement draws the ideologies of those within the movement into concurrence with the ideology of the movement itself. Khadīja and Aḥmad are both acting within the Muslim community and that might indicate a more competitive and a less cooperative attitude towards the majority society. These factors influence what is selected from 'the basket', and it seems apparent that Amal and Ziyād, who are both outside any social movements and moreover are active within the majority society, tend to adopt attitudes which are more compatible with this society.

Riffat Hassan has observed that 'the negative attitudes pertaining to women which prevail in Muslim societies, are in general rooted in theology' (Hassan 1990: 96). She discusses three theological assumptions: first that man is the origin of creation, second that women are by definition temptresses, and third that women were created as a means for men (Hassan 1990: 100–1). It is interesting to note that Hassan with her roots in the cultural sphere of the Indian subcontinent stresses these three theological assumptions, whereas I, as a researcher into the Arabic cultural context, have observed that for all three of the issues identified by Hassan there are various interpretations according to social position and group identity. As I have indicated above, man as the origin of creation is not necessarily an established notion in the Arab Islamist sphere.

The notion of women as temptresses is not common in the *ikhwān* trend, whereas the writings of traditional scholars such as the Egyptian Muḥammad Mutawallī ash-Shaʿrāwī (d. 1998) might lend themselves to such an interpretation (ash-Shaʿrāwī n.d.). In a report on women's issues published by the Muslim Brotherhood in 1994, I found a statement which reflects the general attitude I have found among Arabic-speaking Islamists living in Europe on this matter. In the statement, the Muslim Brotherhood takes care to refute 'all false claims and superstitions that may arise concerning women and their purity' (The Muslim Brotherhood 1994: 4). By referring to the Koran and hadiths, the movement indicates an elevated status for women. By the hadith 'A believer is never impure' (The Muslim Brotherhood 1994: 3; al-Bukhārī, Book of Ablution, no. 274; Muslim, Book of Menstruation, no. 556; Sunan at-Tirmidhī, Book of Purity, no. 112; Sunan an-Nisāʾī, Book of Purity, no. 267; Sunan Abī Dāwud, Book of Purity, no. 199; Sunan Ibn Mājah, Book of Purity and its Sunna; no. 527, Musnad Aḥmad, *bāqi musnad al-muktharīn*, no. 6913) the Muslim

Brotherhood refutes the suggestion that women are impure or inherently evil. Further, their statement rejects the assumption that 'it was Eve who seduced Adam from eating from the tree' (The Muslim Brotherhood 1994: 3) as both of them have to bear responsibility for their transgression. The idea of women as temptresses, although it does exist, is not in my view a pervasive theological assumption in Arab Islamism, such as it might be in an Indo-Pakistani cultural context as observed by Hassan. I would suggest that as the Indian subcontinent was part of the British Empire for a much longer period than any country in the Arab world, there is a high probability of cultural influences from the colonial power's religious traditions, as the notion of women as temptresses has been pervasive in much Christian thinking. This might therefore explain Hassan's observations.

As for the idea that women are created as a means for men, this might be true in some movements, such as for instance among the *salafīs*, and among certain individual Arab Islamists. However, I have observed the attitude that man and woman are complementary to each other, an idea which I believe is much more prevalent among Arabic-speaking Islamists than the attitude that women are a means for men.

In contrast to Hassan's suggestion that negative attitudes towards women are built on theological assumptions, Ḥasan at-Turābī, the leading Sudanese Islamist, offers another explanation. Just as feminist analyses of gender relations are based on structures of power on both the micro and macro levels, at-Turābī sees the suppression of women in Muslim society as a consequence of the abuse of men's power owing to the lack of a correct understanding of Islam. He says:

> The jealousy which men have for women always gives them a reason to strengthen their methods of oppressing and monopolising women and to reinforce the conception that they are in possession of women. Jealousy is one of the male tendencies which can arise in every man, except those to whom God has given strength [through belief]. Jealousy makes men imagine women as weak, and men use this as an argument to prevent women from actively participating in society. This can lead to women becoming characterised by weakness and ineffectiveness, which again men utilise to legitimate and further continue their oppression.
>
> (at-Turābī n.d.: 34–5 [translation mine])

I doubt if at-Turābī's attitude towards the suppression of women is common in an Islamist context. It might be that his cultural heritage led him to draw these conclusions even in 1973, when he wrote the above in a manuscript about women's issues. Sudan, although a country with a large Arabic-speaking population, lies on the border between Africa and the Arab world with influences from both sides. This, together with at-Turābī's stay in Europe at an early stage of the formation both of the feminist movement and of modern Islamist ideology in general, might explain the development of his ideas about gender and gender relations in the Muslim world. The three cultural patterns, the 'western cultural base pattern', the 'Arab cultural base pattern' and the 'African cultural base pattern' have all been active in shaping his ideology and have influenced his selection of traditions and ideas. Moreover, as at-Turābī belongs to a *post-ikhwān* trend since he broke with the Muslim Brotherhood, his position seems to be less dependent on a social organisation.

Women in hadiths

I asked Islamists in discussions or by questionnaire: 'How do you understand the hadith in al-Bukhārī: "The Prophet (p.b.u.h.) said: 'After me I have not left any affliction (*fitna*) more harmful to men than his wife, his children and his neighbours.'" (al-Bukhārī, Book of Fasting, no. 1762; Muslim, Book of Belief, no. 208; Sunan at-Tirmidhī, Book of Afflictions, no. 2184.)[3] Most responses did not point to women as sinful beings. On the contrary, the most common answer was that the hadith indicates a warning to men, as men tend to look upon women in a sexual way. Amal says: 'It is not to blame women, but it is to warn men to control themselves and not to allow themselves to follow their desires when dealing with women.' Ziyād offers a similar interpretation, saying: 'It is a way of telling men to behave well and avoid the behaviour that will lead them to do bad things, such as adultery or having sexual relations before marriage.' One male independent Islamist wrote in the questionnaire:

> Men have to be reminded that women should be respected, and they should not look upon any woman as a sexual object. In men's lower nature there is a tendency to do so. Human beings have basic instincts and sexuality is one of these instincts. Islam came to elevate human beings over their lower nature and the Islamic rules and regulations are part of a training programme so that men and women can raise themselves above the basic instincts and become civilised citizens [my translation].

It is clear from these answers that many Islamists do not understand this particular hadith in literal terms. However, a small group of male respondents, mainly from the *salafī* trend, regarded this hadith from a point of view which saw women as temptations to men. However, their answers did not claim that women were *temptresses per se.* Rather, the idea of a lower versus a higher nature is prominent even in these latter responses.

I believe this is an interesting observation, especially since Hassan's assertion of an Islamic theological assumption about women as temptresses is shared by many Muslim feminists, as well as being an established non-Muslim notion about Islam. In my view this has to do with a lack of subtlety in the interpretation of words and expressions, not only when it comes to the discrepancy between Muslim and non-Muslim interpretations, but also between Muslims of different backgrounds, nationalities or outlooks in life. Thus, when an Islamist says that women are *temptations* to men, a non-Muslim or a common Muslim might seize upon it as an accusation against the nature of women, whereas many Islamists would see it in terms of the weakness of the nature of men. The same statement is also understood by many Islamists as referring to the weakness of the human being in general, and thus their claim that women are *temptations* to men is a general observation aimed at asserting the necessity of Islam as a body of rules and regulations which can enable a human being to transcend these weaknesses. It is worth noting the difference between the active connotation of 'being a temptress' and the passive connotation of 'being a temptation'. One of my informants remarked that the hadith, with its term '*fitna*', actually indicates passivity on the part of women rather than suggesting that women take an active role in the temptation. So as an overall conclusion, the evidence suggests that Arab Islamists in general do not regard women as active agents of temptation.

Another important point is that made by Sajda Nazlee in her book, *Feminism and Muslim Women*, in which she observes that the Arabic word *fitna* also means *trial*. Nazlee points out that the Koran says that children and possessions are also *fitna* for human beings, and this further conveys a sense of inactivity on the part of women in the portrayal of women as *fitna* for men (Nazlee 1996). In this context it is interesting to note that an American convert to Islam who has lived in the Arab world for many years also regards *fitna* in terms of a trial rather than in a sexual way. As a response to the hadith on women, children and neighbours as *fitna* for men, she stated that 'men need to be patient and not be demanding or angry with women, children, and neighbours'. She further added that she cannot understand how *fitna* from women is interpreted in a sexual sense when *fitna* from children and neighbours, who in the text accompany *wife*, is not. The understanding of *fitna*, either as temptation or trial, seems to depend on the cultural context. Despite the fact that *fitna* historically speaking has been understood both as temptation and trial, most Arabic-speaking Islamists tend to interpret *fitna* in sexual terms, thus emphasising the temptation aspect of the term. The American convert's understanding of this particular hadith indicates a reading from the view of the 'western cultural base pattern' in contrast to the 'Arab cultural base pattern', in which *fitna* is understood in respect of women in a way which disregards the last part of the hadith.

The discussion about *temptation* versus *temptress* suggests a cultural dissonance of concepts between Muslims and non-Muslims. The cultural content of *temptation* (*fitna*) tends to change in translation from Arabic to a western language depending on who is doing the translation. As a word like *fitna* has multiple connotations, the text takes on a different meaning according to which term one chooses. The attitude of the translator is thus decisive in conveying the Arabic text in other languages.

It is interesting to note that some of my interviewees were aware of the problem of translating ideas or notions from one cultural sphere to another. Sara, an Arab woman who came to Europe as a little girl and has thus gone through a western educational system, is now a student in a western university. She asserts: 'When it comes to understanding Islam and its sources, we have to be very careful to distinguish between various aspects. What did the Prophet *really* mean with his statements and in which contexts did he express them?' Sara goes on to explore the problem of translation when it comes to Islamic texts. She states:

> The translation of Islamic texts from Arabic to English is a matter of great concern. I believe that sometimes we also have to transform our minds in the act of translation. Look at me, I am an Arab Muslim. When I talk about or listen about Islam in the Arabic language everything seems fine and acceptable. However, when some concepts are translated into other languages, such as English, they are transformed to be understood in a different way. This hadith is particularly a good example of this transformation. When I hear this hadith read in Arabic I immediately understand and comprehend it in a positive way; whereas rendered into the English language the meaning seems to become something else, a text which depicts women in a bad way. Similarly, I also find that some English ideas and notions translated into Arabic change their meanings in a fundamental way in the process of translation.

The problem of translation and the idea that misunderstandings often come about as a result of differences in cultural codes are recurrent themes in the Muslim debate about 'Islam and the West'. Mūnā, a Palestinian woman who has lived in Scandinavia for over eight years, explains that when she went to school to learn the local language, teachers and students used to be curious about Islam. In the class they used to ask her about how Islam views various issues. She found it particularly frustrating when her teacher did not believe her when she said that Islam elevates the position of women. Mūnā explains:

> I kept telling her how God has told men to respect, revere, and protect women. But she [the teacher] always answered me that women should not be protected as they are able to protect themselves. For me to be protected by my husband is part of *my* rights which I as a woman enjoin in Islam, but my teacher regarded her freedom from male protection as *her* main right. She is free to have her own view but it is my right that she and others with her should not consider me as oppressed because I see male protection as essential for *my* life. At least it is *my* personal opinion, and although one might claim that this is a cultural point of view, so is hers [translation mine].

Mūnā's observation is perceptive in view of the cultural relativism she promotes. Mūnā has a substantial theoretical education in humanities from her home country, and her reflective arguments bear evidence of this educational background. Mūnā reinforces Sara's comment about the problem of translation, and she is of the opinion that the understanding of various concepts often differs within Arab and Scandinavian cultures, saying that 'it might be that our controversies have grown out of a misunderstanding or that we are talking about the same thing – but as we use different terminologies we end up disagreeing when actually we are in full agreement'. She further says:

> Another point which I would draw attention to is the way of understanding. When I discuss these issues with Scandinavian people they tend to see everything in black and white, particularly when it comes to the issue of women. When I use the word 'protecting' in the context of the relationship between husband and wife, Scandinavians tend to regard this in a negative, 'black' manner without understanding its nuances. However, protection in other contexts, for instance protection at work or at home by higher institutions, is regarded in a positive, 'white' manner, as part of human rights. When I speak of protection I mean that my husband protects me with those means God gave him; i.e. he is stronger than me, he tends to regard things in a different way than I do, thus we can discuss things in order to find the best solution. However, that does not mean that I do not protect him. I protect him with whatever means God gave me. Actually the Koran states that the woman should protect or guard her husband's secrets. So the act of protection works both ways and one should be aware of nuances in various concepts [my translation].

The above discussion indicates how cultural backgrounds and their emphases tend to dictate the understanding of texts or concepts. There is a cultural dissonance with regard to the Arab term for protection '*ḥimāya*' and the English word 'protection' which makes participants in the discussion talk on different levels. Mūnā's argument about how cultural codes obstruct understanding and agreement between various groups in a society with different ethnic and religious outlooks was repeated by many Islamists in various European countries.

Another hadith which has been given significance in a western context, and which has been used particularly to reinforce the notion of Islam as a religion hostile to women, is rendered by both al-Bukhārī and Muslim. It states that 'Bad omen (*shu'm*) is only in the woman, the house and the horse' (al-Bukhārī, Book of Jihad and Travelling, no. 2646; Muslim, Book of Peace, no. 4128; Sunan at-Tirmidhī, Book of Manner, no. 2749). In the questionnaire I asked for interviewees' understanding of this hadith, and many respondents were actually sceptical of the hadith. Ziyād explained that one has to establish the authenticity of the hadith and then continued to say that he wanted to investigate what the Prophet meant by 'omen' in this context before he was willing to give any personal interpretation of it.

Amal, on the other hand, was more straightforward, saying:

> This hadith contradicts a major Islamic view that nothing and nobody can cause harm to anybody unless it is known to God. Further this hadith contradicts another hadith saying that there is no omen (*ṭīra*) in Islam. This statement might have been said in an unknown context talking about other people who believed in it!

Amal's answer illuminates the problems with a literal reading of the hadith literature. We are presented with two different hadiths which actually contradict each other, as the terms *shu'm* (bad omen) and *ṭīra* (omen) have much the same meaning. The understanding of the hadith literature thus depends on the degree of knowledge a person has of the rest of the hadiths. It is also interesting to observe Amal's last remark that these words have been taken out of context. Mernissi claims the same, referring to the work of a well-established scholar, Imam Badr ad-Dīn az-Zarkashī (d. 1392).[4]

Khadīja gives her explanation of this hadith:

> I understand from these words that a happy man, he is the one who is happy in his marriage with a respectful and well-mannered or refined woman; who owns or rents a nice and comfortable house; and who possesses a riding animal or a horse which today means a nice and comfortable car. The horse indicates the means by which a human being can transfer himself from one place to another. Unhappiness is the opposite of this: if the wife is not well-mannered or refined or if she is in disagreement with her husband; if one does not have a comfortable house; or if one does not have the means of transportation. The meaning of this hadith is thus *not* that there are bad omens in women, but rather that a man's happiness depends on the woman [translation mine].

Aḥmad sees this hadith in a universal perspective. His answer reflects that of Khadīja when it comes to the perspective of the man, but he adds that 'as for a woman, the matter is that there are bad omens in the husband, the house and the horse'.

All these answers, which are representative of those who responded to the questionnaire, indicate a non-literal understanding and a hermeneutic reading of the hadith. In my discussions with the respondents, they all emphasised the need to be careful in the interpretation of hadiths. 'We have to understand every Islamic text in a certain context and regard it according to time and place', Ziyād remarked.

'Women are deficient in intellect and religion'

The hadith which I suspect has been the main reason for prevailing attitudes towards women in a Muslim context is:

> Once the Messenger of God went to offer the Eid prayer. He passed by the place of the women and said: 'O women, give alms as I have seen that you women constitute the majority of the inhabitants of Hell.' They said: 'Why is it so, O Messenger of God?' He said, 'You curse frequently and are ungrateful to your husbands. I have not seen anyone more deficient in intellect (*ʿaql*) and religion (*dīn*) than you. A cautious sensible man could be led astray by some of you.' The women said: 'What is deficient in our religion and intellect, O Messenger of God?' He said: 'Is not the testimony of a woman worth half of that of a man?' They answered in the affirmative. He said: 'This is the deficiency in her intellect. Is it not that a woman can neither pray nor fast during her menses?' They answered in the affirmative. He said: 'This is the deficiency in her religion.'
>
> (al-Bukhārī, Book of Menstruation, no. 293; Book of Almsgiving, no. 1369; Muslim, Book of Faith, no. 114; at-Tirmidhī, Book of Faith, no. 2538; Sunan Abī Dāwud, no. 4059; Ibn Mājah, Fitna 3993; Musnad Ahmad, *musnad al-mukktharīn*, no. 5091)

My own experience has been that in non-Arabic speaking countries in regions such as Southeast and East Asia, one rarely hears any reference to this hadith. This is not to say that this hadith has no role to play in these countries, but in my frequent discussions about women's rights in Islam, at least I never came across it. On the other hand, this hadith does play a role in the debate about gender in the Somali group living in Scandinavia, which might be attributed to the influence of Somali scholars educated in Saudi Arabia.

The hadith above was the most commonly referred to in any discussion about women with Arabic-speaking Muslims during my extensive travels in Arabic-speaking or European countries. Issues raised by this hadith are treated in the many books about women in Islam which have been published lately. I will refer to some of these books published in Arabic and widespread in Muslim communities in Europe, before I turn to the discussion in a European context.

Muḥammad Mutawallī ash-Shaʿrāwī (d. 1998) was previously Sheikh al-Azhar and a Minister of Religious Affairs in Egypt. Until his death, he frequently gave lectures which were conveyed to the whole Arabic-speaking world through radio and television. He used to be a distinguished and recognised *mufti* whose legal rules are followed by a great number of Muslims. As have many other well-known scholars, ash-Shaʿrāwī has analysed the jurisprudence on women. In his booklet *al-marʾa fī al-qurʾan al-karīm* (*The Woman in the Holy Koran*), he gives his explanation of the hadith mentioned above (ash-Shaʿrāwī n.d.). He explains that this hadith points to the fact that women are created in a certain way which is in accordance with the social role that God has destined for them. He emphasises that women are 'emotional' (*ʿāṭifī*), whereas men are 'rational' (*ʿaqlānī*). This notion is prominent in an Arab context among Muslims as well as among Christians, and I would think that the hadith above is partly to be blamed for its huge dissemination not only as a cultural idea but nearly as a dogma. ash-Shaʿrāwī starts his explanation with a warning, saying that some people have used this hadith to insult women and to reduce the nobility of women. His understanding of this hadith is contrary to such a view. 'This hadith,' he says, 'clarifies to us the nature of the woman from the side of creation.' He goes on: 'The nature of the woman's creation makes a woman's emotions master her. And this is not a shortcoming, but it is a distinctive mark which is in accordance with her function in life' (ash-Shaʿrāwī n.d. [translation mine]).

ash-Shaʿrāwī applies the idea of 'emotionality' versus 'rationality' to the division of labour between the sexes. However, he is careful to state that this division of labour and women's 'emotionality' do not mean that men cannot consult women. He refers to stories about how the Prophet consulted his wives in various situations. There is thus an ambiguity in ash-Shaʿrāwī's interpretation which suggests that he is aware of how hadiths like this can be used as a means to oppress women. By taking a wider perspective, he can both reinforce the notion of the sexual division of labour in terms of creation (an approach commonly referred to as biological reductionism), while at the same time educating men to respect women.

ash-Shaʿrāwī's view in this matter is representative of a great majority of Arabic-speaking Muslims, particularly those living in the Muslim world. I find it interesting that this single hadith has been so widely distributed and how a great part of the Islamic social system is based upon a certain understanding of it. The fact that this hadith is so widespread might be due to the fact that its content confirms patriarchal attitudes already present in the Arab cultural context, since the ideas it represents are just as pervasive among the non-Muslim Arab population as it is among Muslim Arabs. It is important to be aware that similar ideas have been pervasive in the western world until at least the 1960s and 70s.

The Muslim Brotherhood has also dealt with the meaning of this hadith, and its position is that the text of the hadith is not to be understood as putting women in a subordinate position. Its report on the role of women in Muslim society says, 'This [women's deficiency in religion] only means that Allah Himself has exempted her from certain forms of ritual worship at certain times, such as prayers and fasting during her menstruation period and during her discharging time after delivery' (The Muslim Brotherhood 1994: 7). As for the idea of women's deficiency in intellect, the Muslim Brotherhood explains this as referring to women's testimony 'in certain matters like debts and sale contracts, and in *ḥudūd* (punishment)' (The Muslim Brotherhood 1994: 7). I demonstrate below that there are various opinions regarding the question of women's testimony and I will come back to the Muslim Brotherhood's view on this matter.

It is obvious that a book written in 1990 by the former member of the Muslim Brotherhood, 'Abd al-Ḥalim Abū Shaqqa (d. 1996), entitled *taḥrīr al-mar'a fī ʿaṣr ar-risāla* (*The Liberation of Women in the Time of the [Muḥammad's] Message*), has been a source of inspiration for the Muslim Brotherhood's report on women of 1994. This is particularly apparent in Abū Shaqqa's interpretation of the above hadith, which the report seems to have taken directly from his book. Abū Shaqqa analyses the hadith in detail and looks at it from three different angles. First, he says that the Prophet's statement is an admonition to women in the way that the Prophet used to give admonitions to all people, men and women. He particularly sees the claim that the majority of the inhabitants of hell are women as an educational statement, intended to make women careful in respect of their actions. He points out that the Prophet also said that the majority of those in paradise are poor people, a statement which in Abū Shaqqa's view does not mean that all rich people are in hell, but is rather meant as a warning to rich people not to make unlawful money (Abū Shaqqa 1990 vol. I: 273). At the same time, Abū Shaqqa discusses how men can best be careful in their actions in order to keep out of hell. He states that they can do this by keeping away from unlawfulness and fulfilling their obligations. One of the obligations which can lead men to paradise is, in Abū Shaqqa's view, offering the best care and guidance to their female relatives in order to make it easy for these women to fulfil their Islamic obligations and secure their place in paradise (Abū Shaqqa 1990 vol. I: 274).

Second, Abū Shaqqa analyses the context in which the Prophet issued this particular statement, and he asserts that it is impossible that the Prophet could be harsh to women or to any person at all on the day of the festival, a day of joy. He then states that the story is from the Medinian period, and thus most of the women present were from the Medinian tribe of al-Anṣār. Abū Shaqqa says that the women of this tribe were known to have strong personalities and to rule their husbands. He refers to the fact that ʿUmar even complained to the Prophet that the immigrant women from Mecca had started to be influenced by the al-Anṣār women. The Prophet then, according to Abū Shaqqa, made this statement as a sort of a joke. He declares:

> As for the [Prophet's] text formulation, it is not a formulation which is a general ruling stipulation or a general rule. It is rather a declaration of the Prophet's (p.b.u.h.) amazement at the existing contradiction in the phenomenon of women's mastery – and they are in themselves weak – over men endowed with firmness, i.e., the [Prophet's] amazement of God's wisdom.
>
> (Abū Shaqqa 1990 vol. I: 275 [translation mine])

Third, Abū Shaqqa points to the biological argument that women are at times subject to circumstances which make them weaker in intellect and in religion, such as during pregnancies and child-rearing when they are preoccupied with these activities and can hardly be of any use in wider society. However, he stresses that these periods are temporary, as there is no reason against a woman being active in society when she is past these stages of life (Abū Shaqqa 1990 vol. I: 276 [translation mine]). Abū Shaqqa's hermeneutics is marked by a psychological approach. Instead of reading the text literally, he tries to understand 'what the Prophet really meant'.

It is important to understand Abū Shaqqa's role in the contemporary debate. Although it is not a new phenomenon to offer a contextual interpretation of either the Koran or the hadith, the innovative aspect of Abū Shaqqa's approach lies in his psychological analysis. His approach is a vivid example of how a 'return to the pure sources' does not mean turning back to the seventh century. Rather, he uses twentieth century methodology to analyse seventh century society in order to reproduce the past in the present. By taking a contemporary view-point, the result is an interpretation suitable for twentieth century society. Moreover, as Abū Shaqqa interprets hadiths in this way, what becomes important is not the text itself but the interpretation of the text. Thus his analysis becomes a weapon against degrading attitudes towards women in Muslim society.

Although Abū Shaqqa has not lived outside the Arab world for any length of time, his ideas at times tend to coincide with western ideas of equality between the sexes. This might be seen as a response to constant criticisms of the degrading position of women in Islam and as a consequence of the globalisation process with its spread of western localism. In common with both Yūsuf al-Qaraḍāwī and Muḥammad al-Ghazzālī, Abū Shaqqa might be regarded as a movement intellectual. Whether inside or outside the organisation of the Muslim Brotherhood, their ideas tend to have a penetrating force among members of the Muslim Brotherhood and among individuals belonging to a *post-ikhwān* trend.

Abū Shaqqa also considers weak or forged hadiths which have commonly been used to raise 'doubts on women's intellect and the practice of her religion'. He says:

> They [the weak or forged hadiths] are only traces of the influence of escapades of the imagination. The roots of this imagination are found in the ancient time of ignorance (*jāhilīya*) which Muslims found it desirable to create [these ideas] from. These influences were unfortunately consolidated, and the result became an overstepping of the limit of the Prophet's (p.b.u.h.) interpretation of the deficiency in intellect and religion. And this led to a great flood of false conceptions about the woman's personality.
>
> Among the forged hadiths are:

1 Do not teach women to write and do not put them in chambers [official positions].
2 Obedience to the woman will be regretted.
3 If no women existed, God would have been worshipped in a true manner.
4 Counsel women and act opposite [to their view].

And from the weak hadiths:

1 Men will be destroyed if they obey women.
2 The worst of your enemies is your wife.
3 Oppose the women, for verily there are blessings in the opposition against them.

(Abū Shaqqa 1990 vol. I: 287 [translation mine])

It is of interest that Abū Shaqqa draws attention to these sayings as they are widespread at least in Muslim society. As he refutes them as forged or weak hadiths, they will probably cease to have any influence on Muslim gender relations in the future as his book is widespread not only among Islamists but among Muslims in general, as well.

The western context

How is the hadith on women's deficiency in intellect and religion understood in a western context? In my discussion with the exiled Islamist, Sheikh Rāshid al-Ghannūshī, who is the Tunisian Islamic opposition leader, I asked him how he understood this hadith. He indicated that there is doubt among some scholars as to whether this hadith is fully authentic or not. He said that these scholars believe that this hadith might be influenced by *isrā'īlīyāt* (i.e. stories particularly from the Talmudic tradition in Jewish thought), as there could be a contradiction between the statement of this hadith and the Koranic message that man and woman are created from one single entity. He continued by saying that, because man and woman are from the same entity, they should be equal and one of the pair could not be deficient compared to the other. I then argued that the well-known scholar of hadith, al-Albānī, has authenticated this hadith with regard to its narrator chain. al-Ghannūshī answered:

> If we suppose that this hadith is authentic – the hadith is to be found in al-Bukhārī and there are some *parts* of hadiths in al-Bukhārī that Ibn Ḥazm and others doubted – however, if we suppose it is authentic, this hadith cannot be regarded as a legal hadith [i.e. to be used as a basis for legal matters], rather it is an educational hadith. It is meant as a guidance and meant to tell that men should not treat women in a harsh way, as women are sensitive. The hadith says that one should

> treat women well and the meaning is not that women are deficient (*intiqāṣ*) [translation mine].

It is important to draw attention to al-Ghannūshī's questioning of the hadith's authenticity. As the hadith is to be found in al-Bukhārī, it is controversial to claim that it is not authentic as there is a strong consensus regarding the authenticity of the hadiths found in al-Bukhārī. However, al-Ghannūshī seems to solve this problem since he does not claim that he himself doubts its authenticity, but he refers to the Islamic scholar, Ibn Ḥazm (d. 1064) whose ideas are accepted on many matters although he is regarded as controversial in others. In addition, al-Ghannūshī does not claim the hadith as such is not authentic but he says that *parts* of it might be not authentic. As for the understanding of the hadith, al-Ghannūshī, similarly to many other Islamists, suggests a hermeneutical interpretation. As will be noted below, Ibn Ḥazm tends to be referred to often in a western context. I believe this has to do with the disintegration of local culture, leading to the encounter between Muslims of different Muslim cultures and between Muslims and the western world-view. In this situation, authors of the past who had been considered non-conformist are now being used to further new arguments influenced by a western point of view. These views might be regarded as acceptable in the new context as they have at least been accepted by some of the classic Muslim scholars. Hjärpe's basket metaphor illustrates this phenomenon as these traditions, although sectarian, are already there, and as they seem to be compatible with the new social context they can be applied within the Islamic framework.

In the questionnaire, the responses were quite similar to those of the scholars above. However, there was a tendency for some men to stress that the reason that the majority of hell's residents are women is that women tend to talk too much. Other answers, however, emphasised that this hadith is to be understood as an admonition for women rather than an argument against women. Amal writes:

> It did not come like that (as a statement). It was said to a group of women on the day of ʿId and it should be regarded in a context. A group of men of Mecca complained to the Prophet that their wives were causing problems to them and they asked the Prophet to talk to them [the women] about it. It is thus said in a context. He was talking to a group of women and he said it to motivate them into doing more good deeds and to work harder.

In my discussion with Amal she further emphasised the importance of recognising that the Prophet addressed this statement directly to women and not to men. She explained to me that when people educate children or even grown-ups, they may draw a fearful picture in order to instil fear. As an example, she pointed to the way in which in contemporary Europe one scares young children with stories of 'dirty men' in order to make sure that they are not tricked into following strangers.

Khadīja offers much the same explanation of the hadith, trying to explain it in terms of an admonition to women. However, Khadīja draws more attention to the latter part of the hadith, explaining that the monthly period hinders women from their religious duties which, according to her, impedes a woman's spiritual development. Khadīja stresses that the hadith only relates to certain periods of a woman's life, and that otherwise women's spirituality is similar to men's. She uses a similar argument with respect to the statement that women have a lower intellectual capacity than men. I recognised this argument as it often recurs in discussions with Arabic-speaking Muslims and also among other Muslims. al-Mawdūdī, in his book *Purdah*, talks in similar terms about women in Islam in general. According to al-Mawdūdī, in women's monthly periods and pregnancies, they are ruled by hormones which render them in a state of emotional imbalance. As for the period of child-rearing, this situation is all-absorbing as women's attention is totally focused on their children (al-Mawdūdī 1972). Khadīja emphasises, however, that women are not less intelligent than men. It is, in her view, a matter which has to do with the social role God has destined for women and it only applies to certain periods in the woman's life.

The examples above, with Khadīja on the one hand and Amal on the other, show yet again how the attitudes of those within organisations or movements tend to reproduce traditional concepts, whereas the attitudes of those outside movements tend to come closer to those of the majority society.

Female testimony

Regarding the validity of female testimony, the various Koranic commentaries coincide in their interpretation. A verse which is referred to in the debate gives the following instruction:

> Whenever you give or take for a stated term, set it down in writing. . . . And call upon two of your men to act as witnesses: and if two of your men are not available, then a man and two women from among such as are acceptable to you as witnesses, so that if one of the women should make a mistake, the other would remind her.
>
> (K.2: 282)

Ābādī has an interesting twist to his interpretation as he says that this passage means that the woman who does not forget should remind the woman who forgets (Ābādī 1988: 48). Ibn Kathīr, in his commentary on the Koran, does not distinguish between various forms of testimony. He explains that two women are needed in contrast to one man due to women's deficiency in intellect according to the above hadith (Ibn Kathīr 1981 vol. I: 254). Muhammad Asad refers to Muḥammad ʿAbduh's commentary, explaining:

> The stipulation that two women may be substituted for one male witness does not imply any reflection on woman's moral or intellectual capabilities: it is obviously due to the fact that, as a rule, women are less familiar with business procedures than men, and, therefore, more liable to commit mistakes in this respect.
>
> (Asad 1984: 63; cf. ʿAbduh in *Manār* n.d. vol. III: 124f)

In Muḥammad ʿAbduh's work, there is a change in the view of women's testimony compared to the classical commentaries. It is interesting that Asad, who is a convert, has followed ʿAbduh's commentaries. ʿAbduh might be regarded as falling within the framework of the cultural encounter between 'Islam' and 'the West' and his ideas tend to coincide with western ideas. In Zainab al-Ghazzālī's commentary on this verse one might expect to find a similar view to that of ʿAbduh, as his perspective might be seen more in terms of a female perspective than that of his predecessors. She does not, however, distinguish between various forms of testimony, and she does not go into detail in her commentary. Instead, she only rephrases the Koranic passage (Z. al-Ghazzālī 1994a vol. I: 182–3). ʿAbduh's approach might be understood according to the model of a 'western cultural base pattern', since during his travels in western countries he came into contact with the intellectual 'rational' milieu of nineteenth century Europe. Zainab al-Ghazzālī, on the other hand, lives in Egypt and in contrast to scholars such as Abū Shaqqa, al-Qaraḍāwī, and Muḥammad al-Ghazzālī, her attitudes coincide to a large extent with the 'Arab cultural base pattern'. The reason for the distinction between her and the three male scholars might be her relationship to the Muslim Brotherhood. In her book, *Return of the Pharaoh*, she is outspoken about her loyalty to the oath which she took with Ḥasan al-Bannāʾ. The social organisation of the movement might therefore make her less prone to change and more directed towards the movement's ideology. Muḥammad al-Ghazzālī, although belonging to the school of Ḥasan al-Bannāʾ, was out of the movement for a long time before his death in 1997. As for al-Qaraḍāwī, he has written a book about the educational aspects of Ḥasan al-Bannāʾ's methodology (al-Qaraḍāwī 1980). Although in the book there are indications of obvious influences from al-Bannāʾ, al-Qaraḍāwī does not mention explicitly that he is a member of the Muslim Brotherhood. The same is true of Abū Shaqqa's book. Thus, Zainab al-Ghazzālī's sense of group belonging is much more explicit than these three male scholars, and I would attribute the fact that she is less amenable to change than they are to the social organisational aspect of her position. Moreover, Muḥammad al-Ghazzālī and al-Qaraḍāwī have both been living outside Egypt for long periods of time; al-Qaraḍāwī became a Qatarian citizen in the sixties during Nasr's persecution of the Muslim Brotherhood and has lived in Qatar ever since, and Muḥammad al-Ghazzālī has lived in various parts of the Arab world. Exposure to other cultural traits, although within the 'Arab cultural base pattern', is an important aspect of change of attitudes.

In contemporary Islamist literature, the issue of female testimony has been dealt with extensively. Muḥammad al-Ghazzālī's book from 1989 and Abū Shaqqa's from 1990 both discuss the matter. They reject many of the common Muslim assumptions, such as that women are not allowed to be a witness in cases of marriage or divorce, and that women cannot be witnesses in criminal cases. They both refer to the fact that Ibn Ḥazm accepted female witnesses alone. They take care, however, to state that most traditional scholars claim that there has to be at least one man's witness in order for a testimony to be accepted (M. al-Ghazzālī 1989: 58–61; Abū Shaqqa 1990: 279). Moreover, Muḥammad al-Ghazzālī points out that Ibn Ḥazm cites the historical examples of ʿUmar Ibn al-Khaṭṭāb and ʿAlī Ibn Abī Ṭālib and their acceptance of female witnesses in various cases. As a rule, al-Ghazzālī speaks in terms of two women for one man. Although he actually refers to an historical example where only two women (not four) witnessed a divorce, he does not comment on this, but rather applies it in order to give evidence of the possibility of women witnessing to divorce at all. Muḥammad al-Ghazzālī looks into some hadiths which reject female testimony in cases of marriage and divorce and falsifies them according to their narrator chains. As a conclusion, al-Ghazzālī mentions that Ibn Ḥazm even accepted women as judges, and refers to Abū Ḥanīfa's acceptance of female judges. In contemporary times, the issue of female judges in the sharia court is still a controversial matter in a Muslim context. The only Arabic-speaking country which presently has introduced female judges in the sharia court is the Sudan, where women are even employed in the federal supreme court.[5] Thus it can be seen that different authors, such as Ghannūshī and Muḥammad al-Ghazzālī, are seeking acceptance of alternative views to resolve controversies in a new cultural context by referring to the controversial writer Ibn Ḥazm.

The Muslim Brotherhood's statement from 1994 reflects some of the ideas of Muḥammad al-Ghazzālī and Abū Shaqqa without specifying whether female testimony alone is accepted or not. As a conclusion, the paragraph which deals with women's deficiency says:

> Indeed, in this regard, it should be pointed out that there are certain matters which only accept the testimony of a woman and not that of a man. Furthermore, women are unanimously accepted as narrators of hadiths, and this means that their testimony in narrating hadiths is treated like that of a man. In addition to this a woman is responsible towards her duties to her faith and she has full independence in her right to possess, and in her right to make contracts. If she was supposed to have a lesser mind, the contracts and other dealings would have required the assistance of a male.
>
> (The Muslim Brotherhood 1994: 7)

The above-mentioned scholars and the movement of the Muslim Brotherhood do not deal with the issue of whether or not it is possible to regard female testimony as the equivalent of one male testimony. Muḥammad al-Ghazzālī actually quotes an example of such a situation without commenting on the issue. On the other hand, Jamal Badawi, the Egyptian–Canadian scholar, raises the issue in his 1995 book, *Gender Equity in Islam*. He notes that most of the Koranic references to testimony do not make any reference to gender (Badawi 1995: 33). He refers to verses 24: 6–9 which deal with the testimony against a spouse, saying that these verses 'fully equate the testimony of males and females' (Badawi 1995: 33). As for the only Koranic reference to gender distinction in testimony (K.2: 282), Badawi explains that this cannot be used as the foundation for a general rule in which one woman's testimony is worth half of that of a man (Badawi 1995: 35). 'This presumed "rule"', he says, 'is voided by the above reference (24: 6–9), which **explicitly equates the testimony of both genders on the issue at hand**' (Badawi 1995: 33 – his emphasis). Badawi further believes that the verse on female testimony, 2: 282 quoted above, relates to testimony on financial transactions 'which are often complex and laden with business jargon,' and therefore it does not constitute a basis for a general rule (Badawi 1995: 35). Badawi goes on to discuss the reason for the variation in the number of men and women, remarking that no reference is made to 'the inferiority or superiority of one gender's witness or the other's' (Badawi 1995: 36). He says:

> The only reason given is to corroborate the female witness and prevent unintended errors in the perception of the business deal. The Arabic term used in this passage, *taḍalla*, literally means 'loses the way', 'gets confused', or 'errs'. But are females the only gender that may err and need corroboration of their testimony? Definitely not, and that is why the general rule of testimony in Islamic law is to have two witnesses, even when they are both male.
>
> (Badawi 1995: 36)

Badawi is claiming that it is not only women who need to be reminded in case of error, but men also as one man cannot be witness alone. He has thus reversed the understanding of this verse. Instead of seeing it as degrading for women he suggests that it is unsuitable for either one single man or one single woman to be a witness as the main principle is to maintain justice. He believes that 'unlike pure acts of worship, which must be observed exactly as taught by the Prophet (P), testimony is a **means to an end, ascertaining justice** as a major objective to Islamic law' (Badawi 1995: 37 – his emphasis).

Badawi gives what he calls 'one possible interpretation' of verse 2: 282. He believes that generally speaking women in many societies, past and present, may not be so involved in economical matters and that makes it necessary for a woman to be reminded. This is the same argument which I have encountered in discussions with Islamists in the Arabic-speaking world and in Europe. He further states that verse 2: 282 is the only exception in the Koran on testimonies, and he links this to aṭ-Ṭabarī's conclusion that there is no evidence in the Islamic sources that women are excluded from being judges, defining a judge as one who hears and evaluates the testimony of others (Badawi 1995: 36). Badawi's explanation implicitly suggests that if a woman can be a judge it would be illogical that her testimony should be regarded as half of that of a man. His conclusion is provocative and it will be interesting to see what it might lead to. He says: 'A witness of a female graduate of a business school is certainly far more worthy than the witness of an illiterate person [read man!] with no business education or experience' (Badawi 1995: 37).

In my discussions with Islamists in Europe, I found that members of the Muslim Brotherhood held a view similar to what was written in the movement's statement on the role of women, which was also the view held by Fu'ād Ḥussain from the Islamic Liberation Party and by many *salafīs*. Amal, on the other hand, who is within a post-*ikhwān* trend, goes much further in her interpretation of the Koranic verse 2: 282. In the questionnaire, she responds as follows to the question 'How do you understand that two female witnesses are equivalent to one male witness?':

> It is only one verse that talks about two female witnesses, namely Surah 2: 282, and this verse refers to dealings with money and debt. The Koran also explains the reason and that is that they should remind each other. Two female witnesses for one male may be as the verse is dealing with money and calculation and numbers and women at that time were not involved much in that sort of business. However, in the Surah *Light* in the Koran [24: 4], there is a mentioning of four witnesses without referring to gender all through the verse.

Ziyād responded to the question in a similar manner, saying that he understood the verse to apply to a certain situation, namely, financial agreements in case of borrowing of money. What can be concluded from the above discussion is that the western context has apparently opened up the possibility of change in this very deeply rooted law in Islamic legislation. As with the other examples above, it is apparent that outside social organisations and within the cooperative group of Muslims there is a greater likelihood of encountering views which coincide with the majority society. While the question of testimony might previously have been regarded as unproblematic in terms of two females for one male, if one delves deeply into the issue it can be interpreted as different rulings according to changing circumstances. Although the new ideas have not yet taken root in a legal context, new rulings might be expected in response to these changing perceptions.

Inheritance

The matter of inheritance is closely linked to the matter of female witnesses. The Koran states that in cases of inheritance a daughter should get half the amount that a son gets. In most books and in the commentaries on the Koran there is unanimous agreement that the reason for this is that men are responsible for the financial maintenance of women – not only wives, but also mothers and sisters who are unprovided for. While men have to use their inheritance to provide for female relatives, a woman's inheritance is for her own extra expenses as she is supposed to be supported on a day to day basis by a male relative. Little, however, has been written about the situation in non-Muslim or rather in non-Islamic societies. Do the rules of inheritance change if the system of provision changes? It is interesting that although social changes in the Arab world have brought a shift in the family system of provision, the question of inheritance has not been on the agenda. Most scholars and Islamists in general usually refer to an ideal Islamic system in dealing with inheritance, and few discuss whether it is possible to change such a system according to changed social circumstances.

The issue of changes in the inheritance system was raised by Amal. After stating that in an ideal Islamic system a woman should be provided for by either a father, a brother or a husband and is thus not entitled to the same inheritance as her brother, she observes that 'if, however, she is not supported financially, i.e. in a non-Islamic society, I think we need to study the subject more and try to find solutions within the sharia framework'. Another important point is that both Khadīja and Amal mentioned that it is not in all cases that a woman's inheritance is half that of a man's, since for instance a mother inheriting from her child inherits the same amount as her husband.

An independent Islamist living in Sweden, responding to my question about whether the law of inheritance could be changed in a European context in which social relations change, answered: 'We are not living in an Islamic society and we can follow the Swedish law of inheritance.' In his view, in the sort of society where both spouses are responsible for the provision of the family, it is unjust that sons inherit more than daughters. 'Therefore', he says, 'it is fully legal, and actually often done, to put aside one third of the inheritance as a testamentary disposition (*waṣīa*). One can testament this money to the daughters, and then there should be justice between the children.'

It seems that both the law of female testimony and the law of inheritance might manifest themselves differently in a European context than in Arabic-speaking countries. However, I would be careful about predicting no change, even in the Arabic-speaking world, as the entire Arab society has gone through great changes of different degrees and forms within various countries. There are rules deduced by the Islamic sources which might be seen as suitable only for an ideal Islamic society, as suggested by many of my respondents and informants. Amal cited an example from the reign of ʿUmar, the second caliph, who terminated the punishment for theft. This, she explained, was due to the drought which struck the Arab Peninsula in a certain period and resulted in famine among the Muslims. Changes even in Koranic injunctions according to different times and circumstances might therefore not be so momentous even for Islamists who regard Islam in totalitarian terms.

Reflections

Many of the above examples demonstrate that those Islamists belonging to social organisations such as the Islamic Liberation Party, the Organisation of the Muslim Brotherhood and the *salafī* trend, tend to reiterate their movements' ideas rather than creating innovative thinking. Ziyād and Amal are two representatives of the *post-ikhwān* trend and it is apparent that both of these tend to break new ground in Islamic thought. In contrast to Khadīja and Aḥmad from the Muslim Brotherhood, these two can be regarded as being in a cooperative position *vis-à-vis* the majority society as they are active in a wider social context. Khadīja and Aḥmad are both active within the Muslim community and have little contact with the majority society. The presence of the 'Arab cultural base pattern' is thus more obvious in the latter's world-view than in the former's. Moreover, the notion of 'the past reproduced in the present' is apparent in most of the answers as well as in literature written by Arabic-speaking Islamists. Worth noting is Ibn Ḥazm's current importance in the Islamist debate. As Ibn Ḥazm was actually a European, this becomes even more significant.

It becomes obvious that much of the debate centred around women and their role in society is built upon biological differences between men and women. What is 'natural' for a woman has to do with how she is created and what is 'natural' for a man is due to his physiology. This is in contrast to western intellectual discussion on gender in general and on women's roles in particular, where men and women are regarded as being on equal footing in all aspects of life. In discussion, Islamists tend to point to the actual situation in most European countries where women in the vast majority of families *are* mainly responsible for housework and child-rearing. One Islamist remarked that the notion of family life in Islam is actually the standard in most European households. However, 'on the ideological level', he remarks,

> they [the Europeans] have other ideas. They do not accept reality. This is how people have lived for thousands of years as it is a natural consequence of creation. They have tried to change, but still they are lingering with the old system despite the fact that the ideological stance is something else [translation mine].

In Sweden, the debate on gender equality [*jämställdhetsdebatten*] is more advanced than in many other European countries, at least in official life. This is apparent in the constellation of the political establishment. Political parties frequently have female leaders, and the Social-Democratic governments of the late 1990s had the policy of 'every second, a woman'. A leading Islamist living in Sweden commented:

> Who picks up the children from the nurseries? Give me the positions in society which have the lowest salaries and I will show you that the majority of the workers there are women. I will tell you that in the end of the day it comes back to what God created and to what God created us for [translation mine].

Islamists thus claim that their ideas are 'natural' as they are 'in accordance with the actual reality', whereas, in their view, 'westerners' tend to create ideological ideas which are in contrast to reality as well as to 'human nature'. This argument reflects the idea of Islam as 'the natural religion' which recognises that God created the social system according to the nature of His creation (Hedin 1988).

It could be said that Islamists tend to observe the gap between theory and practice in the host society, whereas non-Muslims point to the gap between the theory of Islam and the practice of Muslims. This can be explained in terms of in-group/out-group patterns of perception, whereby groups tend to observe the *practice* of other out-groups whereas they only perceive the *ideology* within their own group.

It is important to draw attention to the fact that in matters of gender relations one tends to understand and interpret certain statements in different ways depending on whom they are expressed by. I started this chapter by drawing attention to Paul and to how his statements about Corinthian women have been interpreted. For a Christian, it is easy to look at such statements contextually and to interpret them in a contemporary way. It is also important to be aware that this statement has a wide range of understandings among Christians even today (Eriksson 1998). On the other hand, if a Muslim reads the same statement s/he will read it literally according to the pattern of in-group/out-group perception, pointing to the gender inequality which this text promotes. Likewise, for a Muslim to read some of the above statements, s/he will understand them contextually. However, similarly to the Christian debate there are many different interpretations arising out of different circumstances and also according to each person's biography, but a Christian or a non-Muslim will generally read such Muslim texts literally according to the pattern of out-groups/in-groups.

In the next chapter I examine various concepts in gender relations. Which Koranic verses and hadiths are important in the debate and how are they understood? How are gender relations perceived in an Islamist context?

7 Gender relations

As the Personal Status Law in the Muslim world is one of the few areas where the Islamic texts and Islamic scholars' legislation have been implemented in the official space, the traditional model of gender relations has obtained an almost sacrosanct position within the Islamic creed. In the present chapter I will deal with attitudes and ideas about relations between men and women in micro society – within the family sphere – and in macro society – gender roles in the wider social context. I will look into what can be found in the sources about gender relations, and more importantly I will answer the question: how do Islamists understand the various references to the relationship between men and women?

In the Koran, little is said about gender relations. The most explicit injunctions are given in verse 4: 34, the same verse which states the social role of men as breadwinners of the family. The verse in Alī's translation says: 'Men are the protectors and maintainers of (*qawwāmūn ʿalā*) women, because God has given the one more (strength) than the other, and because they support them from their means' (Alī 1989: 195).

In Asad's translation it says:

> Men shall take full care of women with the bounties which God has bestowed more abundantly on the former than on the latter, and with what they may spend out of their possessions.
>
> (Asad 1984: 109)

The American Islamic feminist and Muslim scholar, Amina Wadud-Muhsin, who is a convert to Islam, has investigated various historical and contemporary Islamic scholars' interpretations of this verse. She indicates that the understanding of *qiwāma* as men's control over women is subject to time and place. She proposes a contemporary interpretation of the verse whereby men's responsibility for women applies only to their economic support of the family. With changes in the socio-economic system, she sees room for a more 'liberal' reinterpretation (Wadud-Muhsin 1992).

The same verse also contains the most controversial statement regarding men's relationship to women. The verse continues:

> And for those women whose disloyalty and ill-conduct (*nushūz*) you have reason to fear, admonish them [first]; then leave them alone in bed [second]; then hit them [third]. And if thereupon they pay you heed (*aṭaʿnakum*), do not seek to harm them. Behold, God is indeed most high, great.

I have observed that the first part of the verse is frequently referred to by common Muslims as well as by Islamists, whereas they tend not to mention the last part. On the other hand, some non-Muslims, particularly within 'popular Orientalism' in western countries, tend to refer to the verse as a whole in order to portray Islam as a religion hostile towards women.

In contrast to this verse, Islamists refer to other passages in the Koran which indicate a more intimate and close relationship between men and women:

1 'The believing men and the believing women are protectors (*awliyāʾ*) to each other' (K.9: 71).
2 'It is He who has created you out of one living entity, and out of it brought into being its mate, so that man might incline [with love] towards woman' (K.7: 189).
3 'And among His signs is this: He created for you mates from among yourselves so that you might incline towards them and he engenders love (*mawadda*) and mercy (*raḥma*)' (K.30: 21).
4 'The rights of the wives [with regard to their husbands] are equal to the [husbands' rights] over them [with regard to divorce]' (K.2: 228).
5 'And consort with your wives in kindness (*maʿrūf*), for if you dislike them, it may well be that you dislike something which God has made a source of abundant good' (K.4: 19).
6 'Your women are a tilth for you, so go to your tilth as you will, and send [good deeds] before you for your souls, and have God-consciousness. For know that you will meet Him. Give glad tidings to the believers' (K.2: 223).

In the hadith-literature there is a similar picture. In some places, the relationship between men and women is portrayed as one of love and intimacy, whereas in other places, women are described in terms which for westerners born and raised in times with a strong notion of gender equality might appear as degrading and disparaging of women as a whole. Below I will render some of the hadiths, both authentic and not authentic, which I have come across in discussions:[1]

1 Ibn ʿUmar said: I saw a woman who came to the Prophet (p.b.u.h.) and said: 'Oh Messenger of God, what is a wife's obligation towards her husband.' Muḥammad said: 'Her obligation is that she does not go out of her house except by his permission, and if she does, God, the Angels of mercy, and the Angels of anger will curse her until she repents or

> until she comes back.' She said: 'And if he oppresses her?' Muḥammad said: 'Even if he oppresses her' (az-Zuḥailī 1989 vol. VII: 336).

The Syrian scholar of sharia, Sheikh Wahba az-Zuḥailī, claims in his book on jurisprudence that this hadith was related by Abū Dāwud from Ibn ʿUmar. I have tried to find this hadith in the computer program, *system al-ʿālamī*, which contains 'The Six Authentics', i.e. al-Bukhārī, Muslim, Sunan at-Tirmidhī, Sunan an-Nisāʾī, Sunan Abī Dāwud and Sunan Ibn Mājah, in addition to the Musnad Aḥmad, Mālik and ad-Dārimī, but I could not find anything similar or close to this text. az-Zuḥailī draws his conclusion mainly based on the above-mentioned hadith, saying:

> And of the [wife's] obedience is: to stay in the house after getting her prepaid dowry and this [the dowry] devotes her to the marital affairs, the house and the care-taking of the children, when they are small and when they are bigger. The woman is not to go out of her house even to perform Hajj, except with the permission of her husband. And he [the husband] has the right to prevent her from going to the mosque and other places with what Ibn ʿUmar stated: [hadith 1 above].
> (az-Zuḥailī 1989 vol. VII: 335–6 [translation mine])

I find it interesting that az-Zuḥailī can make such a statement built upon a hadith which seems not to be well known, and although he claims that it is related by Abū Dāwud, I could not find that it is contained in any of the important hadith collections. Furthermore, he does not mention whether this hadith is authentic or not. Similarly, az-Zuḥailī refers to another hadith which he claims to be from Sunan at-Tirmidhī: 'Verily the woman is *ʿawra* [here: deficient]. If she goes out, Satan will raise a glance at her. She will be closest to her Lord's mercy inside her house' (az-Zuḥailī 1989 vol. VII: 336–7 [translation mine]). When I looked this hadith up I discovered that in Sunan at-Tirmidhī only the first part is present, namely, 'Verily the woman is *ʿawra* [here: deficient], if she goes out, Satan will raise a glance at her'. Moreover, according to at-Tirmidhī this hadith is not authentic (*ṣaḥīḥ*), rather it is a good (*ḥasan*), strange (*gharīb*) hadith which means that there exists only one narrator chain to this hadith and that this narrator chain is not fully authentic (Sunan at-Tirmidhī, Book of Foster Relationship, no. 1093). az-Zuḥailī does not, however, mention at-Tirmidhī's view on this hadith as good and strange, thus not authentic (*ṣaḥīḥ*). His argument in this matter is an outstanding example of a person's ability to select those texts which are compatible with his/her own view on a non-verbalised level. az-Zuḥailī is a scholar of sharia and lives in Syria. It seems apparent that he is influenced to a great extent by the 'Arabic cultural base pattern'. It is interesting to note that the hadiths he selects are not always authentic and this indicates that he tends, in Hjärpe's terminology, to pick those text from 'the Islamic basket' which confirm his own attitudes.

Other hadiths I have come across are:

2 The Messenger of God (p.b.u.h.) said: 'If the husband invites his wife to his bed; she refuses, and he is angry when he goes to sleep, the angels will curse her until morning.'

(al-Bukhārī, Book of Marriage, no. 4794; Muslim, Book of Marriage, no. 2594; Sunan Abī Dāwud, Book of Marriage, no. 1829; Musnad Aḥmad, *bāqi musnad al-muktharīn*, no. 929)[2]

3 The Messenger of God (p.b.u.h.) said: 'I advise you to treat the women well, because they are in your care. You do not have any rights over them other than that [that they are in your care], unless they are evidently adulteresses (*fāḥishāt*). And if they are, separate them in a bed alone, hit them, but not with violence. And if thereupon they pay you heed (*aṭaʿnakum*), do not seek to harm them.'

(Sunan at-Tirmidhī, Book of Foster Relationship, no. 1083; Ibn Mājah, Book of Marriage, no. 1841; cf. K.4: 34)

4 A man asked the Prophet (p.b.u.h.): 'What are a husband's obligations towards his wife?' Muḥammad (p.b.u.h.) answered: 'Give her [food] as you yourself eat. Give her clothes as you yourself dress. Do not hit her face. Do not speak badly to her. Do not separate from her, except in your own house.'

(Sunan Abī Dāwud, Book of Marriage, no. 180; Musnad Aḥmad, *musnad al-baṣrīīn*, no. 19160)

5 The Messenger of God (p.b.u.h.) said: 'Every one of you are protectors, and every one of you are responsible for his/her subjects [herd]. The leader is a protector, the man is a protector of his family, and the woman is a protector of her husband's house and his children. So everyone of you are protectors and everyone of you are responsible for his/her subjects.'

(al-Bukhārī, Book of Friday Prayer, no. 844; Muslim, Book of Signs, no. 3408, Sunan at-Tirmidhī, Book of *Jihad*, no. 1627)

6 The Messenger of God (p.b.u.h.) said: 'Treat women kindly. The woman is created from a rib, and the most crooked part of the rib is in the upper region. If you try to make it straight you will break it, and if you leave it as it is, it will remain curved. So treat women kindly.'

(al-Bukhārī, Book of Marriage, no. 4787; Muslim, Book of Foster Relationship, no. 2671)[3]

7 The Messenger of God (p.b.u.h.) said: 'The Quraish women are the best women: They ride camels, they are tender towards their children, and they take care of their husband and his possessions.'

(al-Bukhārī, Book of Marriage, no. 4692; Muslim, Book of Virtues of the Companions of the Prophet, no. 4589; Musnad Aḥmad, *musnad banī hāshim*, no. 2774)

8 The Messenger of God (p.b.u.h.) said: 'You [pl.] have obligations towards your wives and your wives have obligations towards you [pl.].'
(Sunan at-Tirmidhī, Book of Foster Relationship, no. 1083; Sunan Ibn Mājah, Book of Marriage, no. 1841)

9 The Messenger of God (p.b.u.h.) said: 'The best among you is the one who treats his family in the best manner. And I am the one among you who treats my family in the best manner.'
(Sunan at-Tirmidhī, Book of Virtues, no. 3830; Sunan Ibn Mājah, Book of Marriage, no. 1967)[4]

10 The Messenger of God (p.b.u.h.) said: 'None of you should hit his wife like he hits a slave, then go to sleep with her in the evening.'
(al-Bukhārī, Book of Marriage, no. 4805; Muslim, Book of Paradise, no. 5095; Sunan at-Tirmidhī, Book of the Interpretation of the Koran, no. 3266; Musnad Aḥmad, *musnad al-madinīīn*, no. 15630)

11 ʿĀ'isha said: 'The Messenger of God never did hit any of his wives or any of his servants. Neither did he hit anything with his hand, but for God's sake, or for stopping *maḥārim* [prohibitions], for [in this case] his revenge is for God [not for himself].'
(Muslim, Book of Virtues, no. 4296)[5]

The hadiths above contain various ideas. If one looks upon them in the light of the Koran, they convey the two sides of gender relations which are also evident in the Koran: on the one hand a relationship of mercy and tenderness, and on the other a relationship in which the man has the upper hand. I would divide these hadiths into three categories. Hadiths 1 and 2 can be said to belong to a category of total male superiority. Hadiths 3, 4, 5 and 6 belong to a category of male superiority but at the same time they convey the need to show decent behaviour towards women. Hadiths 7, 8, 9, 10 and 11, on the other hand, give the impression of a relationship of equal rights and obligations from both the man and the woman.

The main ideas which can be extracted from the Koranic verses and the hadiths are, on one hand, the notion of men's 'control' or 'responsibility' (*qiwāma*) over women. Furthermore, there is the idea of women's obedience towards men, and of man's right to hit his wife in case of adultery (as stated in hadith 3 above). On the other hand, both the Koran and the hadith literature indicate a marital relationship of love and tenderness and just treatment of women as the weaker sex.

I will now explore in more depth the ideas about gender relations contained in the Koran and the Sunna and discussed by Islamists. Most literature on Islam conveys an idea of men's and women's similar religious obligations in worship (*ʿibādāt*) such as praying, fasting, welfare work, etc. In contrast to this, historically speaking, men have been regarded as the strongest in all respects in the social model whereas women have had a subordinate position in relation to men.

Men as caretakers of women

Wadud-Muhsin's survey of Koranic commentaries indicates an historical development in the understanding of the term *qiwāma*, which is a verbal substantive (*maṣdar*) of the root *q-w-m*. The present discussion is a complement to her investigation showing how fundamental ideas of women have changed during the course of history. A very important Koranic commentary for contemporary Islamists is the *mukhtaṣar ibn kathīr* (*The Shortened Commentary of Ibn Kathīr*) by ʿImād ad-Dīn Ibn Kathīr (d. 1373).[6] His commentary to the Koranic verse 4: 34 is that men are managers of women, their leaders and their educators, because God has preferred men over women. His main evidence for this is that God has given the privilege of prophethood to men only (Ibn Kathīr 1981 vol. I: 385). A point worth noting is that some contemporary Islamists have stated in our discussions that women such as the mother of Jesus, Maryam (Mary), and the mother of Mūsā are also prophets. They explain this by referring to Ibn Ḥazm, who regards one of the signs of prophethood to be the experience of a divine revelation (*waḥy*); that God speaks to a person either directly or through a mediator. In their view, as God spoke to Maryam through angels (K.3: 42) and to the mother of Mūsā as an inclination of the heart (*idha awḥainā ilā ummika mā yūḥā*; When We revealed to your mother that which We revealed) (K.20: 38) they might be recognised as prophets too.[7]

As Wadud-Muhsin has observed, Sayyid Quṭb (d. 1966) comments on verse 4: 34, saying that man and woman are created from a single soul, therefore they are complementary to each other. In his view, the preference (*faḍl*) of the man over the woman has therefore to be a question of a relationship of responsibility in which love and mercy should dominate. He further claims that the responsibility men have over women is based on the fact that men are economically responsible for their families (S. Quṭb 1986 vol. II: 649–52).

During my stay in Jordan in the summer of 1995, I attended the Monday lectures in the Islamic intellectual club, *The International Institute of Islamic Thought*, headed by Dr Fatḥī al-Malkāwī. As a rule the lecturers were men, but in July a leading female intellectual from the Sudan was invited to give a speech. During the following discussion a heated debate started and one leading Islamist woman, who had previously been close to the Muslim Brotherhood and who obtained her doctoral degree from a western university, stated vigorously that the time had come for Jordanian men to stop taking verse 4: 34 as an argument for male superiority. 'In the Koran', she said, 'it does not say *who* God has preferred over the other. Are men privileged because they are responsible for the family, or are women privileged because their responsibilities are less than men's?' It is relevant to add that in the Koran it does not explicitly say who is preferred, although grammatically speaking it seems to indicate men's preference. On the other hand, with a hermeneutic approach it might be possible to question whether the preference (*faḍl*) is related to being the one in charge or the one who is taken care of. The hermeneutic approach can even lead one to the conclusion that it is the family's breadwinner who is preferred and thus in charge, as implicitly stated by Sayyid Quṭb (S. Quṭb 1986 vol. II: 649–52). This latter interpretation points to a controversial issue in Islamic social thought which has been raised by some Muslims and by many non-Muslims in the western context. I will return to this issue in the discussion with Islamists in Europe.

Another woman at the meeting argued that male preference over women has nothing to do with the intellect but with bodily strength only. She referred to the fact that fourteen girls had been top in the student exam in that year.[8] 'This,' she claims, 'is a scientific proof that women are not less intelligent than men. The male preference is in their bodily strength only.' One of the men asserted that the *qiwāma* is only a matter for the family. In his view the Koranic verse 4: 34 does not claim *all* men are maintainers of *all* women, but on the level of the family, the man is in charge/is responsible.

Zainab al-Ghazzālī, in her commentary on the Koran, explains *qiwāma* as follows:

> In this noble verse is God's decision that the men are in charge/have responsibility (*qiwāma*) for women, and that men have the right of leadership in the family. This, however, does not remove the woman's sovereignty (*wilāya*) in her house and her being the commander (*amīra*), administering freely (*tataṣaraf*)[9] his [her husband's] affairs, in order to protect the interest of the family and the intactness of its unity.
>
> The basis of *qiwāma* is responsibility (*mas'ūlīya*), in the sense that the man is entrusted with making provision for his wife and his children. He is also responsible for participating with his wife in all affairs of the house; taking the Holy Koran and Sunna from our dearest Muṣtafā [the Prophet] (p.b.u.h.) as a method, an example, and a way of behaviour. The family is the primary school for the Umma. The wife is the one in charge of the family (*walīyatu amrihi*) within the home. She is responsible towards God for the soundness of her husband and her children. And all this does not arise without the woman surrendering readily with love and obedience to God and [understanding] that the man's *qiwāma* over her is the source of justice and for her benefit. This is because *qiwāma* demands from the man the best treatment and equity (*inṣāf*) concerning her in every matter whereof she is in need of any service. He is also responsible for protecting her dignity, her honour, and her humanity, because, with the man's sovereignty (*wilāyatihi*) over his wife, she becomes a trust between his hands.

She continues:

> And this is a sound understanding of *qiwāma* which gives the woman trust in her husband and gives her peace of mind. The married life becomes peacefully settled, and by this the wife becomes free to organise her home and take care of the children.
>
> In this manner, Islam wants for the spouses to establish a well-ordered blossoming family tree in a rich garden, for the happiness of those who are under the protection of Islam's sweet smell. This is how marriage is in Islam. And this is the man's degree [over the woman] on the family's scale – to be responsible for the success of the pure happiness of his family. The home will be at peace and society will advance. This is as they are able to understand the Book of God, the understanding of which is the absolute justice. And relevant to this Ibn Kathīr says: 'The man is the caretaker (*qayyim*) of the woman, that is, he is her leader and her superior and governor over her and her educator if she curves [i.e. deviates from the right path].'
>
> (Z. al-Ghazzālī 1994a vol. I: 297–8 [translation mine])

Zainab al-Ghazzālī's understanding of *qiwāma* differs from that of the traditional male commentators. As shown above, the early commentaries portrayed gender relations in terms of male superiority and from a male point of view, with no regard to women's emotions or sentiments. It is interesting to note that although the hadith where the Prophet says that 'the best among you is the one who treats his family in the best way' is often mentioned, this hadith has not influenced the actual legislation concerning gender relations. For instance, in matters of divorce, one can observe that not only in Muslim countries but also in legislation in the various law schools, women obtain divorce with difficulty if there is no documentation of mistreatment (see Chapter 10). In contrast to male interpretations of this Koranic verse, Zainab al-Ghazzālī emphasises not only the material obligations included in the concept of *qiwāma*, she also stresses the humanistic perspective, referring to emotional and psychological factors within domestic life. She further stresses the importance of men's dealing with their wives in a decent way in order to secure a harmonious family life. This is in contrast to Ibn Kathīr's more legal and technical interpretation of this verse. Although there is a shift in approach from the male perspective of Ibn Kathīr to the female perspective of Zainab al-Ghazzālī in this matter, I would claim that her approach in general is definitely *not* a feminist perspective in the sense that she privileges the female point of view in her work. It is interesting to note how she quotes Ibn Kathīr at the end of the passage, even although her previous argument is quite different from his. This gives her work the advantage of an Islamic authority, which she might need being the first female to publish a commentary on the Koran. I would suggest, however, that Zainab al-Ghazzālī's work does not need any Islamic authority, as she is revered by Islamists and common Muslims in general. In my discussions with Islamists in the Arab world as well as in Europe, I discovered that the publication of her autobiography, written while imprisoned by ʿAbd an-Naṣr (Z. al-Ghazzālī 1994b), has elevated her status not only as an Islamist with knowledge of Islam but also as a woman of enormous strength.

The issue of *qiwāma* is much debated and has been taken up in particular by Islamists living in western countries or Islamists with a western education living in Muslim countries. Ḥasan at-Turābī was one of the first of the modern Islamists to raise the issue of women. When he wrote his manuscript dealing specifically with gender relations and women's role in Islamic society in the early 1970s, few Islamic-minded men promoted such views. It is significant that initially the manuscript was launched more as a text for discussion than as a final thesis. The manuscript circulated among Sudanese Islamists, but even well-known Islamists such as the Egyptian Islamic scholar, Sheikh Muḥammad al-Ghazzālī, read and commented on its contents before it was published (at-Turābī 1993: 1). I believe this example illustrates the sensitivity of the issue of women in a Muslim context.

Feminist ideas which had taken hold in the western world from the 1960s onwards spread to Muslim countries, although in most countries only small elites of educated women adopted these ideas. at-Turābī's manuscript has to be regarded in the light of the growing feminist movement. As Sudanese women began to enter higher education, women's consciousness of the need for change in their social status increased. It is obvious that at-Turābī was aware of this, as he writes:

> The modern reality which faces Muslims, the social trends in a continuously changing world, demand an early initiative in order to take command of this change before it takes its own course, so that foreign trends do not take root and assimilate and it will become too late to carry through a rightly guided Islamic reform.
>
> (at-Turābī n.d.: 42 [translation mine])

at-Turābī has lived in England and France where he obtained his MA and his Ph.D. in law. With his experience of western countries he was better equipped than many other Islamists to confront what he regarded as the western influence. From his literary work in general it seems that he combats western influence on 'the West's own premises' (at-Turābī n.d.; 1990; 1993). at-Turābī might be situated in the intersection between three different cultural patterns: the 'Arabic cultural pattern', the 'African cultural pattern', and the 'western cultural pattern', and he tends to select those hadiths and ideas from within these various cultural patterns which are compatible with his specific time and place. The example of the basket metaphor is particularly relevant to at-Turābī, as he often tends to turn traditional perceptions upsidedown.

at-Turābī implicitly demands a new understanding of women's role in society and in Islam in general. At the time when he wrote his text on women, many Islamists were promoting the traditional role of women as mothers and wives only (see for instance M. Quṭb 1985; Yakan 1992). at-Turābī has a different approach to those Koranic verses often cited in Islamist works on the issue of women. In contrast to other Islamists who claim that these Koranic verses are directed to women in order to define their role in society, he claims that these verses are directed to men. He states that 'most rules and regulations in the Koran which deal with female issues were revealed as restrictions for men with the intention of stopping them "from transgressing the borders" towards women'. 'Only a few of the Koranic injunctions', he says, 'introduce restrictions for women' (at-Turābī n.d.: 33 [translation mine]). He illustrates this by pointing out that the rules for divorce and the waiting-period (*ʿidda*) were actually introduced to protect women against men's tendency to repeatedly divorce their wives then take them back again later.

Another example in which at-Turābī inverts commonly held notions is when he refers to the Koranic verse: 'O Prophet! Tell your wives and your daughters as well as all believing women, that they should draw over themselves some of their outer garments [when in public]. This will be more conducive to their being recognised [as decent women] and not annoyed' (K.33: 59). While this verse has often been cited in order to keep women inside the house, at-Turābī refers to it in order to argue that women *can* actually go out. He appeals to verse 4: 15, where the prohibition to go out of the house applies to women who have committed adultery. In his view, women in general have been segregated and isolated from wider society in a way that is only prescribed as a punishment for an adulterous wife.

In the beginning of the book, at-Turābī portrays a picture of the ideal Islamic society as a society in which women play an important part even in the public sphere. Women are themselves responsible for their own lives. No 'specific system of order' applies to women only, rather women and men are brothers and sisters with similar rights and obligations (at-Turābī n.d.: 8). He points out that it is on the basis of a woman's own acts that she will get rewards or punishment on the Last Day, as is stated in the Koran: 'Every one will appear before Him on Resurrection Day in a lonely state' (K.19: 95). This argument is an obvious reaction to the common tendency in much of the Muslim world to interpret the concept of *qiwāma* in totalitarian terms. An example is the pervasive understanding that the man is responsible if his wife or daughters are not following the Islamic prescriptions such as praying, fasting, wearing the head-scarf, etc. A European convert to Islam who is married to an Arab man and lives in an Arab country, said that the understanding of *qiwāma* in a totalitarian sense sometimes even goes beyond men's interference in women's daily religious lives. She suggests that the concept of *qiwāma* 'may explain the license some men take for "honour killings" of wives and daughters, thinking they have divine rights over them.'

at-Turābī challenges the notion of men's responsibility for women's behaviour, pointing to women's right to self-determination. His interpretation of *qiwāma* is:

> They [men] have no authority (*sulṭa*) over women except in marital relations. This relationship is established with the woman's agreement and shall be maintained in a spirit of counsel (*shūrā*) and respect (*iḥsān*). The husband has responsibility for the family but this applies only as a responsibility for sustenance or for guidance or education carried out in a reasonable way. Both parties should be active in the administration of the family's affairs and both have authority over sons and daughters.
>
> (at-Turābī n.d.: 17–18 [translation mine])

The Muslim Brotherhood has also entered the discussion on *qiwāma* in the report I have already referred to, *The Role of Muslim Women in Islamic Society according to the Muslim Brotherhood*, written in Cairo in 1994. In the report the Koranic verse 4: 34 is cited and the report states that 'this should not be understood as an absolute and general attitude in all things and for all men over all women' (The Muslim Brotherhood 1994: 8). It further claims that *qiwāma* as a directing role 'is confined to the family alone and to matters only concerning the husband and wife relationship' (The Muslim Brotherhood 1994: 8). The report defines *qiwāma* primarily in terms of the economic relationship which exists between husband and wife. 'This *qiwāma*', it says, 'is merely a matter of leadership and directing in exchange for duties that should be performed' (The Muslim Brotherhood 1994: 8). The husband's economic responsibilities such as dowry payment, the provision of a house and furniture and daily living expenses are his alone and cannot be claimed from the wife even if she is wealthy. The Muslim Brotherhood also believes that the husband is the best suited to such leadership as in general it is the husband who is usually the oldest and the most experienced (The Muslim Brotherhood 1994: 8). The report goes on to say that this leadership function is to be performed in kindness and that the relationship between a husband and his wife should be one of mutual consultation.

It is important to note that the Muslim Brotherhood actually quotes the verse 'having their affairs in consultation among them' (K.42: 38) describing it as 'a general injunction' (The Muslim Brotherhood 1994: 9). In the past this verse has usually been used to support the idea of consultation (*shūrā*) on a political level. By referring to the verse in support of consultation on a familial level, the Muslim Brotherhood has moved towards a notion of equality of the sexes not only on a spiritual level but on a social level as well. This idea of equality is explicitly stated further on in the report where it says that 'the general rule, therefore, is equality between men and women' (The Muslim Brotherhood 1994: 9). It is worth noting that although this statement is followed by an elaboration of the distinction between males and females, it does not say anything about social inequality.

I sense a modification in attitudes towards women following my fieldwork among Muslim Brothers in Jordan in 1991–2 and this report from the Muslim Brotherhood from 1994. It might be argued that this difference has to do with the distinction between theoretical statements and actual practice, but I do not believe it to be so. During my visits in Jordan in 1995–6 I observed that even there changes had taken place. I think that the report from the Muslim Brotherhood played a great part in this change, and I discovered that arguments on women among members of the Muslim Brotherhood in Europe tended to be the same as those found in the report. This report was written in Cairo, but it is intended to offer guidance just as much to members of the Muslim Brotherhood living in western countries as in the Arab world. The report can be regarded as a result of the globalisation process by which western local ideas have been transferred to other cultural spheres. Although there are apparent changes of attitudes in perceptions of women and the role of women in society, the report is still marked by the patriarchal attitudes of the 'Arab cultural base pattern'.

The Egyptian–Canadian Islamist, Jamal Badawi, exemplifies the change in attitudes towards and perceptions of women among Islamists. He is active in *daʿwa*-work and has travelled widely, giving lectures to Muslims and non-Muslims all over the world. In Badawi's 1995 book, *Gender Equity in Islam*, he exchanges the concept of 'gender equality' with the concept 'gender equity' which in his view is more Islamic. He says:

> Equity is used here to mean justice and overall equality in the totality of rights and responsibilities of both genders and allows for the possibility of variations in specific items within the overall balance and equality. . . . It should be added that from an Islamic perspective, the roles of men and women are complementary and co-operative rather than competitive.
>
> (Badawi 1995: 47)

Badawi regards the only criterion for superiority or inequality to be the relationship the individual has with God, as stated in the Koran and the Sunna. In view of this, he comments on the concept of *qiwāma*:

> Some interpreters of the Qur'an mistakenly translate the Arabic word *qiwāma* (responsibility for the family) with the English word 'superiority'. The Qur'an makes it clear that the sole basis for the superiority of any person over another is piety and righteousness, not gender, colour or nationality.
>
> (Badawi 1995: 13)

Badawi's approach is not uncommon for a Muslim who has lived for a long time in a western country. Moreover, as a *daʿwa* worker who speaks English fluently, he has probably had extensive contact with non-Muslims, something which his book witnesses to as he tends to speak of Islam in terms of an *equality* gender structure. Badawi mixes the spiritual and the social sphere in his analysis, as has also been done by Islamic feminists (Wadud-Muhsin 1992; Hassan 1990). Whereas other male Islamists such as at-Turābī and al-Ghazzālī reinterpret or reselect from the Islamic sources in order to find evidences that prevailing attitudes towards women are a wrong interpretation of the sources, Badawi goes further and more or less tries to eliminate gender differences from the Islamic content. He discusses the spiritual equality between the sexes. He quotes among others the verse: 'Anyone – be it man or woman – who performs good deeds and is a believer, will enter Paradise and will not be wronged' (K.4: 24). For Badawi this verse together with the passage which states that 'the noblest of you in the sight of God is the one who is most deeply conscious (*taqwa*) of Him' (K.49: 13) obliterates any gender distinction. Roald and Ouis have observed that Badawi tends to be selective in his discussion on gender. For instance, he does not cite verse 4: 34 but only refers to it in a brief footnote (Roald and Ouis 1997). They further claim that Badawi addresses the issue of *qiwāma* but tends to leave aside the question of violence against women which is contained in the last part of the verse. I would suggest that this method is in line with modern Christian and Jewish methods of interpretation. By overlooking certain passages or contextualising others, one opens the text up to an interpretation which is more acceptable to a modern audience.

In my interview with Sheikh Darsh in London in December 1995, I asked him how he understood the concept of *qiwāma*. I found it interesting that he expressed an idea which I have often encountered in my interaction with Arabs, Islamists and Muslims alike. He said: '*Qiwāma* is explained as meaning the head of the family. Husband and wife discuss matters among themselves in the family, and when they reach a conclusion, the husband will state this conclusion as the decision of the family.'

What Darsh expressed in this statement is the idea of an outer and an inner sphere. In the inner sphere there exists *shūrā* (consultation), whereas the husband conveys the decision which is based on consultation between the spouses to the outer world as his own decision. I believe this pattern, which indicates a gap between theory and praxis, is a result of the established idea that the husband has the last word.

Darsh further explained *qiwāma* in terms of the supervision of the children's discipline, manners and their education. 'So', he said, 'when we Muslims are talking about the head of the family, it is as if we are talking about the head of a school.' He emphasised, as do many other Islamists, that *qiwāma* does not mean a dictatorial relationship between husband and wife or between parents and children, but that 'it is a matter of taking care of the discipline within the family and seeing to it that everything is functioning in a proper and decent manner.' Darsh's view reflects Badawi's notion of equity, where equity is less a question of role equality than it is a question of justice where all members of the family have their rights fulfilled during the accomplishment of their obligations.

I further asked Darsh whether changing employment patterns, particularly in Europe where many women work whereas their husbands are unemployed, transfers the man's *qiwāma* to the wife. Darsh did not give a direct answer to the question, stating only that this pattern is 'a reversion of the natural order of the human society'. Rather, what concerned Darsh was the lack of attention given to the younger generation when both men and women are working. 'This' he stated 'has resulted in multiple problems with the young and a moral drift in society.' He continued:

> What has become the norm nowadays in Europe in general is the secular point of view which does not care about moral uprightness of society. The idea is that morality is an individual domain which does not need any regulation. Two adults whether they are males or females are allowed to behave in whatever way they like. No! We Muslims do not consider such a way to be for the success and the happiness for the human society. First, the woman is the one who conceives and who goes on carrying the burden and who is supposed to be feeding her children out of her own breasts. And you can read from the medical point of view even nowadays, people are calling for women to breast-feed their children. In the words of the Koran it takes thirty months for the child to be looked after. Now who is to take care of that? Who is to care for the women who is pregnant, who is breast-feeding, who is looking after the child? Can we say: Let her go and work and the husband should sit at home? There has to be a social engineering showing respect to the woman and caring for her agonies and for the stability of the family.

In our further discussion, Darsh stressed that the issue of *qiwāma* is not a matter of economic support only. In his view, women working in wider society is a new development which is a result of industrialisation, and this new development which 'comes in one century at the edge of humanity' cannot change a norm which has prevailed for thousands of years. Darsh was of the opinion that the man always has the *qiwāma* in the family in the framework of 'love and compassion', referring to the Koranic verse 30: 21. 'This verse', he said,

> gives us the background to the family relationship: 'He created for you mates from yourselves that you might find happiness and peace of mind and He ordained between you love and compassion.' So this is the function of the love and compassion between the spouses, the creation of happiness and peace of mind.

In Darsh's view, the *qiwāma* system is the natural order of human society. He stressed that although the *qiwāma* is not *only* due to the husband's economic responsibility, it is still very largely a matter of economic responsibility which women are exempted from. However, Darsh was not against women working or studying, as he said that particularly in European society the economic system is built on both spouses being breadwinners, and thus in many cases women have to go out to work.

In my interview with Sheikh Rāshid Ghannūshī in Manchester in December 1995, he also indicated that the system of *qiwāma* is a system within the family. He spoke in terms of the family as a social institution saying that:

> The family is a social institution and like every social institution the family is in need of administration. But like all administration of social institutions the family is also in need of consultation (*shūrā*). Islam rejects individual administration, and particularly dictatorial administration. The administration is also in need of rules and regulations of which the principle of consultation is the most important. *Qiwāma* is therefore a leadership which has its rules and which is built on the Islamic principle of *shūrā* as stated in the Koran: 'And whose affairs are a matter of consultation among themselves (*wa amruhum shūrā baynahum*)'.
>
> (K.42: 38 [translation mine])

It is important to draw attention to the fact that, apart from what is stated in the report of the Muslim Brotherhood, Ghannūshī and Darsh were the only interviewees who referred to the matter of counsel (*shūrā*) as a family matter. I believe particularly Ghannūshī 's position on female issues is better formulated than that of many other Islamists as he has written a book on the situation of women in Tunis as part of his political agenda.

I further discussed the issue of *qiwāma* with Fu'ād Ḥussain from the Islamic Liberation Party in Britain. Ḥussain has lived in Britain for more than twelve years and his education is in the field of engineering. When I asked him about his understanding of *qiwāma* he said:

> I understand *qiwāma* as an economic responsibility and a protection of the family, not only the wife. The husband has to support and protect the whole family. Thus *qiwāma* is *ri'āya* [keeping, caring] and *ḥimāya* [protection]. According to the Islamic law, however, the husband has no power over those he is responsible for and he has no right to rule them. No created being has any right to claim any power over another created being.

In our further discussion I asked Ḥussain about the husband's right to forbid his wife from going out of the house. Ḥussain pointed out that this was part of the *qiwāma*, and the husband has a right to do so according to Islam. When I asked him whether a husband has the right to prohibit his wife from going out at all, Ḥussain confirmed that a husband has a right to do so. 'However', he said, 'this man does not follow the order and the example of the Prophet who told us to treat our wives well.' There is an obvious contradiction in this statement, at least for a westerner who would interpret a husband's right to deny his wife permission to go out of the house in terms of power. It might be that Ḥussain has a different concept of 'power' from those who understand it in a western context, or it might be that his argument is not well substantiated. I suspect that both alternatives are possible, since there is apparent confusion regarding conceptual meanings between Muslims and non-Muslims, particularly among those coming from different cultural backgrounds, with concepts being invested with different significance. Furthermore, Ḥussain's statement indicates the tension between the legal and the moral aspects of Islamic law. Actual Islamic legislation came into being as a result of interpretations of the sources in different contexts, with specific local traditions (*ʿurf*) constituting the moral norms of society having an influence on this legislation. Today local moral customs (*ʿurf*) differ both from those of ancient Arab society and from one society to another, and this creates tension between what is legal and what is moral.

There is an important problem which has to be raised in the issue of gender relations. In Islamic law there are certain acceptable punishments for women who do not behave in a 'proper' way. To give an example, the husband's corporal punishment of his wife is limited but legally accepted. However, when it comes to a married man behaving badly no legislation exists. I would argue that this lack of punishment in one form or another might explain the power relationship which exists in some Muslim marriages. One important reason why women tend to have such a strong position in Swedish society is that Sweden legislates in favour of women. This does not mean that power relationships do not exist among Swedish couples. On the contrary, there is an abuse of male power among some couples in Sweden as there is among some Muslim couples. However, as Swedish legislation provides women with a certain amount of power, women living in Sweden are able to reject such unbalanced power relationships.

In my further discussion with Ḥussain I confronted him with the fact that the present situation in Europe has led to changes in traditional gender roles. I asked him whether changes in the economic situation, with working women and unemployed men, have any influence on *qiwāma*. He firmly rejected a change in *qiwāma*, and when I challenged him with his own argument that *qiwāma* was to a great extent an economic matter, he stated that

> I did not give a reason for *qiwāma*. What I did was to give my own interpretation (*tafsīr*). We [the Muslims] have not really conducted

any research into the concept of *qiwāma*. When I talk in terms of economy I just give an interpretation.

Ḥasan at-Turābī also gave his own interpretation of *qiwāma* in a discussion I had with him in the Sudan in August 1996. During our discussion at-Turābī was sitting down, and when I asked him how he understood the concept of *qiwāma* he stood up, saying: '*Qiwāma* is just like this: a man has to stand up to serve his wife.' It is interesting to note that the word *qiwāma* is a derivation of the root *q-w-m* with one of its basic meanings being to 'stand up'. at-Turābī's wife, Wiṣāl al-Mahdī, further elaborated upon this idea of *qiwāma*, saying that the Prophet Muḥammad used to serve his wives; at home for instance he cleaned, prepared food and took an active part in daily domestic work.

It is interesting to note that once in a discussion with Arab-speaking women and converts in Sweden I told them about at-Turābī's statement. One Swedish–Arab girl with Egyptian parents, who speaks Arabic fluently, stated enthusiastically that at-Turābī was right as grammatically speaking the preposition *ʿalā* which comes after *qawwāmūn* in the Koranic passage has two meanings. It can mean *over* and the Koranic passage would then mean that men had absolute power over women. 'However', she said, 'if that was so, it would be more natural that the preposition *ʿan* should be used, as *ʿan* has such an absolute meaning' [translation mine]. The other meaning of *ʿalā*, according to her, is *up*, and the Koranic passage would then imply at-Turābī's interpretation. The girl's observation reflects that of Islamic feminist theologians such as Hassan and Wadud-Muhsin, whose hermeneutical approaches to the Koranic text involve similar grammatical considerations.

at-Turābī's understanding of *qiwāma* is also reinforced by Taha Jaber Alalwani, an Iraqi Islamic scholar, who is the director of the graduate School of Islamic and Social Sciences in Virginia, USA. During a visit there in autumn 1999, I asked him about his understanding of *qiwāma*. He answered that a person who is *qawwām ʿalā* is responsible for everything; protection, provision and the development of that which he is responsible for. 'Thus the man is a servant of his wife', he said, 'but it is hard to talk in terms of a human being as a servant, therefore I choose to see the man as the protector of his family and the provider of the family's need.'

Islamists in Europe

In my discussion with Islamists both in the Muslim world and in Europe the argument promoted by Sayyid Quṭb, that men are responsible for women due to their economic support of their families (S. Quṭb 1986 vol. II: 648–57), was often brought up. This argument is particularly forceful in the Muslim world as many women still do not work outside the home.

In the questionnaire, almost everybody gave economic support as either the only reason or one of the reasons for men's *qiwāma* over women. A 38-year-old man who has lived in England for ten years stated:

> Women have a great role in the Muslim society and *qiwāma* means, in my opinion, what is stated later in this Koranic verse (with what God has given men). This means that men have features which allow them to lead the family especially in hard circumstances. This does not mean to ignore the wife's opinion or neglecting her. The couple has to share opinions in any matters concerning their family and future.

Although most of the respondents to the questionnaire emphasised the economic argument, many also saw a consequence of *qiwāma* being that men have the final word. However, the idea of the 'final word' was expressed in different ways. While most answers had an implicitly democratic spirit, stressing that before the final word there has to be consultation between the spouses, one answer was outstanding for its emphasis on men's control over women. It stated that 'men are in charge, in command and in control. He has the final saying after consultation, if necessary'. The striking thing about this answer is that the respondent is a man with a Ph.D. in science who has lived and worked in Europe for more than twenty years. As the questionnaire involved mostly anonymous interviewees, I cannot possibly always investigate the many variables involved such as country of origin, primary and secondary contacts in Europe, or the person's background and characteristics. Nevertheless, this answer is interesting as it differs from most other answers both in the questionnaire and in personal discussions with Islamists in Europe. It indicates that although many Islamists living in Europe are influenced by western concepts of gender relations and thus the 'western cultural base pattern', some still cling to the 'Arab cultural base pattern's' notion of the relationship between men and women.

Amal wrote in the questionnaire:

> Men (in an ideal Islamic society) are responsible for the financial support of the family, since women were created to fulfil other duties in life, that is, they carry babies for nine months, then they take care of them in their early childhood. For a woman to be able to do that perfectly, the worry of the economy and the burden of supporting the family is taken away from her as a sign of mercy and love from God.

Amal, who has a degree in science, has not been working since she came to Europe. She explained that God has instituted a system which is in accordance with human nature. 'There is a meaning behind all creation and God has created men and women with a different biology in order to fulfil a perfect system', she says. Amal stresses the importance of understanding the concept of *qiwāma*, not as a concept of control but as a concept of mutual responsibilities. She states:

> For me, the concept *qiwāma* means that my husband has obligations towards me as I have obligations towards him. God created men with a greater physical strength; whereas women were created with a greater emotional strength in order to be able to carry out the hardship which child-bearing, labour and child-caring demand. In the Koran the word *shūrā* [consultation] is used not only as a political concept but just as well as something which has to do with family matters. *Qiwāma*, for me, is therefore something which claims both a man's ability of consulting his wife as well as it claims his ability to stay firm in his authority in cases of hardship. A man's *qiwāma* in family matters can be compared to that of a democratic leader's authority over the subjects. Another important thing in Islam is that, if for instance two or more persons travel together one should elect a leader for the journey. The leader is not there for controlling the journey but to ensure a secure trip. The same can be said about a marriage, the man should not control his wife but should be responsible for the family's security and comfort.

When I asked Amal what a woman should do if the husband was misusing his authority and utilised the concept of *qiwāma* to control his wife, she answered:

> The woman can choose between two alternatives. Either she can object to his control and divorce him which she has the right to do in Islam, or she can choose to stay with him and be patient. In the latter case, *inshallāh* (God willing) she will get reward from God for her patience as God has promised to reward those who are patient, and her husband has to answer his wrongdoing in front of God on the Day of Judgement. There might be many reasons for her to stay, maybe the couple have children together and the woman does not want to separate them from their father, or she maybe accepts his authority due to other reasons. Anyhow, the social aspect for a married Muslim couple who have problems is similar to a non-Muslim couple in the same situation. However, religiously speaking, human being's responsibility towards God gives the matter of the relationship between a man and a woman another dimension and elevates the relationship onto a level other than a purely material one. My husband is good to me not only because he loves and cares for me but also because he has an obligation towards God to behave in a proper way. The same is for me. God has given us rules to follow so we can behave in a just and decent way towards each other. If one of us misbehaves we have to answer for our misbehaviour on the day of Judgement.

Khadīja's view of *qiwāma* is as follows:

> I think that the understanding of the Koranic verse is that the general *qiwāma* and the administration of life and its direction are the responsibility of men. This does not mean, however, that the woman does not have any role. On the contrary, I strongly believe that the woman has a very important role in the administration of the family and in the direction of her husband's thoughts. *Qiwāma* is not control or oppression and not absolute male authority over women, rather it is consultation (*shūrā*), understanding and partnership in decision-making [translation mine].

She further goes on saying that it is natural that in institutions and in companies there should be a higher administration. But that does not, according to her, mean that there cannot be any advisers and counsellors. Khadīja sees the woman as the adviser in family life and in every aspect of life, whereas *qiwāma* and the higher leadership is for man because God created him like that. 'And', she says, 'He created the woman for other things.'

Although Amal's and Khadīja's view of *qiwāma* is quite similar, there seems to be a difference between the two. In the in-depth interviews I discovered that Khadīja spoke purely from an ideal point of view, whereas Amal often distinguished between an ideal Islamic society and the realities among Muslims in Europe. This was not because Khadīja was unaware of the distinction between Islam and Muslims, but her position as a leading Islamist woman within the ranks of the Muslim Brotherhood means that she tends to view Islam and speak about it in terms of the ideal model. She also tends to reiterate the ideas contained in the Muslim Brotherhood's report on women, particularly that of the different social roles of men and women. In some cases the structure of this social organisation seems to make her less prone to change, whereas in other cases she is apparently influenced by the 'western cultural base pattern'. Furthermore, she lives in a Muslim atmosphere with little primary or secondary contact with either non-Muslims or more secularised Muslims. An important factor is that she does not speak the language of the host country very well, which also limits her contact with the majority society. This might, although not necessarily, make her position conform to a pattern of competition in relation to the majority society.

Amal, on the other hand, lives in a less segregated environment. She has had frequent contacts with the majority society as she is involved in her children's school where the majority of the pupils are non-Muslims. She might thus be regarded as being in a cooperative position with regard to the majority society. Amal also gives lectures to non-Muslims. She told me that during her lectures to non-Muslims, she was always confronted with their view of Muslims. She explained that the bad experiences non-

Muslims have with Muslims are based on contact with marginalised Muslims in European society. She says:

> When I speak with welfare workers or counsellors, I am aware that the Muslims they speak about are people with social problems. Often these people are not even practising Muslims but they cling to their Muslim identity as a contrast to the identity of the majority society. I would also say that most of these Muslims have a very low education which also influences their lack of integration into European society. They follow customs (*ʿadāt wa taqālīd*) prevalent in the Muslim world, instead of following the precepts of Islam.

As a consequence she admitted that these confrontations with non-Muslims had made her change the way she looked upon Islam and Muslims. 'Islam *is* an ideal', she says, 'and today very few Muslims are capable of living up to this ideal. I therefore think it is important to take the starting point from this fact and try to develop Islamic social ideas which can possibly function in our present society.' I believe the difference between these two women is that Khadīja regards the established Islamic social ideas as more or less fixed, whereas Amal regards them as changeable according to time, place and circumstances. I attribute this difference in outlook to the extent of contact and communication with the majority population.

When the reason for *qiwāma* was explained in terms of men's economic support for the family in my discussions with Islamists, men and women, in Europe, I would argue: 'But in Europe many women, even Muslims, are breadwinners in the family. In some cases they are even the only or the main breadwinner. Does that mean that women are in charge (*qiwāma*) of the family?' *All* men I posed this question to pointed to the second proclamation in verse 4: 34, namely that God has given men preference over women. Most women reacted in the same way as men, but some women maintained that women who were main breadwinners had to be in charge of the family.

It is interesting to note that although few of the respondents answered this question in the affirmative, those who did were all women. This indicates how one's own perspective tends to dominate in the process of interpretation. The argument that women might possibly be in charge due to the economic situation of the family is apparently a result of the influence of the 'western cultural base pattern' with its emphasis on female empowerment. This example further suggests the importance of taking into account both male and female perspectives in issues of legislation.

Physical punishment of women

The last part of the Koranic verse 4: 34, as quoted above, deals with the physical punishment of women. The meaning of *nushūz* (translated as disloyalty and ill-conduct) is significant for this verse, as it is this action which determines the circumstances in which a husband can physically punish his wife. How has the term *nushūz* been understood in the Islamic debate through history? Which forms of 'disloyalty and ill-conduct' should be subjected to physical punishment? I will begin by investigating the various meanings this verse has acquired by looking at some prominent Koranic commentaries.

Ibn ʿAbbās, the cousin of the Prophet, is known to have been among the earliest commentators on the Koran. In Ābādī's commentary on the Koran, he explains Ibn ʿAbbās' understanding of the term *nushūz* as 'their [women's] disobedience in sexual matters to you [men]' (Ābādi 1988: 84). He goes on to explain that the infliction of the physical punishment must be 'a non-violent and non-honourable blow' (Ābādi 1988: 84). It appears therefore that the Muslim understanding in the fourteenth century (and ultimately in the first century if one can possibly see this as a first century work) was that physical punishment of women in the Koranic sense had to do with a woman's sexual rejection of her husband, which is also confirmed by aṭ-Ṭabārī's (d. 923) commentary (aṭ-Ṭabārī 1994 vol. II: 452–3). aṭ-Ṭabārī defines *nushūz* as a woman's feeling of superiority (*istiṣlāḥ* [superiority] and *irtifāʿ* [elevation]) over her husband, referring to the essential meaning of the term *nushūz* as being an 'elevated place' or a 'high ground' (aṭ-Ṭabārī 1994 vol. II: 452; also Wehr 1980: 966). aṭ-Ṭabārī regards women's disobedience in this particular context purely in sexual terms, explaining it to mean a woman who refuses to have sexual relations with her husband due to this feeling of superiority or elevation over him. As for the husband's punishment of his wife, aṭ-Ṭabārī interprets this to be a gradual punishment which starts with a husband's verbal reproach of his wife. If this has no effect the husband should sleep in a seperate bed, and as a last step he should hit her with 'a non-violent blow' (aṭ-Ṭabārī 1994 vol. II: 453).

If one turns to Ibn Kathīr, the thirteenth century commentator, he repeats aṭ-Ṭabārī's definition of *nushūz* as 'elevation'. Although Ibn Kathīr emphasises the sexual aspect of a wife's feeling of elevation over her husband, however, he regards *nushūz* in more general terms. For instance, he quotes a hadith which relates that Muḥammad said: 'If I were to order someone to bow down to someone, I would order the woman to bow down to her husband' (Sunan at-Tirmidhī, Book of Foster Relationship, no. 1079; Sunan Ibn Mājah, Book of Marriage, no. 1842)[10] (see hadith 1 on p. 172). Ibn Kathīr refers both to Ibn ʿAbbās' and aṭ-Ṭabārī's writings in his commentary. However, although he builds his argument on previous commentaries, he extends the understanding of this verse to cover not only a woman's sexual refusal of her husband, but to imply a wife's general disagreement with or opposition to her husband.

After repeating aṭ-Ṭabārī's theme of the various stages of punishment of a disobedient wife, Ibn Kathīr ends this section with an exhortation to men that they should *not* hit their wives. He refers to a hadith saying that the Prophet told his companions: 'Do not hit God's servants (*imāʾullāh)* [i.e. here: women in general].' The hadith then tells that some while after the Prophet had said this, ʿUmar complained to the Messenger of God that many women turned against their husbands. Muḥammad gave his permission that the men could hit their wives in cases of rebelliousness. The women then turned to the wives of the Prophet and complained about their husbands. The Prophet said: 'Many women have turned to my family complaining about their husbands. Verily these men are not among the best of you' (Ibn Kathīr 1981 vol. I: 386; Sunan Abī Dāwud, Book of Marriage, no. 1834; ad-Dārimī, Book of Marriage, no. 2122).[11]

Ibn Kathīr's interpretation of the Koranic verse has developed from Ibn ʿAbbās' understanding of female opposition in sexual terms to encompass all female opposition to men in the family. However, although Ibn Kathīr does not *reject* the idea of corporal punishment of women, he encourages men to abstain from such practice, referring to the example of the Prophet.

Twentieth century commentators such as Sayyid Quṭb and Muḥammad ʿAlī aṣ-Ṣābūnī as well as the female commentator Zainab al-Ghazzālī have repeated the ideas of Ibn ʿAbbās, aṭ-Ṭabarī, and particularly Ibn Kathīr with specific reference to these authors. Zainab al-Ghazzālī specifically links the term *nushūz* to rebelliousness towards God in general, and as she also regards a wife's disobedience to her husband as an act of rebelliousness towards God, she maintains the male perspective in her interpretation of the text. Like Ibn Kathīr, Zainab al-Ghazzālī stresses the importance of the stages in the punishment and sees the steps before the hitting as more important than the blow itself, which in her view is merely a symbolic act. She says:

> A light blow is sufficient, because the act of hitting is preceded by admonition and separation and these acts are very hard for them [the women]. And nevertheless, the Prophet expressed while he recited this verse [4: 34]: 'Do not hit, only the evil ones among you [hit].'
>
> (Z. al-Ghazzālī 1994a vol. I: 298 [translation mine])

She continues: 'But the bad treatment some men are giving their wives is backwardness resulting from their enormous incapability of understanding the true nature of Islam and its spirit' (Z. al-Ghazzālī 1994a vol. I: 298 [translation mine]).

I would argue that there is a difference in approach between Ibn Kathīr and Zainab al-Ghazzālī in their understanding of the physical punishment of women. This difference can be interpreted in terms of the transfer from a male to a female perspective in interpretation. Although Zainab al-Ghazzālī and Sayyid Quṭb are careful to stress the importance of delicacy in dealing with marital conflicts, I found the greatest break with the traditional understanding of this matter in the writings of the Egyptian scholar, ʿAbd al-Ḥalim Abū Shaqqa from 1990. Abū Shaqqa belongs to an *ikhwān* trend, and the two prefaces to his book on women are written by Muḥammad al-Ghazzālī and Yūsuf al-Qaraḍāwī. In dealing with a husband's 'right' to hit his wife, he writes:

> If the holy verse came as a general concept, the text of the Sunna came to clarify the situations where this form of disciplinary punishment is demanded. And these situations are when the offence reaches such a high degree that it is possible to label it obscenity (*fāḥisha*),[12] of ignominious speech or an ignominious act, which makes the husband suffer enormously, such as [for a woman] to let men into the house and let them stay there even though the husband detests their presence in the house.
>
> (Abū Shaqqa 1990 vol. VI: 243 [translation mine])

He presents two hadiths in favour of his argument. The first hadith particularly mentions the act of letting men whom the husband detests into the house. The second hadith (hadith 3 on p. 148) is an explanation of the Koranic verse as it has nearly the same wording as the Koranic verse: if a woman makes *fāḥisha* the husband should first warn his wife, then separate from her, and then hit her with a non-violent blow.

After saying this Abū Shaqqa goes on:

> Verily, Islam lays down general comprehensive rules for different times, circumstances, and for a variety of personalities. These [rules] differ also when it comes to levels of culture and civilisation. The practices are linked to their appropriateness to the situation on the one side and to the moral and intellectual levels of the individual on the other side. Maybe a [specific] practice is proper in a certain situation and with a certain individual and produces useful results, whereas it is not proper in another situation and not with another individual where it could lead to harmful results.
>
> (Abū Shaqqa 1990 vol. VI: 244 [translation mine])

Abū Shaqqa goes further in his analysis of the physical punishment of women and this is what makes his text interesting. He says:

> Parallel to the legal texts which report the permission for hitting, there exist other texts which maintain that one should avoid hitting. ʿĀ'isha said: The messenger of God (p.b.u.h.) never hit anyone with his hand, not a woman and not a servant, only when he was fighting on the path of God (*fī sabīlillāh*). He never revenged anything which was done to him, only if God's boundaries were violated. Thus, he was revenging only God.
>
> (Abū Shaqqa 1990 vol. VI: 244 [translation mine]; cf. hadith 11 on p. 149)

Abū Shaqqa's text suggests the tension between the legal and the moral aspects of the law, which was also obvious in the interview with the representative of the Islamic Liberation Party, Fu'ād Ḥussain.

Abū Shaqqa also refers to the hadith mentioned by Ibn Kathīr about the Prophet's permission to ʿUmar for men to hit their wives. In Abū Shaqqa's understanding this hadith indicates that husbands should not hit their wives. To strengthen this view he quotes another hadith where the Prophet urges men *not* to beat their wives as if they were slaves (hadith 10 on p. 149) and then have sexual relations with them in the night.[13] Abū Shaqqa reflects: 'This hadith points out that this practice [of hitting] is not suitable in view of the nature of the relationship between the spouses which attains to the ultimate level of mutual approach and friendly relations' (Abū Shaqqa 1990 vol. VI: 245).

Abū Shaqqa's project is to investigate the sources of Islam but in most cases he also quotes the views of prominent scholars. He demonstrates that Islamic scholars such as Ibn Ḥajar al-ʿAsqalānī (d. 1449) and ash-Shawkānī (d. 1834) regarded the physical punishment of women as applying only to extraordinary cases. It is interesting to note that Abū Shaqqa refers to al-Jaṣṣāṣ (d. 981) who says: 'A non-violent blow with *siwāk* [a small stick used to clean the teeth] or similar. This means that to hit with any other means is legally [Islamically] forbidden' (quoted in Abū Shaqqa 1990 vol. VI: 247 [translation mine]).[14]

Abū Shaqqa's method is to 'turn back to the sources, the Koran and the Sunna', i.e. 'the past reproduced in the present', and he further tends to rely on the earliest commentary of the Koran, Ibn ʿAbbās, as an indicator of early Islamic attitudes. Thus while many medieval Islamic scholars discussed the matter of the physical punishment of women in terms of general disobedience of the wife towards her husband, Abu Shaqqa returns to Ibn ʿAbbās understanding of punishment in matters of adultery or suspicions of adultery.

Contemporary scholars such as al-Ghazzālī, Abū Shaqqa and also al-Qaraḍāwī all belong to the *ikhwān* stream of thought and are all Egyptians. The works of these three scholars must be understood in terms of change. It is interesting to note that all three have lived in the Arab world and their tendency towards change might therefore be seen in terms of the general globalisation process of western local thought. Particularly in Abū Shaqqa's work, the results of his method of 'the past reproduced in the present' seem to be influenced by the 'western cultural base pattern'. This might not be the whole picture as one can deduce that due to the globalisation process there is an awareness among Islamic scholars, even in the Muslim world, of the non-Muslim or western notion of Islam as a religion hostile to women. The western influence on the one hand and the awareness of non-Muslim hostility towards Islam on the other, seem to be driving forces in the scholars' selection of hadiths and the interpretation of these hadiths. This process of selection and the reasons behind it can once again be understood in terms of Hjärpe's basket metaphor.

Islamists in Europe

In my discussions with Arab Islamists in Europe I often met the same attitudes as I found in the works of Abū Shaqqa. Khadīja wrote in the questionnaire:

> The Messenger of God said that the best among you do not hit, and he himself did never hit any woman or any servant in his whole life. When God and His Messenger lay down rules, then they lay down these rules for the whole humanity, to be suitable for all times to come, and for what is inside every human being. There are some men who have a hot temper, and there are women who are not kept straight with nice words only. But physical punishment is the last step in treating a problematic relationship, as the Koran says: (1) warn them, (2) separate from them sexually, (3) then hit them. And the blow has to be with *siwāk* or with the corner of a scarf.

It is interesting to note that the reference to the *siwāk* is very common among contemporary Islamists in Europe and even in the Muslim world. All the Islamists I interviewed from the various Islamic directions referred to the *siwāk*. I have, however, still not found any hadith in support of this, and it seems that Jaṣṣāṣ' regulation, which is most probably an *ijtihād*, has penetrated Islamic thought in this matter. In my discussions with Khadīja I asked her what she meant by 'a woman who does not keep straight'. She answered that the matter of physical punishment for a disobedient wife is of a sexual nature. 'A woman who does not keep straight' means in her view, a woman who talks and deals with men without her husband's approval and in a way that gives her husband reason to be suspicious of her. However, Khadīja does not believe this to pertain to women in general as most women are chaste and keep up a strict moral life. 'The matter of physical punishment', she says, 'is only for very particular cases.'

In this statement it seems obvious that Khadīja has adhered to Abū Shaqqa's rather than Ibn Kathīr's and even Zainab al-Ghazzālī's ideas.

Amal, in her answers to the questionnaire, explained:

> The matter of physical punishment was mentioned in the context of *nushūz* which in my understanding means the very bad behaviour when dealing with other men (without reaching the act of adultery). Hitting comes after the advice and other methods. Many scholars have explained that the beating should be very gentle without causing any bodily harm.

It seems that most Islamists see this matter in sexual terms, linked to acts of sexual immorality. This is also confirmed by the late Muḥammad al-Ghazzālī when he was interviewed by Akbar Aḥmad in the television programme, *Living Islam*, in the early 1990s. In the programme he explained that a man could only hit his wife for two reasons: either if she rejected him sexually or if she let men whom her husband despises into the house. Muḥammad al-Ghazzālī's view therefore coincides with that of Ibn ʿAbbās interpreted through Ābādī. The emphasis on husbands' sexual rights might be attributable to the idea of chastity in Islamic society. Many Islamists referred to the sexual relationship between the spouses as part of the worship of God (*ʿibādāt*). One respondent said: 'If a man has sexual intercourse with his wife before he goes out of the house, he has no need of looking at other women in a sexual manner.'

In the case of the physical punishment of women, there seems to have been a development from early Islamic history, when female 'disloyalty and ill-conduct' were regarded as sexual offences towards the husband, to include women's disobedience in general. However, as Abū Shaqqa and Muḥammad al-Ghazzālī return to an ancient understanding of the term *nushūz*, so do most Islamists living in Europe. On the one hand, this might be seen as a result of the globalisation process by which western local ideas come to dominate and in which physical punishment might be regarded as understandable in case of adultery. Due to the influence of these ideas, the selection from 'the basket' tends to involve those traditions compatible with them. On the other hand, the method of 'returning to the Koran and Sunna', i.e. 'the past reproduced in the present', is also a factor as this return to an earlier form of understanding is more compatible with the contemporary moral norm (*ʿurf*).

A wife's obedience to her husband

A Muslim woman's obedience to her husband as a religious obligation is suggested in the Koran in verse 4: 34. However, as I have already pointed out, this verse has been interpreted in terms of adultery or the threat of adultery. One other reference to wives' obedience to their husbands is found in the hadith-literature in Ibn ʿUmar's story of the woman who came to the Prophet and asked him about a wife's obligation to her husband (hadith 1 on p. 146). I suspect that it is from this hadith that the notion of *ṭāʿat az-zawj* (obedience to the husband) has become prominent in 'Arabic' Islam. The need to ask the husband's permission to go out of the house is probably also derived from this particular hadith. A common notion in Islamic law is 'the house of obedience' (*bait aṭ-ṭāʿa*), a merging of the two notions of obedience to the husband and the requirement for the husband's permission to be sought before a woman goes out of the house, which has come to mean, 'the husband's house to which a woman, in case of unlawful desertion, must return' (Wehr 1980: 573).[15]

It is interesting to note that despite the strong notion of women's obedience in the 'Arab cultural base pattern', I have observed that the hadith by Ibn ʿUmar, which has an authentic (*ṣaḥīḥ*) narrator chain, is less referred to in contemporary Arab Islamist literature and in discussions than two other hadiths which are not classified as authentic but merely as good (*ḥasan*). These are often repeated in literature and in discussions about gender relations as well as in Friday sermons. Both of these hadiths are rendered in az-Zuḥailī's jurisprudential work, and although he writes in a footnote that their narrator chains are not authentic (*ṣaḥīḥ*), he uses them to explain the marital relationship in Islam. This is an example of the tendency to use even hadiths which are not authentic (*ṣaḥīḥ*) in order to fortify well-established beliefs. The two hadiths related from the Prophet are as follows:

1 If I were to order someone to bow down to someone, I would order the woman to bow down to her husband.
(Sunan at-Tirmidhī, Book of Foster Relationship, no. 1079; Sunan Ibn Mājah, Book of Marriage, no. 1842)[16]
2 If a woman dies and her husband is satisfied with her she will enter Paradise.
(Sunan at-Tirmidhī, Book of Foster Relationship, no. 1081; Sunan Ibn Majah, Book of Marriage, no. 1844)[17]

The first hadith has been used as evidence of men's superiority over women and women's obedience to their husbands, and I have come across this particular hadith in many of my discussions. The question is whether the content (*matn*) is compatible with the Islamic message that human beings should only bow down to God (K.41: 37; 27: 24; 22: 77; 41: 37). In my discussion with a leading Arab Islamist living in France, I asked her opinion about this hadith without mentioning that it was not authentic (*ṣaḥīḥ*). She explained that the hadith had to be understood in metaphorical terms: 'It does not mean that we should actually bow down to men, but it is only a picture of the strong relationship between men and women in marriage, and men's great responsibility in marital life.' I then told her that the hadith was not authentic, and she reflected:

> For me that does not matter, as I never understood this hadith to mean that men should have power over women. For non-Muslims, however, I suppose it matters, as they have difficulties in distinguishing between images and the reality, particularly when it comes to Islamic issues. They tend to take the texts literally without understanding that the span in time and place changes the way to look at the text.

This woman's ability to understand this particular text as compatible with the present situation of life in France is not shared by many women living in Arab countries. When it comes to Islamists in Muslim countries, I have observed in my fieldwork that even female Islamists tend to accept and promote a traditional understanding of hadiths of this kind. In my fieldwork in Jordan in the beginning of the 1990s, it was my experience that many women stressed 'a wife's obedience to her husband'. My meeting with foreign Muslim students in Jordan also reinforced this picture. A group of female sharia students, who had come from various non-Arabic speaking countries in order to learn Arabic, expressed their frustration with what they called 'the Arab's obsession with women's obedience to men'. From an outsider's view, Arab Islamist women can be regarded as having internalised an androcentric world-view. Although it would be easy to agree with this explanation, one should be aware that the same applies to men. Men are usually brought up and educated by women, and men's traditional world-view is therefore very much a product of an education given by women. In a wider perspective, indoctrination by and internalisation of a world-view, whether male-centred, female-centred or gender-neutral, applies to most societies and cultures.

It is interesting to note that Sara Johnsdotter, a Swedish anthropologist who has conducted fieldwork in an immigrant area in Sweden, has observed that although on an ideological level most Muslim women would express the necessity of obedience towards their husbands, on a practical level the situation is different. In her interviews with Arab Muslim women they expressed the belief that their obligation was to obey their husbands. With the follow-up questions, however, she discovered that this obedience means to do 'their duties', i.e. what is expected of them within the framework of traditional gender roles. If their husbands demanded duties outside this framework they would not agree. She further observed that most women's acceptance of their husbands' authority to make certain decisions for them was built on a respect for their husbands and a belief that the husbands had more experience in certain areas, and therefore were in a better position than themselves to judge right from wrong in these particular areas. In those cases where the man used his authority against the will of the woman, she would frown for some days until he came and asked her forgiveness.[18] Johnsdotter's observations indicate how certain concepts are manifest and how various patterns of behaviour are moulded within such concepts.

As for the second hadith which states that a husband should be satisfied by his wife, it has been referred to and used as an argument *against* female activities in the wider society. I will discuss this matter below, but first I will give a brief account of how this hadith has been used to reinforce the idea of male superiority over women. During a stay in Jordan in 1991 and 1992, this hadith was often referred to in order to explain the role of women and it is worth noting that women stressed this more than men. Among Muslims in general, I discovered that the main idea of a woman's role was to stay at home and perform domestic work, often with reference to this hadith. Likewise, in the circles of the *salafī* movement this notion of the woman's domestic role was maintained. However, among many other Islamists I observed another pattern. Islamists close to the Muslim Brotherhood regarded this hadith more in terms of general gender relations in which women should accept their husbands' decisions in matters of disagreements between the spouses. As for female activities in wider society, this was promoted by most members and sympathisers of the Muslim Brotherhood at least on the ideological level.

Similarly to many other Islamists, al-Ghannūshī expressed an opinion concerning the issue of female obedience to the husband: that this obedience is 'obedience which is not in disobedience to sharia'. However, in continuing his argument al-Ghannūshī showed himself to be at odds with many other Arab Islamists. While other Islamists tend to regard the matter of obedience in legal terms, that which is allowed and that which is forbidden, al-Ghannūshī looks upon it mainly in moral terms. He explains that 'a wife's obedience has to be in *maʿrūf*, i.e. that which is canonised and that which is common (*mutaʿārif*) in customs (*ʿurf*).' He gives the example that in some environments there is a custom (*ʿurf*) that women should not do housework. In this situation the husband cannot force her to do the housework, and it is not disobedience if she refuses. He states that 'what is meant by *maʿrūf* is that which is common (*mutaʿārif*) in the frame of sharia.' al-Ghannūshī's statement is wholly indicative of the connection between *ʿurf* and *maʿrūf* where *ʿurf* refers to *moral* verbalised or non-verbalised customs relevant for any particular time and place. I believe his interpretation opens up the possibility of a reinterpretation or a reselection of legal decisions which emphasise contemporary moral codes acceptable within Islamist discourse. In the European context, the gap between *what exists*, i.e. legal decisions, and *what should be*, i.e. moral judgements, might be narrowed through such reinterpretation or reselection for the establishment of a minority legislation.

Islamists in Europe

In my discussion with common Arab Islamists in Europe they tended to regard a wife's obedience to her husband as a matter which was solely about conflict resolution. In the questionnaire I asked: 'How do you understand the Islamic concept of "a wife's obedience to her husband"?' Most answers were vague, indicating that a woman should obey her husband within the limits of the Koran and Sunna. Some people also wrote about the necessity of one head in order to maintain peace and harmony in the family. Notably, there was no great discrepancy between male and female answers. Some, men and women, expressed the view that this obedience does not indicate a master/slave relationship. Amal explained that 'it is not a matter of blind absolute obedience. It may be a prevention of a never-ending argument.'

Khadīja's answer is of interest as she introduces an emotional and dialectical understanding of the concept. She says:

> I understand by 'a wife's obedience to her husband' that mutual understanding, mutual consultation and understanding must as far as possible be within the framework of love and mercy. If it happens that there is a disagreement between me and my husband and he persists in his view, then I would obey him as far as it is not in disobedience to God. I obey him one time and the next time he surrenders to my view. This is how married life is [translation mine].

I find Khadīja's answer interesting as in her other responses she is more bound to the views of the Muslim Brotherhood. She sometimes even tends to have a literary and not a psychological approach to the Islamic sources. One could also add that her approach is androcentric, as she adheres to the Muslim Brotherhood's understanding of Islam, an understanding which is mainly based on male interpretations. In this matter, however, her answer is based less on the sources and more on her own practical experience. When I confronted her with my impression of her answers, she claimed that she had also been literal in this answer. She said:

> In the Koran I found all the terms I have stated here, mutual understanding, mutual consultation and understanding. Is this not to be literal in approach? However, this is what I understand of the concept [a wife's obedience to her husband]. For me obedience has nothing to do with terror and oppression. For me obedience to my husband means mutual understanding because we have a common aim in life [translation mine].

Maryam, a natural scientist from the Middle East, has lived in Scandinavia for more than ten years, and she has no group affiliation. When I discussed the matter of a wife's obedience to her husband, she said:

> For Scandinavians and westerners in general the word obedience has a negative connotation. Obedience to somebody is something terrible in their eyes. One who obeys is weak, and I believe this has to do with the idea of equality which is very strong in Scandinavian countries. It thus has to do with attitude. For us Muslims it is a virtue to obey parents, older people, etc. The problem with the translation from Arabic to Scandinavian languages is thus not the problem of finding the correct wording but it has to do with attitudes [translation mine].

A Scandinavian convert to Islam who was taking part in the discussion remarked that even in Scandinavia people are obedient, but this particular obedience is a form of invisible obedience. 'Scandinavian people,' she says, 'tend to obey non-personal injunctions.' She claimed that Scandinavians will often follow with blind obedience what is stated in advertisements or what non-personal institutions recommend. Her conclusion is thus that it is more the concept of obedience that Scandinavians reject, rather than the practical act of obedience. It is interesting to observe how differences in attitudes and differences in perceptions of concepts create misunderstanding and hostility between various social groups. In Scandinavia it is particularly the idea promoted by many Muslims of a wife's obedience to her husband which fuels the debate about whether Islam is a religion hostile to women or not. This matter must be linked to the problem of translating concepts from one language to another, as concepts which convey cultural values tend to change when they encounter different values in a new cultural context.

In my discussion with Darsh, I linked the issue of a wife's obedience to her husband to the question of a woman's work outside the home. I asked him whether a woman who goes out to study or work against her husband's will might be considered disobedient to her husband. He answered by referring to books written by Islamic scholars of *fiqh*, that some decades ago in Egypt there was a woman who went to court as her husband forbade her to work as a teacher. The sharia court judged that she was not disobedient to her husband as the husband was fully aware that she was a teacher and that she was working as a teacher at the time of their marriage. Darsh referred to a principle which says that *al-maʿrūf ʿurfan kal-mashrūṭ sharṭan.* He explained this principle as meaning that the fact that this woman was working was regarded as the normal custom, so that the norm becomes the dominant factor. The husband accepted that she was teaching when he married her and that implies his agreement that she should have the full right to continue working even after marriage.

The importance of education in a western context might have led Darsh to conclude that women are not disobeying their men if they continue to work or study despite their husbands' disapproval. During our discussion he also mentioned the importance of women being educated as women are the educators of the children. If the mother does not understand the society around her she might not be able to fulfil her educational role. It is interesting to note that although the question I posed was a general one, Darsh's answer pointed to a particular legal case which probably cannot be used to form a general ruling on women's work. As Darsh was an independent scholar and not bound by any 'social organisation' according to Barth's conceptualisations, he seems to have been free to select and reformulate notions to a great extent, as will also be shown in later chapters of this study.

In the discussion of the education of women, it is important to be aware that hadiths about the importance of education for women and men alike have come to play a role in the modern Islamic conception of the Muslim woman's role in society. This illustrates the basket metaphor, where traditions and texts which reflect social norms are selected in order to foster a religious practice compatible with society. The influence from western society seems to be stronger than the 'Arab cultural base pattern' in this matter, where few women were entitled to an education up to as late as the 1960s and 1970s in certain Arab countries.

Islamist gendered division of labour

How does the 'male/female' pattern manifest itself among Arab Islamists in western countries? Islamist culture is outstanding in a Muslim context in that a great number of women have higher education. With the exception of many *salafīs* who do not attach any specific importance to formal higher education for females, most other Islamists, particularly those belonging to the *ikhwān* and *post-ikhwān* trends, regard higher education for male and female alike as an individual religious obligation (*farḍ ʿayn*). In the Koran men are given an explicit social role, namely that of the provider for the family (K.4: 34), and many Muslims are therefore of the opinion that even if a woman works outside the home the money she earns is hers to use and should not be part of the household's spendings. As Wadud-Muhsin has observed, the role of women, on the other hand, is not explicitly stated in the Koran (Wadud-Muhsin 1992). In the hadith literature there are some indications of the woman's role as the *administrator* of the household. One of the few hadiths on the issue is narrated by Ibn ʿUmar in hadith 5 on p. 148.

as-Sayyid Sābiq's jurisprudential work in three volumes, *The Jurisprudence of Sunna* deals with the daily worship of God (*ʿibadāt*) as well as social matters such as marriage, divorce, custody of children, etc. (*muʿāmalāt*), and is a guide for Muslims' everyday life. The work is widely read not only by Islamists but also by Arabic-speaking Muslims in general, and as parts of the work have recently been translated into English it has acquired a wider audience.

Sābiq discusses rules and regulations within the framework of the four Sunnī law schools, but his own preferences clearly influence his emphases and conclusions. In the chapter 'The woman's service towards her husband', he refers to two hadiths which justify his view of women's domestic role, not only as managers of the household but also as workers responsible for cooking, cleaning, taking care of children, etc. (Sābiq 1985 vol. II: 201–3). The first hadith tells the story of how Fāṭima, the daughter of the Prophet, came to her father and asked for a domestic servant as she had heard that he had acquired some new slaves. As the Prophet was not at home, he received her message and later he went to her home and addressed both Fāṭima and ʿAlī:

> Should I not guide you [ʿAlī and Fāṭima] to something which is better than that which you asked for: when you go to your beds, say: *subḥānallāh* (God be praised) thirty-three times, say: *al-ḥamdulillāh* (thank God) thirty-three times and say: *allāhu akbār* thirty-three times. This is better for you than a servant.
>
> (Sābiq 1985 vol. II: 202 [translation mine]; al-Bukhārī, Book of Virtues, no. 3429 and Book of Provision, no. 4942; Sunan Abī Dāwud, Book of Manners, no. 4403; Musnad Aḥmad, *musnad al-ʿashara*, no. 1085)[19]

It is interesting to note that although the grammatical use of dual references suggests that this hadith is directed to both ʿAlī and Fāṭima, Sābiq sees the hadith in a social context only and as directed particularly to Fāṭima. He thus interprets its content as a divine evidence of women's destined domestic role. However, it is apparent that this hadith can be viewed from different perspectives. From a spiritual point of view, the hadith can be interpreted as showing how the Prophet, who himself was modest and pious, wanted his own daughter and son-in-law to be examples of modesty and piety in a time of economic strength. The interpretation of this hadith depends on whether one emphasises its spiritual or its social message.

The story of Fāṭima's request for a servant indicates that *grinding of corn* was part of women's work at that time. However, does that imply that all domestic work is a divine decree destined for women in general? The story rather gives a picture of general social roles in seventh century Arabia, and there is nothing in it which indicates that domestic work was only for women. On the contrary, the fact that the Prophet speaks to both ʿAlī and Fāṭima, in grammatical duals, might indicate that household management and work could be a common responsibility for men and women. A hadith dealing with how the Prophet participated in domestic work points to such an interpretation. ʿĀʾisha is reported to have been asked about what the Prophet used to do at home. She answered: 'He used to sew his garment, repair his sandal, and do what men used to do in their homes.' (Musnad Aḥmad, *bāqi musnad al-ansār*, no. 23756 and no. 25039). We also know that Khadīja, the first wife of the Prophet, was a rich businesswoman. Although she hired men to lead her caravans, she was herself active in the trade business (Ibn Isḥāq, translated by Guillaume 1990: 83). It seems that at the advent of Islam there were no absolute *fixed* gender roles placing only men in the public sphere, and only women in the private, domestic sphere. Furthermore, the lack of Koranic injunctions or hadiths specifically defining the social role of women indicates flexibility of gender roles in society.

The second hadith to which Sābiq refers in order to give evidence from the Islamic sources that women's main social role is domestic work, is a hadith about Asmāʾ, the daughter of Abū Bakr, the second Caliph. After her marriage she had to help her husband with his horse, and she had to walk a long distance every day in order to feed and water it. After a while Abū Bakr sent her somebody to take over the horse's daily care. When she was released from this responsibility, she said: 'And it was as if he [Abū Bakr] had relieved me from bondage.' (al-Bukhārī, Book of Marriage: no. 4823) Sābiq concludes from these two hadiths: 'And in these two hadiths are that which points out that a woman's obligation is to do the domestic work, as also it is obligatory for the husband to spend [his money] on her' (Sābiq 1985 vol. II: 202 [translation mine]).

It is interesting to note that, whereas Sābiq refers to the latter hadith to prove that women's place is in the domestic sphere, at-Turābī, in his book on Muslim women, points to this hadith as proof that women *can* work outside the home, because Asmāʾ went out of the house every day to care for the horse (at-Turābī n.d.: 16). I believe that these two opposite interpretations of one single hadith do not indicate anything other than that these texts have various messages, and one person in a certain time and place might emphasise one aspect of the text whereas another person in another time and place might emphasise other aspects. Moreover, I see this hadith in terms of a reinforcement of the flexibility of gender roles in Islam. Because at-Turābī intends to promote a view of female participation in wider society, he pays attention to those matters in the Koran and the hadiths which can support his arguments, while Sābiq looks for those which support his view that women should stay within the domestic sphere. In this particular hadith he draws attention to the fact that Asmāʾ's work outside the home was with her *husband's* horse. Thus, in his view her work was still within the domestic sphere. Sābiq says:

> The foundation which Islam establishes for the cooperation between the spouses and the organisation of life between them is a biological and natural foundation. The man is capable of doing the hard labour and earning outside the house. The woman, on the other hand is capable of household management, bringing up the children, promoting means for homely comfort and homely peace. So, the man is charged with that which is suitable for him and the woman is charged with that which is natural for her. In this manner the household is organised in the domestic and the public fields in order that neither of the spouses can find any reason for splitting the household.
>
> (Sābiq 1985 vol. II: 201–2 [translation mine])

The belief that women's main responsibilities are within the domestic domain which implies housework and childcare is widespread among Muslims, particularly in the Arab world. However, it is important to draw attention to the fact that with regard to the upbringing of children, many of the hadiths concerning this are directed to men as well as to women (Roald 1994: 153). Thus, men and women might be seen as having a shared responsibility in childcare despite the traditional Muslim claim, which is influenced by the 'Arab cultural base pattern', that children's upbringing is mainly the responsibility of women.

The question to pose is whether it is possible to find any indication in the Islamic sources that there is a divine order of female responsibilities. As Wadud-Muhsin has observed, no specific female social role is mentioned in the Koran. As for the hadith literature, on the other hand, women are told to be 'managers' of the domestic sphere as laid down in the hadith above, which states that 'the woman is a protector of her husband's house and his children'. However, except for this hadith and some scattered remarks on what women used to do in seventh century

Arabia, I have not found any specific injunctions directed towards women in general. This might have to do with the fact that it was mainly slaves/servants who did most of the domestic work, and there was therefore no need to give much detail on this aspect of daily life. Such an argument, however, might lead to an understanding of the hadith literature as either time-bound in all aspects and therefore not valid in Islamic legislation, or socially time-bound and spiritually universal, meaning that in social matters one should not necessarily follow the social pattern which was particular for seventh century Arabia except that which is mentioned by the Prophet to be a specifically Islamic injunction. Asghar Ali Engineer has discussed this question, saying: 'The problem was that the sociological often became the theological and was defended as such even when the sociological conditions changed' (Engineer 1992: 6). He further states: 'The sharia should be seen both in its cultural context as well as in its normative transcendental spirit. Unfortunately, at present it is viewed more in its cultural context' (Engineer 1992: 14).

It is important to note that despite the ideal Islamic division of labour advocated by traditional forces and also by some Islamists, women have in general taken an active part in breadwinning activities although these activities can rarely be found in official statistics. In rural areas women have worked in the fields, whereas in urban areas many women have carried on trades on a smaller or larger scale. Women have sewed for each other, made food for each other and received either money or other services in return.

With social changes arising from new economic patterns, women have started to play a more active part in the official sphere of society. As in the western world, women in the Muslim world have invaded the official labour market. I have already suggested that this is first due to the fact that one salary is no longer regarded as enough to support a family, and second to the rise in female education. In the 1970s and the beginning of the 1980s female education tended to be a luxury for privileged members of Muslim society, but recently it has become the source of an enhancement in the household's economy. During my frequent visits to Jordan from 1985 onwards I observed that up to approximately 1992, it was common for women to work until they married or until they gave birth to their first child, whereas since then it has been more and more common for women to keep working even after having children. On my visit to Jordan in 1995 I also discovered that there is a new tendency for men largely only to marry women who have degrees, with a university degree favoured over a college degree. With Jordan facing increasing economic problems, the trend towards marrying well-educated women seems to be in the hope that women will be breadwinners together with their husbands.

Within the Islamic framework domestic work is idealised. In Muslim literature in general the woman as a housewife and an educator of her children is portrayed as the ideal woman whose fulfilment of domestic duties is just as much worship of God as is the man's breadwinning. However, Muslim women have said that in practice it seems that many Muslim men tend to 'judge according to a western standard', i.e. to have disrespect for women doing domestic work whereas women working outside the home are held in higher esteem. At one of the Islamist women conferences I attended in Britain in 1995, I met Fadhīla, an Iraqi woman, who had recently become interested in Islamic work. Her husband, she explained, was 'a common Muslim' (*muslim ʿādī*), an expression which according to her meant a person who performed his/her daily prayers and the obligatory fasting but was not active in any *daʿwa* work.[20] Fadhīla claimed that many common Muslims tend to value women in economic terms. She said that when she was working at home, her husband would not always trust her opinions whereas when she started to work she felt that he appreciated her judgements more. Likewise, before he would interfere in her affairs. She gives an example that sometimes he would forbid her to visit certain friends or he would decide matters on her behalf. She feels that he is much more perceptive to her social freedom than before. 'In Islam', she says, 'my value as a woman does not depend on whether I am part of the household's breadwinning or not. On the contrary, my role as a mother and a housewife is my main role in Islam and that which first and foremost grants me rewards in this world as well as in the Hereafter.'

Fadhīla further explained that what is needed among Muslims is a change of attitude:

> We [Muslim women] have to be judged according to the Islamic standard, which means that a woman who works at home and educates her children should just as much be regarded as being capable of deciding her own affairs as does a woman working outside of the home.

Fadhīla's ambition was that her husband would become more active in Islamic work as that would 'change his attitude towards women'. This comment was part of a larger discussion among a group of women at the conference. Another woman whose husband is an Islamist confirmed that among 'common' Muslims disrespect for women was often the case. In her view, Islamists have another standard of values. She asserts:

> Among Islamists it is not so much the economic matter which is important. Islamic activism and higher education for women count more. A woman who on the one hand is active in Islamic work, giving lectures on different levels, and has a substantial knowledge of Islam, or on the other hand has a higher education which she uses on the path of God (*fī s-sabīlillāh*), she will be highly respected, not only

> by her own husband but also by Islamists in general. Thus, it does not come down to such a simple matter as economy but how one is evaluated depends on one's actions. This, in my view, is the right attitude, as the role of a Muslim woman is not only to stay at home doing domestic work. God the Almighty asks us to work for Him, and in divergent societies different activities are demanded and He will judge us according to our actions [translation mine].

It seems that in Muslim society as in most other societies women who have their own source of income will be more free to follow their own paths, both as they do not feel economically dependent on their husbands and as they are not threatened by the loss of economic security, for instance through divorce. However, I believe that this does not always have to be the case. During my discussions with female Islamists I realised that in the Islamic understanding of the division of labour many of them had a notion of a common economy in marriage. Amal said that 'the money my husband earns is as much mine as his'. In her opinion, a woman's pregnancies and the child-rearing that follows are all-consuming tasks which tend to absorb most of her energies. She therefore believes that if the economic situation allows a woman to stay at home in these demanding periods it is better for both her and the children. I have observed that Amal's view of the division of labour and the economics of marriage is typical of many Islamist women and men living in Europe. At the same time, in nearly all my interviews with Arab Islamists, they pointed out that there is nothing wrong with a woman working if she wants to or if the economic situation of the family demands two incomes.

A matter of importance which I gradually came to realise is that female Islamists have a different view of paid work than what I had expected. Most of them stressed the importance of being active in society, but by this activity they did not necessarily mean paid work. This might of course have to do with the fact that many male Islamists living in Europe are highly educated and thus capable of supporting their families without the help of an extra salary. However, I believe that it has less to do with these women's actual economic situation than with a general attitude towards paid work for Muslim women – an attitude which I observed not only among Islamists but also among many Muslim women in general. For instance, in densely populated immigrant areas in Sweden, the Swedish authorities make an effort to give migrant women the opportunity to get out of their houses to learn Swedish or to work in one form or another. However, the women themselves are usually not interested in such projects as they regard their domestic work and activities within the Muslim community as more important. This, together with Amal's statement that 'the money my husband earns is as much mine as his', gives an indication of how the man's role as provider for the family is accepted by many Muslim women.

There are two issues at stake in the matter of Muslim women in paid work. First, we have to look at situations where women have to work in order for the family to have a decent lifestyle as is the case in many western countries. In this matter most Islamists recognise the necessity of sharing economic responsibilities as well as domestic activities. However, as was pointed out by many women, this acknowledgement was mainly theoretical in the case of many men, since in practice domestic activities were regarded as first and foremost a woman's responsibility. Nasra, a Tunisian woman with small children who lives in Europe, sees her situation in a general perception of women's oppression. She claims that the consequence of women working outside the home is that at the end of the day Muslim women are just as oppressed as western non-Muslim women, who have to face a double burden of responsibilities. She continues, saying that while women share men's economic responsibilities, men do not share women's. She says: 'You will always hear husbands, Muslims and non-Muslims alike, saying, "We are helping at home", but how can help be more than a drop in the ocean, when what we need is shared responsibilities?'

But while Nasra is forced into the labour market much against her will, some female Islamists living in western countries want to work outside the home when their children are grown up. In Britain, for instance, many female Islamists do voluntary work in Islamic corporations such as Islamic schools, Islamic publishing houses, Islamic welfare organisations etc. In these cases, women would not expect men to share their domestic work since they regard their work outside the home as being done in their spare time.

The pattern of an ideal gendered division of labour among Islamists is regarded as being based upon a divine decree, based mainly on traditional Koran interpretations, sharia rulings and on scholarly works, such as for instance Sābiq's and az-Zuḥailī's. As discussed above, the Koran explicitly states that men are responsible for the economic support of the family. In the Koran the only explicit task mentioned for women is child-bearing, but in hadiths women are given the responsibility of being managers of the domestic domain without any further specifications. The Islamic sources offer no rationale for this division of labour, but immediately preceding the statement about men's economic responsibility it is stated: 'Men are responsible for/in charge of women with what God has preferred some of them over others' (K.4: 34). The interpretation of this statement has varied. The most common interpretation is linked to the hadith where the Prophet says first that 'the majority of people in the hell-fire are women' and second that 'women are incomplete in intellect and religion' (*ʿaql wa dīn*), as discussed on pp. 131–5.

Reflections

In matters of gender relations there are various ideas in the Islamic sources. As with gender attitudes, the prevalent ideas are based on texts which in different contexts have been latent in the debate. It is important to note that existing social attitudes are unconscious factors in the interpretation of social issues in the Islamic texts, as the debate on the verse 4: 34 indicates. When circumstances change, attitudes are modified to fit the existing situation. The various cultural patterns actively influence the interpretation of the text. As has been shown above in the example of the physical punishment of women, where previous Islamic attitudes seem to have been more compatible with contemporary attitudes than the classical scholars' interpretations, the method of 'returning to the Koran and the Sunna' makes it possible to select alternative interpretations more in line with the 'western cultural base pattern' which totally condemns physical punishment in general. This again conforms to the basket metaphor where those traditions and texts relevant to the present situation and in conformity with existing attitudes are selected and used in the discussion. It is noteworthy that there is a correspondence in attitude between the classical scholars of early Islam and modern Islamists, whereas many established medieval scholars' arguments tend to be dismissed in the modern debate.

The tension between ideological concepts and actual practices is also important to bear in mind. As the texts on *qiwāma*, physical punishment, and 'obedience to the husband' exist, it seems necessary to agree with the common interpretation at least on an ideological level. On a practical level, however, the situation is different. I believe that in this tension between ideology and practice, new interpretations of social issues in the existing texts will emerge and modify the conceptual content.

In this chapter I have dealt with gender relations on a micro level. In the next chapter I will turn to gender relations on the level of macro society. Can a woman possibly be the leader of a Muslim state?

8 Women's political participation in Islam

With the coming of female Muslim leaders such as Benazir Bhutto, and with the increased demand for extended female political participation in the Muslim world in general and in the Arab world in particular, the matter of female involvement in politics on various levels has become a much debated issue. The hadith of the Prophet which says that the people who have a female leader will not succeed has been the foundation on which Islamic scholars have built their prohibition of female leadership (M. al-Ghazzālī 1989; az-Zuḥailī 1989; Sābiq 1985). Despite the sharia prohibition of female leadership, there have been many highly respected female leaders in Muslim history. Bouthaina Shaaban has researched this issue and she mentions names such as Shajarat ad-Durr from the times of the Crusades, Queen Orpha (d. 1090) in Yemen and Sultana Radia (thirteenth century) in Delhi (Shaaban 1995: 62–3). In our own time there have also been examples of female leadership in Muslim countries, such as in Bangladesh, Pakistan and Turkey. However, in Arabic-speaking countries no woman has yet been a leader of the state, although many Islamists remarked on the presence of women such as Jihān as-Sadāt, the wife of Anwar as-Sadāt in Egypt and Wasīla Burqība, the wife of Ḥabīb Burqība in Tunis, who have strongly influenced their husbands in their dealings with matters of state.

When it comes to female leadership, there seems to have been a contradiction between the ideal expressed in sharia and actual practices in Muslim state policies in certain periods of history. It is interesting to ask if there have been any writings about this historical controversy. Did the Islamic scholars react to female leadership or did they accept it either through appealing to an Islamic standard or for reasons of their own interest? These are questions which need an in-depth investigation into ancient manuscripts and this is outside the scope of my study. Instead I will focus on the contemporary debate and look into how the issue of female leadership is treated in a modern context.

The first incidence of importance was in Pakistan in the beginning of the 1960s. During the presidential election the Islamic movement in Pakistan, the Jama'at-i-Islami, supported Fāṭima Jinnāh, the sister of Muḥammad ʿAlī Jinnāh, the first president and founder of Pakistan. According to Saulat, the biographer of al-Mawdūdī, Jama'at-i-Islami 'after discussing the religious aspects of the issue in a detailed resolution, opined that under the present extraordinary circumstances it would be permissible in Islam to accept this selection' (Saulat 1979: 60). Jama'at-i-Islami met substantial criticism, mostly on religious grounds. al-Mawdūdī wrote an article in response to the criticism in the monthly journal, *Tarjuman al-Qur'an*, in which he produced quotations from the Koran, the hadith literature, and from Islamic law (al-Mawdūdī 1965: 2–16). However, rather than opening the way to an acceptance of female leadership in general, Jama'at-i-Islami treated Fāṭima Jinnāh's leadership as a special case due to her particular position and personality.[1]

The political empowerment of women can be looked at from various perspectives. Secular Muslim feminists focus on the top of the political ladder and thus promote female leadership, whereas Islamist women seek empowerment on the lower rungs of the ladder so that many women are politically activated. This was confirmed by my fieldwork in Jordan in 1991–2, when I discovered that Islamist women would regard female political empowerment in terms of political participation exclusively at the lower levels. The blockage of women's entry into politics was the major problem noted, followed by the lack of political education among women. When I asked a leading member of the Muslim Brotherhood why women were not involved in politics, he said that women in Jordan lacked sufficient political consciousness to be involved in official political activities. Leading Islamist women agreed with this statement, but they blamed it on the male Islamists who, in their view, had failed with respect to the educational programme for women in the movement.

The Muslim feminist, Fatima Mernissi, has dealt at length with the issue of female leadership. Her book *Women and Islam*[2] was originally published in French in 1987. In 1993 it was translated into Arabic under the title *al-ḥarīm as-siyāsī: an-nabī wa n-nisā'* (*The Political Woman: The Prophet and the Women*). On the first page Mernissi asks the question: 'Can a woman be a leader of Muslims?' In contrast to Islamist women who do not raise the question of top level leadership, Muslim feminists headed by Mernissi have made the leadership question a major issue in the battle for female empowerment in the Muslim world.

Mernissi investigates the hadith literature, and she finds that the only hadith which deals with this matter is a hadith included in al-Bukhārī's hadith collection. She remarks that as al-Bukhārī's collection is regarded as authentic (*ṣaḥīḥ*), the hadiths included in it are 'unassailable without proof to the contrary' (Mernissi 1987: 49). However, Mernissi has observed that this particular hadith on female leadership was transmitted by one person only, namely a manumitted slave, Abū Bakra. The hadith is related in at least three of the 'six authentic hadith-collections' in addition to in the hadith-collection *Musnad Aḥmad*. It states that Abū Bakra at the time of the Battle of the Camel said that when the Prophet Muḥammad heard that the Persians were ruled by a woman, he said: 'A people which has a woman as leader will never prosper.' (al-Bukhārī, Book of Maghāzī, no. 4073; Sunan an-Nisā'ī, Book of the Manner of Provision, no. 5293; Sunan at-Tirmidhī, Book of Trials, no. 2188; Musnad Aḥmad, *musnad al-baṣrīīn*, no. 19542)[3]

Mernissi goes into details of Abū Bakra's background in order to explore why he should make such a statement. As it is stated in the hadith that Abū Bakra recorded this saying of the Prophet during the period when ʿAlī ibn Abī Tālib was in conflict with ʿĀ'isha, she concludes that it came a quarter of a century after the death of the Prophet (Mernissi 1987: 50). Mernissi uses the classical non-controversial sources, such as aṭ-Ṭabarī (d. 923), Ibn Ḥajar al-ʿAsqalānī (d. 1449) and Ibn al-Athīr (d. 1233) to expose the weaknesses of Abū Bakra's hadith transmission. First, she suggests that Abū Bakra recorded this remark of the Prophet as an answer to ʿĀ'isha's pledge of allegiance against ʿAlī after the Battle of the Camel. According to Mernissi, by saying this he avoided becoming involved in the conflict (Mernissi 1987: 50–1). Second, Mernissi suggests that Abū Bakra should not be regarded as a reliable hadith transmitter as he was once flogged by the second caliph, ʿUmar, because he officially gave evidence in an adultery case where one of the four witnesses withdrew the testimony.[4] Mernissi concludes that Abū Bakra does not meet the required standards according to the rules concerning the reliability of a hadith transmitter (Mernissi 1987: 60–1). In addition to her discussion on Abū Bakra, Mernissi also notes that some of the classical Islamic scholars, such as for instance aṭ-Ṭabārī, took a position *against* the rejection of female leadership (Mernissi 1987: 61).

Mernissi's discussion of female leadership is of interest in an Islamist context. Although she is a secular feminist, Mernissi has entered the Islamist debate by using much the same methods and arguments as Islamists. First, she 'returns to the sources' as she investigates the hadith literature, thus by-passing the development of Islamic law. Second, she uses the classical method in hadith criticism of looking at the narrator chain (*isnād*) in order to authenticate hadiths. A significant difference is that she psychologically analyses the narrators in terms of a male/female perspective, claiming that some important narrators, such as the much revered Companion of the Prophet, Abū Huraira, are misogynists. This has aroused the anger of Islamists, particularly in Morocco, Mernissi's native country, and I would argue that although she stays within the broader limits of the Islamist discourse, she is balancing on the borderline. Many Islamists tend to disregard her work due to her 'disrespect' towards Islamic historical personalities. However, at the same time the content of her work has also become part of the ongoing discussion in contemporary Islam.

In Ḥasan at-Turābī's book on women, he not only consults the Koran and the hadiths but also other Islamic historical sources, and this is probably why he offers a greater rationale for female political participation than can be found in other Islamist literature. He refers to the incident of ʿUmar's death and the intense negotiations for finding a new leader after ʿUmar. According to at-Turābī, one of the Companions of the Prophet, ʿAbd ar-Raḥmān ibn ʿAuf, went around to Muslim tribes and listened to their opinions on the two candidates, Uthmān and ʿAlī. at-Turābī says: 'He consulted individuals and groups, privately as well as officially, and he even reached the Muslim women's private quarters' (at-Turābī n.d.: 16–17 [translation mine]).

In Arab Islamist literature the most prominent scholarly work on female leadership is Sheikh Muḥammad al-Ghazzālī's 1989 book, *as-sunna n-nabawīa bayna ahl al-fiqh wa ahl al-ḥadīth* (*The Prophetic Sunna between the People of Jurisprudence and the People of Hadith*). In this book, al-Ghazzālī gives his reactions to various common ideas about women concerning issues such as female leadership, the place of Muslim women in society, etc. In his discussion on female leadership, he takes as his starting point Ibn Ḥazm's (d. 1064) claim that Islam does not prohibit women from occupying any position except that of caliph (M. al-Ghazzālī 1989: 47). al-Ghazzālī writes that he has heard that scholars appeal to the Koranic verse that men are in charge of women (K.4: 34) to argue that it is forbidden for a woman to be a leader of any men in any activities. al-Ghazzālī strongly refutes this position, arguing that men's *qiwāma* applies only within the family. He then goes on to quote the hadith which says that 'A people which has a woman as a leader will not succeed', pointing out that according to Ibn Ḥazm's view, this hadith is solely a matter of the leadership of the state. al-Ghazzālī continues:

> I would like to give a more profound view of this hadith. We are not aiming to make women heads of countries or heads of governments, but we are aiming at one thing: namely, that the person who governs the country or the government is the best fitted person in the Umma.
> (M. al-Ghazzālī 1989: 48 [translation mine])

al-Ghazzālī regards the hadith on female leadership as authentic (*ṣaḥīḥ*) both in the narrator chain (*isnād*) and in content (*matn*), but he asks, 'what is its meaning?' He explains the background to the incident when the Prophet was supposed to have uttered this statement. According to al-Ghazzālī, it was expressed as a reaction to the news that a young Persian princess had inherited the throne after her father. al-Ghazzālī explains that this royal family 'did not know *shūrā* [consultation], neither did they respect opposing views' (M. al-Ghazzālī 1989: 49), and the Prophet's words have thus to be understood in the light of these historical facts. al-Ghazzālī then goes on to analyse the matter from a Koranic perspective. The Surah *Bee* in the Koran contains the story of Bilqīs, the queen of Sheba. al-Ghazzālī tells how this queen is depicted as a just and wise ruler. When the Prophet Sulaymān asks her to become a Muslim, she gathers her advisers to counsel her in the matter. al-Ghazzālī compares this Koranic story with the hadith, asking: 'Will a people fail who has a woman of this particular kind as a leader?' (M. al-Ghazzālī 1991: 50). Having offered this defence of female leadership, al-Ghazzālī continues:

> One more time I want to confirm that I am not among those who are supporting female leadership. . . . All I aim to do is to interpret the hadith and react against what is written in books. I also aim at preventing a contradiction between the Book [the Koran] and some common heritage.
>
> (M. al-Ghazzālī 1989: 50 [translation mine])

The manner in which al-Ghazzālī treats the issue of female leadership indicates its sensitivity. Whereas, on the one hand, he points at how a certain Koranic passage has been 'misunderstood', on the other, he finds it difficult to go the whole way and accept female leadership *in toto*. It might seem that al-Ghazzālī is just using the story of Bilqīs as it actually is a good indication on how a hadith has come to overrule the Koran. At the same time it might be that the idea of female leadership in Muslim society is too revolutionary a matter to be considered and al-Ghazzālī's turn-around has to be understood in this context.

It is interesting to note that al-Ghazzālī's main point is that women should stay at home taking care of their children as he thinks it is dangerous to leave childcare to others, for instance to maids, in order for women to pursue a career. However, in spite of this stance, al-Ghazzālī offers evidence in support of female leadership. I think this is because the book is a response to the growing *salafī* movement in the Arab world, and his main objective is to argue against the way in which the *salafīs* interpret the hadiths. While they often understand hadiths in a literal sense, al-Ghazzālī attempts to show that hadiths have to be understood within a context. It is interesting that in arguing his case, he particularly accentuates hadiths on women's issues. This would seem to confirm the Muslim feminist claim that it is particularly the hadiths on women which historically speaking have been most 'misinterpreted' by classical Muslim scholars.

With regard to the hadith cited above, it should be noted that whereas Mernissi is mainly traditional in her approach, i.e. she emphasises the narrator chains of the hadiths that she discusses, al-Ghazzālī has an hermeneutical approach to hadiths. He relates the hadith to its historical context and compares it to the Koranic text. Although this is also part of a traditional methodology, al-Ghazzālī exemplifies how new perceptions and selections from Islamic sacred and historical sources can bring new understanding of hadith material.

Jamal Badawi's book, *Gender Equity in Islam*, also deals with female leadership.[5] He rejects the idea that the Koranic verse 4: 34, which has been used to denounce female leadership, is sufficient evidence against it. Similarly to al-Ghazzālī, he regards the verse as applying to the family system rather than to the political system in society (Badawi 1995: 38). As for the hadith related by Abū Bakra, Badawi assumes that

> the Prophet's response to this news [of the Persian ruling family] may have been a statement about the impending doom of that unjust empire, which did take place later, and not about the issue of gender as it relates to leadership of the state in itself.
>
> (Badawi 1995: 39)

Concerning interpretations of hadiths, Badawi relies on a contemporary scholar, Zāfir al-Qāsimī, who wrote a book in 1974 entitled *niẓām al-ḥukm fī sh-sharīʿa wa t-tarīkh* (*The System of Rulings in Sharia and in History*). Badawi concludes according to al-Qāsimī's analysis that:

> One of the rules of interpretation known to Muslim scholars is that there are cases in which the determining factor in interpretation is the **specificity of the occasion** (of the hadith) and **not the generality of its wording**. Even if the generality of its wording is to be accepted that does not necessarily mean that a general rule is applicable, **categorically**, to any situation. As such, the hadith is not conclusive evidence of categorical exclusion.
>
> (Badawi 1995: 39 – his emphasis)

Badawi further rejects the argument used by many Islamic scholars that as women are not allowed to lead prayers in mixed gatherings, this means that they are not allowed to lead the state as well. Badawi argues that prayer is a 'purely religious act', whereas leading the state is a 'religiously based political act' (Badawi 1995: 40). He concludes in accordance with the above statement of the 'specificity of the occasion' as against 'the generality of its wording' that 'exclusion of women in one instance does not necessarily imply their exclusion in another' (Badawi 1995: 40). Although he states that 'given the format of Muslim prayer and its nature, it is not suitable for women to lead a mixed congregation', Badawi also mentions that there are exceptions to this rule. He refers to a hadith from Sunan Abī Dāwud, where a woman leads her household consisting of both men and women in prayer. He also writes in a footnote that particularly within the Ḥanbalī school, and as stated by Ibn Taimīya, 'it is permissible for an illiterate man to be led in prayers by a woman who is the reciter of the Qur'an in prayers in Ramadan, according to the more commonly known opinion of Aḥmad (Ibn Ḥanbal)' (Badawi 1995: 57–8, footnote 27).

Referring to al-Qāsimī's work, Badawi notes that a famous jurist (whose name is not mentioned) in Islamic history did not include being a male among the qualifications of the Imām (here: head of state) (Badawi 1995:

40 [al-Qāsimī 1974: 342]). Badawi further refers to a contemporary scholar who supports female leadership, M. I. Darwazah, who rejects the common argument that as few women in Muslim history actually participated in official social life, this should mean that women in general are not fitted to such a task. According to Badawi Darwazah argues that women did not participate in social life due to 'the nature of social life at that time' (Badawi 1995: 40).[6] Badawi does not explicitly state his own opinion on the question of female leadership but rather builds on the arguments of others, referring to scholars such as al-Qāsimī and Darwazah. He does, however, imply a vague objection to female leadership when he talks about the obligations of leaders, such as being involved in confidential meetings with other state leaders who are mostly men. He says:

> Such heavy and secluded involvement of women with men and its necessary format may not be consistent with Islamic guidelines related to the proper interaction between the *genders* and to the priority of *feminine* functions at home and their value to society.
>
> (Badawi 1995: 40 – italics mine)

It is worth drawing attention to Badawi's use of concepts common in the western debate, such as gender. *Gender* as a term is generally used to depict the social sex, i.e. the social construction of sex roles, but Badawi uses the term as synonymous with sex, i.e. the biological sex. Moreover, Badawi's use of the term *feminine* to depict certain domestic activities reinforces the idea that, despite his rapprochement with the 'western cultural base pattern', the 'Arab cultural base pattern' influences his view of sex roles in society.

In his conclusion to the chapter on female leadership, Badawi becomes more outspoken as he reflects on reasons for the exclusion of women. He considers the main reasons to be 'individualism, ego-satisfaction, and the rejection of the validity of divine guidance in favour of other man-made philosophies, values or "isms"' (Badawi 1995: 41). He states:

> The ultimate objective of a Muslim man or woman, however, is to selflessly serve Allah and the Ummah in whatever appropriate capacity. In the incident of al-Hudaybiyah, Umm Salamah, a wife of the Prophet (P), played a role equal to what we would refer to today as 'chief advisor of the head of the state'.
>
> (Badawi 1995: 41)

Although Badawi seems to be in favour of female leadership, he is rather vague expressing his position. His stance must be understood in the light of the sensitivity of this matter in a Muslim context, in which the common view has generally been against women as heads of states. However, as Badawi has shown, the view among scholars in this matter has not been one of 'complete unanimity' (Badawi 1995: 58, footnote 28), as there are examples in Muslim history when contradictory views have been promoted. I think Badawi's book must be seen in the context of its audience. The book is written in English, to an English-speaking Muslim and non-Muslim public. The question to ask is whether Badawi would have been just as outspoken in an Arabic-speaking context? It is obvious that he builds on the heritage of al-Ghazzālī, as many of the ideas promoted by al-Ghazzālī in 1989 can be found in Badawi's work from 1995. In my view, Badawi has 'westernised' al-Ghazzālī's ideas in such a way that they have become culturally compatible with western society. I believe this 'westernisation' of ideas and the emphasis on the challenge posed by the views of historical Islamic scholars to commonly established notions, such as for instance Ibn Ḥazm's work, have to do with the minority situation of Muslims in the western world. In countries where Muslims are the majority population, one does not have to investigate matters which are working and functioning according to established cultural practices. In the new situation of being in a minority position, Muslims have to search more deeply to find ways of dealing with issues according to the existing cultural standards of the host society. Norms of Islam that were held by a minority in the past are preserved in texts that justify their position by referring to the Koran and hadiths. In the hands of contemporary writers these historical texts might suggest new norms which are more appropriate to the new cultural context than the norms imported from the old cultural context. Badawi's book is a prominent example of this as in most of the book he is actually presenting views opposed to established Islamic norms. On the question of leadership he can, by presenting scholarly differences of opinion in the matter, imply the possibility of female leadership in Islam, as Islamic jurisprudence is open to alternative possibilities in matters where there is no unanimous prohibition.

Rāshid al-Ghannūshī is also of the opinion that women can be leaders of states. In his own party *ḥaraka an-nahḍa* (the Renaissance Movement), al-Ghannūshī has opened the way for female participation on a high level, as women are part of the party's Advisory Council (*al-majlis ash-shūrā*). When I asked him about leadership, he distinguished between prayer leadership and state leadership, which he regarded as belonging to two different spheres. 'Prayer', he said, 'has to do with worship, whereas state affairs have to do with *maṣlaḥa* [welfare or common interest].' He went on:

> As for leading prayers, the rule is that men should lead, as the Prophet said 'Pray as you see me pray,' and we did not see any women as prayer leaders at that time. There might be some situations where women should lead men in prayer. For instance, if a woman is a learned person and her husband is totally ignorant of Islam, she might lead the prayer at least for a period until she has taught him. However, this is an extraordinary situation and not the Islamic origin [translation mine].

al-Ghannūshī sees state leadership as something totally different since what has to be considered in this matter is the most suitable person for the administration of Muslim affairs. He said, 'Generally, we see that in most institutions, men are more competent [than women] to take decisions as a whole'. He did not say whether he saw this as a result of biological factors or of socialisation or education, but in our further discussion it became apparent at least that he did not regard decision-making as subject to biological factors. al-Ghannūshī acknowledged that many scholars have decided that women cannot be leaders of states due to the Koranic verse on *qiwāma* and the hadith on female leadership. 'But', he said, 'there are other opinions about this matter. I have discussed this matter and the conclusion is that this is a *mubāḥ* (permitted) matter which has to be subject to the general Islamic view in Islam that one should elect the best person for leadership.' He continued:

> So if a woman supersedes all men in knowledge and political capacities, she can be a leader. In state leadership today there are no individual leaderships but partial leaderships. Ruling (*ḥukm*) is distributed in the parliament, in the army, in the high court etc. The president today has become a symbol of the state rather than having the power (*sulta*) of decision. As ruling has become spread out or diversified, the matter has become one of consultation (*shūrā*). A decision is not only a matter for one individual whether it is a man or a woman. This is an opinion of Sheikh Muḥammad al-Ghazzālī and other contemporary scholars. We can also find it in the Sunna of the Prophet and his Companions, as ʿUmar, the second caliph, appointed a woman as a judge of the market. Also, ʿĀ'isha was a leader of the army and under her leadership were a large group of Companions. If there was a clear proof that women should not be involved in politics such as some people say, we could not have found such examples among the Companions. What happened then was that scholars made *ijtihāds*, and these scholars were influenced by their own times. At that time women in general in Muslim society as well as among non-Muslims did not play an official role in society. Thus, this [that few women were in leading positions] was a matter of traditions (*ʿurf)* and not a matter of legislation [translation mine].

al-Ghannūshī represents a trend with a positive attitude towards female leadership. Moreover, his emphasis on *shūrā* is also remarkable. As shown above, he sees *shūrā* not only as a political matter but as a family matter as well. It is interesting that he also points to how scholars of earlier Islamic periods were influenced by traditions of their time, a point also made by Muslim feminists. I mentioned earlier that al-Ghannūshī's formal education is in philosophy, he studied both in Syria and in France, and he is presently living in Britain. I believe that his perspective has changed due to his western education, a change which is most apparent in his political ideas and particularly in his development of the concept of *shūrā*. It is also significant that al-Ghannūshī has put some of his ideas into practice since he was one of the first Islamists to introduce female participation in high positions in his own party. al-Ghannūshī is an example of how the 'western cultural base pattern' tends to influence Islamists living in western countries. This might be particularly true for him as he obtained his degrees in humanities from western universities and has thus been exposed to secular academic thought in a different way than have Islamists with degrees in natural sciences.

Sheikh Darsh, on the other hand, was of the opinion that a woman cannot be the leader of a state, although women can hold high positions in society. In my interview with him, Darsh emphasised that his rejection of female leadership does not mean that he is against female participation in wider society. He stated that his own daughters are highly educated. Darsh's view coincides with the view promoted by the Muslim Brotherhood in its issued statement from March 1994. The statement discusses women's right to vote and women's right to be members of representative councils. It refers to two Koranic verses: 'The men believers and the women believers are responsible for each other. They enjoin the good and forbid the evil' (K.9: 71), and 'Let there arise out of you a group of people inviting to all that is good and forbidding all evil. And it is they who are the successful' (K.3: 104). From these verses the Muslim Brotherhood draws the conclusion that women have the right both to vote in elections and to be elected (The Muslim Brotherhood 1994: 11). The statement further analyses various arguments for and against female participation in political affairs.

First, the report addresses the claim that women lack the necessary knowledge for participating in public affairs and thus are easily misled. The Muslim Brotherhood rejects this idea, saying that 'an ignorant woman is like an ignorant man. Not all women are ignorant and not all men are educated or experienced in public affairs' (The Muslim Brotherhood 1994: 12). The report further states:

> We are dealing with the basic right, not with the conditions that must be present in every candidate whether they be male or female. This is quite another issue. We call for the education and the enlightenment of both women and men, and the exertion of all possible efforts in this connection, this being an important objective and duty made binding by the sharia.
>
> (The Muslim Brotherhood 1994: 12)

It seems that the Muslim Brotherhood has recently changed its view on female participation in official political work. During my fieldwork in Jordan in 1991–2, I spoke with an Islamist woman who wanted to join the Islamic Action Front, the Islamists' political branch in Amman. She was not allowed to join the party, and she told me that this was because the more conservative block of the party was against female political participation (Roald 1994). Only two years later the Muslim Brotherhood in Egypt, which is the head of all regional branches of the movement, officially stated its support for female political participation in the report on women. The Muslim Brotherhood's call for the political education of both women and men indicates a change in attitude. My fieldwork experience from Jordan was that the leadership was less concerned about the political education of members in the female branch of the movement than in the male branch. This impression was confirmed by leading Islamist women, some of whom had left the movement but were still part of the Islamist environment, and some of whom were active within the movement but were critical of the leadership's policies towards the female branch. When I met some of these women in 1994–5 during my re-visits to Jordan, they told me that there had been 'revolutionary improvements' and that in their view the most important change was the change in leadership. It is also worth noting that the Islamic Action Front opened up to participation by women at around the same time as the publication of the Muslim Brotherhood's statement in 1994.

Second, the report deals with the commonly held belief that the female biological cycle and life cycle in general with menstruation, child-bearing and pregnancies might obstruct women's performance in councils to which they are elected (The Muslim Brotherhood 1994: 12). The Muslim Brotherhood refutes this argument as it says that even men might be 'subject to misjudgement or illnesses which may impair their performance' (The Muslim Brotherhood 1994: 12). It further argues that statistically speaking most official politicians or council's representatives are mature people in their thirties or their forties. Women who have reached their forties have generally completed the periods of child-bearing and child-rearing and have 'attained to a phase of mental and psychological maturity, as well as emotional stability' (the Muslim Brotherhood 1994: 12), the report states. By taking this position, the Muslim Brotherhood has partly turned away from its most common argument against female participation in society. Previously the biologically based argument that women were mentally unstable due to menstruation and child-bearing provided the main rationale for the Islamist rejection of women occupying high positions. The fact that the Muslim Brotherhood has revised its attitude to women's life cycles is significant. The static image of women *always* having small children around them has yielded to a more inclusive awareness of women in other parts of the female life cycle.

Third, the Muslim Brotherhood analyses the argument that female participation will necessarily lead to immodesty and intermingling between the sexes. The movement stresses that a woman who participates in politics has to adopt the Islamic dress-code. Although it does not elucidate upon the matter, it is an understatement that the Islamic dress-code is a protection against free mixing of the sexes. This argument is in line with those of the Islamist women I met in Jordan. They pointed out the paradox that in the Islamist movements in Jordanian society, women who actually dressed in 'a proper way' were excluded from official participation by male Islamists' arguments about the danger of free mixing between the sexes, whereas women who did not follow the Islamic dress-code had free access to many fields of society (Roald 1994).

Fourth, the Muslim Brotherhood responds to the argument that the need to travel as part of her official duties would obstruct a woman's participation in politics, as a woman cannot travel without a *maḥram* (the husband or a male unmarriageable relative). This argument is rejected by the Muslim Brotherhood, as the report states: 'She need not be in a situation without secure company nor in any situation which is not within the boundaries of the sharia' (The Muslim Brotherhood 1994: 13). The Muslim Brotherhood does not go into detail as to what this means. What is 'secure company'? Does it refer to any company and not necessarily a *maḥram*? What are exactly the 'boundaries of sharia' in this particular matter? The issue of women travelling alone is a matter of controversy among Islamists, and the Muslim Brotherhood has avoided the discussion by being sparse with details. In the contemporary debate I have encountered various arguments, such as that at the time of the Prophet travelling was dangerous as one travelled on camels through isolated areas. The prohibition against women travelling alone was therefore a natural response to the situation. Today, on the other hand, travelling is generally safe. Modern vehicles and transport services make it possible for women to travel in a group or with other women. The opposing argument is also prominent in the debate, claiming that the sharia rules on women travelling are universal in nature and have to be followed strictly even today. The discussion on this issue will probably not end with the Muslim Brotherhood's statement, but the relaxed attitude taken by the movement might encourage an increase in women's mobility not only in matters of political participation but also with regard to social activities in general.

Finally, the Muslim Brotherhood's report takes up the discussion of whether or not it is possible for women to hold public office. It states: 'The only public office which it is agreed upon that a woman cannot occupy is the presidency or head of state' (The Muslim Brotherhood 1994: 13). It is important to draw attention to the expression 'it is agreed upon' in this statement. Is the Muslim Brotherhood suggesting that all scholars both in the past and in the present are in agreement with this statement, or does it mean that the Muslim Brotherhood's leading members have agreed among themselves that currently they choose to exclude women from presidency? As Badawi has demonstrated, there are different points of view throughout Islamic history on this matter, and the leading members of the Muslim Brotherhood are surely aware of this fact. Ibn Ḥazm holds the view that women can occupy every position except that of *khalīfa* (the leader of all Muslims). It is obvious that a *khalīfa* is different from a head of a nation-state. The fact that there are various opinions in this matter opens up the way for new interpretations. As for the Muslim Brotherhood, one can conclude that the organisation has chosen to take a stand against female presidency, and the rationale for this decision might be implied in the concluding remark of the movement's statement. It says:

> We, the Muslim Brothers, wish to draw attention to the need of distinguishing between a person having a right and the way, the conditions, and the appropriate circumstances for the use of that right. Thus, if today's societies have different social circumstances and traditions, it is acceptable that the exercise of these rights should be gradually introduced in order for the society to adjust to these circumstances.
>
> (The Muslim Brotherhood 1994: 14)

The Muslim Brotherhood has in the report accepted female participation at all levels of society except the presidency or as the head of the state. At the same time it states that social circumstances and traditions can prevent such participation. I believe that the insertion of this reference makes it easy to obstruct women's access to official life. By blaming the backwardness of others and claiming that society is not yet mature enough for female political participation, one can protect the existing male hegemony which is pervasive in most Muslim institutions.

In my discussion with Darsh, I asked him whether a woman can be appointed judge in sharia courts, and Darsh answered very decisively, 'yes, she can.' He referred to aṭ-Ṭabarī who has expressed the opinion that women can be judges. Darsh's own view was that a woman would be particularly suited to be a judge in the family division of Islamic law 'as she is much more qualified, much more able to look into family matters, and it will be much easier for a woman to talk to a female judge about her problems'. Fu'ād Hussain from the Islamic Liberation Party also answered in the affirmative when asked whether it is possible to have a female judge in sharia courts. This is interesting as the Party's constitution implicitly excludes the possibility of women as judges (Taji-Farouki 1996: 201–3).[7]

When discussing Muḥammad al-Ghazzālī's book dealing with female leadership, Darsh criticised his approach to hadiths, referring to Sheikh al-Qaraḍāwī's book about how to understand the Sunna as a more mature example of scholarship (al-Ghazzālī 1989; al-Qaraḍāwī 1990). I understood this criticism of al-Ghazzālī's book to also be an implicit rejection of female state leadership, although Darsh never explicitly referred to al-Ghazzālī's stand on this issue. Darsh's ideas are in line with the Muslim Brotherhood's understanding of women being able to occupy higher political positions with the exception of the office of state leadership.

Islamists in Europe

In my discussions with Islamists in Europe I discovered that al-Ghazzālī's book had been widely read, whereas when I asked about Badawi's book, few Arabic-speaking Islamists had actually read it although many had heard about it and its concepts, particularly that of 'gender equity'. On the other hand, many of the people I spoke with had not even heard about Mernissi's book. In the questionnaire I posed two questions linked to female leadership:

1 Can a Muslim woman in your opinion have high positions in society?
2 Can a Muslim woman in your opinion become a leader of the state?

Seventy-five per cent of the respondents answered yes to question (1), whereas for question (2), 80 per cent of the respondents answered no and only 20 per cent said that women could be state leaders. Among the latter respondents were mainly those belonging to the *post-ikhwān* trend. Khadīja, who adheres to the *ikhwān* view, accepts women in leading positions but not as leaders of the state. In the questionnaire she writes:

> As for women in higher positions, sharia does not prohibit it. A woman can be a minister or she can be a member of parliament, but I believe that a woman cannot be a leader of the state. However, there are different views among the scholars in this matter, and some directions even accept a woman as a leader of the state. In my view, as men are in charge of the family (*qawwāmūn ʿalā*), men are most fitted to be the leaders of the state [translation mine].

Aḥmad, who also promotes an *ikhwān* view, was of the same opinion as Khadīja. A woman can hold any position except that of leader of the state. Aḥmad in his answer tends to portray women stereotypically and describes women as 'emotional' whereas men are 'rational'. He says:

> A woman cannot be a leader as her emotions tend to overtake her. She spends most of her time in her house, either pregnant or breast-feeding or educating her children. All this time she is at home and she is far from what happens in society. These matters also influence her and will influence her decisions. Those women who are leaders of the state, they are exceptions rather than rules. In those situations where women are ruling one should evaluate their work and see whether they have been doing a good job or not. This is my personal view.
>
> However, when it comes to the Islamic legal point of view, there is the hadith that people will not succeed with a female leader, and there is the Koranic verse about men's *qiwāma* and the verse on female testimony which is half that of a man. In addition, all Prophets were

> men and we also have to look at the practice of the Prophet's Companions [translation mine].

Aḥmad's statement reflects the 'Arab cultural base pattern' with his emphasis on men being superior to women. He further reinforces Ibn Kathīr's point of view that all prophets were men. His statement perpetuates the traditional stereotype which sees a woman as the pillar in the home.

Reflections

In the debate about female leadership there are a variety of opinions. I discovered during the in-depth interviews that independent individuals belonging to the *post-ikhwān* trend, members of the Muslim Brotherhood and members of the Islamic Liberation Party tended to accept women in high positions in society, whereas *salafīs* categorically rejected not only women as heads of state but also women in high social positions. Their rationale for this was that as men are in charge of wider society, there is bound to be mixing between the sexes if women are to work in such positions. Regarding the question of women as heads of state, there are opposing opinions between members of the Muslim Brotherhood and individuals in the *post-ikhwān* trend. As the view of the Muslim Brotherhood is that women cannot possibly be heads of state, every individual from the movement with whom I discussed the idea rejected it, although in this group there was an open attitude towards female leadership in general. Both Ziyād and Amal were of the opinion that a woman can hold all positions of leadership, even leadership of the state. As a general remark I would point out that in contrast to Muslim feminists, Islamist women stressed that they are not striving for presidency but rather that they are in the first place working for female political participation on a lower level.

In the interview with Sheikh Rāshid al-Ghannūshī, he expressed the belief that women can hold all leadership positions even at the highest level. I suspect that the idea of women as heads of state had its breakthrough in Muḥammad al-Ghazzālī's book, an Islamist who although he has had extensive contact with Islamists living in western countries has actually lived his whole life in the Arab world. He was originally from Egypt, but was a lecturer at universities in Algeria and Saudi Arabia for many years. I believe that his considerable influence on modern Islamism is the reason why the discussion about female leadership at the level of the state has intensified in recent years in the Islamist debate. Badawi's book must be seen in its context as it is written in English and aimed at an English-speaking audience. As for Islamists in general, what is most prominent is the general *ikhwān* view, that women can occupy any position except that of head of state. This was unanimously upheld by all Muslim Brotherhood members and is in accordance with the Muslim Brotherhood's programme on women. Islamists belonging to the *post-ikhwān* trend promote female leadership at all levels. I expect that the development in understanding which these Islamists have experienced will also occur among members of other Islamist movements at a later stage, in accordance with Barth's theory of the clear boundaries found in social organisations as opposed to the constant flux of 'culture'.

As European members of the Muslim Brotherhood tend to adhere to the report which is shaped mainly by members living in Arab countries, one can conclude that the report is influenced to a great extent by the 'Arab cultural base pattern'. However, as the globalisation process with its spread of western local thought is strong even in non-western societies, the change in attitudes towards women which I have observed might be seen in terms of a response towards western notions of Islam as hostile to women. However, on the question of leadership, the Muslim Brotherhood's stance tends to be more in line with the 'Arab cultural base pattern' with its stress on male leadership, whereas al-Ghannūshī together with individuals belonging to a *post-ikhwān* trend have gone much further in this matter. I believe that al-Ghannūshī's western education in the humanities and independent Islamists' interaction with majority societies in Europe have effected such fundamental changes as to make possible the proclamation of female leadership in Islam. Their adopting such a bold stand signifies a turn away from a traditional Islamic model towards the 'western cultural base pattern' which promotes gender equality.

I will now turn to a discussion of polygyny, which is another controversial subject in Islam. In a non-Muslim perspective polygyny tends to be seen as one of the symbols of repression of women in Islam. Even within Islamist discourse there is a variety of views on polygyny, as will be shown in the next chapter.

9 Polygyny[1]

The question of polygyny in Islam is a matter of great concern, not only as an argument *against* Islam for non-Muslims, but also for many Muslim women who dread the prospect of their husbands taking a second wife. Badawi writes in his book, *Gender Equity in Islam*, that 'associating polygyny with Islam, as if it were introduced by it or is the norm according to its teachings, is one of the most persistent myths perpetuated in Western literature and media' (Badawi 1995: 26).

In Islamist writings and discussions of polygyny the two following verses are referred to:

1 And if you have reason to fear that you might not act equitably towards orphans, then marry from among the women such as are lawful to you – two, or three, or four; but if you have reason to fear that you might not be able to treat them with equal fairness, then marry only one – or from among those you possess. This will make it more likely that you will not deviate from the right course (K.4: 3).
2 And it will not be within your power to treat your wives with equal fairness, however much you may desire it. Do not allow yourselves to incline towards one to the exclusion of the other, leaving her in a state, as it were, of having and not having a husband. But if you put things right and are conscious of Him – behold, God is indeed much-forgiving, a dispenser of grace (K.4: 129).

In the traditional commentaries on the Koran two alternative interpretations of verse 4: 3 are suggested. One interpretation is built on a hadith related back to ʿĀʾisha, saying that for a man who is tempted to marry a rich orphan girl due to her wealth and then would treat her badly, it would be better for him to marry other women of his liking, one, two, three or four (al-Bukhārī, Book of Trusteeship, no. 2557; Muslim, Book of Interpretation; no. 5335; Sunan an-Nisāʾī, Book of Marriage, no. 3294; Sunan Abī Dāwud, Book of Marriage, no. 1771). Ābādī quotes Ibn ʿAbbās' explanation of the verse as meaning that just as men are afraid of not dealing in an equitable manner with orphans, in the same way they should be afraid of not dealing justly with their wives and treating them in an equal manner (Ābādī 1988: 77).

Historically speaking, it seems that polygyny was quite common in many Muslim societies, and from Muhammad Asad's writings it would appear that even in the twentieth century polygyny was widespread in the Arab Gulf states (Asad 1956). One of the first signs of public disapproval of polygyny came with Muḥammad ʿAbduh's commentary on the Koran. ʿAbduh's commentary is marked by a 'modern approach' as suggested by Muhammad Asad's observation that 'His [ʿAbduh's] importance in the context of the modern world of Islam can never be sufficiently stressed' (Asad 1984: v). In his commentary to the above verses ʿAbduh goes through the traditional literature, quoting hadiths and various scholars' views on the matter. He concludes that 'Polygyny is in contrast to the original nature of marriage. Verily the origin is for a man to have one woman, and he is towards her as she is towards him' (ʿAbduh n.d. vol. IV: 350 [translation mine]). At the same time, however, ʿAbduh stresses the need for the option of polygyny to remain open in case of necessity, such as for instance in times of war or when the woman is infertile. He further suggests that it is up to the rulers in the various countries to legislate according to specific circumstances. If there is a need in a society for polygyny the ruler should allow this option, whereas if there is no need the ruler should forbid it. This is a thought-provoking suggestion, particularly in view of the fact that the state of Tunis has actually prohibited polygyny, a matter which has aroused the anger of Islamists. In Senegal there has also been a development towards a more cautious attitude towards polygyny as the state has introduced a law saying that the first wife has to give her consent if her husband wants to marry a second wife.

Sheikh Muḥammad Mutawallī ash-Shaʿrāwī (d. 1998), the famous Egyptian scholar, debates the issue of polygyny and attempts to justify it rationally. He remarks that men tend to be in the minority in a society because in times of war it is men who fight and die, and he asks: 'Then, what are the surplus women going to do?' (Shaʿrāwī n.d.: 32). ash-Shaʿrāwī does not, however, prohibit or disapprove of polygyny in other circumstances and he does not even discuss the consequences of polygyny in 'normal' circumstances. For him, polygyny is allowed and since it is a law laid down by God human beings cannot question it. His argument is based on the Islamic view of men as providers for women, so unmarried women have difficulty finding economic support.

It is interesting to note that Zainab al-Ghazzālī's comment on these two Koranic verses does not give what I would call 'a female perspective'. Instead, she merely quotes the above hadith from ʿĀ'isha and paraphrases the Koranic verses. In my discussions with Islamists in the Muslim world, as well as in Europe, I have observed that there is a tendency to view this issue in economic terms, seeing women's need for economic support as a justification for polygyny. It would therefore be interesting to discover to what extent social changes in the family economic model might have affected this idea, as women in contemporary society are often themselves breadwinners.

It is not surprising that Badawi, who lives in a western country, has dealt at length with the matter of polygyny. In his *da'wa* work among non-Muslims, he has experienced the western notion of a strong link between Islam and polygyny. He attempts to challenge this notion by saying: 'No text in the Qur'an or Sunna explicitly specifies either monogamy or polygyny as the norm, although demographic data indicates strongly that monogamy is the norm and polygyny the exception' (Badawi 1995: 26–7).

He offers a 'rational' explanation, saying that globally speaking women and men are almost even in numbers and, as polygyny as a norm requires that women outnumber men, it is impossible that the Koran should set up a norm which contradicts reality. 'No Qur'anic "norm" is based on an impossible assumption', he says (Badawi 1995: 27). Badawi goes on to say that Islam did not outlaw polygyny, but it regulated and restricted it. He remarks that it is neither required nor encouraged, but is simply permitted and not outlawed. He further argues that the Koranic verse 4: 3 was revealed after one of the battles of the Prophet in which many Muslims were slain, leaving behind widows and orphans. Badawi expresses the opinion that

> *This seems to indicate* that the intent of its continued permissibility, at least in part, is to deal with individual and collective contingencies that may arise from time to time (e.g., imbalances between the number of males and females created by war).
>
> (Badawi 1995: 28 – my italics)

Badawi is cautious of appealing to general principles. As indicated by my italics, he treads a very thin line in trying to satisfy all parties – which one might guess could be identified as the *salafīs* on the one hand since they tend to take a strict view on matters concerning women, and Muslims brought up in 'the West' or a western audience on the other hand. Badawi's approach, which I would interpret in the context of a cultural encounter between Arab Islamism and western values, is a balance between these two extremes and I think he manages to remain within both 'Islamic discourse' and 'western discourse'.

I questioned above if social changes in the family economy might challenge the acceptance of polygyny, since the common defence offered by Islamists was based on an economic system in which men are the sole providers. Badawi's explanation might provide an answer to this question. He says:

> This [polygyny] provides a moral, practical and humane solution to the problems of widows and orphans, who would otherwise surely be

> more vulnerable in the absence of a husband and father figure in terms of economics, companionship, proper child-rearing and other needs.
> (Badawi 1995: 28)

It is interesting to note that although Badawi refers to economic factors, this is just one aspect and other factors are seen as just as important. Badawi's position is somewhat idealistic, given that many Muslim women emphasise that most men who marry a second or a third wife do so not in order to protect widows or orphans, but rather to satisfy their sexual needs. In this context polygyny is regarded as a means of preventing divorce and adultery.

Badawi further considers the options of the parties involved in such a polygynous marriage. In contrast to Sheikh ash-Shaʿrāwī who does not touch on this sensitive issue, Badawi suggests that as the man and the second wife are free to choose polygyny, all women are allowed, according to sharia, to include the condition of being the only wife in their marriage contracts. Moreover, even if a woman has not claimed such a condition, she is free to claim a divorce (*khulʿ*) if her husband wants to take a second wife. However, in spite of Badawi's argument, in my experience the question of female divorce even in a western Islamic context is still extremely sensitive (see Chapter 10).

A question commonly asked by westerners is why polygyny is permitted in Islam but polyandry is forbidden. This is one of the main issues for those who regard Islam as a religion hostile to women. Badawi's answer is in line with a common Islamist view, namely:

> In the case of polygyny, the lineal identities of children are not confused. They all have the same father and each of them knows his or her mother. In the case of polyandry, however, only the mother is known for sure. The father could be any of the 'husbands' of the same wife. In addition to lineal identity problems, polyandry raises problems relating to inheritance law. For example, which of the children inherits or shares in the estate of a deceased 'probable' father?
> (Badawi 1995: 29)

Overall, it seems that although Badawi regards polygyny as a suitable alternative in certain circumstances such as when there is a surplus of women, one has the impression that he disapproves of it as a general rule.

Muhammad Asad follows in the footsteps of Muḥammad ʿAbduh in his commentary on the Koran. This book is of interest in a European perspective as it is in English and is thus accessible to second-, third- and fourth-generation immigrants. The former Swedish diplomat, Knut Muhammad Bernström, has incorporated large parts of Asad's commentaries into his Swedish translation of the Koran (1998). Asad implicitly disapproves of polygyny. Although he does not go as far as ʿAbduh in demanding local legislation on this matter, the conditions that he puts forward as necessary for a polygynous marriage indicate that he regards it as undesirable in an Islamic society. In his commentary on verse 4: 3 he quotes the standpoints of both ʿĀ'isha and Ibn ʿAbbās.[2] However, by stressing that aṭ-Ṭabārī preferred the latter interpretation, he indirectly puts forward his own bias which is towards stressing the rights of women. Asad states:

> As regards the permission to marry more than one wife (up to the maximum of four), it is so restricted by the condition, 'if you have reason to fear that you might not be able to treat them with equal fairness, then [marry only] one', as to make such plural marriages possible only in quite exceptional cases and under exceptional circumstances.
>
> (Asad 1984: 101)

Asad reinforces this view of polygynous marriages as exceptional cases in his commentary to the second verse in the Koran which deals with polygyny. In his commentary to verse 4: 129 he refers back to his commentary to verse 4: 3, saying that although the former verse stipulates the necessity of treating the wives equally, the second verse provides 'judicial enlightenment' as it states that feelings are beyond human control and this equal treatment refers to outward behaviour only (Asad 1984: 130). He goes on to say:

> However, in view of the fact that a man's behaviour towards another person is, in the long run, almost inevitably influenced by what he *feels* about that person, the above passage – read in conjunction with verse 3, and especially its concluding sentence – imposes a *moral* restriction on plural marriages.
>
> (Asad 1984: 130)

These two passages clearly demonstrate Asad's disapproval of polygyny, which I would attribute to his European cultural background. In his book, *The Road to Mecca* (1956), it is also apparent that despite his love for Arab Muslim Bedouin life, he found it difficult to understand the attitudes he encountered concerning marriage and divorce.

As for the question of why only polygyny and not polyandry is allowed in Islamic law, Asad explains:

> Still, one might ask why the same latitude has not been given to women as well; but the answer is simple. Notwithstanding the spiritual factor of *love* which influences the relations between man and woman, the determinant *biological* reason for the sexual urge is, in both sexes, procreation: and whereas a woman can, at one time, conceive a child from one man only and has to carry it for nine months before she can conceive another, a man can beget a child every time

> he cohabits with a woman. Thus, while nature would have been merely wasteful if it had produced a polygamous instinct in woman, man's polygamous inclination is biologically justified. It is of course, obvious that the biological factor is only one – and by no means always the most important – of the aspects of marital love: nonetheless, it is a basic factor and, therefore, decisive in the institution of marriage as such. With the wisdom that always takes human nature fully into account, Islamic Law undertakes no more than the safeguarding of the socio-biological function of marriage (which includes also care of the progeny), allowing a man to have more than one wife and not allowing a woman to have more than one husband at one time; while the spiritual problem of marriage, being imponderable and therefore outside the scope of law, is left to the discretion of the partners.
>
> (Asad 1984: 101–2)

Asad ends this section by emphasising that as marriage in Islam is a civil contract, it is possible for both men and women to ask for a divorce, thus indicating that if the woman is not happy with her husband taking a second wife she is, according to sharia, free to seek a divorce. Asad makes a point of explaining that the task of Islamic law is to safeguard 'the socio-biological function of marriage' rather than to cater for the emotional state of the spouses. Asad might therefore be seen as appealing to the biological argument which is common among Arab Islamists, but I believe that his position is more refined than this. He does not pursue the idea of what is 'natural' for the two sexes but refers instead to the sexual function of men and women, thus regarding Islamic law as a code of legislation based upon the needs of human beings as biological individuals. He therefore makes a distinction between what is strictly biological and what is emotional in the sharia legislation. I regard this tension between biology and emotions in Islamic legislation as arising out of the fact that the emotions and needs of *women* have to a great extent been excluded from the codified Islamic law. This is most evident in the way that the frequent prophetic sayings on how to treat women well have not been incorporated into the law, whereas sayings concerned with male privilege such as those about a wife's obedience towards her husband have been codified and often strictly followed in legal procedures.[3] This is another example of the tension between the legal and the moral aspects of Islamic law. The moral aspect is mostly based on androcentric claims, pervasive at the time when legislation was being formed, whereas contemporary moral attitudes which are sympathetic to women are not found in the existing form of sharia.

In Sheikh Darsh's 1984 booklet, *An Outline of Islamic Family Law*, he expresses the opinion that, although allowed, polygyny is not recommended but 'is looked upon as a remedy in exceptional cases' (Darsh 1984: 9). This is a common attitude found not only in Darsh and Badawi but also in other important Islamist scholars' literature, even outside the western world. az-Zuḥailī writes in his book on Islamic jurisprudence that 'verily the system of one wife in marriage is the best and it is the most common' (az-Zuḥailī 1989 vol. VII: 169). The norm according to Darsh is 'one man, one wife'. Darsh also observes that if a man remarries his first wife can seek a divorce, and he too suggests the possibility that a woman might make it a condition of the marriage contract that her husband should not remarry. Like other Arab Islamists, Darsh does not specify conditions for polygyny because most of them argue that as polygyny is permitted in the Koran, human beings cannot prohibit it. In my personal discussion with him Darsh further reinforced the idea that there are no legal conditions for taking a second wife, although in his book he lists what he views as 'considerations' for polygyny, which he is careful to state are not prerequisites but rather 'point the way in which Islam has moved with regard to this issue' (Darsh 1984: 9). His 'considerations' are:

1 If the first marriage does not produce children.
2 If the first wife becomes sick and needs someone to look after her and her husband.
3 If, for one reason or another, she cannot satisfy the sexual needs of the man.
4 In case of there being surplus women, especially after wars.

(Darsh 1984: 9)

Darsh offers a further rationale for the practice of polygyny. The first point is that if a husband wants another wife for one reason or another and she has been given the choice of divorce which she refuses, then it is more humane to let her stay with her husband who will see to her 'protection, maintenance, and satisfaction' (Darsh 1984: 10). The second point is that instead of a man having a secret relationship, if it becomes necessary for him to marry it has to be done openly with all the obligations married life demands (Darsh 1984: 10). When I met Darsh in his home in December 1995, I asked him if he lived in a monogamous or polygynous marriage. Being a humorous person, he laughed and said, 'I have more than enough with one wife'. I think this comment illustrates his attitude towards polygyny as suggested in his 'considerations' above. In Islamic law, a man does not have to have any reasons for marrying a second wife, whereas in the contemporary debate conditions and 'considerations' are identified. This is yet another example of how influences from the 'western cultural base pattern' make Islamists find new explanations more compatible with the society they live in.

In our further discussion Darsh explored the issue of polygyny. He referred to cases in the British media about women who had been the secret mistresses of married men for years with all the accompanying problems. He also mentioned the cases of children who cannot take their fathers' names as they are products of secret relationships. He said:

> That is what we are considering when it comes to the Islamic attitude. If you are emotionally involved as an accident of life, it is better for the woman that you marry her in the fully glaring light of the society to give her the respect and honour of a decent woman.

He continued:

> To go on there is a bad [Arab] proverb which says: 'a thousand girlfriends but not another wife.' That is not the Islamic attitude. The Islamic attitude is dignified and gives respect to the woman. Every wife has the same rights like the others. Who is losing in the above attitude? It is the woman, it is she who loses her chastity, her dignity, and she becomes some sort of person without any order. The Islamic attitude is that once you are involved, bring the woman into the relationship in a clear, moral, responsible way.

Darsh gave the impression of being a man who interprets the Islamic rules in the context of the existing environment. While some Islamists tend to see the issue of polygyny in purely legal terms, emphasising that it is permissible for a man to marry more than one wife without the consent of his existing wife/wives, Darsh was concerned with the relationship between the spouses within such a polygynous marriage. In his answer to the question of whether a man has to seek permission from his wife to marry another wife, he answered:

> We do not like to have a conflict within the family, and we like to do things in the open. We do not like to do things in a hidden way because this means a denial of the rights of the second wife to be respected and to be treated as a full wife.

It is significant that Darsh emphasised the second wife's rights instead of the more common view that the first wife is the one to suffer in a polygynic marriage as she has been 'rejected'. I think Darsh's statement must be understood in the light of his perception of how mistresses are treated in British society. It seems that for Darsh, the first wife's rights are automatically secured by her status as a respectful wife.

In my discussions with Islamists living in Europe I found that a small group, particularly those coming from the *salafī* trend, tended to regard polygyny as the original Islamic model. For example, one remarked that 'what is first mentioned in the Koran is [to marry] two, three, or four, then it comes that one should marry one.' This interpretation suggests a literal reading of the text. Even within this trend, however, there is no unanimous view. Bashīr, one of the *salafīs* I interviewed, sees both polygyny and monogamy as the norm. He explained that it all depends on the situation, first and foremost on the man's ability to ensure justice. In my discussion with a *salafī* woman from Saudi Arabia who has been living in Europe for a short period, she expressed the belief that due to all the Egyptian films and television series which are presently shown on Saudi television, attitudes towards polygyny have changed among young Saudis. In her view many of these films and series treat polygyny as a huge social problem, and this has made young Saudis reject it. She adds that the same films and series stress love and strong emotions between men and women, a second factor that she thinks gives young Saudis an unfavourable view of polygyny. 'The negative effect of this,' she says, 'is that many women are unmarried and have no prospect of marriage.' I have observed the same phenomenon in Jordan, where many families have one or more unmarried daughters sitting at home. As statistically the number of men and women is more or less even, this phenomenon might have another explanation than that there is a surplus of women in society.

In contrast to the main *salafī* view, I found that within most of the other groups the majority shared the view of Badawi and Darsh that polygyny should only be resorted to in exceptional cases. Sheikh al-Ghannūshī, for instance, was of the opinion that monogamy is original, but as human society sometimes goes out of step with what is 'natural' such as in times of war or if there is an imbalance in the proportion of men and women in society, there has to be a mechanism for solving the problems which arise. al-Ghannūshī says

> Islam is a religion which suits human nature and in cases when human society is in a non-natural state it is possible for men to marry more than one wife, but this is in extraordinary situations, the origin is monogamy.

All of the individuals presented in the above discussion have different perspectives on polygyny that vary along a scale of acceptance or rejection. ash-Shaʿrāwī's position might be located within the framework of the 'Arab cultural base pattern', whereas Darsh, Badawi and al-Ghannūshī represent a pattern of change in which they introduce new interpretations to established norms. These scholars are in a cooperative position with regard to the majority society as they are active at various levels of western social life. Asad is the one whose views conform most closely to western intellectual thought. As a European convert he has merged Islamic ideas with western ideals. It is particularly in matters such as polygyny and women's veiling that Asad signals his belonging within the 'western cultural base pattern'. The question of polygyny has the capacity to provoke strong feelings between Muslims and non-Muslims, and Asad's approach to the issue is marked by a rapprochement with the 'western cultural base pattern'.

Islamists in Europe

In the questionnaire I gave three options for which respondents could tick more than one answer, asking whether:

1 A man can freely marry a second, a third, or a fourth wife.
2 A man can marry more than one wife only under certain circumstances.
3 A man *cannot* marry another wife *without* the consent of the first wife.

Half of the male respondents ticked alternative (1) and the other half alternative (2). As for the women, it was interesting that the majority ticked alternative (1). Khadīja, whom I would have expected to tick alternative (1), instead ticked alternative (2). Both Ziyād and Amal ticked alternative (3), but few of the other respondents ticked this alternative. Those who did were young people born and brought up in Europe. This does not mean, however, that all those who were brought up in Europe had a view corresponding to alternative (3), as some of this category actually ticked alternative (1). My impression is that in this particular area opinions are very divergent, and it was difficult to find any correspondence between views on this matter and views on other issues which were raised in the questionnaire.

It seems that the issue of polygyny raises the emotions of Muslims in general, and Islamists tend also to have an emotional reaction to it. During my discussions I had the feeling that for many men it was a criterion of good faith for a woman to accept the idea of polygyny. On the other hand, women tended to judge men's faith on the basis of their acceptance of living in a monogamous relationship in spite of their right to remarry. At the end of the day it seems to come back to whether one's perspective is that of the male or that of the female. It is, however, important to draw attention to the fact that even male respondents acknowledged the problematic situation of women living in polygynous relationships, and both men and women acknowledged that a polygynous relationship could be just as difficult for a man. One man noted that the obligation of the husband to treat all his wives equally was a test and a trial, and he believed that few men could actually do it. He further explained that as God was to judge his acts he would be reluctant to complicate his life in this way, and he wondered whether 'what one gains in the roundabouts one loses in the swings'. Ziyād believed that it would be psychologically harmful for the first wife to have another woman in the house to share her husband, an opinion which was shared by some of the second-generation Muslims.

As a second question on the issue of polygyny, I quoted a hadith and asked the respondents' reaction to it. The hadith goes:

> The Messenger of God was on the pulpit, saying: 'The tribe of Hishām bin al-Mughira has requested me to allow them to marry their daughter to ʿAlī bin Abī Ṭālib. I do not give permission and I will not give permission unless ʿAlī divorces my daughter in order to marry their daughter, because Fāṭima is a part of my body and I hate what she hates to see, and what hurts her, hurts me.'
>
> (al-Bukhārī, Book of Marriage, no. 4829; Muslim, Book of Virtues of the Companions, no. 4482; Sunan at-Tirmidhī, Book of Virtues,

no. 3802; Sunan Abī Dāwud, Book of Marriage, no. 1773; Sunan Ibn Mājah, Book of Marriage, no. 1988)[4]

Most of those who had ticked alternative (1) above suggested in their answers that this was a special case, applying only to Fāṭima as she was the daughter of the Prophet. Those who had ticked alternative (2) gave various explanations for this hadith. One man who had lived in Europe for more than twelve years remarked that this hadith showed that the original idea in Islam is that a man should have only one wife. Some others, among them Khadīja, interpreted the hadith contextually, saying that the leader of the tribe in question was an unbeliever and the Prophet rejected the marriage on these grounds. One respondent wrote that there were no reasons for ʿAlī to marry another woman, whereas a male engineer who had lived in Europe for six years wrote that 'it is terrible for the wife to get a co-wife. What hurts a woman also hurts her father or her parents, and the Prophet (p.b.u.h.) was very frank as a human being.'

Amal uses this hadith to reinforce her answer to the former question that a man cannot marry another wife *without* the consent of the first wife, as the remarriage affects the first wife and causes her a great deal of distress. According to the Islamic law, however, a man has the legal right to marry without even telling his first wife. This example points out the discrepancy between the established Islamic law, which reflects a moral order of a certain time in history on the one hand, and on the other, the moral sentiment in present time. I find it of interest that the hadith above has not provided the Muslim scholars with sufficient legal evidence necessary for making it obligatory to get the first wife's permission to marry a second wife. It is obvious that selection and 'picking from the basket' according to world-view and personal disposition has influenced such legislation. One can speculate about whether this particular legislation would have been different if women had had a voice in the early development of Islamic legislation,

Bashīr, the *salafī* who responded that both polygyny and monogyny were the origin of the Koranic injunction, answered that the Prophet forbade the marriage of his son-in-law to a second wife, as 'the Prophet (p.b.u.h.) understood that in this situation it would be unjust for ʿAlī to remarry'. Bashīr interprets the Koranic verse 4: 3 as giving more than one option and argues that there are degrees of permissibility[5] for a man to marry more than one wife according to his own personal needs. Thus for Bashīr the principle of justice becomes the prominent principle, and in this particular case he preferred the principle over the text, a matter which I found of great interest as those belonging to the *salafī* stream of thought tend to prefer texts and literary interpretations of texts over Islamic principles.

Reflections

The various positions adopted by Islamists living in Europe over this issue reflect the diversity of views found among scholars from the formative age of sharia as well as in modern times. The variations in understanding of the Koran and hadiths and the selective use of texts indicate the influence of the individual's background and personal characteristics on the perception of the text (Hjärpe 1997). As shown above, despite the pervasive practice of polygyny in early Islamic history, prominent Companions such as Ibn ʿAbbās and Saʿīd ibn Jubair seem to have discouraged polygyny. By turning back to the sources and reproducing the past in the present, one can find attitudes which are more compatible with the 'western cultural base pattern' than traditional attitudes.

It is important to be aware that hadiths are interpreted in various ways and often particular hadiths are taken to affirm certain ideas or practices. This is obvious in the hadith about the marriage of ʿAlī, which traditionally seems to have been interpreted according to a bipolar model of Islam versus *jāhilīya* (time of ignorance) (see Roald 1994: 179–84), with the controversy between the Prophet and Hishām ibn al-Mughīra, who is more commonly known under the nickname of Abū Jahl (Father of ignorance), representing these two poles. Abū Jahl is depicted by Muslim historians of the classical age as one of the greatest opponents of the Prophet's mission. He was among the few of the Prophet's contemporaries who died a non-Muslim. It is interesting to note how this hadith tends to be interpreted in a specific context and its content has not acquired universal significance, whereas the hadith about female leadership in Islam which can be regarded in much the same way has greatly affected the ability of Muslim women to attain positions of leadership. With a different approach in a new cultural context in which the 'western cultural base pattern' dictates attitudes, it is possible that traditional ideas will yield to other interpretations.

What is most obvious from the above discussion is that the notion of polygyny is discouraged among Arab Islamists in general both in the Arab world and in Europe. It is important to be aware that the various Arabic-speaking countries have different cultural practices when it comes to polygyny, and without proper statistics it is impossible to comment on the frequency of polygyny in the various countries. However, from my personal observation in my frequent travels in the Arab world, I would conclude that polygyny is not very common in most countries. I have come across most polygynous marriages in the Arabian Gulf states. Muhammad Asad's book, *The Road to Mecca*, gives the impression that polygyny was quite common in the Arabian peninsula even in the early 1920s before the coming of oil wealth, but as indicated above, the globalisation of the media even in this part of the world means that the practice of polygyny is on the decline.

Having discussed marriage in the context of polygyny, I now turn to a discussion on divorce and the issue of child custody in the next chapter.

10 Divorce and child custody

The easy access which Muslim men have to divorce in contrast to the difficulty which Muslim women have in obtaining a divorce has become a matter of interest particularly for Muslim feminists (cf. Afkhami 1995; Yamani 1996). Even Islamist women have raised the issue, although with a slightly different approach. Unlike Muslim feminists, Islamist women do not consider that Islam or Islamic law is to blame but rather local customs based on pre-Islamic habits which still influence practice in the Muslim world. Below I will consider various views on divorce and child custody and investigate alternative interpretations of the Islamic sources.

In general, Muslims regard marriage as an essential of life. Many hadiths affirm that to marry is the Sunna of the Prophet Muḥammad and that every man who can afford it should marry (al-Bukhārī, Book of Marriage, no. 4677; Muslim, Book of Marriage, no. 2485; Sunan an-Nisā'ī, Book of Marriage, no. 3155; Sunan Abī Dāwud, Book of Marriage, no. 1750; Musnad Aḥmad, *al-ʿashratu al-mubasharūna bi l-janna*, no. 388). The family, whether the extended or the nuclear family, is considered to be the main institution of society. The Islamist concern over the issue of Islamic education, which stresses the importance of family stability for the future of Muslims, reflects the emphasis on the family's significance for the structuring of Islamic society. Marriage in Islam is a secular contractual act and not a divine union initiated by God. According to hadiths recorded by Bukhārī and Muslim, the woman has to give her consent to the marriage (al-Bukhārī, Book of Marriage, no. 4741; Muslim, Book of Marriage, no. 2543; Sunan at-Tirmidhī, Book of Marriage, no. 1025; Sunan an-Nisā'ī, Book of Marriage, no. 3213; Musnad Aḥmad, *bāqi musnad al-mukhtirīn*, no. 9232) or the marriage is regarded as void (al-Bukhārī, Book of Marriage, no. 4743; Sunan an-Nisā'ī, Book of Marriage, no. 3216; Sunan Abī Dāwud, Book of Marriage, no. 1797).

al-Qaraḍāwī quotes a frequently mentioned hadith in his book *Contemporary Legal Opinions* (*fatāwā muʿāṣira*): 'Divorce is that which God has permitted which He hates most' (al-Qaraḍāwī 1996: 517; Sunan Abū Dāwud, Book of Divorce, no. 1863 and in Sunan Ibn Majāh, Book of Divorce, no. 2008). This hadith reflects the attitude towards divorce among Arab Islamists. However, we also read in the hadith literature and in historical documents from the early period of Islam that the Companions of the Prophet divorced and remarried frequently. Even today I have noticed that in some parts of the Muslim world, divorce and remarriage are widespread among both men and women.[1] In Jordan, on the other hand, I observed that divorces are not common but whereas divorced men remarry easily, divorced women rarely have any chance of remarrying.[2] The practice of divorce and attitudes towards it are thus different within the various Muslim countries.

There are different forms of divorce within the law schools, three of which are important for Muslims living in western countries, *ṭalāq*, *khulᶜ* and *taṭlīq* (granting a woman divorce). Other forms of divorce include *liᶜān* (an oath of condemnation in relation to the accusation of adultery), divorce by conversion, etc., but I will not go into these in this study.

ṭalāq

The Koranic term for divorce, which is regarded as a right for men only (Sābiq 1985 vol. II: 246), is *ṭalāq* which is derived from the root *ṭ-l-q*, meaning 'being released' or 'being set free'. There are many verses of the Koran which deal with divorce. The most important are the following:

1 And the divorced women shall undergo, without remarrying, a waiting period of three monthly courses: for it is not lawful for them to conceal what God may have created in their wombs, if they believe in God and the Last Day. [In this situation] their husbands are fully entitled to take them back, if they desire reconciliation. In accordance with justice, the rights of the wives [with regard to their husbands] are equal to the [husbands'] rights with regard to them, although men have precedence over them [in this respect]. And God is almighty, wise.

A divorce may be [revoked] twice, whereupon the marriage must either be resumed in kindness (*maᶜrūf*) or dissolved in a goodly manner. And it is not lawful for you to take back anything of what you have ever given to your wives unless both [partners] have reason to fear that they may not be able to keep within the bounds (*ḥudūd*) set by God. Hence, if you have reason to fear that the two may not be able to keep within the bounds (*ḥudūd*) set by God, there shall be no sin upon either of them for what the wife may give up [to the husband] in order to redeem herself. These are the bounds (*ḥudūd*) set by God. Do not, then, transgress them. Those who transgress the bounds (*ḥudūd*) set by God – it is they who are the evildoers.

And if he divorces her [finally], she is then not lawful for him unless she first takes another man for her husband. Then, if the latter divorces her, there shall be no sin upon either of the two if they return to one another – provided that both of them think that they will be able to keep within the bounds (*ḥudūd*) set by God: for these are the bounds (*ḥudūd*) of God which He makes clear unto people of innate knowledge.

And so, when you divorce women and they are about to reach the end of their waiting-term, then either retain them in kindness (*maʿrūf*) or let them go in kindness (*maʿrūf*). Do not retain them against their will in order to hurt [them], for he who does so wrongs himself. Do not take [these] messages of God in a frivolous spirit, and remember the blessings with which God has graced you, and all the revelation and the wisdom which He has bestowed on you from on high in order to admonish (*yaʿiẓūkum*) you thereby. Remain conscious (*attaqū*) of God, and know that God has full knowledge of everything.

And when you divorce women, and they have come to the end of their waiting-term, hinder them not from marrying other men if they have agreed with each other in kindness (*maʿrūf*). This is an admonition (*yūʿaẓu bih*) unto every one of you who believes in God and the Last Day. It is the most virtuous for you, and the purest. And God knows, whereas you do not know (K.2: 228–32).

2 O Prophet! When you [plural form] intend to divorce women, divorce them with a view to the waiting-term appointed for them, and reckon the period [carefully] and be conscious (*attaqū*) of God, your Lord. Do not expel them from the homes, and neither shall they [be made to] leave unless they become openly guilty of immoral conduct.

These then, are the bounds (*ḥudūd*) set by God – and the one who transgresses the bounds (*ḥudūd*) set by God does indeed sin against himself, for you know it not that after that God may well cause something new to come about.

And so, when they are about to reach the end of their waiting-term, either retain them in kindness (*maʿrūf*) or part with them in kindness (*maʿrūf*). And let two persons of [known] probity from among your own community witness [what you have decided]; and do yourselves bear true witness before God. Whosoever believes in God and the Last Day are exhorted to (*yuʿaẓu bih*) act in such a way. And unto everyone who is conscious (*yattaqi*) of God, He grants a way out [of unhappiness].

And provides for him in a manner beyond all expectation, and for everyone who places his trust in God. He [alone] is enough.

Verily God always attains to His purpose, and indeed, unto everything has God appointed its [term] and measure.

Now as for such of your women as are beyond the age of monthly courses, as well as for such as do not have any courses, their waiting-term – if you have any doubt [about it] – shall be three [calendar] months, and as for those who are with child, the end of their waiting-term shall come when they deliver their burden.

And for everyone who is conscious of God, He makes it easy to obey His commandment.

> All this is God's commandment (*amr*), which he has bestowed upon you from on high. And unto everyone who is conscious (*yattaqi*) of God will He pardon one's bad deeds, and He will grant vast reward.
>
> Let the women live in the same manner as you live yourselves, in accordance with your means. And do not harass them with a view to making their lives a misery. And if they happen to be with child, spend freely on them until they deliver their burden. If they nurse your offspring [after the divorce has become final], give them their due recompense, and take counsel with one another in kindness (*maʿrūf*). And if both of you find it difficult [that the mother should nurse the child], let another woman nurse it on behalf of him [who has begotten] it (K. 65: 1–6).

In the hadith literature, particularly in Bukhārī's collection, there are detailed discussions of different situations such as pronouncements of divorce during a rage; when there are suspicions of adultery; the situation of women during their waiting-term after the divorce; the situation of women who are pregnant, etc.

There are various subdivisions of *ṭalāq* in Islamic law.[3] The jurists talk about *ṭalāq as-sunna*, the form of divorce which is according to the Prophet's Sunna, and *ṭalāq al-bidʿa*, which is an invented form of divorce. In the first form, first a woman should not be having her menstrual period when her husband divorces her (Sābiq 1985; al-Qaraḍāwī 1996). Second, the husband utters a single pronouncement of divorce and the couple abstains from sexual intercourse during the waiting period (*ʿidda*) which lasts for three months (three menstrual cycles). If the husband chooses to uphold his divorce they are divorced, and if they want to remarry they have to arrange a new marriage contract. This form of *ṭalāq* is called *aṭ-ṭalāq ar-rajaʿī* (revocable divorce) and it can be done twice. However, after the third time the divorce becomes irrevocable (*aṭ-ṭalāq al-batta*; irrevocable divorce). The couple can then only remarry after the woman has married another husband in a legal, consummated marriage.

Another alternative is that the man can pronounce the divorce after each menstrual period and at the last and third pronunciation the couple is irrevocably divorced. Sābiq explains the reason behind the definitiveness of three divorces. He renders a hadith from at-Tirmidhī, where ʿĀ'isha talks about a woman whose husband divorced her again and again and always took her back again before the waiting-term was ended. She came to the Prophet to complain and the Koranic verse on two divorces was sent down (Sābiq 1985 vol. II: 246).[4] Thus the Koranic regulations on divorce are regarded as an improvement for women and a protection against male abuse and control.

aṭ-Ṭalāq al-bidʿa is a more controversial matter. The husband pronounces three divorces in one sitting, either saying 'I divorce you thrice' or saying three subsequent times, 'I divorce you'. Esposito states that this particular form of divorce contradicts the Koranic prescription:

> When you divorce women, divorce them at their prescribed periods, and count their prescribed periods. . . . And fear God your Lord. . . . Those are limits set by God: and any who transgresses the limits of God, does verily wrong his own soul.
>
> (K. 65: 1)

It is interesting to note that although this form is actually labelled 'the invented form of divorce' and despite the fact that this form of divorce is not mentioned in the prophetic Sunna, some scholars actually permit it in Islamic law (cf. Sābiq 1985 vol. II: 265). Engineer has dealt at length with the invented form of divorce. He has observed that in traditional Islamic law, ash-Shāfiʿī is the only one of the classical jurists who regarded three divorce pronouncements in one sitting as both legitimate and in accordance with the Koran. Other classical jurists maintain, according to Engineer, that this form of divorce is not permissible. However, at the same time, permissible or not, many of these jurists would legitimate this form of divorce (Engineer 1992: 125). Engineer has an interesting theory, based on among others the ideas of the twentieth century author Muhammad Husain Haikal, as to how the invented form of divorce entered sharia. Muslim expansion brought captured women to the Arab Peninsula. Arab men wanted to marry them but as these women were not used to living as co-wives, they often made the condition that the men should divorce their former wives thrice first. The Arab men would pronounce three divorces in one sitting as the foreign women did not know the Koranic conditions for divorce. When they were well married to the new wife, they would take their former wives back and this created problems. ʿUmar Ibn al-Khaṭṭāb thus made the three divorces in one sitting valid as a revocable divorce to overcome such problems (Engineer 1992: 125–6).[5] Engineer claims that although this form of divorce is opposed to the spirit of Islam, it is pervasive in the Muslim world and is a great problem, particularly on the Indian subcontinent.

A women can get a divorce if her husband agrees. The man can give the wife the choice of getting a divorce and if she chooses to do so, the couple is divorced. The woman can also stipulate her right to divorce in the marriage contract. These forms of divorce are called *ṭalāq at-tafwīd* (delegated divorce).

Within the law schools, the matter of divorce has been seen within the five classifications of actions: *ḥarām* (prohibited), *makrūh* (not recommended), *mubāḥ* (acceptable), *mustaḥabb* (recommended) and *farḍ* (obligatory). The Arab scholar, ʿAbd al-ʿAṭī, for instance, has observed that divorce is obligatory 'where there is no conceivable way or reconciliation or hope for peace between the parties'. It is recommended 'if the wife is unfaithful or defiantly inattentive to her religious duties'. It is 'forbidden legally and/ or religiously during the wife's monthly course', and it is 'strongly undesirable or nearly forbidden where there is no good reason for it' (ʿAbd al-ʿAṭī 1977: 219).

khulʿ

Khulʿ is derived from the form *kh-l-ʿ* which means to 'take off' or to 'dismiss'. In the Koran there is one derivation of the root, *ikhlaʿ*, which means 'take off'. It is mentioned in the story of Moses when he was ordered to take off his shoes in the Holy Valley (K.20: 12). The Koranic verse which is understood to be dealing with the wife's right to divorce is 2: 229:

> Hence, if you have reason to fear that the two may not be able to keep within the bounds (*ḥudūd*) set by God, there shall be no sin upon either of them for what the wife may give up [to the husband] in order to redeem herself.

In this verse there is no mention of any derivation of the root *kh-l-ʿ*. In Islamic law the *khulʿ* form of divorce is the divorce for women. Bukhārī has a subchapter in his Book of Divorce which is called the section of *khulʿ*, and in the introduction to this subchapter Bukhārī cites the Koranic verse 2: 229. He states that 'ʿUmar allowed *khulʿ* without the permission of the authorities', whereas 'Uthmān allowed the husband, in case of *khulʿ*, to take back every gift except the ribbon of her hair' (M. M. Khān 1985 vol. VII: 149; al-Bukhārī, Chapter of *khulʿ*). After the introduction Bukhārī records the hadith which is used as evidence of women's right to divorce:

> The wife of Thābit ibn Qais came to the Messenger of God and said: Oh Messenger of God! I do not blame Thābit for any defects in his character or his religion, but I cannot endure to live with him. The Messenger of God then asked her: 'Will you return his garden? [which was given to you as dowry]' She said: 'Yes'. Then he [Muhammad] said to Thābit: 'Accept the garden and divorce [*ṭallaqhā*, release] her one divorce [with one divorce pronouncement]'.
>
> (al-Bukhārī, Book of Divorce, no. 4867; an-Nisāʾī, Book of Divorce, no. 3409; Ibn Majāh, Book of Divorce, no. 2046; Musnad Aḥmad, *musnad madanīīn*, no. 15513)

It is important to draw attention to the fact that in this hadith the Prophet does not use the term *khulʿ*, and it is probably used as a legal term only by later jurists. This is confirmed by Aḥmad's transmission of this hadith, in which Aḥmad Ibn Ḥanbal himself adds that this was 'the first *khulʿ* in Islam (Musnad Aḥmad, *musnad madanīīn*, no.15513).' In the Prophet's terminology however, according to the hadith, the man is ordered to divorce (*ṭallaq*) the woman, i.e. 'to release her'.

There are two more hadiths referred to in Koranic commentaries which I have encountered in discussions with Islamists. Ibn Kathīr refers to these two hadiths (Ibn Kathir 1989 vol. I: 280):

1 The woman who asks her husband to divorce her where there is no harm done, the smell of Paradise is forbidden for her.

(Musnad Aḥmad, *bāqi musnad al-anṣār*, no. 21404; Sunan Ibn Majāh, Book of Divorce, no. 2045; Sunan Abī Dāwud, Book of Divorce, no. 1899; Sunan at-Tirmidhī, Book of Divorce and Oath of Condemnation, no. 1108)[6]

2 The women who make *khulʿ* are hypocrites.

(at-Tirmidhī, Book of Divorce and Oath of Condemnation, no. 1107; Sunan an-Nisāʾī, Book of Divorce, no. 3407; Musnad Aḥmad, *bāqi musnad al-mukhtirīn*, no. 8990)[7]

Neither of these hadiths is regarded as authentic (*ṣaḥīḥ*). With regard to the first, at-Tirmidhī claims it to be good (*ḥasan*) only. As for the second, according to the hadith system *al-ʿālamī*, which contains the 'Six Authentic' hadith collections in addition to Musnad Aḥmad, Mālik and ad-Dārimī, its narrator chain is not authentic (*ṣaḥīḥ*). Moreover, according to Ibn Kathīr, at-Tirmidhī claims the latter hadith to be *gharīb*, i.e. with only one first narrator and one narrator chain. In addition its narrator chain is weak (Ibn Kathīr 1989 vol. I: 280). In spite of this lack of strong authenticity, these two hadiths have been actively used in order to weaken women's claims for divorce. Moreover, Ibn Kathīr adds that those belonging to the three first generations of Muslims and later scholars have judged that *khulʿ* is not allowed except when a woman suffers hardship in the marriage (Ibn Kathīr 1981 vol. I: 280). It is interesting how some scholars have deduced rules and regulations according to a patriarchal value system using weak legal evidence such as the two hadiths mentioned above, while disregarding stronger legal evidence such as the Koranic verse 2: 229 and the hadith about the wife of Thābit ibn Qais.

Although Esposito mentions evidence from the Koran and the Sunna in his study, *Women in Muslim Family Law*, it seems that he mostly bases his descriptions and arguments on legal material, particularly from *qanūn*, so it would appear that he has not distinguished between the three levels of legislation, sharia, *fiqh* and *qanūn*. He sees *khulʿ* in terms of a divorce in which there is mutual consent between the man and the wife. He further explains that *khulʿ* can be executed *with* the wife's financial compensation to her husband, either through paying back her dowry or by offering an agreed sum or object, or *without* any financial compensation (Esposito 1982: 33–4).

It is a fact that female divorce is a controversial matter in most Muslim countries, where divorces for women have been difficult to obtain without establishing strong evidence of mistreatment or male sexual impotency (Yamani 1996: 16; 259). In contrast to this, the Koranic verse 2: 229 and the hadith about the wife of Thābit ibn Qais quoted above offer substantial legal evidence that a woman can easily get a divorce even without any strong reasons. It seems, however, that in the development of Islamic law, scholars have tended to pay less attention to this latter evidence than to the two former hadiths quoted by Ibn Kathīr and regarded as not authentic (*ṣaḥīḥ*). This is confirmed by the writings of Sābiq who quotes the hadith which says that women who ask for *khulʿ* are hypocrites, without mentioning that it is not regarded as an authentic hadith. Sābiq also states that a woman has to obtain an acceptance of divorce from a judge, and he offers as evidence the fact that the wife of Thābit ibn Qais went to the Prophet to ask for a divorce (Sābiq 1985 vol. II: 299). In contrast to this interpretation of the hadith, I suggest that although the hadith about the wife of Thābit does not deal with a situation in which the husband objects to a divorce, one can presume that the Prophet's Companions would not reject or oppose any of the Prophet's judgements. This hadith therefore, could, in my view, not only refer to a situation in which the husband agrees to a divorce, but could hypothetically also refer to a situation in which he refuses. The treatment of divorce both within the various law schools and in the legal regulations in the various Muslim countries, i.e. *qanūn*, indicates a male reading and an androcentric interpretation of the Koran and the Sunna. This male reading is in accordance with patriarchal attitudes based on the 'Arab cultural base pattern' prevailing in the society where these rules were formed. This is indicated in the above discussion which shows that certain hadiths have been preferred over others not according to their strength in narrator chains but according to their content. The selection of certain texts in preference over others points to 'the basket metaphor' by which ideas and notions are selected from available resources according to their cultural relevance. Thus, the interpretation of social issues in the Islamic sources was influenced by the social organisation and structures which prevailed at the time of the formation of the law.

As indicated above, Esposito sees *khulʿ* as a matter of mutual consent only, and I suspect that his study of legal texts in contemporary Muslim countries has made him draw this conclusion (Esposito 1982: 135–43). Esposito's observation actually reinforces the Muslim feminists' claim that the woman's right of divorce is denied in Muslim countries (cf. Yamani 1996; Afkhami 1995), a denial which is more a consequence of *qanūn* than of Islamic jurisprudence.

In the *fiqh* works by Sābiq and az-Zuḥailī, a second form of *khulʿ* when the husband objects to a divorce is presented. In this case a judge can release the wife from her husband despite his opposition. If there are not any substantial reasons for divorce, such as sexual impotence, mistreatment or lack of financial support, the woman will have to pay back the dowry. However, if there are such reasons, the judge can grant the woman a divorce. This latter form of divorce is called *taṭlīq*. In this case the husband has no right to financial compensation.

As for non-Muslim countries, many Islamists claim that a Sheikh, Imam or a learned person could take the role of a judge in this matter. When I went into detail however, I discovered that there was disagreement about *who* could actually function as a judge in this situation. Some Islamists with whom I discussed the issue believed that anyone with sufficient knowledge of Islamic law could function as a judge. Others claimed that only Islamic-educated scholars could perform such a role.

I would claim that the practice of female divorce (*khulʿ*) despite the objection of the husband is more common in a western context than in Muslim countries. As noted by many female Muslim researchers, divorce for a woman is difficult to obtain in Muslim countries due to what they define as strict patriarchal practices (Yamani 1996; Afkhami 1995). Najla Hamadeh has discussed the situation of divorce in Muslim countries. She writes:

> The Islamic family laws [here she probably refers to *qanūn*] governing divorce are not in harmony with what is generally known about the life of the Prophet. The Prophet considered a wife's disinclination to be his wife as tantamount to breaking the marriage contract, as happened with Amrah bint Yazid al-Kilabiyyah on their wedding night. Moreover these laws are not in line with the principle implicit in the Prophet's acceptance of the marriage proposal made to him by Khadija. The implied principle here is that women can initiate marriage by their independent will, and, as a corollary, it may be argued that women can end the marriage on their own initiative. The fact that Sukainah, the Prophet's great-granddaughter, stipulated in her marriage contract that she retain the titular right of divorce, together with the precedent of Khadija and Amrah, offers Muslim society enough leeway to revise the existing family laws. In fact, these precedents impose on it the duty to recognise the wife's will and her right to decide her own fate in this most crucial and most intimate aspect of her life, especially since the Qur'an, though giving the husband the right to divorce his wife, nowhere denies such a right to the wife.
>
> (Hamadeh in Yamani 1996: 335–6)

Hamadeh criticises those Muslim writers who 'romanticise Muslim family life', saying:

> Even if such portrayals were true about the prevailing state of affairs, it is to be kept in mind that the function of the law is to deter, not nice people and doting husbands, but transgressors and criminals. The law is there to protect the weak from the tyranny of the strong, when the latter

> choose to use their power to oppress the former. By putting powerful legal weapons in the hands of *every* husband, no matter what his mental or moral qualities happen to be, the wife is left at the mercy of her luck; and family law, which is supposed to protect the weaker member in the marriage, does the opposite, leaving her in a precarious position.
>
> (Hamadeh in Yamani 1996: 336)

This is how the Personal Status Law in Muslim countries is viewed by Muslim feminist activists. In Hamadeh's portrayal of the situation it seems that the legal provision for *khulʿ* is rarely used. On the other hand, it is important to draw attention to the fact that, while Muslim feminist activists are fighting for the right to divorce, many common Muslim women are concerned with how to *remain* married and how to prevent their husbands from divorcing them. Moreover, Rosander has observed that in a certain area in Morocco women view Moroccan family law as 'an instrument for embittering their lives' (Rosander 1991: 51). Rosander says that these women 'in particular stress men's right to repudiation and to polygyny as the great threats to a married woman's existence' (Rosander 1991: 51). This is reinforced by Hamadeh's arguments as she attacks the ease of access to divorce by men rather than criticising the absence of a female right to divorce.

Discussion

An interesting observation is that verses dealing with divorce are often followed by a warning: 'These are the bounds (*ḥudūd*) of God, do not, then, transgress them'. *Ḥudūd* is a legal term used to denote corporal punishment such as flogging or stoning for adultery, and cutting off hands for theft. In contrast to this, by exploring the Koran I discovered that the term *ḥudūd* was applied mainly to matters concerning the treatment of women (K.58: 4; 2: 187), divorce (K.2: 229–30; 65: 1) and inheritance (K.4: 13–14), i.e. matters which we now define within the legal sphere of Personal Status Law. The other matter linked to *ḥudūd* in the Koran is the striving for 'God's cause' with regard to one's possessions and one's life (K.9: 97; 112). The issue which arises therefore is how a matter such as divorce which the Koran treats so seriously, has been treated so casually by many Muslim men and has even been sanctioned by the law, as observed by Hamadeh and Rosander. Moreover, the term *ḥudūd* has come to convey issues of grave significance in Islamic law. In spite of this, male divorce and men's treatment of their wives in divorce situations have not acquired any real importance although this matter is obviously linked to the concept of *ḥudūd allāh* (the boundaries of God).

It is interesting to note that in my discussion with Sheikh Aḥmad ʿAlī al-Imām, a presidential adviser for authentication (*taʾṣīl*, i.e. what is present in the Islamic sources) in the Sudan, we discussed the question of divorce. I argued that I found it strange that there is no punishment attached to *munkar* behaviour (behaviour which is not generally accepted) in divorce cases, given that in the Koran the matter is regarded as serious. al-Imām suggested that what might possibly be introduced in such cases is *taʿzīr* (reprimand). *Taʿzīr* is described, for instance in the classical manual of Shāfiʿī Law, *The Reliance of the Traveller*, as a disciplinary action imposed on a person who commits an act of disobedience against God, which has no specific legal penalty or expiation. This disciplinary action (*taʿzīr*) is not specified and might be decided by the authorities (N. Keller 1991: 619). al-Imām was the only one of my informants and interviewees who accepted that there could possibly be a form of punishment for men in matters of misbehaviour within marriage. Sudanese Islamists might be placed within the 'normative field', where three main cultural base patterns are active: the 'Arab cultural base pattern' as Sudan is part of the Arab world; the 'African cultural base pattern' as Sudan is on the borderline between the Arab world and South of the Sahara; and, lastly, the 'western cultural base pattern' is active as a frame of reference since most leading Sudanese Islamists have pursued higher degrees in Europe or the USA. My experience of Sudanese Islamists is that they are inclined towards reform and renewal in the understanding of Islam as well as in Islamic jurisprudence. The social organisation within such a broad cultural sphere seems to be conducive to an open attitude towards change.

In my daily relations with Arab Muslims in particular, but also with Muslims belonging to other ethnic groups, I have observed that men tend to treat the matter of divorce lightly and that even some scholars support this attitude. In Muslim countries, marital problems tend to be dealt with within the extended family. In western countries, with the spatial separation of Muslim extended families, Muslims turn to other bodies in order to solve their social problems. It seems that although Muslim women in western countries have less social protection than in Muslim countries, the majority society tends to favour the Muslim woman over the man. This is usually the case in Sweden, for instance, where the authorities tend to favour Muslim women in disputes of divorce and child custody.

As for the Muslim community in general, in my experience there is often an initiative taken from within the community when it comes to resolving marital problems. If a man has a problem with his wife, his friends would send their wives to talk her into better behaviour. If this does not work, the issue of divorce is easily raised. Contrary to this, if a woman has difficulties within her marriage few men would take the responsibility of talking to the man in question. The common notion in such cases is that one should avoid interfering in family affairs. Moreover, if a woman wants a divorce, there is a tendency to urge her to be patient (*ṣabr*) even in matters where the man has transgressed what in the Koran is called 'the bounds of God'. The issue at stake is thus that men are often supported in their pursuit of a divorce, whereas women are most often dissuaded from pursuing a divorce from within the community.

Although I observed this same attitude among Islamists in Europe, I also noticed that well-educated Islamists regard divorce as a much more serious matter than common Muslims do. The great majority of my interviewees and scholars belonging to this category emphasised men's responsibilities in divorce cases and women's right to divorce.

As mentioned above, at the time of the Prophet and the Companions, divorce and remarriage were common even among women. The Prophet himself was mainly married to divorced women or widows, which indicates that there was no stigma attached to divorced women. In addition, issues surrounding child custody were different then than they are today. It is probable that children were regarded as adults at an early age, and the provision of custody within the extended family was probably less of a problem than it is today when the span of childhood is prolonged and the nuclear family has taken the place of the extended family. Moreover, it seems obvious that attitudes towards divorced women in the Muslim world have changed dramatically from early Islamic history until today, with fewer opportunities for women to remarry.

It would be interesting to study reasons for these changes in attitude towards divorced women. Although this question is well beyond the scope of this study, I would like to suggest that one possible reason might have to do with the matter of polygyny versus monogamy. As polygyny, which was quite common in early Islamic history, decreased and monogamy came to be the most common form of marriage, the marriage bond tightened and marital breakdown became less common. This idea first occurred to me when I was reading Muhammad Asad's book, *The Road to Mecca*. This book gives an impression of the Arab Peninsula in the 1920s and 1930s, at a time when traditional attitudes and practices were widespread and polygyny flourished. Asad refers specifically to the prevalence of marriage, divorce and remarriage which in my view concurs with attitudes found in hadith and in the biographies of the Prophet and his Companions, where frequent marriages and divorces happened with the active participation of both sexes. In my discussion with a Saudi Arabian Islamist, she told me that she remembered how in her grandparents' generation, marriages and divorces and remarriages were common and that her grandmother for instance had been married up to four times. In contrast to this pattern, she said that in Saudi Arabia today monogamous marriages are increasing and divorced women rarely remarry. 'However', she added, 'even women who have not previously been married are these days not getting married, and in many families young girls have not any prospect of getting a marriage partner.' Her statement reinforces the suggestion that changes in attitude towards divorced women and their possibilities for remarrying have to do with changes in polygynic practices. As more women are available, men tend to choose more carefully and divorced women take second rank in this competition.

As it is apparent that attitudes towards divorced women have changed, I will consider the two Koranic terms *maʿrūf* (that which is generally acceptable) and *munkar* (that which is *not* generally accepted). These are terms which I think indicate the possibility of change *per se*. In the section on sharia, I raised the question of what happens when that which is 'generally accepted' and 'right' or that which is 'not generally accepted' or 'wrong' changes from one period of time to another or from one society to another. I draw attention to this matter here because the term *maʿrūf* is frequently linked to the matter of divorce. This is evident in the Koranic verse: 'And so, when they are about to reach the end of their waiting-term, either retain them in kindness (*maʿrūf*) or part with them in kindness (*maʿrūf*).' Bearing in mind Christensen's model of the 'normative field', I would pose the question as to whether the content of what is *maʿrūf* is necessarily constant or if it is subject to change. In discussion with many Islamists, they claim that what is *maʿrūf* and what is *munkar* is defined according to sharia. This indicates a view of sharia as homogeneous and static which is contrary to reality, since in Islamic jurisprudence most cases include a variety of views.

Esposito has observed that the form of sharia applied in the Egyptian Personal Status Law allows for few possibilities of a woman obtaining a divorce. This, he claims, has to do with the predominance of the Ḥanafī law school in Egypt, which according to him is the Islamic law school which allows fewest rights for women in issues of family law. The Mālikī law school, on the other hand, he sees as offering greater protection for the rights of women (Esposito 1982). The differences between the law schools in matters of family law indicate that there is a discrepancy in the interpretation of Islamic sources. The Koranic terms *maʿrūf* and *munkar* might therefore be seen to have different meanings in the various regions of the Muslim world.

What happens then in a western context? Does the content of *maʿrūf* and *munkar* change? What are the possibilities for change regarding attitudes towards divorce among Islamists living in Europe? It was in my interview with Fu'ād Hussain from the Islamic Liberation Party that I first became aware of the Islamist tendency to distinguish between what the sharia says (*sharʿan*) and what is morally acceptable in Islam (*akhlāq islāmī*), and it was in the discussion about divorce that this distinction became obvious. I asked Hussain whether a man could divorce a wife for no reason and without involving a judge. When he started to give the legal arguments I asked him what *his* opinion was, not what the law said. He answered that in his view it was not moral in terms of Islam for a man to treat his family badly by divorcing in this way. I trace this obvious distinction between the legal sphere and the moral sphere back to the legislation of the ninth century when non-verbalised moral customs (*ʿurf*) of the time were canonised. As these customs were patriarchal in form and emphasised male rights, legislation concerning the protection of women's rights was not included, as indicated by the difference between a man's right to divorce and a woman's lack of the same right. The question is whether the reinterpretation or reselection of the Islamic texts or injunctions in a European context will lead to contemporary verbalised or non-verbalised moral customs associated with women's rights which are compatible with the letter or the spirit of Islamic sources being incorporated into legislation. I believe that selection from 'the basket' will be carried out according to the ideology of the 'western cultural base pattern', depending on the degree of involvement with majority society and on whether the interpreter's social grouping is an Islamist movement or a particular network group.

The hadith about the Prophet's acceptance of the wife of Thābit's plea for divorce where there was no obvious mistreatment has played a minor role in traditional Islamic legislation within the law school system. However, I assume that in a reinterpretation or reselection of the Islamic texts this hadith will become more prominent with the Islamist methodology of 'returning to the Koran and the Sunna'. By 'reproducing the past in the present', hadiths which are compatible with European society may be brought to the forefront. Thus, there is a possibility that moral customs which are in line with Islamic principles will be taken into consideration in the development of new Islamic legislation in Europe.

Islamists in Europe

I asked two questions about divorce in the questionnaire: one about *ṭalāq* and one about *khulʿ*. For the question about *ṭalāq* I gave five alternatives with the possibility of ticking more than one. The alternatives were as follows:

1 The husband can divorce his wife only *through* a judge.
2 The husband can divorce his wife *without* a judge.
3 The husband can divorce his wife whenever he wants, without any reason and without discussing the matter first with her.
4 The husband can only divorce his wife if he has good reasons, but may do so without discussing it with her first.
5 The husband should not divorce his wife without good reasons and not until he has discussed the matter with her.

Among the respondents, 75 per cent ticked alternative (5). Even divided into sexes, 75 per cent of the men and 75 per cent of the women ticked alternative (5). Within the group who ticked this alternative, 40 per cent had it as the only alternative whereas 25 per cent had this answer as a second alternative. The rest of this group, 35 per cent, had alternative (2) as a second alternative. In the other main group which constituted 25 per cent of the respondents, alternatives (2) and (3) were ticked.

What do these figures tell us? Neither Sābiq nor az-Zuḥailī in their widespread works on *fiqh* have attached any conditions to a man's right to divorce his wife (Sābiq 1985 vol. II; az-Zuḥailī 1989 vol. VII). As both these legal works are based on traditional *fiqh* literature, it can be assumed that in traditional law, i.e. within the legislation of the four law schools, there are *no* conditions which must be fulfilled for a man to divorce his wife. This was reinforced in the interviews I conducted with Islamist scholars who explicitly stated that a man can divorce his wife without any reason at all. Likewise, according to traditional works on *fiqh*, a man has an exclusive right to divorce his wife without any reason and without discussing the matter with her. In spite of this, 75 per cent of the respondents, who were all well-educated Arabic-speaking Islamists with easy access to works on *fiqh*, ticked alternative (5) which stated that a man should not divorce his wife without good reasons and not until he has discussed the matter with her. Their answers are not in conformity with the legal understanding of a man's right to divorce and they point to the tension between the legal judgements and contemporary moral thought.

As for alternative (1), that a man can divorce his wife only through a judge, this was ticked by 25 per cent of all the respondents (also in this case by 25 per cent of the women and 25 per cent of the men). In Islamic literature there is an emphasis on the husband's right to freely seek a divorce, as shown in Sābiq's and az-Zuḥailī's work. Within Shīʿī legislation, on the other hand, Mir has observed that a man can only obtain a divorce through a judge (Mir-Hosseini 1993). It is important to be aware that even in many Sunnī Muslim countries a man has to get a divorce acceptance from a judge as this is part of the countries' actual legal code. In Sunnī legislation, however, there is no need for a judge in the case of a man's pursuit of divorce. Thus for 25 per cent of the respondents to claim that a judge is needed for a man's divorce might either mean that they take their starting point in their countries' actual legislation, or it might imply a change in attitudes towards male divorce in general.

I further pursued the matter of male divorce (*ṭalāq*) in an in-depth interview with Nasra, who had ticked alternative (1) in the questionnaire, that a judge is necessary even in cases when it is the husband who wants to divorce. When I asked her why she had ticked this alternative, she answered:

> Many men tend to use the law of divorce to their advantage, although in the Koran the matter is one of great seriousness. When I see how many men misuse the right God gave them, I become very sad. They will be in big trouble as they misuse a benefit given by God. On the other hand, God will deal with them when their term is out [when they die]. Everything God gave us, whether bad or good, is a test of how we can handle it. However, I think it is important to know that men who do take advantage of God's benevolence are people who do not fully understand what Islam is. My experience is that it is mostly men with generally low education and little understanding of Islam

> who actually misuse the law of God. That is why I think that all cases of divorce whether initiated by the husband or by the wife *should* always go through a legal body [translation mine].

Although the attitudes of some of the Islamists I spoke to as well as some respondents to the questionnaire conformed to the 'Arab cultural base pattern', it is apparent that there is a modification in attitudes. I believe that Islamists with traditional (*taqlīdī*)[8] attitudes are those who either work in closed Muslim environments or have little contact with majority societies. Another variable is the kind of education that the various Islamists have. Those with an Islamic education tend to be more influenced by the 'Arab cultural base pattern' than those with a secular education. It is interesting that the change in attitudes did not necessarily depend on how many years the interviewees had been in Europe. Among the 25 per cent of respondents who ticked alternatives (2) and (3), that a man can divorce his wife without a judge and that a man can divorce his wife whenever he wants, without any reason and without discussing the matter with her first, most had spent more than ten years in Europe. My impression is that modifications and changes in attitude and the selection from 'the basket' have to a great extent to do with one's primary and secondary contacts and with matters of personal disposition, such as whether a person is open-minded or whether s/he is closed to external influences.

Islamist attitudes towards divorce and the modification of these attitudes in the encounter with western society are another indication of a change of the normative base pattern. In the western context the 'Arab cultural base pattern' tends to be eclipsed by the 'western cultural base pattern'. Traditional interpretations of the Islamic sources have given way to an interpretation which places greater emphasis on women's rights in keeping with the 'western cultural base pattern' in which the ideal of gender equality is prominent.

Female divorce

When it came to the question on *khulʿ*, I gave three alternatives in the questionnaire:

1 A woman can divorce (*khulʿ*) her husband through a judge (*qāḍī*) *with* the consent of her husband.
2 A woman can divorce (*khulʿ*) her husband through a judge *without* the consent of her husband.
3 A woman can divorce (*khulʿ*) her husband *without* the consent of a judge and *without* the consent of her husband.

None of the respondents ticked alternative (3). As for alternatives (1) and (2), 33 per cent ticked alternative (1) only whereas 67 per cent ticked both (1) and (2). There is a link, although not unanimous, between those who ticked alternative (5) in the question on male divorce (*ṭalāq*) and those who ticked alternative (2) in this section. It is interesting that all females who ticked alternative (3) in the section on male divorce, thus accepting that a man is free to divorce his wife whenever he wants without any reason, and without the consent of a judge, ticked alternative (1) above, accepting female divorce only *with* the man's acceptance. This means that they actually denied the woman her right to divorce if the husband objected. This is very much in line with the practice in Muslim countries, where women's right to divorce is limited even with strong evidence of mistreatment, as observed by many Muslim female researchers (Yamani 1996; Afkhami 1995).

In European countries, what seems to happen is that Muslim women who do not find acceptance for their plea for divorce through a Muslim mediator tend to go to European authorities, pursuing their cases through European courts. Farūq is a Palestinian who has lived in various countries in Europe for nearly fifteen years. He has a scientific education, but in Europe he holds a position as Sheikh in the Muslim community. He issues marriage and divorce certificates and is active in *daʿwa*-work. When I asked him why it is easier for women in European countries to obtain a divorce (*khulʿ*) in the face of the husband's refusal than in the Muslim world, even with a Muslim mediator, he stated:

> There are various reasons for this. In our Muslim countries, the social system is totally different from the European system. There, the husband is working and supports his family, whereas the wife stays at home. If she seeks a divorce, she usually does not have any economic security. I believe that women in Muslim countries do not think about divorce as women in Europe, even Muslim women, do. Ideas and attitudes differ. In addition, the actual legislation in Muslim countries is rigid and traditionalist (*taqlīdī*). If the woman does not have a *very* good reason for divorce, the judge would send her home to her husband's house. Here in Europe on the other hand, most women work, and due to their economic security, it is easier to consider divorce in difficult situations. Moreover, in the European legal system, even judges themselves encourage women to divorce. Muslim women in Europe obtain divorces from the European system. We Muslims want to solve the problems of Muslims, and we are therefore more open to divorces initiated by women. In addition, we are open towards change and we are reform-directed. We want reform (*tajdīd*) in *fiqh*, we do not want to maintain traditional practices which are not compatible with Islamic principles [translation mine].

As for the financial compensation the wife has to grant her husband in case of *khulʿ*, Farūq says:

> It is justice that the woman should give back her dowry (*mahr*) to her husband. A man *has to* give his wife dowry. It is an obligation in Islam. If she wants a divorce, it is *her* obligation, and *his* right to get it back. As far as *khulʿ* is concerned, it is usually not a matter of mistreatment on the husband's part, but rather a matter of maladjustment on the part of the wife, and the husband should not suffer in this case.

With regard to *khulʿ*, there is an apparent discrepancy between people's attitudes and what actually happens. Despite the fact that most Islamists maintain views influenced by the 'Arab cultural base pattern', that women are rarely entitled to divorce, the social system in Europe might force through changes. As divorce for women is relatively easy in the European countries where I conducted my fieldwork, there is greater acceptance of female divorce even within Muslim communities in these countries. The Islamist methodology of 'returning to the Koran and the Sunna' thus 'reproducing the past in the present' might generate a reselection from the Islamic sources, bringing to the forefront those hadiths compatible with the 'western cultural base pattern' and adjusting Islamic rules to the social reality. There is however a problem when it comes to *khulʿ*. If the wife is mistreated either in a psychological or in a physical manner and she cannot provide sufficient evidence she has to return the dowry her husband gave her. I believe, thus, that the increase in dowry, particularly in the Muslim world recently, might actually function to obstruct the ability of women to divorce.

Child custody

In the Koran there is no mention of which parent should have custody of the children in case of a divorce. According to the view of Islamists, however, it is the father who is responsible for the child's and the mother's economic sustenance for as long as the child is with the mother. They referred to the verse 2: 233:

> And the mothers may nurse their children for two whole years, if they wish to complete the period of nursing. It is incumbent upon him who has begotten the child to provide in kindness (*maʿrūf*) for their [the mothers'] sustenance and clothing. No human being shall be burdened with more than one is well able to bear; neither shall a mother be made to suffer because of her child, nor, because of his child, he who has begotten it. And the same duty rests upon the heir. And if both parents decide, by mutual consent and counsel (*tashāwur*), to end the sucking, they will incur no sin thereby. And if you decide to entrust your children to foster-mothers, you will incur no sin provided you ensure, in kindness (*maʿrūf*), the safety of the child which you are

handing over. But remain conscious of God (*attaqū allāh*), and know that God sees all that you do.

When I remarked that this verse refers to the nursing period, they stated that the support should be extended to the whole of the *ḥiḍāna* period, which means up to the time when the child is supposed to be with the mother according to the Islamic law schools.

In the hadith literature I have found four hadiths related to the Prophet's handling of matters of child custody (*al-ḥiḍāna*)[9] after a divorce. In addition there is a story about ʿUmar's custody dispute with his former wife which is narrated by Ibn Abī Shaiba. The hadiths from the Prophet are:

1 A woman came to the Messenger of God (p.b.u.h.) and said: 'O messenger of God. Verily, my son here was in my womb, my breasts give him milk, and from my lap he gets affection. His father divorced me and he wants to take him away from me.' [Muhammad] said: 'You are most entitled to him if you do not remarry'.

(Sunan Abī Dāwud, Book of Divorce, no. 1938)

2 The Messenger of God (p.b.u.h.) said: 'The one who separates a mother from her child, God will separate between him and his beloved one on the Last Day.'

(Sunan at-Tirmidhī, Book of Buying, no. 1204; Sunan Ibn Majāh, Book of Trade, no. 2241; Musnad Aḥmad, *bāqi musnad al-anṣār*, no. 22401)

3 Narrated by Abū Huraira: A woman said: 'O Messenger of God, my husband wants to take away my son, who has availed me and provided me with drinking water from Abū ʿInaba's well.' Then her husband came and the Prophet said: 'Lad, this is your father and this is your mother, so take whoever of them you wish by the hand.' He took his mother's hand and she went off with him.

(Sunan an-Nisāʾī, Book of Divorce, no. 3439; Sunan Abī Dāwud, Book of Divorce, no. 1939)

4 Rāfiʿ ibn Sinān told that he became Muslim but his wife refused to become a Muslim. The Prophet then made the mother sit down on one side and the father on another side and made the son sit down between them. The boy inclined to his mother. The Prophet then said: 'O God, give him guidance.' The boy then inclined to his father and he took him.

(Sunan Abī Dāwud, Book of Divorce, no. 1916)

The story about ʿUmar goes:

ʿUmar ibn al-Khaṭṭāb divorced his wife, Umm ʿĀṣim (the mother of ʿĀṣim). ʿUmar came to her and ʿĀṣim was on her lap. ʿUmar wanted to take ʿĀṣim from her. They pulled ʿĀṣim back and forth between

> each other until the boy started to cry. ʿUmar went to Abū Bakr who said to him: 'Her caresses, her lap and her smell is better for him than you are, until he grows up and he can choose for himself.'
>
> (az-Zuḥailī 1989 vol. VII: 761)

Law schools on child custody

The four law schools have deduced various rules for child custody after a divorce from these few examples in the Islamic sources. According to az-Zuḥailī, the main principle of the Islamic legal material in the matter of custody is 'the welfare of the child' (*maṣlaḥa al-maḥḍūn*) (az-Zuḥailī 1989 vol. VII: 743–5; Darsh 1984).

In *fiqh* there are two stages of child custody. The first stage, called *ḥiḍāna* (nursing), applies to small children and in this stage there is unanimous agreement among scholars that children should in the first place be cared for by women: first, the mother if she has not remarried, and second the mother's mother. The scholars differ about who should come next. Some say the mother's grandmother, then the child's paternal grandmother, the sister, etc., whereas in the Ḥanbalī school for instance the father of the child is second after the maternal grandmother (az-Zuḥailī 1989 vol. VII: 744–5). All law schools have long lists of preferences in the matter of custody, but it is important to be aware that many of these are individual judgements (*ijtihād*) based mainly on the hadiths I have rendered above.

As for the second stage of child custody when children come of age, there are different opinions among the scholars about who should have custody. The hadiths above suggest that children should be able to choose for themselves, but they do not mention any age at which this should come into effect. In contrast to these vague suggestions in the Islamic sources, the four law schools have detailed regulations for child custody. Within the legislation of the Ḥanafī law school a boy should move to his father when he is no longer in need of 'women's caring' (az-Zuḥailī 1989 vol. VII: 742). This school defines this age as 7, from the hadith 'Order your children to pray at seven', and claims that when the child is able to keep his [state of] purity (*ṭahāra*), at 9 years at the latest, the stage of *ḥiḍāna* is ended (az-Zuḥailī 1989 vol. VII: 742). As for a girl, she should stay with women for a longer period as she needs a female education, and at the start of menstruation at either 9 or 11 she should move to her father (az-Zuḥailī 1989 vol. VII: 742).

Within the legislation of the Māliki law school, it is considered that a boy should stay with his mother until his puberty, then he should move to his father. The girl should stay with her mother until she gets married. This applies even if the mother is a non-Muslim. Both the Ḥanafī and Mālikī law schools reject the possibility of the child's choosing between the parents as they say that the child would choose the one who 'plays' with it, not the one who takes the child's education seriously (az-Zuḥailī 1989 vol. VII: 743).

Within the legislation of the Shāfiʿī school, the period of *ḥiḍāna* is considered to end when the child is 7 or 8 years old. At that time, the child should choose between the mother and the father if the parents have not come to an agreement. The Ḥanbalī law school has similar regulations for the boy. When he is 7, he should choose between the parents. However, the regulation for girls differs. When a girl turns 7 she should live with her father. The school bases this legislation on the principle of the welfare (*maṣlaḥa*) of the child. At the stage of *ḥiḍāna* the child is in need of care so the mother should be the care-giver, but at the end of *ḥiḍāna* the child is in need of protection. According to the Ḥanbalī law school the father is the one who is most capable of protecting the girl (az-Zuḥailī 1989 vol. VII: 744–5).

What is interesting in this matter is the differences between the various law schools, and since legal evidence is scarce their regulations are based mainly on scholarly opinions. It can thus be anticipated that the regulations with regard to child custody are liable to change, and in my discussion with Sheikh Darsh I found this to be the case. In 1984 Darsh wrote a booklet called *An Outline of Islamic Law*. He discusses the matter of child custody and asserts that 'the welfare of the child' is the main principle. Further on he categorically states that 'if a woman remarries she cannot get the custody of her children' (Darsh 1984: 13). In the early 1990s Darsh had a column responding to readers' queries in an Islamic magazine, *Q-News*. This magazine is directed towards Muslim youth, particularly second-generation Muslims. In one issue Darsh was asked who should have child custody after a divorce. He again asserted that the main principle is the welfare of the children. However, as he went into detail and pointed out the rules and regulations which exist in the Islamic law concerning child custody, he expressed the opinion that if it is better for the welfare of the children, they can live with their mother *even if she remarries* (Vogt 1995). This case indicates how attitudes become modified and how these modifications can restructure actual Islamic legislation. In my interview with Darsh in London in January 1996, I asked him how he could possibly say that children can live with their mother even if she remarries, when most other Islamic scholars would claim the opposite. He answered:

> I make it very clear, I am not qualified to make a statement of my own. What I have seen is what is written in the standard available textbooks. I refer particularly to three books dealing with family life; one written by Sheikh Muḥammad Abū Zahra, the second is written by Professor Salām Madhkūr, the third is written by Professor Abū al-ʿAinain Badrān. The three of them are professors of the Islamic sharia and the Faculty of Law. Thus I am reflecting the standard of

> the Islamic point of view. In their books they are discussing the question of guardianship of the minor. They are talking about whose rights should be considered; is it the right of the children alone; or the right of the mother alone; or the shared right of the children and the mother? There is a recent point of view saying that custody is primarily the right of the children. Another point of view is that it is the right of the mother. A third standpoint which is much more in line with Islam says that it is a shared right for, on the one hand, the mother, as she is the one who brings them up and is psychologically qualified for the children's upbringing, and, on the other hand, the children. Islam takes into consideration these basic points of view as one point. And as such, the three scholars say that the mother, if she is trustworthy and a woman of integrity, she is entitled to the guardianship. So as for the question of custody of the minors, I am reflecting the Islamic point of view which is taken by the Egyptian courts as far as children are concerned. They do not differentiate between whether the mother is a Muslim or a non-Muslim. The basic question is: is she trustworthy and a woman of integrity? The answer is, if she is qualified and she is not standing in the way of their Islamic education she has the right to keep them. So I am saying this [the saying above] is not an *ijtihād* or a change in attitude. However, here in Britain, in this community everything is speculation. In this community we do not have jurisdiction in this question, that is why we have established our organisation, The Islamic Sharia Council, which is dealing particularly with family affairs. In this organisation, we are not tied up to a particular school of thought. For instance, in matters of divorce, we take the Mālikī point of view which is much more liberal in this issue than the other law schools. As for the children's guardianship it is what is for the benefit (*maṣlaḥa*) of the children which matters.

Darsh emphasised that although children might stay with the mother after a divorce, this does not mean that the husband escapes his responsibilities as the main educator of the children. In Darsh's view the husband is still mainly responsible for the discipline and morals of his children and he has the right to full access to his children even though they live with their mother.

Both in 1984 and in the 1990s Darsh claimed that he was following Islamic law, but in spite of this he has changed his opinion in this fundamental matter of Islamic legislation. The conclusion might be that time and place play an important part in determining potential interpretations. I believe that this process of change might be a non-deliberate process, which can be understood within the model of Hjärpe's 'basket metaphor' in which the whole Islamic content is latently present but one tends to select on the basis of that which has relevance in any given situation (Hjärpe 1997: 267). Furthermore, as the sources lend themselves to different interpretations, what is perceived in the text differs according to the context. The process of perception functions in such a way that when one searches for legal evidence, one tends to perceive that which accords with one's own ideas and attitudes, and with a certain cultural base pattern. As for that which one does not accept or which is not compatible with one's own ideas, one tends to disregard it either deliberately or non-deliberately. In this particular situation, Darsh claimed that when he judges he never promotes his own ideas but follows the intention of the Islamic sources and judges according to these sources. I believe that this is only partly true. I would suggest that as Islamic legislation is flexible and open to individual differences in the interpretation of the sources, it is possible that changes in attitude also influence legal decisions, as the example of Darsh indicates. During his stay in Europe he was influenced by the 'western cultural base pattern'. What is important to note, however, is that Darsh did not hold *salafī* ideas, so his methodology was not that of 'reproducing the past in the present'. Rather, he looked into previous scholarly judgements and selected from these. In spite of this, however, he was not opposed to new ideas and practices which would benefit the development of Islam, so his selection from 'the basket' reflects a search for solutions compatible with modern society. Although Darsh worked mainly within the Muslim community in Britain, his fluency in English and his engagement with current happenings in Europe also seem to have been factors which influenced his attitudes towards the issue of divorce and child custody. As he was also involved with actually solving Muslims' family problems, it would appear that this contact with 'the real world' led him to select a different judgement from 'the basket' in the matter of child custody.

While Darsh's change in attitude might be a non-deliberate process, other Islamists are more conscious of the process of change. In my discussion with al-Imām in the Sudan I discovered that he held the same opinion as Darsh in matters of child custody, expressing the opinion that sometimes children can stay with their mother even if she remarries if it proves that her new husband would be better at educating the children than their own father would be. However, al-Imām stated clearly that in the sharia, rulings on child custody are *ijtihāds* only and there is therefore the possibility of making new *ijtihāds* in this matter as societies change. When I suggested that he might have been influenced by the 'western cultural base pattern' during his stay in Great Britain where he pursued a higher degree, he rejected this by saying that what he *is* doing is to turn back to 'the true Islam'. This is an example of how 'the past reproduced in the present' might create less patriarchal legislation. Although it is easy to interpret al-Imām's position only in terms of 'West' and 'East', I have already suggested that the Sudan's geographical and cultural setting plays an important role in recent changes among Sudanese intellectual Islamists. Positioned on the borderline between two distinct cultural spheres, Arab and African, external cultural patterns are more likely to influence the ideology than in more closed societies. Moreover, as many Sudanese Islamists tend to have a degree from Europe or from the USA, the 'western cultural base pattern' also comes to play a role in perceptions and attitudes.

Reflections

In terms of Christensen's concept of the 'normative field', it is apparent that Darsh operates within the intersection between the 'western cultural base pattern' and the 'Arab cultural base pattern'. The 'Arab cultural base pattern' is a latent influence as it has played a significant part in the formation of that form of sharia which later Islamic legislation is based upon, and Darsh as an Islamic scholar has a traditional Islamic education built on this form of legislation. In Darsh's actual legislation in the western context, however, the Arab cultural pattern seems to recede and to play a smaller part in the restructuring of his perceptions of Islamic legislation than the other base pattern.

The above examples suggest that matters of divorce and child custody tend to change in a western context. Pressures from the majority society as well as modifications in basic attitudes promote changes in legislation. Some Islamists show a greater potential for change whereas others remain traditional in their outlooks and their perspectives on gender relations have not changed considerably from the Arabic context to the western environment.

In the next chapter I will turn to the controversial issue of female circumcision, an issue which has aroused the emotions of the various factions within the Muslim community as well as in European society.

11 Female circumcision

Female circumcision (*khitān*), which is more commonly labelled 'female genital mutilation' or 'female genital cutting' (Kassamali 1998: 39), is an issue of extreme sensitivity. In the Muslim world various attitudes towards it have been promoted, and the great variety of its practice in the different regions and disagreements among scholars put a question mark over its religious rationale. Although female circumcision was identified as an issue at the NGO's forum at the United Nations Mid-Decade Conference for Women in Copenhagen in 1980, it was at the Habitat Conference in Cairo in 1994 that this centuries-old tradition proved to be explosive in the western as well as in the Muslim debate. The report by CNN of a genital cutting operation in Cairo and the death of two young Egyptian girls, 3 and 4 years old, allegedly as a consequence of such an operation, prompted worldwide reaction to such an extent that even the Egyptian authorities were forced to make a statement against the practice. In October 1994 the then Grand Mufti, Muḥammad Sayyid Ṭanṭāwī, one of the highest Islamic authorities in Egypt, made an official statement in which he challenged the belief that there are any authentic (*ṣaḥīḥ*) hadiths or even good (*ḥasan*) hadiths which permit female circumcision or make it compulsory (al-Zuhairī 1996: 14). This statement is interesting as many Sheikhs al-Azhar, the highest Islamic authority in Egypt, have made *fatwās* (legal decisions) in favour of compulsory female circumcision (al-Zuhairī 1996: 76).

The most common types of genital operation differ from region to region, but they can be described as follows:

1 Circumcision: the removal of the prepuce or hood of the clitoris.
2 Clitoridectomy: the removal of the clitoris.
3 Excision: the removal of the clitoris and of all or part of the labia minora.
4 Infibulation: the removal of the clitoris, labia minora and all or parts of the medial part of the labia majora (The Minority Rights Group 1985: 3). This form is referred to by many Muslims as 'the pharaonic circumcision'.

In the discussion that follows I use 'circumcision' as a general term. However, in the more specific discussion I will refer to 'female circumcision' when it is a matter of the removal of the prepuce of the clitoris, whereas I will refer to 'genital cutting' to refer to other forms.

According to the 1985 report of the Minority Rights Group, clitoridectomy, excision and infibulation are the most widespread in Africa and these practices follow a geographical belt, often referred to as the nomadic belt, which covers the centre and north-east of Africa and the far south of the Arab Peninsula. Circumcision, on the other hand, is practised by the Muslim population in Indonesia and Malaysia (The Minority Rights Group 1985: 6).

Although the most drastic form of genital cutting, infibulation, is found in the Sudan which is an Arabic-speaking country, Arabic-speaking Islamists do not claim any Islamic rationale for this operation. During my visits to Sudan in 1995–8, I discussed female circumcision with many Islamists, men and women, and I discovered that although there is a common rejection at least of infibulation, female circumcision is not an issue in the general Islamic debate in the Sudan. Some Islamic activists, however, had a more conscious approach to female circumcision, among them Wiṣāl al-Maḥdī who explained:

> There is nothing in the Koran and Sunna which says that a girl should be circumcised. I am very much against the practice. In Sudan, if a midwife is caught doing the operation of circumcision, she will be imprisoned. The problem is that they are doing this in secret and it cannot be traced. Often men are against this practice, but their wives, mothers and grandmothers would make their daughters or granddaughters go through the operation without their husbands' knowledge.

Wiṣāl further quoted the Koranic verse: '[Satan says] And surely I will command them and they will change Allah's creation. Who chooses Satan for a patron instead of God is verily a loser and his loss is manifest' (K.4: 119). 'When I read this Koranic verse', she said, 'I clearly see this awful practice of circumcising girls to be the work of Iblīs [Satan] – the changing of what God has created.' She went on to say that 'in Sudan we have fought against this practice for years, but education and illumination and Islamic knowledge are the only means to put an end to it'. She ended by saying categorically: 'But definitely it will take years and years to change this practice in the Sudan.'

Wiṣāl's statement is interesting first and foremost due to her position in the Sudan as the wife of the leading Islamist, Ḥasan at-Turābī, and also because she belongs to the Maḥdī family with its historical ties with the Sudanese power elite. Her last point, however, indicates how difficult it might be to change a tradition which has survived for more than three thousand years. Although female circumcision is prohibited, the female network within Muslim countries make it almost impossible to enforce this legal prohibition.

The question of how to eradicate the various forms of female genital cutting has been raised by many educated Muslims. What is interesting to note is that most of them prefer a debate from within, refusing western meddling in the matter. Noor J. Kassamali, an African physician, claims that with western interference it might take longer to get rid of the practice. Kassamali believes that eradication of female genital cutting 'can only occur when the myths and misconceptions that surround it are understood and dispelled' (Kassamali 1998: 39). This suggests that to look at the practice in exclusively sexual terms by regarding it as a form of male sexual repression of women, an approach which is common particularly among western feminists, is not the solution. One has to address social myths which have built up around the practice of female genital cutting, such as that it prevents promiscuity, that circumcised girls are 'pure' and 'clean', etc.

Kassamali also refers to leading African women in the debate, one of whom stated: 'Let the indigenous people fight it [female genital cutting] according to their own traditions. It will die faster than if others tell us what to do.'[1] An American convert to Islam, Eric Winkel, is of the same opinion. In his view there is a stark polarisation in the debate about female circumcision, with public health professionals, development organisations and feminists on one side, and conservatives and 'fundamentalists' on the other. He says:

> The two sides seem to be characterized by observers variously as good and bad, pro-woman and anti-woman, or forward and backward. Perhaps it is more accurate to say that female circumcision and issues of the Cairo conference divide people into two groups, those who believe that the western model of development is universal and universally beneficial and those who do not.
>
> (Winkel 1995: 2–3)

He goes on to explain how as a Muslim, he and many other Muslims are in a position between the two, saying 'we agree with the points of the first side without accepting their agenda; and we agree with the agenda of the second side without accepting their points' (Winkel 1995: 3). 'Development', he says, 'includes paternalistic and racist notions of who stands in need of education and development, and why.' Winkel suggests that, as Muslims would regard western interference in the circumcision debate in terms of conspiracy theories, it is important for Muslims themselves to become involved in the eradication of female circumcision.

'The Islamic legal discourse' is, he proposes, built on a holistic view of Islam such that various texts should be regarded in the light of one another. Winkel does not explicitly reject female circumcision in terms of removal of the clitoral prepuce, rather he regards it to be an optional Sunna practice.[2] On the other hand, he categorically rejects clitoridectomy which he regards as similar to amputation of the penis, for which there are special punishments in Islamic law. The search for Islamic injunctions which take into consideration all aspects of Islamic texts and legislation might, in Winkel's view, bring about 'meaningful social change'. Winkel's main message is that Muslims should depend only on their own resources as he says that 'we [Muslims] need to apply our own traditional practices and to support an indigenous Islamic legal discourse' (Winkel 1995: 6).

That a change of attitude towards female circumcision is most effective when it is instigated from within the Muslim group is indicated by research done among Somalis in Sweden. The Swedish anthropologist Sarah Johnsdotter has observed how the Somali group has entered an Islamic legal discourse in order to put an end to the practice of infibulation among Somali girls in Sweden. In an investigation in cooperation with a male anthropologist, a male Somali medical doctor and a female Somali psychologist, they discovered that it is the Islamic argumentation which has effectively changed the attitude towards such practice in Sweden (Johnsdotter, Carlbom, Geesdiir and Almi 2000). Likewise, as with Wiṣāl above, the Somali group referred to the Koranic injunction which indicates that one should not change God's creation (K.4: 119).

The four researchers discovered how the Somali group unanimously stand up against infibulation, but how some within the group would accept what they call the 'Sunna circumcision'. The main understanding of 'Sunna circumcision' is according to them a spotting of the clitoris, which means using a small stick with a needle. As many Somalis, men and women, tend to look at women in bipolar terms of 'circumcised' or 'uncircumcised', where the circumcision means to enter the grown-up world, the spotting becomes an alternative practice to infibulation. Such a symbolic circumcision means the girls are regarded as grown-up women. The report suggests that the way to campaign against infibulation should be through religious Sheikhs, who they discovered often oppose infibulation as well, as they are aware of the 'Sunna circumcision' as not compulsory in Islam (Johnsdotter, Carlbom, Geesdiir and Almi 2000: 49–52).

Western research

Although female circumcision is customary among non-Muslims as well as Muslims and in spite of its historical origins before the advent of Islam, the practice has often been linked to the Islamic creed. In the non-Muslim debate, female circumcision has been seen as an Islamic tradition, and in the Muslim debate in those areas where circumcision is common, the debate has centred around whether circumcision is an Islamic tradition or not. In Muslim areas where female circumcision is not a common practice, the intellectual debate on female circumcision is a response and a resistance to what are regarded as western allegations linking female circumcision to Islam. It is important to be aware of the different attitudes which prevail in the various Muslim regions. While Islamic scholars in some regions promote the practice, scholars in other regions refuse to recognise it as an Islamic tradition or regard it as an individual matter in which every person is free to choose.

The problem is whether female circumcision can be regarded as belonging to Islam or not. Some western researchers claim that it does since it is considered by many Muslims to be an Islamic custom, and in the view of these researchers, if Muslims regard it as Islamic then it is Islamic (Stowasser 1994; Otterbeck 1997). Many Muslims, on the other hand, refute the allegation that female circumcision is part of the Islamic creed (cf. Ahmad 1992: 175–6).[3] For instance, the Egyptian scholar, Muḥammad al-Ghazzālī (d. 1996), is reported to have held the view that female circumcision is an evil custom which there is no evidence of the Prophet practising on his own daughters, thus indicating that this is not an Islamic custom.[4] As Peter Habbe observes in his graduate dissertation thesis, 'The significance of definition in the study of religions', the problem of whether female circumcision is an Islamic phenomenon or not depends on *how* one defines religion. Habbe refers to various voices in the debate and points out that whether one sees female circumcision as sanctioned by Islam or having no link to Islam depends on one's definition of religion. Habbe refers to various definitions, such as the *analytic* definition of religion, which he describes as a definition or a typology of religion with the emphasis on what religion *is* (Habbe 1997: 39 [translation mine]). However, it is the *operational* or the *contextual* definition of religion, which makes western researchers see female circumcision as part of the Islamic creed. Habbe identifies the *contextual* definition of religion in terms of what religion *is* and what it *does* in a discursive context (Habbe 1997: 5). Female circumcision, thus, becomes Islamically sanctioned or not Islamically sanctioned depending on which *Islam* one refers to, i.e. *how* one interprets the Islamic sources (Habbe 1997: 39). The *operational* or *contextual* definition of Islam takes into consideration not only what Islam *is*, according to the sources, but also what Muslims *do*, i.e. how Muslims understand and interpret their sources.

Thus, in a contextual definition of Islam, which is the definition applied by some western researchers, female circumcision tends to be regarded as part of the Islamic creed. Islamists and many Muslims, on the other hand, tend to define Islam in a broader manner, looking at what the texts say and then interpreting these texts. So how can it be possible to generalise and see female circumcision as an Islamic phenomenon when it is obvious that this is not a universal phenomenon among Muslims? According to the Swedish researcher on Islam, Jonas Otterbeck, it is not possible to generalise any interpretation of Islam as interpretations of social issues in the Islamic sources are variable in different Muslim societies and within the various Islamic directions in these societies. He says that as long as Muslims practice female circumcision and regard it as an Islamic custom, one cannot deny that it is part of the Islamic creed. If the custom dies out it will cease to be part of Islam, and according to him, this is what is actually happening. He explains that 'through removing it [female circumcision] as a possible Islam, one attempts to put an end to its practice' (Otterbeck 1997: 40).

I believe that Habbe's analysis of the various definitions of religion highlights a significant problem in the study of Islam in particular. The discussion of Muslims and Islam has mostly been a meta-debate in which Muslims have not had a voice. Moreover, in situations where Muslims *have* been active in the debate, the debate has been conducted on various levels in which Muslims and non-Muslims tend to talk at cross-purposes. With Habbe's definitions of religion in mind, it might be easier for those involved in the debate not only to understand each other across religious and ideological borders, but also for Muslims to understand the various directions of Islam as socio-cultural expressions which can be regarded within one all-encompassing entity which is Islam.

Islamic law schools on circumcision

The Islamist debate in an Arab context is conducted on two levels. On one level there is a discussion as to whether the reference to circumcision (*khitān*) which is found in the hadith material can be considered authentic or not. On another level the question is *how* to understand these hadiths. The terms *khitān* (circumcision) or *ṭahāra* (purity) are used as broad terms to denote both male and female circumcision, whereas there are subterms which distinguish between the two. Female circumcision is referred to as *khafaḍ* (lowering; reduction) as this term was used by the Prophet in a hadith (see below). Male circumcision, on the other hand, is referred to as *iʿḍār*.

With regard to the discussion about whether the hadiths on female circumcision are authentic or not, as-Sayyid Sābiq explains in his book written in the 1940s,[5] *The Jurisprudence of the Sunna* that circumcision for women is 'the removal of the upper part of the female pudendum', but he goes on to say that 'this is an old custom' (Sābiq 1985: 37 vol. I [translation mine]). His definition applies to a more extensive circumcision than a removal only of the prepuce of the clitoris. As Sābiq is an Egyptian, one might expect that he would put this tradition into an Islamic framework as female circumcision is pervasive in Egypt. It is important to note, however, that although Sābiq usually does not comment on the authenticity of the various hadiths he refers to, in this particular case he adds a footnote saying that 'the hadiths which order circumcision for women are all weak hadiths and the content is therefore not authentic' (Sābiq 1985: 37 vol. I [translation mine]).[6]

Sābiq's view is interesting when considered in the light of the four Islamic law schools. According to az-Zuḥailī, who often refers to existing points of view and the evidence for them, the Ḥanafī and the Mālikī law schools regard circumcision for men as Sunna and 'noble' (*makrama*) for women. Their view is built on the hadith which says that 'Circumcision (*khitān*) is Sunna for men and noble for women' (Musnad Aḥmad, *musnad al-baṣriīn*, no. 19794). az-Zuḥailī then writes in a footnote that this hadith is related by Aḥmad and al-Baihaqī, and that al-Baihaqī has rendered this hadith weak (az-Zuḥailī 1989 vol. I: 306). In the Ḥanbalī law school circumcision for men is considered to be obligatory, whereas circumcision for women is regarded as 'noble' only, due to the hadith stated above and to another hadith related by Umm ʿAṭīya al-Anṣārīya, recounting how the Prophet told her, as she used to perform female circumcision in Medina: 'If/when (*idhā*) you reduce (*khafaḍ*), then remove only a little[7] and do not ruin it (*tunhik*), because this is better (*asrā*) [more beautiful][8] for the face and more favoured by the husband (az-Zuḥailī 1989 vol. I: 307. Sunan Abī Dāwud, Book of Manners, no. 4587).'[9] It is important to note that in az-Zuhailī's book where he as a rule states the strength of the hadiths, he does not mention that this particular hadith is regarded as weak by Abū Dāwud, who is the one who has transmitted it.

The Shāfiʿī law school, on the other hand, regards circumcision as obligatory for both men and women. Shāfiʿī scholars base their argument on those hadiths which talk about male circumcision. One of these hadiths which, according to the 'Six Authentics', Musnad Aḥmad and ad-Dārimī, has many narrator chains but has Abū Huraira as the only first narrator, says that five things come from a human being's *fiṭra* (nature or instinct): to cut the pubic hair; to pluck [the hair] of the armpit; to cut the nails; to cut the moustache, and to circumcise (az-Zuḥailī 1989 vol. I: 306–7; al-Bukhārī, Book of Clothing, no. 5439; Muslim, Book of Purity, no. 377; Sunan an-Nisāʾī, Book of Purity, no. 11; Sunan Abī Dāwud, Book of Masculinity, no. 3666; Ibn Mājah, Book of Purity and its Sunna, no. 288). It is of interest to note that in the English translation of the book, *ʿumda as-sālik* (*The Reliances of the Traveller*) by Aḥmad Ibn Naqīb al-Miṣrī (d. 1368), which is a manual of the Shāfiʿī law school's rules and regulations, female circumcision is given as obligatory. In the Arabic text the word *baẓr* is used, which refers to the clitoris. In the English translation Keller has added that this means 'for women removing the prepuce (*bizr*) of the clitoris (n: not the clitoris itself, as some mistakenly assert [remark by the translator])' (N. Keller 1991: 59). This is an example of how certain ideas change when transferred into a western context. In the Arabic text it is obvious that what is meant is clitoridectomy, whereas in the English translation it has come to mean removal of the clitoral prepuce only, a practice which has occurred even in the western world.

The first question to ask is why countries belonging to the same law school have such variation in the practice of female circumcision. For instance, female circumcision is not practised in the North African countries of Morocco, Algeria and Tunisia, despite the fact that they adhere to the Mālikī law school which encourages female circumcision. In contrast, the Sudan, which belongs to the same law school, is one of the countries where female circumcision has the firmest hold. Similarly, one has to ask why female circumcision is not widespread in many of the Arab countries which adhere to the Shāfiʿī school, since this school prescribes female circumcision as compulsory. Egypt and Yemen are the only countries in the Arab world belonging to the Shāfiʿī law school which actually practice female circumcision. In other Arab countries such as Palestine, the Lebanon and Syria, however, where significant parts of the population adhere to the Shāfiʿī law school, the practice of female circumcision is practically unknown. Conversely, it is important to be aware that in Malaysia and Indonesia, countries situated in a region where female circumcision is uncommon, it has become part of the Islamic creed because of the dominance of the Shāfiʿī law school. However, the female circumcision which is practised in these countries is what the Southeast Asians label 'the Sunna circumcision' which means the removal of only the prepuce of the clitoris, as is also noted by The Minority Rights Group Report (1985: 6).[10]

The above discussion indicates that female circumcision, except in Southeast Asia, has less to do with the Islamic law schools than with socio-cultural customs in the various countries. az-Zuḥailī reports the views of the four law schools concerning female circumcision, but it is important to be aware that the law schools manifest themselves differently in the various countries according to customary practices in those countries, as demonstrated above.

What is important is to draw attention to the fact that the four law schools have used the hadith, 'Circumcision is Sunna for men and noble for women' as a rationale for accepting female circumcision, a hadith which the great scholar of hadith, al-Baihaqī, has referred to as being a weak hadith. The other hadith used in support of female circumcision is the one related by Umm ʿAṭīya al-Anṣārīya and even this is regarded as weak. However, this latter hadith has become the most prominent in the modern debate on female circumcision and has been understood in various ways as indicated below.

The Islamist debate

According to the understanding of the Ḥanbalī law school, this hadith related to Umm ʿAṭīya al-Anṣārīya did not render female circumcision obligatory but rather indicated the opposite, that female circumcision is acceptable but is not an act which is to be encouraged (az-Zuḥailī 1989 vol. I: 307). Moreover, female circumcision is not prevalent in areas with an adherence to Ḥanbalī, such as for instance in Saudi Arabia. This Ḥanbalī view is also held in Europe among *salafī* Islamists. One leading *salafī*

Islamist who is a medical doctor stated that the hadith about Umm ʿAṭīya al-Anṣārīya indicates that female circumcision is not obligatory but is merely acceptable. He stresses that what he means by female circumcision is the removal of the prepuce only, and in his opinion such an operation increases the sexual sensitivity of women rather than decreasing the sexual urge. His view is therefore that this hadith encourages such an operation but that the operation should be the same as for men, i.e. that only the prepuce is removed. That the *salafīs* in general tend to not reject, although not necessarily promoting, female circumcision is due to the fact that the *salafī* scholar, al-Albānī, has rendered the hadith related to Umm ʿAṭīya al-Anṣārīya strong. According to him, although the hadith's narrator chains are weak, it has come through various narrator chains and that makes the hadith strong (al-Albānī 1972: hadith no. 722). In this respect it is important to note that Ibn Jawzī (d. 1201) quotes two versions of this hadith in his book on women, claiming that both of these versions have weak narrator chains (Ibn Jawzī 1988: 28).

Egyptian *salafīs* have a different view of the issue of female circumcision. The practice has deep roots in Egyptian society and is pervasive even among the Christian population. The Great Mufti's campaign against female circumcision, which was prompted by western protest, has caused reactions within Egyptian society both among scholars and among common people. Abū al-Ashbāl az-Zuhairī, an Egyptian *salafī* adherent, wrote a booklet in 1996 in response to the Grand Mufti's statement. In this booklet, az-Zuhairī analyses those hadiths he regards as supporting circumcision, and among them is the hadith related by Umm ʿAṭīya al-Anṣārīya. In his view this hadith offers strong evidence of female circumcision, and instead of interpreting it as discouraging female circumcision, as is the view of the Ḥanbalī school, he sees this hadith as a strong evidence that it is an Islamic obligation. Moreover, when az-Zuhairī discusses female circumcision he speaks in terms of that which is superfluous, and this implies for him parts or the whole of the clitoris. He states that the reason for female circumcision is to reduce female sexual desire, arguing that 'what is intended by female circumcision is to set right her sexual desire, for if she is uncircumcised she would be seized by a strong sexual desire' (az-Zuhairī 1996: 45). However, later in the text he contradicts himself, since he says that a girl does not always have to be circumcised. If there is nothing which is superfluous, there is no need to remove anything. One could ask, what about these girls' excessive sexual desire? Does az-Zuhairī indicate that the size of clitoris has something to do with high or low sexual desire? It might be that this is what he implicitly suggests, as he goes on to talk about the difference between women living in hot regions and women living in cold regions. In response to the argument against female circumcision on the grounds that it causes sexual frigidity, he argues that the size of clitoris depends on the climate. He believes that women living in cold regions do not necessarily need circumcision due to the small size of their clitoris, whereas women in hot regions need circumcision due to its larger size (az-Zuhairī 1996: 33). It is obvious that az-Zuhairī is talking about clitoridectomy, and he is thus promoting the genital cutting of women. It would be interesting to know on what he builds his 'theory' of difference in the size of clitoris in hot and cold areas, but he does unfortunately not bring forward any scientific evidence which could support such a theory.

An important implication of az-Zuhairī's argument is the issue of beauty, since he actually refers to the size of clitoris as a condition for whether a girl should be circumcised or not. That beauty and appearance form part of the whole issue of female circumcision was reinforced in my discussions with women coming from areas where female circumcision is common. Muslim women have explained to me that it is part of a woman's beauty to be circumcised. One Muslim woman stated: 'Female circumcision is similar to the cosmetic operations western women go through. Women always suffer in order to make themselves beautiful in the eyes of men.'[11] In Aman's narrative in the book, *Aman: the Story of a Somali girl*, the idea that circumcised women are superior in the eyes of men is further reinforced when Aman expresses her surprise at being confronted with an uncircumcised woman in the delivery room at the hospital. She says:

> That part of a Somali woman is covered and closed – it looks better. I have brothers, cousins, and friends who have dated European women, or women who have a clitoris, and they say we have the best one – they say it's smaller, hard, clean, it's clean and it's less wet. I know myself we smell better and are less dirty than women who are uncircumcised.
>
> (Barnes and Boddy 1995: 280)

Aman expresses many of the social and hygienic myths about female circumcision which Kassamali presented in her discussion on how to eradicate the practice. However, Aman's belief that circumcised women have an advantage over uncircumcised ones is less often expressed in many of the studies about female genital cutting.

az-Zuhairī continues with the analysis of a story related back to the famous Islamic scholar, Ḥasan al-Baṣrī (d. 782), which tells that one person who had been close to the Prophet was invited to eat. He was told that the reason for the celebration was that a girl had been circumcised. The man said: 'We did not see this thing during the time of the Prophet', and he refused to eat from the food (az-Zuhairī 1996: 46; Musnad Aḥmad, *musnad shāmīīn*, no. 17232). az-Zuhairī explains this story as meaning that male circumcision should be an open and visible matter whereas female circumcision should be a hidden matter, i.e. there should be no public party attached to female circumcision. It is interesting to note that az-Zuhairī interprets this hadith to mean that female circumcision should not be celebrated in the same way as male circumcision. In the hadith there is absolutely no indication that this is what is meant, but as az-Zuhairī is already operating within a certain conceptual framework, it is natural that he would interpret this hadith as supporting evidence for female circumcision.

az-Zuhairī refers to one more hadith which in his view confirms that circumcision is part of the Islamic creed. The hadith tells of how people came to ʿĀʾisha to ask in what circumstances associated with sexual intercourse one should perform the major ritual ablution (*ghusl*). ʿĀʾisha answered that she had heard the Prophet say that one should perform this ablution 'when the two circumcised meet' (*al-khitānayn*) (al-Bukhārī, Book of Ablution, no. 282; Muslim, Book of Menstruation, no. 526; Sunan at-Tirmidhī, Book of Purity, no. 101; Sunan Abū Dāwud, Book of Purity, no. 186; Musnad Aḥmad, *musnad al-anṣār*, no. 20182; Mālik, Book of Purity, no. 92).[12] This hadith might indicate that female circumcision existed during the time of the Prophet, but contrary to az-Zuhairī, I do not believe that it necessarily proves that the practice is Islamic in form. One could compare it with the case of slavery, a pagan custom which was not abolished but both in the Koran and in the Prophetic example there is an encouragement to free slaves. Similarly, in the hadith from Umm ʿAṭīya as well as in the hadith where the Prophet's Companions would not eat food at a party for a girl's circumcision, there is no encouragement for the practice of circumcision and in both hadiths there is an apparent dissociation from the practice.

On the other hand, if we look at the hadith from a different point of view, it does not necessarily mean that the expression *al-khitānayn* refers to the female sexual organ as circumcised. In Arabic grammar there is a concept named *taghlīb*. According to Wright's *A Grammar of the Arabic Language*: 'when two objects are constantly associated, in virtue either of natural or opposition, a dual may be formed from one of them, which shall designate both, and the preference given to the one over the other is termed *taghlīb*' (Wright 1981: 90). The example highlighted is that in classical literature ʿUmarān (the two Umars) is often used to designate the first two caliphs in Islamic history, Abū Bakr and ʿUmar, thus making ʿUmar, who was regarded as the 'strong' one, dominant over Abū Bakr. If *khitān* was a common synonym for the male sexual organ, which is not improbable, then the use of the word *al-khitānayn* might be a grammatic *taghlīb* form where the 'stronger', i.e., the male sexual organ, is linguistically preferred over the 'weaker', i.e., the female sexual organ. This understanding is not far-fetched, as in classical Islamic literature male sexuality is regarded in active terms in contrast to female sexuality which is regarded in terms of passivity (cf. for instance K.2: 222). In this sense the Prophet's expression of 'the two circumcised' implies only that the male sexual organ is circumcised; it does not necessarily imply a circumcision of the female sexual organ (personal communication with Nora Eggen).

As for pre-Islamic practices, Wilfred Thesiger, who travelled in the Arabian desert in the first half of the twentieth century, observed a certain form of male circumcision in the Ḥijāz, the area where Mecca and Medina are situated. Thesiger calls this practice 'the flaying circumcision', claiming it to be a pagan custom. He writes: 'In the flaying circumcision, the skin is removed from the navel down to the inside of the man's leg' (Thesiger 1959: 91–2). Thesiger goes on to tell how this form of circumcision was regarded as a proof of manhood. It was inappropriate to scream during the operation as a 'real man' should endure pain without showing any emotions. The practice was prohibited by Ibn Saʿūd (d. 1953) (Thesiger 1959).

I should point out that I have found it difficult to verify Thesiger's information, probably because circumcision in general is a sensitive issue. However, given this reservation I want to dwell on this matter briefly, first by asking whether this practice was common at the time of the Prophet. If Thesiger's observation is accurate, one can assume that the custom might have been prevalent in ancient times. The second question which then arises is, if it was a common practice at the time of the Prophet, did the Prophet know about this practice? And if he knew, why did he not prohibit it? If he knew about it and did not prohibit it, does that indicate that this form of circumcision is acceptable (*mubāḥ*) in Islam? Or one can pose a more radical question: does it mean that 'the flaying circumcision' is a Sunna practice (*mustaḥabb*) as the Prophet did not forbid it?

I believe these questions are important in the context of female circumcision, since the same problem arises with regard to the ancient customs of both female and male circumcision: are such practices that were common during the time of the Prophet necessarily Sunna insofar as the Prophet did not explicitly forbid them? Is it not true that in Medinian society there were customs which the Prophet accepted (*mubāḥ* practices), either because they were acceptable (*mubāḥ*) within a broader framework of Islam or because they were so deeply rooted in society that the Prophet avoided creating a direct confrontation, choosing instead to implicitly dissociate himself from the practice. As for the hadith related by Umm ʿAṭīya al-Anṣārīya, the introductory word of the sentence (*idhā*), might indicate both 'if' and 'when', and it is therefore *not* an obvious commandment. The hadith about the Companion of the Prophet who stated that 'we did not see this thing [female circumcision/a party to celebrate a female circumcision] during the time of the Prophet' might further be an indication of discouragement of female circumcision.

What is worth noting in the various *salafī* approaches is the contrasting arguments of various supporters of the movement. While the non-Egyptian *salafī* adherent living in Europe sees circumcision as a means to heighten female sexual desire, Egyptian *salafīs* living inside Egypt regard female circumcision as a tool to reduce sexual desire. Moreover, *salafīs* with whom I have discussed the matter in Arabic-speaking countries other than Egypt and Sudan, do not regard female circumcision as an Islamic tradition at all.

As for the Muslim Brotherhood, there is also a variety of views according to the informant's country of origin and according to the interpretation of the hadiths. When I visited Egypt in the spring of 1997 I met highly educated women belonging to the Muslim Brotherhood and I discussed the matter with them. One of them claimed that female circumcision was something which was not obligatory but which she regarded as 'noble' for women. It is interesting to note that this woman's family comes from rural areas, whereas other Islamist women I talked to in Cairo from urban backgrounds tended to take the opposite view, that female circumcision was an unnecessary practice. The issue is thus affected by class and also by background, whether rural or urban. The Muslim Brotherhood's official position on female circumcision is that the hadith about Umm ʿAṭīya al-Anṣārīya might exist but that the content of this hadith does not indicate that female circumcision is obligatory, rather it is a matter in which individuals are free to choose their own preferences.

An Egyptian woman who is a member of the Muslim Brotherhood and lives in Europe explained that in Egypt, female circumcision is mostly practised in rural areas or among the urban population which has its roots in rural areas. She further stated that with the increase in education among Egyptian youth, this tradition will fade. I discovered that the issue of female circumcision was not a matter of great importance among Egyptian Islamists living abroad, whether scholars or ordinary members of the Brotherhood, and they neither defended it nor rejected it. However, inside Egypt female circumcision seems to be quite a different matter and it has to be regarded in view of the tense situation between Islamists and the Egyptian government, a struggle which Islamists often represent in terms of the opposition between Islam and 'the West'.[13] It is also of importance that in my discussions with Egyptian Islamists, there was no concern to distinguish between circumcision and clitoridectomy. The most common opinion was that *if* such an operation should take place one should remove only 'a little bit', but what this meant was not specified.

On the whole, however, it is important to note that among non-Egyptian members of the Muslim Brotherhood, female circumcision is strictly rejected. All the women and men I spoke to represented it in terms of 'old customs' which flourish in certain regions, and they remarked that the Prophet did not order female circumcision but rather encouraged people to put an end to the custom.

As for the other group of Islamists, those who belong to a *post-ikhwān* trend of thought, the attitude I met was one of fierce opposition to female circumcision. One leading male Islamist living in Sweden said during our discussion of the hadith related by Umm ʿAṭīya al-Anṣārīya :

> I understand this hadith to discourage female circumcision. At that time some people practised this old tradition and when the Prophet (p.b.u.h.) discovered that, he explained that *if* you have to remove

something, remove as little as possible. The Prophet's explanation has to be regarded in view of how he always was very careful not to break any custom abruptly. Look at for instance how God in the Koran does not forbid alcohol all at once, rather the prohibition was performed in stages. Similarly, Islam does not prohibit slavery, rather it urges a gradual cancellation of slavery by encouraging the release of slaves as a religious action [translation mine].

The same person, when I showed him az-Zuhairī's argument concerning the story of Ḥasan al-Baṣrī about the celebration party for a girl's circumcision, said:

> It is strange, is it not, that when I read this story I understand that female circumcision was not common during the time of the Prophet (p.b.u.h.). az-Zuhairī, on the other hand, understands exactly the opposite. Certainly, it has to do with his Egyptian background that he looks for evidence, as this is part of his cultural education [translation mine].

That the issue of female circumcision has become a matter of concern even within the rank and file of Islamists is evident in Jamal Badawi's book *Gender Equity in Islam*. In the 1995 edition female circumcision is not mentioned, whereas in the 1999 edition he has inserted a whole chapter dealing with its various aspects. His conclusion is to reject female circumcision and as Badawi is himself an Egyptian it seems obvious that in this matter, the 'western cultural base pattern' has had the strongest influence.

Imān is a convert from Scandinavia. She lives in Egypt, speaks Arabic, and has therefore often been confronted with the issue of female circumcision. It is interesting to look at how she experiences this debate as she is a person in between, both belonging and not belonging to the Egyptian Muslim cultural sphere. She explains:

> In Egypt it is the secular forces who have involved themselves in the debate on female circumcision. They claim that as sex is taboo in Muslim society the whole issue of female circumcision has become very sensitive. In my view, sex is far from being taboo among the Muslim population in Egypt, rather it is sexuality which has been covered up and has become a taboo subject.[14] In films and television women are exposed as sex objects. Likewise, in shop exhibitions sexy women's underwear is displayed freely in a sexually provocative manner. On the other hand, sexuality, for instance sex education for young people, is regarded as shameful and thus ignored. This is the opposite of what can be found in the Islamic way of thinking where the exposure of sexual behaviour is *harām*, whereas sexuality as part of human nature is of great concern for the well-being of the individual, the family, and society in general. The norms have thus been

> turned upside-down. This complicates the process of finding solutions to the deep-rooted tradition of female circumcision [translation mine].

It is interesting to note that Imān, who experiences the Egyptian cultural context in the light of her Scandinavian background, interprets cultural behaviour differently from indigenous Egyptians. The encounter between various cultural spheres is once again seen to entail a confrontation which might result in change of one form or another.

Imān further sees Islamic ethics, education and training rather than female circumcision as the way to prevent immoral behaviour in Muslim society, saying:

> Many Muslims believe that female circumcision is the only way to control female promiscuity. In my view, the Islamic cure for promiscuity in general in our Muslim society is Islamic upbringing and education which promotes *ḥayā'* (modesty) and which channels sexuality into its rightful place which is within wedlock. In one of my discussions with an Egyptian woman she expressed her concern about the un-Islamic behaviour of young Egyptian women who mixed freely with the opposite sex. I responded that these women she referred to are all circumcised as nearly 90 per cent of Egyptian women are still circumcised in one way or another. I asked her with astonishment whether she never thought about the fact that sexual behaviour can only be controlled through *tarbiya* (education, upbringing, training) as sexual irritation starts from the brain. A circumcised woman can still feel a sexual urge which can be expressed through different kinds of behaviour. Female circumcision is thus not a means to obliterate immoral behaviour in society. As sexuality is part of human nature (*fiṭra*) it is only through Islamic *tarbiya* human beings can possibly know how to deal with it in a proper way [translation mine].

Imān reflects the views of Eric Winkel when he calls for an Islamic legal discourse within the Muslim community. She says:

> It is against Islamic *ḥayā'* (modesty) that non-Muslims should interfere with the privacy of Muslim women. It is time that Muslims themselves start to objectively analyse and discuss the subject of female circumcision in a proper manner. We have to be independent in knowledge and seriously investigate the consequences of this pre-Islamic tradition. We have to look for an Islamic solution which takes into consideration all aspects of human nature and human life to make a balance in the relationship between men and women [translation mine].

These two converts' call to Muslims to involve themselves in the debate about female circumcision might seem like an easy task, but the reality is different. From my discussions with Imān and in my own experience of Arab-speaking Muslims both in the Muslim world and in Europe, it is obvious that female circumcision is a sensitive issue and few Islamists willingly take the initiative to discuss the issue. I believe, however, that by reflecting on the consequences of leaving the discussion to non-Muslims, many Muslims might start to investigate the matter in order to find Islamic responses to the various arguments in the debate on female circumcision.

Reflections

The overall impression both from the written material and from my discussions with Islamists in the Arab world and in Europe is that female circumcision is regarded as a cultural phenomenon, and the interpretation of the texts concerning the matter takes place through the lenses of culture. Thus Egyptian Islamists either defend the practice or have an indifferent attitude towards it, whereas Islamists from other Arabic-speaking countries tend to have a strong emotional reaction against it. The 'Arab cultural base pattern', or in this particular issue the 'Egyptian cultural base pattern', influences the understanding of female circumcision, since even Egyptian Islamists living in Europe who encounter strong reactions from western society concerning this matter tend to have an indifferent attitude towards it. In contrast to this, Islamists from areas where female circumcision is not practised tend to be influenced by the 'western cultural base pattern', so that they strongly condemn female circumcision in all its forms. The most interesting argument I encountered in the debate was that of the *salafī* medical doctor who actually stated that although not compulsory, female circumcision was a means of heightening the sexual response of women, as the operation according to him meant a removal of the prepuce. This *salafī's* statement might be explained as an extension of the belief that male circumcision heightens the sexual desire of men. However, I believe that even *his* comment shows the influence of the 'western cultural base pattern'. As a *salafī* he cannot condemn female circumcision because the scholar of hadith, al-Albānī, has accepted the hadith from Umm ʿAṭīya al-Anṣārīya, and *salafīs* rarely understand hadiths in their context but tend to interpret them literally. In this case, by turning the issue upside-down, he can accept and rationalise the practice of female circumcision.

The debate about female circumcision is highly emotive both among those for and against the practice. I believe this is due to the reception the issue of female circumcision has had in western society where it is often associated with Islam, thus reinforcing the image among non-Muslims of Islam as a religion hostile towards women. Islamists living in Europe who see this as just another attack on Islam attempt to reject all allegations which link female circumcision to Islamic tradition. The problem seems to revolve around the authenticity of the hadiths relating to female circumcision, in particular the hadith related by Umm ʿAṭīya al-Anṣārīya, as al-Albānī has rendered it authentic, whereas other well-known scholars such as Ibn Jawzī from the twelfth century and Sābiq from our own century have rendered it as weak due to weak narrator chains. The controversy about these hadiths' authenticity might mean that female circumcision will continue to be a heated issue in the near future among Muslims who differ in their understanding of the Islamic sources. However, it seems that the strongest trend in the Arabic-speaking Islamist debate is against female circumcision. What can be observed is that in large cities and with an increase in education, people tend to turn against the practice.

Having dealt with a controversial issue in this chapter, I will follow this up with yet another controversy in the next chapter by discussing various approaches to the issue of female 'veiling' in Islam. The issue of the veil has come to be one of the most highly-charged issues in the cultural encounter between Islam and 'the West'.

12 Islamic female dress

Few religious manifestations have aroused such strong feelings as has Islamic 'veiling'. Muslims and non-Muslims alike have produced books, articles, television programmes, etc., discussing various aspects of veiling. As I wear a head-scarf myself, I have personally been on the receiving end of both positive and negative reactions and I have often been surprised by the intensity and depth of people's attitudes.

'The veil' has various connotations in a western context. A Christian nun wearing a veil might be seen as an image of sincere religiosity, purity and peace, whereas a Muslim woman wearing a veil is likely to be seen as a symbol of the oppression of women and as making a political-religious statement. She may evoke anger from non-Muslim westerners because they believe her to be betraying the struggle for women's rights by submitting to her own oppression in wearing the veil. Furthermore, she is perceived to be displaying the fact that she is at odds with the prevailing social and religious norms. An extreme reaction might even see her as dangerous for she might support or participate in so-called 'Islamic terrorist organisations' that threaten social stability. The visibility of her religious commitment may be seen to signal a 'holier than thou' attitude and thus evokes resentment in the non-Muslim. In Sweden and many other western countries, religion is regarded as a private matter. Thus a common statement is that 'religiosity should not be visible but should be a matter of the heart and one's innermost feelings'.[1] The acceptance of the nun's veil seems unaffected by such complaints against the Muslim woman's veil, even although both share the same visibility. Why? Because the nun represents commitment to the prevailing religious tradition. She is an 'insider'. The Muslim woman, on the other hand, symbolises the intrusion of alien beliefs contrary to the prevailing religious tradition. This response is further reinforced by negative media reports about Muslim immigrants or Muslims in other countries.

The Muslim feminist debate on 'the veil'

Within the Muslim Umma there is extensive discussion about the veil, and Muslim feminists have launched a variety of attacks against the practice of veiling. Some such as Mai Yamani, Haleh Afshar and Maha Azzam discuss it in an academic context from the perspective of social researchers describing Muslim social realities. Others such as Fatima Mernissi, Nawwal El Saadawi and Leila Ahmad criticise it in the context of social, political or religious activism. The debate is hard to follow largely due to the lack of any clear definition of whether a veil is understood as a head-cover or face-veil. In order to better understand the discussion, I will give the Koranic verses which participants in the debate about the veil refer to. As feminists rarely refer to the hadiths, I will introduce hadith references at a later stage of the discussion.

There are four passages in particular in the Koran which are regarded as dealing with behaviour between men and women who mix outside kinship bonds:

1 Tell the believing men to lower their gaze and to be mindful of their chastity [guard their private parts]. This will be most conducive to their purity. Verily, God is aware of what you do.

 And tell the believing women to lower their gaze and to be mindful of their chastity [guard their private parts], and to not display their adornment beyond what may [decently] be apparent thereof. Let them draw their coverings [*khumur*; sing. *khimār*] over their bosoms and let them not display their adornments to any but their husbands, or their fathers. . . . Let them not stamp their feet so as to reveal what they hide of their adornments. O believers, turn unto God all of you so that you may succeed (K.24: 30–1).

2 Women, advanced in years, who do not hope for marriage, incur no sin if they discard their garments (*thiyābahunna*), provided that they do not aim at a showy display of their charm. But it is better for them to abstain from this. God is All-hearing All-knowing (K.24: 60).

3 O Prophet! Tell your wives and your daughters and the wives of the believers, that they should draw over themselves some of their outer garment (*jilbāb*). That will be better, so that they will be recognised and not annoyed. God is ever Forgiving Merciful (K.33: 59).

4 O you who believe! Enter not the Prophet's dwellings unless you are given leave. . . . And [as for the Prophet's wives] when you ask of them anything that you need, ask them from behind a curtain (*ḥijāb*). That is purer for your hearts and for their hearts. You should not cause annoyance to the Messenger of God and you should not ever marry his wives after him. That would, in the sight of God, be an enormity (K.33: 53).

The first three Koranic passages above are directed towards women in general. The fourth passage deals with how men should behave towards the wives of the Prophet only. Before I proceed, therefore, I think it is appropriate to quote the Koranic verses dealing specifically with the special position of the wives of the Prophet, verses which are often referred to in the debate about veiling:

> O wives of the Prophet! If any of you are to become guilty of manifestly immoral conduct, she will have double punishment [in the Hereafter]. This is indeed easy for God.
>
> But any of you who devoutly obeys God and His Messenger, to her We shall grant her reward twice and We have prepared for her a most excellent Sustenance [in the Hereafter].
>
> O wives of the Prophet! You are not like any of the [other] women. If you are conscious of God let not your speech be over-soft, in case any in whose heart is a disease should desire [you]. So speak in a right (*maʿrūf*) way.
>
> Stay in your house and do not flaunt your charms as they used to do in the former times of ignorance (*jāhilīya*). Establish regular prayers and give regular charity and obey God and His Messenger. O members of the Household! God wishes to remove from you that which is loathsome and He wants to purify you to utmost purity (K.33: 30–3).

These Koranic passages indicate that the wives of the Prophet were regarded as having a special status. In the Islamic discussion one main conflict has arisen: does this mean that the injunctions given to the Prophet's wives were directed only to them, or should all female Muslims be expected to follow the example of the wives of the Prophet? Divergencies over women's issues in the various Islamic approaches arise out of this particular dilemma.

Nawwal El Saadawi and Fatima Mernissi both oppose the use of the veil. El Saadawi, in her many lectures in Scandinavia, particularly at the end of the 1980s, used the idea of 'veiling the brain', building on a sort of simple fieldwork methodology. Her main argument drew on the account of a young relative who had been intelligent and brave until she put on the veil. After that, according to El Saadawi, it was impossible to conduct a normal discussion with her. This story was presented as evidence of how veiling not only comes to mean covering the hair but also 'veiling the brain'. Fatima Mernissi, who has taken a more scientific approach to the study of veiling, attacks the use of the veil, claiming that there is no Koranic evidence that the wearing of a veil is an Islamic obligation (Mernissi 1987: 85–101). Leila Ahmad, in her book, *Women and Gender in Islam*, argues that veiling for women was a requirement only for the wives of the Prophet (Ahmad 1992: 55).

In contrast, the idea of veiling as a symbol of oppression has been refuted by many leading Islamists, among them Samīra Fayyāḍ, a leading

Islamist who has been active in the struggle for female influence in the Islamist movement in Jordan. She writes:

> There are many roots of this insignificance in woman's position. The first of which is the divergence of women's liberation movements away from the essence of the problem. Those involved in the movement should have joined the mainstream of a general liberation movement working for the liberation of man and woman in times when both were suffering. Upholding her banner of woman's liberation emphasized her peculiarities as female and overlooked her integral nature as a rational and sensible human being. Rather she should have concerned herself with the national problems side by side along with men bearing full responsibility, ignoring marginal matters such as changing dress-styles and other trivialities.
>
> (Fayyāḍ 1992: 3)

Fayyāḍ's appeal for liberation within the framework of Islam using the language of western feminism can be seen as a consequence of her studies in western countries. The quotation above indicates that in the 'normative field' between the two cultural base patterns, she tends to choose those Islamic options which might be regarded as belonging to the 'western cultural base pattern' with its emphasis on female responsibility in society and women's participation in political life.

The debate about Islamic dress is conducted on various levels. First, social researchers tend to analyse Islamic veiling in scientific terms, thus excluding its religious rationale. Muslim feminists turn to the Islamic sources in order to find evidence that Islamic veiling is an ancient custom which has nothing to do with Islam. In contrast to these two approaches, the Islamist discussion on the issue tends to focus on whether Islamic veiling includes a face-veil, gloves and stockings or whether it means only the covering of the hair and most of the body, with the exception of the hands and the feet.

The analysis of Islamic veiling by social researchers must be understood in the context of recent social research which abandons religion as an instrument of analysis. Beckford, a sociologist of religion, observes that the sociological classics relegated an important role to religion in the understanding of society in the nineteenth century, and that they treated religion as a unitary phenomenon (Beckford 1989: 6–7). However, in his view later social scientists tend to modify this unitary outlook on religion and distinguish between phenomena such as religious organisation, knowledge, beliefs and rituals. He argues that 'the differentiation of religion in society has been mirrored in the differentiation of the concept of religion in society' (Beckford 1989: 8). In the debate about the veil, it seems that Beckford's observation has proved true. Much research dealing with Islamic veiling tends to analyse it in socio-political terms (Zuhur 1992;

Broch-Due and Rudie and Bleie 1993; El-Solh and Mabro 1994; Göçek and Balaghi 1994). Mai Yemeni, a researcher on women in Islam and herself a Muslim, states that 'the *ḥijāb* is central to this Islamist movement. In general, women who choose to wear it are aware of its social and economic advantages. These range from more possibilities for getting married (since men 'prefer' *muhajjabat*) to economic practicalities (low-cost dress)' (Yamani 1996: 11). Haleh Afshar, a researcher on Iranian women, also sees the veil in socio-political terms. She claims that

> Islamist women are particularly defensive of the veil. The actual imposition of the veil and the form it has taken is a contested domain. Nevertheless, many Muslim women have chosen the veil as the symbol of Islamisation and have accepted it as the public face of their revivalist position. For them the veil is liberating, and not an oppressive force. They maintain that the veil enables them to become the observers and not the observed; that it liberates them from the dictates of the fashion industry and the demands of the beauty myth. In the context of the patriarchal structures that shape women's lives, the veil is a means of bypassing sexual harassment and 'gaining respect'. In Iran it is seen as a means of liberation from the plight of being the unveiled, exploited 'slaves of imperialism' and facilitating their full participation in the public domain.
>
> (Afshar in Yamani 1996: 201)

This instrumentalist interpretation of the phenomenon of Islamic veiling has its base in the nature of in-group/out-group communication. I believe that when Islamist women meet non-Islamist or even non-Muslim women, their discussions are governed by what they perceive are the 'premises of the other'. For example, in discussions with a researcher, Islamist women might try to convince her of the benefits of veiling on rational, apologetic grounds. Thus socio-political arguments are used, whereas in other contexts with different people, other arguments might be used. This becomes apparent in Maha Azzam's article which is part of the anthology edited by Yamani. Azzam, who is herself of Muslim origin, breaks with the practice of offering socio-political explanations of veiling. She records that 'when women are asked why they wear the *ḥijāb*, they frequently respond by simply saying that they are merely complying with a Qur'anic injunction' (Azzam in Yamani 1996: 224). This is the same answer which I have usually been given in my discussions with Islamist women.

In order to understand why the same person can give different answers to the same question from different people, it is necessary to appreciate that a phenomenon might lend itself to various levels of explanation. Hjärpe explains this by saying that on one level there is the person's drive which might be hard to assess. On the second level there is the person's motivation, which in this particular case might be to follow a Koranic injunction. On the third level there are the apologetics, i.e. the various arguments a person offers to explain a practice. These arguments might vary according to whom the person is speaking to.

Azzam explores the Koran looking for texts on veiling, and she quotes verses 33: 59 and 33: 32–3 (see pp. 254, 255). In quoting these verses, Azzam states that 'literally, these verses are directed to the wives of the Prophet'. Although she is right with regard to verse 33: 32–3, it should be noted that she has overlooked the fact that verse 33: 59 explicitly states 'O Prophet, tell your wives and daughters and the women of the believers', which means that covering is not just an injunction for the Prophet's family members but is directed towards the believing women in general. Moreover, Azzam also quotes verse 24: 30–1 which contains a reference to women wearing 'coverings' (*khumur*). Despite the fact that this is the verse most Islamists would refer to in matters of veiling, Azzam does not mention the term *khumur* but interprets these verses in terms of their reference to proper Islamic modesty which requires both men and women to lower their eyes. Azzam's selectivity indicates her intention to render Islam compatible with a western world-view. Her feminist approach situates her within the 'western cultural base pattern' since her interpretations are in line with a western notion of gender equality. Azzam further goes on to discuss socio-political reasons behind the new veiling, but in summary she states:

> Despite these explanations, it is important not to overlook the fact that the *ḥijāb* is worn by women out of sincere religious conviction and it is primarily meant to convey piety and respect for religious values rather than political radicalism and anti-westernism, but the potential for it to symbolise a political stand is very powerful.
>
> (Azzam in Yamani 1996: 226)

Azzam thus weaves together the two themes, the religious and the political, in the debate on women's veiling, but by putting the religious argument first she has changed the emphasis of the debate. As will be indicated below, in the Islamist discussion on veils and veiling, the religious rationale seems to be in the forefront, although one should not overlook veiling's symbolic value in the Islamist struggle for a more moral society.

Muslim feminists tend to reject the suggestion that the use of the veil is Islamic, claiming instead that it is an ancient tradition which has crept into the present understanding of Islam. Also, as I mentioned above, they and others involved in the debate fail to define clearly what comprises a veil, which causes confusion especially with regard to the interpretation of Koranic verses. It is important to bear these issues in mind when giving an account of the different points of view.

Fatima Mernissi, who might be regarded as the most prominent of the Muslim feminists – or at least the most widely read in a western context

– devotes a whole chapter of her book, *Women and Islam*, to a discussion of the veil, which she entitles, 'The Hijab, the Veil.' It should be noted that Mernissi discusses the concept of Hijab (*ḥijāb*) not from a contemporary perspective but from the perspective of the Koran, and so she fails to acknowledge the important point that the term '*ḥijāb*' has acquired a variety of meanings. Her choice of the term '*ḥijāb*' might be explained by the fact that today it is often used to denote the female head-cover, but in Koranic language it refers not to female clothing but to the curtain which was ordered to be set up between the Prophet's wives and men in Medina. It might be that Mernissi is aware of this and wants to draw attention to the issue of segregation between men and women – the Muslim construction of a female versus a male world which might be seen as a consequence of the verse on *ḥijāb*. But if she wants a word synonymous with 'veil', the Koranic term '*khimār*' is a more specific term used to denote a covering cloth worn by women. That Mernissi wants to portray the discussion of *ḥijāb* as pertaining specifically to the Prophet's wives is indicated by her reference to verse 33: 59 in which the term '*jilbāb*' is used, since she twists the meaning in such a way that readers without sufficient knowledge of the text might be misled. She says that verse 33: 59 is the verse '*in which* He [God] advised the wives of the Prophet to make themselves recognized by pulling their *jilbāb* over themselves' (Mernissi 1987: 180 – my italics). While this is not entirely inaccurate since the verse is partially directed to the wives of the Prophet, Mernissi does not give the full meaning since the verse actually says: 'O Prophet, tell your wives and your daughters and *the women of the believers* to draw their cloaks close around them' (K.33: 59 – my italics).

There are possible explanations for this: either Mernissi has misunderstood (or chosen to misunderstand) the terminology in the debate, or she has decided to disregard the Koranic verse about *khimār* (see p. 254), in order to focus only on the concept of 'segregation' (i.e. *ḥijāb*). In either case, her discussion is marked by a lack of specific terminology with regard to female veiling and a certain selectivity from the source material. By interpreting *ḥijāb* as 'the veil' she uses the word as it is sometimes used in contemporary debate, but by confining her discussion only to the Koranic verse which mentions the term '*ḥijāb*' she limits the issue to the veiling of the wives of the Prophet. I see it as a Muslim feminist strategy to associate veiling exclusively with the wives of the Prophet, as can also be seen in Azzam's text above. In Azzam's article she actually quotes verses about female covering while at the same time claiming that these verses are directed to the wives of the Prophet only, thus contradicting one of the verses she quotes. By arguing that veiling applies only to the wives of the Prophet, Muslim feminists attempt to neutralise the claims of Islamists and of traditional Islamic jurisprudence that veiling is an Islamic injunction. Mernissi's discussion on veiling is a prominent example of how the arguments of feminists, similarly to those of Islamists, 'reproduce the past in the present'. However, the differences in outlook make the two factions arrive at different conclusions. In the 'normative field', the 'western cultural base pattern' governs the feminist approach and feminists tend to overlook or ignore relevant Koranic statements. The selection from 'the basket' seems to be dictated by a verbalised attempt to introduce new legislation based on disregarding certain passages of the text.

Mernissi looks at *ḥijāb* in its Koranic context. By referring to aṭ-Ṭabarī's explanation of the *ḥijāb*-verse (K.33: 53), she claims that this verse came into being as a consequence of the Prophet's politeness, which she explains 'bordered on timidity' (Mernissi 1987: 86). She further discusses the context in which this verse was revealed, suggesting that this revelation followed a different course of events from previous revelations and that it does not correspond to the Prophet's character (Mernissi 1987: 88). She goes into a detailed discussion of how the difficult circumstances at the time of the revelation of the verse might have disturbed the equanimity of the Prophet, making him change his former approach. From this discussion it is clear that Mernissi sees Islam in historical-critical terms, attributing the Prophet's sayings and actions to human circumstances rather than to divine inspiration. This makes her approach different from that of the Islamists and has resulted in considerable criticism of her work by Islamists.

Mernissi further indicates that the *ḥijāb* was a direct consequence of the situation in Medina where the Prophet lived with his wives close to the mosque, which was the public space in Medina. In her view the Prophet had created a space which was not divided into a dichotomous public/private sphere, but it was ʿUmar, the second caliph, who insisted on such a division of Islamic space. By saying this, Mernissi creates an element of doubt as to whether this verse is reliable or not, as well as suggesting to the reader that this Koranic verse needs to be understood only in the context of the Prophet's time, thus allowing her to dismiss its significance for today. It is, however, important to remember that she does not even mention verse 24: 31 (the *khimār* verse) which puts female covering in a wider context, and moreover is the verse which many contemporary scholars see as the most essential in matters of female covering.

Leila Ahmad is another Muslim feminist who has discussed female veiling. In her book, *Women and Gender in Islam*, one chapter is called 'The discourse of the veil' (Ahmad 1992: 144–68). Ahmad's main argument is that the use of a veil is a cultural rather than a religious custom which existed in Arabia and was associated with a high social status. Ahmad's treatment of veiling in an Islamic context is superficial and suggests either that she is ignorant of Islamic discussion about the veil, or that she wants to simplify the matter in order to make it irrelevant to the contemporary debate. She states that

> It [veiling] is nowhere explicitly prescribed in the Koran; the only verses dealing with women's clothing, aside from those already quoted

> [33: 59; 33: 53], instruct women to guard their private parts and throw a scarf over their bosoms (Sura 24: 31–32).
>
> (Ahmad 1992: 55)

Like Mernissi before her, Ahmad tends to interpret the Koranic verses about veiling as context-related. Thus they both present veiling as a practice specifically prescribed for the Medinian time when hypocrites tended to abuse the wives of the Prophet because they mistook them for slaves. Ahmad strengthens her argument by saying that veiling was a sign of social prestige at the time. Similarly to Mernissi, she claims that during the lifetime of the Prophet veiling and seclusion were observed only by his wives, and she observes that the phrase ' "[she] took the veil" is used in hadith to mean that a woman became a wife of Muḥammad'. Thus she concludes that 'for some time after Muḥammad's death, when the material incorporated into the hadith was circulated, veiling and seclusion were still considered peculiar to Muḥammad's wives' (Ahmad 1992: 54). It is important to note however, that Ahmad does not give references to the hadith she refers to, thus making it difficult for the reader to accept her argument.

As with Mernissi, Ahmad confuses the concepts and manifests a strong desire to discredit the use of the veil, whatever that means in their discussions, as an Islamic phenomenon. This confusion of concepts in the discussion about Islamic veiling is a problem which has created misunderstandings since the discussion *should* have been conducted on various levels. At least among western-educated researchers, there is a failure to distinguish between the face-veil, which covers either the whole face or parts of it, and the head-scarf which covers the hair but leaves the face free. In the Islamic and the Islamist intellectual debate the discussion of the veil and veiling is much more specific and I discuss below some of the concepts which are common in this debate.

Regional differences in terminology

I believe that one reason for the confusion is that in practice Muslims tend to use a variety of terms. In non-Arab speaking countries the terms for veiling in various forms are usually, but not always, drawn from local languages. Thus, in Southeast Asia the terms for head-scarf are *telekong* and *mini-telekong* according to the size of the scarf. In Urdu, the small transparent head-scarf is called *dupetta*, whereas the word for face-veil or complete covering is *burqa* and the institution of segregation is called *purdah*. In Arabic, on the other hand, there are various terms drawn from both the Koran and from hadiths, whereas other terms are derivations of Koranic terms. The terminology differs not only in various Arab countries but also within each particular country. In Jordan, for example, some would understand the term *ḥijāb* to mean the head-scarf, whereas others would understand it to mean the long overcoat which women frequently wear.

The face-veil on the other hand is usually referred to as *niqāb* or *khimār*. In other Arab countries, for instance in many of the Gulf states and in North Africa, *khimār*, although little used, denotes the head-scarf. In Algeria, the traditional dress is called *ḥaiak*, which is a white sheet wrapped around the body. *Ḥijāb* denotes Islamic clothing without specifying what should be covered and what should be exposed. The term *niqāb* refers to a cloth covering the lower part of the face with the eyes exposed, and *sadl* refers to the covering of the whole face. In Algeria a new understanding of the Koranic term *jilbāb* has been introduced with the coming of the *salafī* ideology. Whereas *jilbāb* has usually been used to refer to a long cloth in general, the word is now used to refer specifically to a covering in *one* piece from top to toe, in addition to a face veil. In Saudi Arabia, the terminology conforms more to that of Algeria than that of Jordan for instance, although the latter is closer geographically and relationally speaking. The most common term for head-scarf in Saudi Arabia is *ṭarḥa* which is used synonymously with *khimār*. In Saudi Arabia there is also a similar distinction to that found in Algeria between various forms of face-veil: while *niqāb* denotes the covering of the lower part of the face with the eyes exposed, the term *ghaṭā* denotes the cloth which covers the whole face. *Ḥijāb* on the other hand denotes the long coat together with a headscarf. As Saudi Arabia is the birthplace of the *salafī* ideology, the idea of the long covering in one piece is most prominent there. In many Muslim countries such as Iran and in countries in South Asia and Southeast Asia a two-piece suit with either a skirt or wide trousers is common, a form of dress which is not fully accepted everywhere as 'proper Islamic dress'. Followers of the *salafī* trend, for instance, tend to regard *jilbāb* as referring to a covering in one piece, thus regarding the former clothing as improper according to an Islamic standard. In African countries, a long piece of material which women wrap around themselves is common and in the Sudan for instance this piece of material is called *thawb*, which actually corresponds to the Koranic verse 24: 60. I believe that this diversity in terminology is due to the different understanding of what 'Islamic veiling' or 'female Islamic covering' means in various parts of the Muslim world. Moreover, it is also probable that pre-Islamic terminology linked to certain forms of veiling has entered local Islamic expressions for veiling.

Veiling in the hadith literature

In the Islamist debate certain hadiths have been highlighted in support of one standpoint or another according to different points of view.

In order to form a picture of what the hadith literature says about veiling, I looked up the various Koranic terms in the computer programme al-ʿālamī containing the 'Six Authentic' hadith collections in addition to Musnad Aḥmad, Mālik and ad-Dārimī. It is interesting to note that in this important part of the hadith literature very few details have been given as to the actual form of female veiling. I further looked into the chapter in al-Bukhārī's hadith collection dealing particularly with dress (*bāb al-libās*) and the chapter in Muslim's hadith collection which deals with clothes and decorations (*zīna*). al-Bukhārī's chapter on dress is divided into 103 sub-chapters and of these only a handful are concerned with female issues, whereas the chapter's main theme is the dress of the Prophet and his Companions. Most of the hadiths concerning women deal with prohibitions against artificial lengthening of hair, tattooing and the wearing of jewellery outside the home. Only two hadiths talk about women's clothing and both refer to the same incident, but they are narrated in two different versions. The reference to clothing in the story says that the woman is wearing a *jilbāb* in one of the versions and a green *khimār* in the other without any specific reference to the exact form of this clothing. The same is true for the third term *thawb* (garment) referred to in the latter hadith (al-Bukhārī, Chapter on Dressing, no. 5346; no. 5377; M. M. Khān 1985 vol. VII: 459 and 479–80). In Muslim's chapter on dress and decorations, the prohibition against women wearing artificial hair and practising tattooing is repeated. In addition there is a hadith which prohibits women from plucking their eyebrows. As for clothing, there is one hadith saying that the women who are dressed but appear as if they are naked will go to hell (Muslim, Book of Dressing and Decoration, no. 3971). The rest of the hadiths in this chapter deals with the decoration of houses and male dressing.

As for the widespread book *riyāḍ aṣ-ṣāliḥīn* (The Garden of the Righteous), in which Imām an-Nawawī (d. 1277) has compiled and systematised hadiths, the same pattern which can be found in the early hadith collections is maintained. In the 'Book of Dress', an-Nawawī quotes hadiths about how the Prophet used to dress and what guidelines the Prophet gave to the believers on how to dress. These hadiths are almost exclusively directed towards men and, except for the Prophet's statement that silk is forbidden for men and permissible for women, there is only one hadith which talks about female dressing. This is a hadith which is related by an-Nisāʾī, and it reads as follows:

> The Prophet said: 'On the Day of Judgement, God will not look at the person who drags his clothes along out of pride.' Umm Salama asked: 'What should women do with their skirts (*dhuyūl*)?' The Prophet answered: 'Shorten it the span of a hand.' She said: 'Then their feet will be exposed.' He said: 'Then they should lower it an arm's length and not more than that.'
>
> (an-Nawawī 1983: 432; Sunan an-Nisāʾī, Chapter on Decoration, no. 5242.)

This hadith was explained to me on the one hand by a female *salafī*, who claimed that it indicates that a woman can and should wear clothes covering the feet, thus for a woman to 'drag her clothes' is recommended. On the other hand, a member of the Muslim Brotherhood explained this hadith to mean that a woman's skirt should be a little longer than a man's, without specifying that the feet should be completely covered. It is interesting to observe how ideological presuppositions to do with the individual's position in the 'normative field' and her/his biography are factors in such interpretations.

This hadith introduces yet another term, namely *dhuyūl* (sing. *dhīl*) which might be translated by the English word 'skirt'. The Koranic term *thawb* which means a cloth is also pervasive in the hadith literature, but *thawb* was just as often worn by men as by women. Just as references to the Prophet's clothing suggest that he used to wear a variety of different garments, the few references which can be found to female dress indicate diversity in attire, rather than the uniformity promoted by some contemporary Islamic groups.

The major concern to do with dress in the hadith literature is therefore not with female dress but with male dress, with an emphasis on how the Prophet and the Companions used to dress. In the 'Chapter on Prayer' in al-Bukhārī's and Muslim's hadith collections the same tendency is evident. They give details of how the Prophet and the Companions used to dress for prayer but there are only a few references to women's dress in prayer. There is an indication that one changed one's way of dress in prayer. The Prophet is said to have taken off his waist-cloth, tying it around his neck during prayer. Another hadith tells about how one of the Companions, Jābir ibn ʿAbdullāh, was praying wrapped up in a garment (*thawb*) whereas his cloak (*ridāʾ*) was lying beside him. When asked about this, he explained that this was how he had seen the Prophet praying (al-Bukhārī, Chapter on Prayer, no. 357). There is, however, no reference as to *how* the garment was wrapped.

As for female attire in al-Bukhārī's 'Chapter on Prayer', which has more references to ways of dressing during prayer than Muslim has, there is one reference to women who used to pray the dawn prayer in the mosque wrapped up in their sheets (*murūṭ*, sing. *mirṭ*), (al-Bukhārī, Chapter on Prayer, no. 359) but this hadith gives no indication of *how* the sheet was wrapped either. In Muslim's hadith collection there is also a reference to the fact that the Prophet was wearing such a sheet (*mirṭ*) one day, (Muslim, Chapter on Dressing and Decoration, no. 3881) but even in this hadith nothing is said about *how* he used to wear it.

In his 'Chapter on Interpretation of the Koran', al-Bukhārī refers to the background of various Koranic verses (*sabab an-nuzūl*). In the commentary to verse 24: 31 'Let them draw their head-coverings (*khumur*) over their bosoms', he narrates a hadith from ʿĀ'isha saying: 'May God be merciful towards the first emigrant women. When God revealed "Let them draw their head-coverings (*khumurahinna*) over their bosoms", they tore their aprons and covered themselves [*ikhtamara*; from the root *kh-m-r*]' (al-Bukhārī, Chapter of Interpretation of the Koran, no. 4387; Sunan Abī Dāwud, Chapter on Dressing, no. 3579).

When I searched in the computer program for the Koranic terms, *ḥijāb*, *jilbāb*, *thawb* and *khimār*, I found one hadith with various narrator chains talking about *jilbāb*, saying that if a woman goes out for the ʿId-prayer and she does not have a *jilbāb*, she should cover herself with parts of her sister's *jilbāb*. With regard to *ḥijāb*, I found that this term was used for the wives of the Prophet, whereas I found that most of the hadiths where the term *khimār* is used in connection with female clothing have weak narrator chains.[2] It is interesting to note, however, that the term *khimār* is used in hadiths about the Prophet where it is said that the Prophet, when he did his ablutions, used to take water and wipe his *khimār* (Musnad Aḥmad, *bāqi musnad al-anṣār*, no. 22791; Sunan an-Nisāʾī, Chapter on Purity, no. 105). That the Prophet used a *khimār* indicates that it is not a face-cover, but rather a cloth covering the head.

In the Islamist discourse on female covering the hadiths referred to are first those addressing women in general:

1 ʿĀ'isha told that once Asmāʾ the daughter of Abū Bakr entered the house of the Prophet (p. b. u. h.), and she was wearing transparent clothes. The Prophet said: 'O Asmāʾ! When a women comes to the age of menstruation she should only show this', and he pointed at his face and his hands.

(Abū Dāwud, Chapter on Dressing, no. 3580)[3]

2 When the Koranic verse [the *jilbāb*-verse 33: 59] was revealed, the women of *al-ānṣār* tribe [in Medina] went out [of their houses] with a black cloth on their heads (*ruʾūsihinna*).

(Sunan Abī Dāwud, Chapter on Dressing, no. 3578)[4]

3 ʿĀ'isha narrated that the Messenger of God (p.b.u.h.) used to pray the morning prayer and with him were believing women who were shrouded in their sheets (*murūṭ*). Then they went back to their houses and nobody knew them.

(al-Bukhārī, Chapter on Prayer, no. 359)

4 The Messenger of God (p.b.u.h.) ordered that on the day of ʿīd [festival] all mature women, the virgins and menstruating women should go to the place of prayer in order to look at the good (*khayr*) and the message of the Muslims. One woman asked: if one of them does not have a *jilbāb*? He answered. Then her sister should cover her with her *jilbāb*.

(al-Bukhārī, Chapter on Menstruation, no. 313, Muslim, Chapter of the Two 'Ids' Prayer, no. 1475; Sunan at-Tirmidhī, Chapter on Friday Prayer, no. 495; Sunan Ibn Mājah, Chapter on the Call to Prayer and its Sunna, no. 1297; Musnad Aḥmad, *musnad al-baṣrīīn*, no. 19863)

Hadiths which refer specifically to the wives of the Prophet are:

5 Umm Salama relates that she and Maimūna once were together with the Prophet. She said: 'When we were with him, the son of Umm Maktūm approached. He entered the house and this incident was after we had been ordered to *ḥijāb* [separation with a curtain]. The Messenger (p. b. u. h.) said: "Hide from him (*iḥtajabā minhu*)". I said: "O Messenger of God! Is he not blind and can neither see us nor know us?" The Messenger of God (p.b.u.h.) said: "Are you blind? Can you not see him?"'.[5]

6 ʿĀ'isha narrated that when the wives of the Prophet went to Hajj they brought travel escorts with them. When these escorts passed by them they used to slip down their overcoat (*jilbāb*) from their head over the face, and when the escorts had passed them they would uncover.
(Sunan Abī Dāwud, Chapter on Hermitage, no. 1562; Musnad Aḥmad, *bāqi musnad al-anṣār*, no. 22894)[6]

The hadith literature seems to give the impression that there are some basic rules about decency for both men and women, but nothing of what I have read gives any indication of a uniformity of dress. What is described is a general style of dress rather than a fixed form.

The Islamic debate on veiling

The four law schools differ concerning female veiling. Three of the law schools, Shāfiʿī, Mālikī and Ḥanbalī promote the view that the face-veil is obligatory (N. Keller 1991: 512; 899). In the Ḥanafī law school, however, the face-veil is not obligatory.

In the discussion below I will turn to both ancient and contemporary commentaries on the Koran and I will then consider the contemporary debate. It is amazing how Islamic writers tend to concentrate on female dress. Given that male dress is a major theme in the hadith literature, one might expect that there would be much written about it in the contemporary Islamic movement, particularly as there is an obvious conflict between the guidelines given in the hadiths and how male Muslims dress today. However, I have rarely found anything written about how men should dress in general. Writings on male dress tend to be paragraphs dealing with the prohibition against men wearing silk and the special dress men should wear during Hajj, incorporated in general books on Islam. In contrast, books on 'proper female Islamic dress' have flooded the market. Usually the books list conditions of *jilbāb* and these conditions differ according to Islamic directions and geographical locations. Thus, for instance, one fundamental schism between the *salafī* movement in the Gulf area and the *salafī* movement outside, led by al-Albānī, concerns the question of female dress, a discussion with theological implications which I refer to below.

Traditional Islamic literature

One of the first, if not the first, work dealing with the women issue in general is Ibn al-Jawzī's (d. 1201) book called *kitāb aḥkām an-nisā'* (*The Book of Jurisdiction for Women*). In this book Ibn Jawzī discusses various issues concerning women in worship and in social life. The book is divided into numerous chapters, each dealing with a specific subject. Thus one chapter might extend to only one page, whereas others might extend to four or five pages. It is important to note that not one single chapter deals with female dress, neither is the term *ḥijāb* mentioned at all. The only mention of female dress is when Ibn Jawzī quotes the hadith about the festival prayer, that if a woman does not have a *jilbāb* her sister should cover her with her *jilbāb*. Ibn Jawzī does not discuss how women should dress when they go out of the house but concentrates instead on the possibility of women going out of their houses at all and of their communicating with men other than their husbands. According to him a woman should not go out if she might cause any temptation (*fitna*) and this is in my view a strong indication that women were not in general covering their faces. He devotes a further chapter to 'The virtue of the home for women', where he quotes hadiths from Ibn Ḥanbal in which the Prophet is related to have said that 'the best mosque for woman is her home'. It is interesting to note that Muḥammad al-Ghazzālī has discussed this hadith and claims that it is not authentic according to its content although its narrator chain is of an authentic standard (M. al-Ghazzālī 1989: 54–6). al-Ghazzālī bases his argument on references to other hadiths telling about how women used to pray at the mosques on various occasions. He further refers to the fact that the Prophet established a special entrance for women in his mosque, adding that it is generally accepted among Islamic scholars that a hadith which contradicts stronger hadiths is a deviated hadith (M. al-Ghazzālī 1989: 55).

It is obvious that Ibn Jawzī calls for segregation between women and men, but surprisingly enough he does not speak of this segregation in terms of dress. The question is why he does not discuss women's dress in his book. Could it be that female dress was not an issue at that time? Was it simply that all women covered themselves either with the face or hands exposed or with a complete covering? Could it possibly be that Ibn Jawzī's contemporaries regarded women in terms of Muslim women on the one hand and 'other women' on the other, with 'other women' constituting a group that included slaves, prostitutes and non-Muslims? Which women were present in the official 'male' world? These are questions of importance to the contemporary debate on female veiling, but the answers are beyond the scope of the present research. To investigate this matter would require archaeological and historical research into customs surrounding housing and dress rules, which might give an indication of the situation as it was then.[7]

In *lisān al-ʿarab* the three terms of interest, *ḥijāb*, *jilbāb* and *khimār* are explained. As for *ḥijāb*, Ibn Manẓūr (d. 1311), the author of this lexicographic work, explains it as something which separates one thing from another (Ibn Manẓūr 1955 vol. I: 298). He further explains *khimār* to be 'that which the woman covers her head (*ra's*) with' (Ibn Manẓūr 1955 vol. I: 257). *Jilbāb* is in his view a 'shirt' or 'a garment which is wider than a *khimār*'. He does not in any of his explanations of these three terms refer to the covering of the face or the hands. Ibn Manẓūr lived in the thirteenth/fourteenth century, and Ibn Jawzī in the twelfth/thirteenth century. Both seem to have a fairly unproblematic attitude towards female dress, in contrast to twentieth century scholars who give various detailed explanations of 'Islamic female dress'.

By turning to the Koranic commentaries, we find that aṭ-Ṭabārī (d. 923), in his discussion of verse 24: 31, includes various scholarly opinions on female attire. He concludes that in his view the Koranic passage 'only that which is apparent thereof' refers to the face and hands. He adds that as the face and hands might be exposed it follows that also kohl (black colouring of the eyelids), rings, bracelets and dye (i.e. henna colouring of the hands) might be exposed too (aṭ-Ṭabārī 1994 vol. V: 419). aṭ-Ṭabārī's argument is based on a consensus (*ijmā'*) among scholars that in prayer and during Hajj women expose their hands and their faces. That means, according to him, that the rest of a woman's body is her *ʿawra* (that which should not be exposed). Thus, he concludes that it is not forbidden (*ḥarām*) to show that part of the body which is not *ʿawra*. As a woman's face and hands are not *ʿawra*, this means that the Koranic passage in question refers to the face and hands. aṭ-Ṭabārī explains the sentence 'let them draw their coverings (*khumur*) over their bosoms' as meaning that women should cover their hair and their necks and their earrings. His view is thus the opposite of that of Ibn ʿAbbās who in Ābādī's interpretation demands full covering, and although aṭ-Ṭabārī refers to those who view complete covering as the correct form of female dress, he chooses the exposure of the face and the hands as the most prominent understanding.

As for the *ḥijāb*-verse 33: 53, aṭ-Ṭabārī interprets this as expressing a concern for both the wives of the Prophet and the wives of the believers. He explicitly states that one should not enter houses of women one is not married to, and if one has to ask them something one should ask from behind a curtain. This might appear to contradict his former statement that women should expose their faces and hands, but I think that he is discussing two separate issues. The former refers to how women should appear outside the home, whereas the latter describes how men and women who are not married to each other should relate to one another indoors. aṭ-Ṭabārī's view actually reflects a common practice among Muslims, particularly Islamists. Many women who appear outside the home with their faces and hands exposed observe total segregation inside the home. If husbands or fathers have male guests, women will keep to their private rooms which the guests are not allowed to enter. Thus, segregation within the homes differs from segregation outside the homes.

In the *jilbāb*-verse 33: 59, aṭ-Ṭabārī mentions two possible interpretations: complete covering or the covering of the face with an opening for one eye. He does not give his own view as he does for verse 24: 31, but he explains that the reason for women to cover themselves in such a way was that they should not be taken for slaves and thus be molested by men on the street (aṭ-Ṭabārī 1994 vol. VI: 200). aṭ-Ṭabārī specifies that the intention of this verse is that believing women should be identified as free women. What is interesting about this explanation is that he tends to refer to others' points of view and abstains from offering his own opinion. It is also important to note that in this verse he actually contradicts his earlier explanation of verse 24: 31, where he explicitly states his own view in favour of exposing hands and face. Would it not be natural in a commentary on the Koran to link similar contexts and interpret them in the light of each other? Does aṭ-Ṭabārī's caution about putting across his own ideas concerning this verse reflect his uncertainty over the relationship between the two verses? It is interesting to note that, in contrast to aṭ-Ṭabārī, Ibn Kathīr links these two verses. However, for Ibn Kathīr there is no contradiction between the two as his view is that women should cover their faces outdoors. Ibn Kathīr refers to Muḥammad Ibn Sīrīn (d. 729) who thought that women should cover the whole body and expose only one eye (Ibn Sīrīn mentions the left eye), and he also refers to Ibn ʿAbbās who mentions the face and hands and the ring. In response to Ibn ʿAbbās' explanation, Ibn Kathīr discusses whether Ibn ʿAbbās really means that the face and hands and the ring are beauty (*zīna*) which the Koran says should be covered, or that these should be exposed. Ibn Kathīr does not present his own opinion but one can deduce from the references he uses, that he prefers full covering (Ibn Kathīr 1981 vol. II: 114). In the explanation of verse 24: 31, Ibn Kathīr refers to the hadith from Abū Dāwud about Asmāʾ who was dressed in transparent clothes, but he classifies this hadith as *mursal* (an incomplete transmitted hadith resting on a chain of authorities that goes back only to the second generation after the Prophet) (Ibn Kathīr 1981 vol. II: 114).

If one looks at the commentary on the Koran according to Ibn ʿAbbās by Fīrūz Ābādī who belonged to the Shāfiʿī school, it is possible to investigate how Ābādī perceived female dress according to a fifteenth century view, authenticating it by referring back to Ibn ʿAbbās. His explanation of verse 24: 31 is that the adornments which women should hide are the bracelets and ornamented belts which they used to wear at that time. The sentence which immediately follows the expression, 'only that which is apparent thereof', he explains as referring to women's clothes. As for the phrase, 'let them draw their coverings over their bosoms' Ābādī states that women should let loose their *qināʿ* (veil or a mask) over their breasts and their necks (Ābādī 1988: 353). With regard to *jilbāb* in verse 33: 59, he explains this to mean *muqannaᶜ* (veil, mask) and a cloak. Ābādī thus suggests that according to Ibn ᶜAbbās there already existed a face cover to be loosened or lengthened in order to cover the breasts and the neck. Ābādī's explanation is an example of how one's own opinion is confirmed through the selection of texts. That Ibn ᶜAbbās' text is not as clear as Ābādī claims it is, would seem to be substantiated by the fact that Ibn Kathīr had problems ascertaining what Ibn ᶜAbbās meant. As Ābādī was a scholar in Shāfiᶜī jurisprudence which holds that women should wear a face-veil, he incorporates fifteenth century Shāfiᶜī ideology into Ibn ᶜAbbās' interpretation. This is an example of how history is usually written, not only in the Muslim world but generally. The discussion above indicates a variation in practice in different times and places. As aṭ-Ṭabārī from the ninth century holds a different view from that of Ibn Kathīr from the thirteenth century and Ābādī from the fifteenth century, it seems that ideals and practices varied over time. Diverse cultural base patterns seem to have been active in the interpretation of the Islamic sources in different historical contexts.

Contemporary Islamic literature

With regard to classical commentators on the Koran, there is a consensus that women should cover in one way or another. The controversy between the scholars is the extent to which women should cover: should a woman cover her hair but expose the face and the hands, should she cover everything except for one eye, or should the covering be complete? Contemporary scholars are involved in the same controversy. Among Islamic scholars there is consensus with regard to female covering but there is no consensus for the actual form of covering.[8] Similarly, as the Muslim feminist discussion focuses on whether the segregation between men and women instituted by the *ḥijāb*-verse 33: 53 is directed only to the wives of the Prophet or to Muslim women in general, some Islamic scholars have questioned the universality of the verse. Abū Shaqqa says in his book that 'the verse [33: 53] speaks unambiguously about the household of the Prophet (p.b.u.h.) and not about the household and the general wives of the Muslims' (Abū Shaqqa 1990 vol. III: 70 [translation mine]). Abū Shaqqa is careful to speak about *ḥijāb* in Koranic terms, and he sees *ḥijāb* as a curtain behind which something is hidden. In the Prophet's house there was to be a 'boundary' between men and the Prophet's wives. When the Prophet's wives went out, this 'boundary' was to be maintained as no men should see the wives of the Prophet. It was therefore obligatory, according to Abū Shaqqa, for the wives of the Prophet to cover completely when they went out of the house. He uses the term '*ḥijāb*' to refer to the actual 'segregation' or the 'boundary' between men and women but he also uses it to refer to the dress which functions as a 'boundary', namely a dress which covers the whole body including the face and hands (Abū Shaqqa 1990 vol. III: 69).

Other scholars are less careful in their use of terminology. Sheikh ash-Shaʿrāwī, for instance, talks about *ḥijāb* as the 'head-cover', whereas he sees *niqāb* as the face-veil. ash-Shaʿrāwī points out that every Muslim woman *should* wear a head-cover, whereas he regards a face-veil as necessary only for a woman whose face is so beautiful that she might cause temptation (*fitna*). This view is common among Muslims in general. The problem which arises is who should define this beauty and what degree of beauty actually causes temptation. I believe this idea has arisen in parallel with the idea of women as temptresses. As I have not often encountered the idea of women as temptresses in Arab Islamism, I find it interesting that in ash-Shaʿrāwī's book this idea is prominent. He states that 'the whole issue [of head-cover and face-veil] circles around the fact that women should not be *fitna* to men' (ash-Shaʿrāwī n.d.: 97 [translation mine]). ash-Shaʿrāwī does not represent the Islamist movements but rather he is a *madhhabist*, (i.e. he adheres to one Islamic law school), and he thus represents a traditional understanding of Islam.[9] It is interesting to note that in verse 33: 59 the Koran mentions that women should cover so as not to be molested *by* men, whereas ash-Shaʿrāwī has turned the whole issue around to suggest that women should cover so as not to be temptations *to* men. I believe that the way these ideas are presented is decisive in the formation of attitudes. In the former case men are the aggressors and women the victims, whereas in the latter, women are the actors and men the victims. However, as I have discussed before we should bear in mind the possible change in cultural content of a concept in the translation process, and it might be the 'western cultural base pattern' which makes me interpret ash-Shaʿrāwī's argument in such a way.

ʿAbdullāh Jārullāh, a Saudi scholar, consequently uses the term *ḥijāb* for women's complete covering (except for one eye). However, in contrast to ash-Shaʿrāwī who I believe is less aware of the distinction between the terms, Jārullāh's use of *ḥijāb* reflects his point of view that the *ḥijāb* verse (33: 53) is directed to all women and not only to the Prophet's household (Jārullāh 1983: 47–61). Jārullāh is representative of the Saudi point of view, thus belonging to the 'Arab cultural base pattern' which is a particularly strong feature of the Saudi Arabian understanding of Islam. It is interesting to note that his booklet is printed and distributed by the Ministry of Information in Saudi Arabia. Jārullāh's ideas on female covering, moreover, represent a *salafī* approach to Islam. Two other *salafī* scholars who hold the same view are Muḥammad Muḥṣin Khān and Muḥammad al-Hilālī, both linked to the Islamic University in Medina. In an English translation of al-Bukhārī's hadith collection, Khān, who is the translator, has translated the hadith about the interpretation of the Koranic verse about *khimār* to mean 'to cover the face' (M. M. Khān 1985 vol. VI: 267). Although the Arabic text does not indicate any veiling of the face, the translator has incorporated his own view in the translation. One can deduce that the cultural surroundings, the 'Arab cultural base pattern', of these two authors have made them interpret the Koranic term *khimār* to mean a face-veil. The same subjectivity can be observed in a translation of the Koran into English, called *Interpretation of the Meaning of the Noble Qur'an in the English Language*, by these two *salafī* authors, Khān and Hilālī. In the translation of verse 24: 31 they write:

> [A]nd not to show off their adornment except only that which is apparent (like palms of hands or one eye or both eyes for necessity to see their way, or outer dress like veil, gloves, head-cover, apron etc.) and to draw their veils all over *juyūbihinna* (i.e. their bodies, faces, necks and bosoms, etc.).
>
> (Hilālī and Khān 1993: 542)

It is of interest to note that the literal interpretation of *juyūb*, according to Wehr, is 'breast' or 'bosom', whereas Hilālī and Khān translate it as 'bodies, faces, necks and bosoms' as this translation suits their particular view which is that women should cover even their faces.

As for verse 33: 59 (the *jilbāb* verse) the two authors have a similar argument, saying that what should be visible of the body are the eyes or one eye 'to see the way' (Hilālī and Khān 1993: 657).

In contrast to the *salafī* approach of the Saudi scholars, the famous Jordanian *salafī* scholar, al-Albānī, takes the opposite view. He is engaged in polemics with the Saudi scholars, particularly over the matter of female covering. Jārullāh's main argument for covering both the hands and the face is the weakness of the hadith about the Prophet's order to Asmā' to cover all her body except the face and the hands, as there is a discontinuity between the first and the second chain in the narrator chain (*isnād*) (Jārullāh 1983: 56). al-Albānī claims that although there is a problem with the narrator chain, the content of this hadith comes in so many shapes and so many ways (different narrator chains) that it is possible to categorise it as authentic (*ṣaḥīḥ*) (al-Albānī 1994: 57–8).

al-Albānī's discussion focuses on whether the face of a woman is *ʿawra* or not. It is of interest that he does not discuss the *ḥijāb* verse at all but concentrates instead on the other two Koranic verses dealing with female covering: 24: 31 (the *khimār* verse) and 33: 59 (the *jilbāb* verse). al-Albānī first published his book *ḥijāb al-mar'a l-muslima fī l-kitāb wa s-sunna* (*The Woman's ḥijāb in the Koran and Sunna*) in 1951–2 (1370–1371 AH). In 1994 he republished the book and changed the term *ḥijāb* in the title to *jilbāb*. In the text, however, he continues to use the term *ḥijāb* to denote female covering. In the preface to the new edition he explains that the difference between the first and the second edition is that the second contains thirteen pieces of evidence (*dalīl*; pl. *adilla*) that a woman's face is not *ʿawra* instead of the eight pieces of evidence he presented in the first edition. He does not explain the reason why he changed the term '*ḥijāb*' to '*jilbāb*' in the title of the book. I would hazard a guess that as the term '*ḥijāb*' originally meant total segregation, al-Albānī wanted to make a point with regard to the Saudi scholars who advocate segregation for all women, that *ḥijāb* is something which is linked exclusively to the wives of the Prophet. However, as al-Albānī has decided to adhere to the term *ḥijāb* in the text his point gets lost. Given that he is the contemporary scholar who tends to be most scientific in terms of always thoroughly referencing his work, I would have expected him to show greater care with regard to the choice of terminology than he has in his book.

al-Albānī's main argument concerns the hadith about Asmāʾ. He also refers to other hadiths but none of these specifically discuss dress as such and the issue of clothing is often only implicitly referred to. al-Albānī devotes the great part of the preface of the 1994 issue of the book to attacking the Saudi scholar, at-Tuwaijrī, who has accused him of opening the way for a display of women's beauty (*tabarruj*) in official life. al-Albānī quotes at-Tuwaijrī as saying:

> Those who allow women to expose themselves (he means by this the exposing of the face only [al-Albānī's remark]) and provide evidence for this as al-Albānī has done, have left the door wide open for displaying (*tabarruj*). They have encouraged women to perpetrate blameworthy behaviour such as non-covered women are doing these days.
> (al-Albānī 1994: 10 [translation mine])

This attack on al-Albānī and al-Albānī's counterattack, which is at times quite fierce, suggest the emotional potential inherent in the debate about veiling. al-Albānī, like the Saudi scholars, belongs to the *salafī* movement, which does not regard adherence to a school of Islamic law as acceptable practice in Islam. However, it seems that al-Albānī's break with the law schools is more fundamental than that of many Saudi scholars, given that the Ḥanbalī school has such a firm status in Saudi Arabia. It might also be that as scholars belonging to the Ḥanbalī school, in spite of their ideal of turning back to the Koran and the Sunna, they have difficulty with liberating themselves from the rules of the law school because ideologically speaking it is closest to the *salafī* ideas, and it tends to build its jurisdiction mainly on the Koran and hadiths. I further assume that as most Saudi scholars are trained in Ḥanbalī thought, it might be easier to turn to those hadiths which they already are familiar with in content and narrator chains. al-Albānī implies that this is the position of the Saudi scholars when he states that although many *salafī* scholars (i.e. Saudi scholars) know that the hadith related by Ibn ʿAbbās about how women should show only one eye is a weak hadith, they present it as authentic (al-Albānī 1994: 11).

al-Albānī goes on to discuss the Koranic verses and he refers to the traditional Koranic commentaries. He shows that, for instance, al-Qurṭubī

(d. 1273) and many other classical scholars interpreted the Koranic passage 'except that which is apparent thereof' as the hands and face. He argues with reference to al-Jaṣṣāṣ (d. 981) that it is impossible that clothing or jewellery are the beauty of women referred to in the Koran as *zīna*, as these can be seen by men when women are not wearing them. Thus he claims that what is meant by that which is apparent is the place of jewellery and clothing, i.e. the hands and the face (al-Albānī 1994: 54).

al-Albānī also engages with the discussion about the term *khimār*. He claims that linguistically speaking it does not mean the covering of the face but the covering of the head only (al-Albānī 1994: 6–7; 72). He points to how many Koranic commentators have explained the reason behind this revelation (*sabab an-nuzūl*) as being that women used to cover their head with *khimār* and then they let the cover hang down their backs leaving the necks, shoulders and ears uncovered. 'God the Almighty then ordered the *khimār* to be bent over the chest,' he says (al-Albānī 1994: 78). al-Albānī refers to another hadith about a woman who came to speak to ʿUmar. She was wearing a *jilbāb* with which she covered herself (*wa ʿalayhā jilbāb mutaqanaʿ bih*). The story ends by saying that ʿUmar told her to remove the *jilbāb* from her head (*ra's*) as she was a slave and the *jilbāb* was for free believing women to wear (al-Albānī 1994: 99–100). al-Albānī notes that as ʿUmar knew this woman and knew that she was a slave she obviously exposed her face, otherwise he would not have known her.[10] It is important to draw attention to the fact that the word *mutaqanaʿ* which is mentioned in the hadith comes from the same root *q-n-ʿ* which Ābādī used when he referred to Ibn ʿAbbās' interpretation of the Koranic verses on female covering. The root *q-n-ʿ* means in a contemporary context 'mask', as the particular face-mask which many women wear in certain Gulf-states is called *qināʿ*. However, al-Albānī changes this interpretation of the word by pointing out that in the early Islamic period *qināʿ* or the adjective *mutaqanaʿ* referred to the covering of the head rather than the covering of the face.

I have only referred to a few examples from al-Albānī's book in order to demonstrate his argument. His discussion is convincing in that his method is scientific in the sense of giving accurate references. He is careful to present all hadiths with accurate narrator chains and to say in which hadith collection they occur. He also goes into detail by explaining the positions of the various persons involved in the narrator chains. What is interesting to note is that after al-Albānī has made such an effort to establish that a woman's face is not *ʿawra*, he refers to a court case from the third century of Islam, where the woman involved in the case covered her face. He concludes that as there is evidence that women at that time used to cover their faces, it is acceptable (*mubāḥ*) for those who choose to cover, although the primary position is that covering the face is not obligatory (*farḍ*) (al-Albānī 1994: 114). I would argue that by allowing for the use of face-covering in spite of concluding from the sources that there is no obligation to cover, al-Albānī goes against his own principle that everything not found in the Islamic sources is innovation (*bidaʿ*) in Islam. Although covering the face cannot be called an innovation as such since there are indications that the Prophet's wives observed the practice, the extension of this practice to *all* Muslim women may be regarded as a form of innovation. al-Albānī is living outside Saudi Arabia. Although the 'Arab cultural base pattern' is influential even in Jordan where he lives, perceptions about women are less rigid in Jordan than in Saudi Arabia. For instance, in contrast to Jordan where women can freely expose both the face and the hair, in Saudi Arabia a woman can hardly be in public places without covering herself with a face-veil. 'The social organisation' within Saudi Arabia, and I use the concept here in terms of the local ideology, is a factor which obstructs change in the matter of female veiling. In contrast to this, the various options about veiling within the social organisation of Jordanian society seem to have influenced al-Albānī's selection from 'the basket' in this issue.

In Muḥammad al-Ghazzālī's (d. 1996) book *as-sunna n-nabawīya bayna ahl al-fiqh wa ahl al-ḥadīth* (*The Prophetic Sunna between the People of the Jurisprudence and the People of Hadith*) he devotes a chapter to female covering named 'The battle of ḥijāb'. Although al-Ghazzālī's text is a reaction to the *salafī* stand, it seems obvious that al-Ghazzālī has read al-Albānī's book and uses his references to argue against covering of the face. Many of the hadiths which he refers to, hadiths containing only incidental remarks on female clothing, seem to be picked up from a reading of al-Albānī's book. He starts this chapter with a general remark which indicates his aims:

> We want two things of the Islamic awakening (*ṣaḥwa*). The first is: to stay away from the faults which deviated the Umma and removed its strength and encouraged its enemies. The second is: to give a practical image which will please the observers and remove ancient obscurity [misunderstandings] (*shubahāt*), and be just to the divine revelation.
>
> (M. al-Ghazzālī 1989: 36 [translation mine])

In al-Ghazzālī's view, 'some participants of the Islamic awakening' have failed to realise these two aims. He regards 'the battle of the face-veil (*niqāb*)' as an example of this failure. al-Ghazzālī specifically mentions scholars in the Gulf countries who state that it is forbidden for a woman to expose the face in public (M. al-Ghazzālī 1989: 36). In his argument, al-Ghazzālī discusses the authenticity of some of the hadiths about female covering. He also refers to other hadiths which in his view indicate that women, with the exception of the wives of the Prophet, did not cover their face and hands during the time of the Prophet and the Companions. He refers to a book he read by a Gulf scholar who writes that Islam has forbidden fornication (*zinā*) and that the uncovering of the face necessarily leads to fornication. al-Ghazzālī opposes this view with the argument that Islam has made obligatory the uncovering of the face during Hajj and during prayers. He states that 'is it that by this uncovering [of the face] in two pillars of Islam's five pillars, the [sexual] instincts are aroused and the way to criminal acts is cleared? How deceitful is this reasoning?' (M. al-Ghazzālī 1989: 36).

al-Ghazzālī then discusses the two hadiths narrated by ʿĀ'isha; the one about Asmāʾ in which Asmāʾ is told to expose only the face and the hands and the hadith about ʿĀ'isha's saying that the wives of the Prophet used to hide their faces from the travel escorts when they travelled to Hajj. al-Ghazzālī claims the latter to be weak (*ḍaʿīf*) according to its narrator chain and deviated (*shādhdh*) according to its content. He raises the question of why this latter hadith, which is far less authentic than the former hadith on Asmāʾ, has gained such prominence among certain scholars. He adds that he is aware that the former hadith is incompletely transmitted (i.e. the narrator chain stops with the second generation of Muslims) but he states that the content of the hadith on Asmāʾ is fortified as other narrators have related it in various forms. 'Anyway', he says, 'this hadith is stronger than the other one' (M. al-Ghazzālī 1989: 40).

As for further evidence that women are not obliged to cover their face and their hands, al-Ghazzālī quotes various hadiths which in his view indicate that women exposed their faces. He further points to the Koranic injunctions that men should lower their gazes (K.24: 30). 'Should one lower the gaze from the clothes and the [women's] back?' he asks. He relates a hadith where the Prophet talked to the women and a woman among them who had 'burnt spots on her cheeks' answered the Prophet (M. al-Ghazzālī 1989: 37).[11] al-Ghazzālī interprets this as evidence that women used to expose their faces. Another hadith he refers to is about a woman who came to ask the Prophet about something and 'one of the Companions looked at her and she looked at him, then the Messenger of God turned the Companion's face' (M. al-Ghazzālī 1989: 39). al-Ghazzālī explains that this took place at the Prophet's last pilgrimage and therefore no hadith came after it (M. al-Ghazzālī 1989: 38–9).[12]

It is important to draw attention to the fact that al-Ghazzālī quotes Ibn Kathīr's interpretation of the Koranic verses 24: 30–1, where Ibn Kathīr refers to Ibn ʿAbbās' saying that 'what may [decently] be apparent thereof' means the face and the hands. al-Ghazzālī explicitly states that Ibn Kathīr is a *salaf* scholar. He thus manages in a rhetorical way to point out that a great historical authority who moreover is a *salaf*, as are al-Ghazzālī's opponents to whom he addresses his arguments, was opposed to the covering of the face and hands. What he does not mention, however, is that Ibn Kathīr actually discusses Ibn ʿAbbās' view and believes that his explanation 'the face and the hands' refers to a woman's beauty rather than suggesting that these parts of the body should be exposed (Ibn Kathīr

1981: 114 vol. II). al-Ghazzālī's discussion of Ibn Kathīr's interpretation might be an example of how one tends to omit parts of an argument in order to reinforce one's own point of view. This is the same phenomenon that I observed in the debate by Muslim feminists, where the 'western cultural base pattern' influenced what was selected from 'the basket'. However, this disregarding of certain obvious statements in texts might alternatively be a non-verbalised omission whereby the process of perception works in such a way that a person observes only that which is in accordance with his or her own view. Without entering into a psychological discussion of this matter, I would point out that a person's preconceived ideas, based on world-views and cultural base patterns, tend to be confirmed through such a process.

al-Ghazzālī ends the chapter by stating on the one hand the importance of dressing decently according to the standard which God has given, and not in the standard, as he says, 'of European society' (M. al-Ghazzālī 1989: 42). On the other hand he combats common Muslim concepts about female behaviour, resisting in particular the widespread idea that women should not go out of their houses. He refers to one of the famous Islamic preachers (without mentioning any names), who proclaimed that a woman should only go out of her house twice: to her husband when she marries and to the grave when she dies. The hadith he refers to in this matter tells about a man who left home to go to war and told his wife not to leave the house until he came back. His wife refused to visit her father during his illness and then to go to his funeral, due to her husband's order. When the Prophet heard about this he is related to have said: 'Verily, God has forgiven your father his sins due to your obedience to your husband' (M. al-Ghazzālī 1989: 43).[13] al-Ghazzālī fiercely opposes this hadith stating that it is not authentic. Concerning the preacher who spoke of this hadith in his speeches, he asks: 'Is this how he opposes our religion? A prison for the woman, cutting [the bonds] which God has ordered to be linked?' (M. al-Ghazzālī 1989: 43).

It is important to be aware that in the 1970s and 1980s many speeches by Imams and other Islamic scholars were widely disseminated on cassette recordings in the Muslim world and in Europe and the United States. Many of these recordings were made during Friday prayers or lectures (*durūs*) in mosques when the speakers' main aim is to get people enthusiastic and rouse their feelings for the sake of Islam, so many of the speeches tend to be emotive. However, with the expansion of satellite television and the increase in Arab channels these cassettes have come to have less influence on Arab Islamists than they had in the 1970s and 1980s.

The writing of al-Ghazzālī has had a great influence on Islamists of various shades, except maybe on those belonging to the *salafī* trend. His book aroused emotions among *salafīs* as it was a response not only to traditional conceptions of Arab society but also to the *salafī* movement's methodology in matters of jurisprudence. al-Ghazzālī's style of language is, as I have indicated above, highly rhetorical and provocative. Until his death in 1996 he was regarded by a great many Islamists, particularly those with *ikhwān* and *post-ikhwān* sympathies, as '*the* great Islamic scholar of the time [*al-ʿallāma*]'. With the death of al-Ghazzālī, Yūsuf al-Qaraḍāwī has in many Muslims' view been raised to this position. In his 1996 work entitled *fatāwā muʿāṣira* (*Contemporary Legal Decisions*), al-Qaraḍāwī answers questions which as a Sheikh and a mufti he has received from various parts of the world, one of which was posed by a young man from Aden in Yemen:

> A long dispute has arisen among us about uncovering (*sufūr*) and covering (*ḥijāb*) in particular the woman's face:
> Is the face *ʿawra*? Is it obligatory to cover the face or not? Neither of the two factions has succeeded in convincing the other and we therefore turn to you in order to find a final answer provided to us from the sharia text and its evidence.
>
> (al-Qaraḍāwī 1996 vol. I: 431 [translation mine])

al-Qaraḍāwī responds by referring to the various opinions on this matter, before pointing out that no text has claimed that the face is *ʿawra* except one hadith from Ibn Ḥanbal which in al-Qaraḍāwī's view is not a well-known (*maʿrūf*) hadith. When al-Qaraḍāwī discusses the implication of the Koranic injunction to 'lower the gaze', his argument resembles that of al-Ghazzālī's. He explains:

> The lowering of the gaze which is an order from God does not mean the shutting of the eye, or the bowing of the head in order that the human being does not see anyone. This is not possible. For verily the meaning of the expression lowering [of] the gaze (*al-ghuḍḍ min al-abṣār*) does not mean the lowering of [the whole of] the gaze (*ghuḍḍ al-abṣār*).
>
> (al-Qaraḍāwī 1996 vol. I: 431 [translation mine])

al-Qaraḍāwī makes the point that by appealing to the rules of grammar, one can deduce that it is possible to look at the other sex within the limits of other Islamic rules, explaining:

> It is permitted for a man to look at that which is not *ʿawra* in a woman with a look which is without sexual desire. . . . And for the woman, as for the man, it is permissible for her to look – with decency and with lowering [of the gaze] on that which is not a man's *ʿawra*.
>
> (al-Qaraḍāwī 1996 vol. I: 431)

Although al-Qaraḍāwī explicitly states that if a man is afraid of temptation (*fitna*) he should not look at the woman, he does not emphasise this point as does ash-Shaʿrāwī in his discussion of female covering (ash-Shaʿrāwī n.d.: 97).

al-Qaraḍāwī's main argument against covering the face is that much of what is said in this respect is addressed directly to the wives of the Prophet. Thus he believes that the hadith related by Umm Salama in which she and Maimūna, another of the Prophet's wives, were told not to look at the blind man, is a matter for the wives of the Prophet only, whereas for ordinary women another hadith applies. This hadith is the story about Fāṭima bint Qays who was told by the Prophet to complete her *ʿidda*-period (waiting-period after divorce) at a house where a blind man lived. The Prophet is related to have said that 'he is a blind man so you can lay down your clothes in his house' (al-Qaraḍāwī 1996 vol. I: 432).

In al-Qaraḍāwī's response as to whether the woman's face is *ʿawra* or not, he refers to a Ḥanbalī scholar's answer to the question of whether a woman should show her face or not, bearing in mind society's moral deficiency, when she is performing Hajj. This scholar is reported to have said:

> It is one of the symbols of Hajj that women should expose their faces. To abolish a fixed Islamic ruling because of new events is not allowed, because this will lead to abolition due to circumstances and we will arrive to a situation where Islamic laws are abolished just like that. It is not innovation (*bidʿa*) to ask the woman to expose her face and order the man to lower his gaze.
>
> (al-Qaraḍāwī 1996 vol. I: 433 [translation mine])

It is interesting to note that al-Qaraḍāwī refers to a Ḥanbalī scholar who permits the uncovering of the face during Hajj, indicating that in this scholar's view, the face cannot possibly be *ʿawra*. The Ḥanbalī scholars are known among Muslims to be rigid in *fiqh* matters and they are regarded as those who keep most strictly to the prophetic traditions. Thus by citing this scholar's view as being most in accordance with his own, al-Qaraḍāwī establishes that the face is not *ʿawra*, as understood by even the strictest scholars of Islamic jurisprudence. It should also be noted that in the above quotation the Ḥanbalī scholar refutes the common argument among *salafī* scholars (even among those who do not promote the covering of the face as obligatory) that in times of moral deficiency women should cover their faces. Although al-Qaraḍāwī does not explicitly state his own view, his argument implies his support for women showing their hands and faces. This is in line with most scholars within the *ikhwān* and *post-ikhwān* trends, although in countries such as Egypt where Islamist forces are suppressed and persecuted, many women of the Muslim Brotherhood tend to cover their faces not mainly for ideological reasons but as they see the veiling of the face as a protection.

Muḥammad Fu'ād al-Barāzī, a Syrian scholar from the Muslim Brotherhood living in Denmark, wrote a book called *ḥijāb al-muslima* (*The Muslim Woman's Ḥijab*) while living in one of the Gulf states. al-Barāzī is convinced that the covering of the face is the original commandment (*aṣl*) of female Islamic dress. He starts with an analysis of terms, such as *ḥijāb*, *jilbāb*, *niqāb* and *khimār*, according to the Islamic sources and to Islamic scholars. He further refers to Ibn Manẓūr's work *lisān al-ʿarab* (*The Arabic Tongue*), but interestingly he interprets Ibn Manẓūr's explanation of *khimār* as being in favour of the covering of the face and hands. In his discussion of *khimār*, al-Barāzī points out that Ibn Manẓūr quotes a hadith from Umm Salama, the wife of the Prophet, in which she is related to have said that the Prophet used to wipe his hands (for ablution) over his shoes and his *khimār*. Ibn Manẓūr explains that what is meant by *khimār* is the turban as 'the man covers his head with the turban similarly as the woman covers her head with the *khimār*' (al-Barāzī 1995: 36; Ibn Manẓūr 1955 vol. IV: 257–8). The *khimār* has also obviously been used by men as Ibn Manẓūr relates the Prophet as having worn one, an issue which al-Barāzī does not take up in the discussion as he only looks into al-Manẓūr's explanation of what *khimār* is. al-Barāzī also refers to another lexicographic work, *tāj al-ʿarūs* (*The Bridal Wreath*) by az-Zubaidī (d. 1791), which describes *khimār* as 'everything which covers something' (al-Barāzī 1995: 36). The third authority which he refers to is Ibn Ḥajar al-ʿAsqalānī (d. 1448), who in his commentary on al-Bukhārī's hadith collection (*fatḥ al-bārī*) defines *khimār* as meaning that which a woman covers her head and her face with (al-Barāzī 1995: 37). In conclusion al-Barāzī states that the definition of *khimār* is 'that which a woman covers her head and face with, concealing herself from the eyes of the men' (al-Barāzī 1995: 37). It is interesting to note that of the three historical authorities cited by al-Barāzī, al-ʿAsqalānī is the only one who explicitly states that *khimār* refers to the covering of a woman's face. Neither of the two lexicographic works, *The Arabic Tongue* and *The Bridal Wreath*, mention the covering of the face in interpreting *khimār* to mean covering (*taghṭiyya*) the head. Since Ibn Manẓūr also refers to a hadith which indicates that even men could wear *khimār*, this further reinforces the idea that according to Ibn Manẓūr, *khimār* indicates covering the head only and not, as al-Barāzī interprets him as saying, the covering of the face. In spite of this, al-Barāzī implicitly concludes that there is unified agreement in the historical sources that *khimār* means the covering of the face as well.

It is important to note that instead of acknowledging the various opinions about how a woman should cover herself, al-Barāzī indicates that the 'right' opinion is that which advocates covering the head and the face. This attitude is reflected in the subtitle of his book, *The Muslim Woman's Ḥijab: Between the Unwarranted Assumption of the Liars and the Interpretation of the Ignorant*. al-Barāzī's methodology is in contrast to that of al-Qaraḍāwī who acknowledges that there are different opinions, but who goes on to say that in his view the strongest evidence suggests that a woman can expose her face. al-Barāzī's point of view reflects the view of the *salafī* scholars in Saudi Arabia. Thus, the 'Arab cultural base pattern' seems to have been influential in shaping his ideas about veiling. It is interesting that although al-Barāzī has lived in Denmark for more than seven years, he has not changed his views on veiling. In an interview he stated that according to the text (*naṣṣ*) the only alternative is that of covering the face and the hands, although he did explain that there are various views among scholars. With regard to Europe, he recognises that there are certain circumstances which require the exposure of the face, for example when women have professional jobs as teachers, doctors, lawyers, etc. The example of al-Barāzī clearly indicates that being in a European context does not necessarily in itself promote change, since one might have assumed that after seven years in a European country at least some modifications about an issue as fundamental as veiling of the face would have occurred. I believe, however, that one has to bear in mind that al-Barāzī is active only within the Muslim community, working as a spiritual guide and *muftī* (assigning legal decisions), and therefore having little contact with majority society. The 'Arab cultural base pattern' is thus the most influential in his world-view, making him select that legal evidence from 'the basket' which is compatible with his ideas.

In western countries most Islamic scholars regard the covering of the body and the head as sufficient. Sheikh Darsh wrote a booklet in 1995 called *Hijab or Naqab*. In the preface Huda Khattab, a Muslim woman convert living in Canada, explains how the booklet came into being. In the summer of 1994 there was a discussion among Muslim women in western countries about whether it was obligatory to cover the head and the face or the head only. Some women had investigated the vast literature on *ḥijāb* and they discovered that there were various trends in the debate. One of the observations was that literature designed for Muslims living in western countries tended to conclude that covering of the head was sufficient, whereas literature designed for Muslims living in the Muslim world tended to conclude that the covering of the head and the face was obligatory. In order to get a comprehensive perspective on the matter, the women wrote down their questions and sent them to Darsh. They describe Darsh in these terms: 'His deep Islamic knowledge, combined with years of experience of life in the West, makes him particularly qualified to relate the teachings to Muslims who are settled in Western societies' (Foreword by Huda Khattab in Darsh 1995: 3). Huda Khattab ends her preface by stating that the booklet 'sheds much light on the issue of Niqab', but she adds:

> However, the fact remains that there are differences among the classical scholars of Islam as to whether or not the face is *ʿawra* (but it is worth remembering that these scholars refrained from denouncing those who held different views as Kafirs [non-Muslims] and such like!). Human nature being what it is – different people will always choose to follow different interpretations.
>
> (Foreword by Huda Khattab in Darsh 1995: 4)

In the booklet, Darsh discusses two of the suras of the Koran dealing with female covering, Sura Parties 33 (*al-aḥzāb*) and Sura Light 24 (*an-nūr*). In his view the former deals 'with certain circumstances which needed specific treatment', whereas the latter is the Sura 'in which were revealed the definitive rules and regulations clearly prohibiting fornication . . . and the command to lower the gaze, preserve chastity, and cover the body properly' (Darsh 1995: 14). This leads him to conclude that Sura Light may be considered as 'the final and universal statement' about the covering of Muslim women. He goes on:

> All other previously-revealed regulations, as in Surah al-Ahzab, may be considered as either (1) pertaining to the noble household of the Prophet (SAAS), as is clear from the Ayah [verses] themselves or (2) intermediary steps necessitated by the lewd behaviour of the local thugs before specific severe punishment for such acts had been revealed.
>
> (Darsh 1995: 15)[14]

Darsh states two opinions in this statement. First, he indicates that the *ḥijāb* verse is aimed at the Prophet's wives only, and second that the verse in the same Sura about the wearing of *jilbāb* is to be understood specifically in the context of a certain limited period during the lifetime of the Prophet. He assumes that the Sura Light abrogates former injunctions as it also prohibits the behaviour which was the reason for the revelation of the Sura Parties. Further down he explicitly states that 'in general terms, the latter revelation abrogates the former' and that 'Surah al-Ahzab was sweeping away the former bad ways, preparing the ground for the final statements on these matters' (Darsh 1995: 15).[15] Darsh gives historical evidence of the sequence of revelation of these two Suras. According to him, the incident in which ʿĀ'isha was accused of indecent behaviour mentioned in Sura Light happened after the injunction of *ḥijāb* for the wives of the Prophet, since at the time of this incident Zainab was already married to the Prophet (Darsh 1995: 16). Darsh then questions the judgement of Ibn Taimīya who was of the opinion that the verse of *jilbāb* (33: 59) abrogates the verse of *khimār* (24: 31) as 'the historical evidence shows that the reverse is true, and that Surah al-Nur was the final statement on the matter, Surah al-Ahzab was an earlier step towards the final, universal rules' (Darsh 1995: 16).

Darsh concludes this chapter by referring to a common principle among Islamic scholars that if there are two contrasting texts which deal with the same matter 'the later parts of the revelation are the final word' (Darsh 1995: 16–17). He states, however, that in this particular matter he has not come across any clarification according to the two texts, except that of Ibn Taimīya whose conclusion is 'the reverse of that which is indicated by the historical evidence' (Darsh 1995: 17). Darsh claims that even

Ibn Taimīya does not give any evidence in support of covering the face, 'other than what may be described as a sort of custom among some of the Arabs', and he further states categorically that 'a local custom cannot be taken as the basis for legislation which is to be universally applicable' (Darsh 1995: 17).

Darsh goes on to discuss how the classical scholars of the Koran and the hadiths have treated female covering. He refers to, among others, aṭ-Ṭabārī and Ibn Kathīr, and he deduces that the most common opinion favours the exposure of the hands and face. It is interesting to note that even Darsh, like al-Ghazzālī, suggests that Ibn Kathīr advocates the exposure of the hands and face, whereas my own reading of Ibn Kathīr is that he supports covering them.

Similarly with regard to the hadith literature, Darsh concludes that the strongest evidence supports the exposure of the hands and face. He refers among others to Ibn Ḥajar al-ʿAsqalānī's commentary of hadiths, and *nayl al-awṭār* (*The Obtainance of the Aim*) by ash-Shawkānī (d. 1834). Darsh quotes ash-Shawkānī in his explanation of the hadith about how the women of Medina, shrouded in sheets, used to attend the morning prayer together with the Prophet, then dispersed 'unrecognised because of the darkness':

> al-Baqi said: This shows that women used to unveil their faces. For if they were used to covering their faces, it would have been difficult to recognise them whether it was dark in the early morning or it was light (i.e. the fact that it was dark would have made no difference [Darsh's commentary]).
>
> (Darsh 1995: 25)

Furthermore, Darsh refers to al-ʿAsqalānī's reference to the same hadith in which, according to Darsh, al-ʿAsqalānī points out that women are allowed to attend the mosque for prayer even at dawn and dusk when it is dangerous for women to move freely in the streets (Darsh 1995: 26). Darsh's conclusion from his reading of the Koran and the hadith literature and their commentaries is that the majority of Islamic scholars are of the view that a woman's hands and face are not *ʿawra* and that there is 'not an obligation or a strong recommendation to cover her face' (Darsh 1995: 30: 38). However, he stresses that 'the consensus of all Muslim scholars is that the Muslim woman must cover her body'(Darsh 1995: 38). In his view, those who are of the opinion that Muslim women should cover their faces 'rely on the special rules given, clearly and specifically, to the members of the Prophet's household to safeguard their honourable and special position which they had in society'(Darsh 1995: 38). He adds ironically that 'those who would extend this privilege should, perhaps, add that ordinary women are also Mothers of the Faithful and are not to remarry after being divorced or widowed!' (Darsh 1995: 38). 'Alternatively,' he says, 'they should accept that Niqab was a sign of some sort of class distinction, or a social habit of some of the Arabs during the times when slavery existed' (Darsh 1995: 38).

Darsh is pragmatic in his approach to the issue of whether women should cover their faces or not. He says:

> The wordings of the two Texts – i.e., the Book of Allah and the Sunnah of the Prophet (SAAS) are constructed in such a way as to protect the dignity and honour of the Muslim woman; at the same time, she is given the practical opportunity to go about her daily life – in education, in work, and in participation in public life, in a decent, proper and relaxed manner.
>
> (Darsh 1995: 38)

This picture of Islam's 'practical' message is maintained when Darsh answers specific questions posed by Muslim women at the end of the book. A Muslim woman asks:

> More recently, it has been suggested that those who go out quite often/too much (?!) are more in need of Niqab than the stay at homes for their own good and protection. Is this true?
>
> (Some of us have to go out virtually every day to take children to and from school, do shopping etc. Some husbands work extremely long hours, and if the wife didn't undertake some of the out-of-house chores, then nothing would be done!)

Darsh answers:

> It is agreed that what is required for those women who work, study, go shopping, go out regularly (or indeed rarely) is decent Islamic dress. Those who talk about Niqab for the category of women mentioned in the question are those who are obsessed with the question of sexuality, who are sitting in the security of their homes or organisations, who are not aware of the needs of human society (regardless of geographical location), who are well looked after, who rarely labour even for a piece of bread, who do not go out to work, whose minds are totally locked and blocked. These people are talking about class ideas, not the Islamic view.
>
> (Darsh 1995: 42)

In spite of this harsh attack on his opponents, Darsh does not attack those women who choose to cover their faces. He states that those who choose to do so have freedom of choice (Darsh 1995: 44). It seems obvious that Darsh takes as his starting point a western context, where many women are forced to work outside the home and where such practices as veiling the face and even covering the head are rarely accepted in the labour market. Although he tends to use the same method of selection as many other Islamic scholars (and I would claim the same method that many other scholars, Muslims and non-Muslims, use in all fields of scientific study) he is less categorical than for instance al-Barāzī. On the other hand, he is less tolerant towards others' views than is al-Qaraḍāwī who tends to discuss matters in a broad manner with references to various opinions, ending up by giving his own preference. It is important to draw attention to Darsh's attack on those who see the present time as a time of moral deficiency so that women should cover their faces in order to protect themselves. This is a common argument in the *salafī* movement all over the world. During my many visits to Jordan I heard it in many forms, and the *salafī* Imam at the local mosque I used to visit repeatedly stated that, although there are different points of view regarding covering the face, the temptations of the present time (*fitna*) require that women *should* cover their faces. The same sort of argument has also been used in local mosques in Sweden, where the Imam of one of the *salafī* mosques argues that although women are allowed to go to the mosques, the risk that they might be molested in the street makes it preferable for them to stay at home. The question of authority about who should judge when it is dangerous for a woman to go out without covering her face or whether to go out at all, becomes a question of power with the possible misuse of male superiority.

In my personal discussion with Darsh we went into the matter of *fitna* (temptation). Darsh regarded *fitna* as part of a biological pattern in which the basic instinct is the attraction between the sexes. He explained:

> Fitna means that innate feeling, that innate inclination a human being has towards the other sex. This is inside the person and we cannot get rid of it and it is hard always to control it. *Fitna* means that attraction is inside human beings and it is part of human nature. Thus the Prophet (p.b.u.h.) said these beautiful words – that if you feel attracted to another woman, go to your wife because she has the same thing as this woman has.

As an answer to the question, 'Can we say that men are *fitna* to women in the same way as women are *fitna* to men?' Darsh stated that 'It is the same thing'. *Fitna* for Darsh was thus not something which is particular to women, and it is not identified with women as such. I believe that when Darsh and other scholars with a traditional Islamic education speak of Islamic issues, the idea of the segregated spheres of men and women is incorporated into their world-view. Thus, although ideas and perceptions change in another cultural sphere, the language of their traditional education contains connotations and expressions which for them might convey other meanings than for westerners, Muslims or non-Muslims.

When Darsh stressed that women can cause *fitna* in the male sphere, this did not in his view mean that women are responsible for such *fitna*. His reaction to the question of men as temptation to women made me understand how difficult it is for traditional Islamic educated scholars to change their perspectives as they move into a new cultural sphere. The Islamic idea of women as expressed by Darsh as 'valuable' and 'respectful' does not imply that women are a temptation for men but rather that *fitna* must be understood in a wider perspective in which human beings' instincts sometimes tend to control the intellect instead of the other way round. As suggested earlier, the concept of *fitna* is one of those concepts which are difficult to translate from one cultural sphere to another. Although there is an incommensurability in the translation of the concept, its actual translation into languages other than Arabic has laid the foundations for a fundamental assumption about gender relations in Islam among non-Arabic-speaking Muslims in the Indian subcontinent as noted by Hassan (1990), as well as among non-Muslims.

In contrast to Darsh's detailed elaboration on female covering, Jamal Badawi discusses the matter only briefly and in a superficial manner. This is interesting as female covering is such a 'big issue' in western countries. Badawi does not mention the word 'veil', but discusses segregation in general. He contrasts the two opposing practices: 'unrestricted mixing' and the total seclusion of women (Badawi 1995: 31–2), saying 'Both extremes seem to contradict the normative teachings of Islam and are not consistent with the virtuous yet participative nature of both men and women in society at the time of the Prophet Muhammad (P)' (Badawi 1995: 32).

He states that the injunctions for 'proper modesty' for men and women are based on 'revelatory sources (the Qur'an and authentic Sunnah)' and thus accepted by believers as 'divinely-based guidelines with legitimate aims and divine wisdom'. It is interesting to note that Badawi includes the Sunna of the Prophet in the 'revelatory sources'. This might either be 'a slip of the pen', or it might be that Badawi's understanding of the authentic Sunna is that it is divine or divinely inspired. If the latter is the case, this would imply that Badawi believes the Sunna to be as strong as the Koran in matters of jurisprudence. Such a belief would require a strong hermeneutic tradition in the development of jurisprudence in a new cultural setting such as in the new Muslim presence in the western world. However, this matter is beyond the scope of this study so I will leave it to others to investigate it further.

Badawi goes on to state that Islamic dress and behaviour 'are not male-imposed or socially imposed restrictions' (Badawi 1995: 32). This statement is interesting as it seems to be a reaction to western attacks on Islam as a male-dominated religion which oppresses women. A common argument in western contexts is that women are forced to wear head-scarves or face-veils by male relatives, thus implying that covering is a male invention. By linking the injunctions of Islamic dress not only for women but also for men to the religious sources, Badawi manages to turn female covering into a religious rather than a social matter.

Badawi turns his fire on Muslims in his discussion of decency, covering and seclusion. He believes that the problem of interpretation concerning gender relations and women's place in society is a matter of different cultural influences and circumstances in various parts of the Muslim world (Badawi 1995). In this, he reflects al-Albānī's position when he challenges 'strict scholars' for interpreting the matter of veiling in terms of their own culture rather than in terms of the Islamic texts. Badawi's book gives an indication of how the cultural encounter between Islam and 'the West' results in corresponding views among the various groups. His argument reflects the antagonism between Muslims and non-Muslims when his statements are clearly intended as explicit answers to non-Muslim criticisms of Islam as a religion. But his position also reflects how the 'western cultural base pattern' has influenced his selection from 'the basket', as Badawi is in close contact with non-Muslim society and is thus concerned with presenting Islam as compatible with the modern world.

Islamists in Europe

In my discussions with Arab Islamists living in Europe, I found that most were in favour of women covering the body and the head only. However, some but not all of those from the *salafī* group preferred that women should also cover the face and hands. Among these, some practised veiling the face even in western countries, whereas others indicated that although they favoured such a practice they thought it was difficult in a western context where the face-veil tends to provoke aggression among non-Muslims. Other *salafīs* remarked that they accept al-Albānī's view regarding the exposure of the hands and face, but in spite of this preferred a face-veil because it is 'more proper in Islam'. This view reflects the 'Arab cultural base pattern' built particularly on a Gulfian understanding of the matter of female veiling.

The *ikhwān* view on veiling approves of exposing the face. In most countries where the Muslim Brotherhood is active, its female members cover the body and the head only. When I visited Egypt in 1997, however, I found that many female members covered their faces. Some of these were professional women, but they explained that they did not find any difficulties in working with a face-veil. When I asked why they preferred wearing a face-veil when the classics within the movement such as Ḥasan al-Bannā' and Sayyid Quṭb never spoke in favour of veiling the face, they claimed that the face-veil functions as protection for women in a society where even women can be harassed on the street because of their political and religious convictions. One woman explained:

> We are working in a democratic manner. We never talk of violence. Still, the authorities suspect us and they do not leave us in peace. This

> is why I chose to wear the face-veil, in order to protect myself in this turbulent society [translation mine].

I asked Khadīja from the Muslim Brotherhood in Europe about Islamic female dress and why she adopted it. In her view, it is sufficient to cover the head and the body. 'When I was in my home country one of the great female leaders told me that my face is *daʿwa*', she said. The same idea was expressed by many other Islamists, men and women, who explained that when a woman wears a face-veil it is difficult for her to make contact with the rest of society. Many Islamists regard *daʿwa* as a major obligation in Islam (Roald 1994). Thus the face-veil is seen as an obstacle to this obligation. This might explain why Islamic scholars living in Europe or America, such as Darsh and Jamal Badawi, are such fierce opponents of the practice of veiling the face.

As I mentioned above, social scientists tend to regard Islamic veiling in its various forms in socio-political terms. Khadīja promotes a different view. 'I wear the head-scarf (*ḥijāb*) first and foremost because it is part of the worship of God', she said. I asked her what reasons there are for wearing specific Islamic dress, and she explained that for her the main and only reason is that the injunction for Islamic female dress is stated in the Koran. 'Then', she said, 'I can deduce some reasons with an intellectual effort.' She continued:

> Islamic female dress is for me a sign of distinction (*tamiīz*). A woman with the head-scarf (*ḥijāb*) represents respectfulness and she is a sign of a healthy and decent society where sexuality is restricted to take place inside a marriage, where everybody fulfils their obligations and obtains their rights. A woman with the head-scarf is a woman who is respected and is treated as a human being not a sexual object [translation mine].

Similarly to Khadīja, Sumāya, who comes from North Africa and has lived in Sweden for more than seven years, pointed to personal conviction as the driving force behind the wearing of Islamic dress. She asserted:

> Our religion, Islam, is both a belief and a way of life. The belief (*imān*) gives meaning to life and it is the first and the foremost part for a Muslim. Umar, the second Caliph, said: 'The belief was the first we built in our souls, thereafter did we learn the Koran.' If we believe in God, we have to believe in everything in the book of God, the Koran. In the Koran, the Islamic female dress is stated. The hadiths from the Prophet confirm this dress and clarify which parts of her body a woman should cover. When a woman has reached puberty she should cover the whole of her body except her hands and her face [translation mine].

Sumāya reinforced the notion that uncovered women are seen as sexual objects:

> For me, the head-scarf (*ḥijāb*) is a part of myself, it indicates who I am and which identity I have. It is also a boundary mark for all foreign men [*ajnabī* i.e. men not belonging to the family] that my body is not for sale. In my head-scarf I have freedom. I am not ruled by the needs of men. Tell me, who is more often than not behind fashion? Is it not the men? When they are tired of one fashion-doll, there are unfortunately so many other fashion-dolls who are prepared to fulfil their desires . . . the head-scarf has only advantages. Although we do not know at the present time all the advantages of it, I am convinced that covering (*ḥijāb*) is for the best for women [translation mine].

Sumāya further believes that the increase of rape in what she calls 'the modern society' is provoked by women's way of dressing which tends to cover as little as possible of their bodies. This is not an uncommon idea among Islamists and other Muslims, since they regard the public exposure of the female body as a form of provocation of the male sexual instinct. Many Islamists have expressed the belief to me that from a biological point of view men's sexuality is different from women's. Some of them referred to the book *Brain Sex* as offering scientific evidence for this point of view (Moir and Jessel 1989). One male Islamist also believed that as rape and the sexual abuse of women are often committed by men under the influence of either drugs or alcohol, men in such a condition tend to have less control of themselves, especially if they are sexually provoked by lightly dressed women. He further expressed the view that not all men are able to live out their sexuality in satisfying relations with women and that might lead men into committing such crimes. One female Islamist from North Africa believes that non-Muslims and particularly feminists tend to speak in idealistic terms. 'They claim', she says,

> that women can dress as they want and that women are masters of their own bodies. Look at the reality, however, how many women are not raped? How many women are not sexually molested at work or on the street? This is the reality! Idealistic ideals are marvellous, but the reality is not always as we want it to be.

The people referred to above are all ideologically based in the *ikhwān* tradition and their arguments coincide to a great extent. Moreover, in my discussion with Islamists from both the Liberation Party and those with no explicit group identification I encountered many of the same arguments.

Maryam, who has lived in Scandinavia for more than ten years and has no group affiliation, responded immediately to my question as to why she wears a head-scarf: 'Because I believe in it as it is stated in the Koran.' Upon further questioning she reflected:

> I think it is pretty for a woman to wear the head-scarf (*ḥijāb*). But it also gives her a tough (*töff*) look. Sometimes at my work I can reflect that I am the only one with *ḥijāb* and it gives me the feeling that the head-scarf is something majestic and dignified. It gives a woman dignity (*waqqār*) and it reflects that which is inside her. I see the head-scarf as a protection for women, giving them space. At the same time, a woman with a head-scarf conveys the image of the Muslim woman as an entity [translation mine].

Khālid belongs to the *post-ikhwān* trend. In response to my question about why women should cover, he answered,

> I firstly want to stress that women are not the only ones who should cover and dress decently. In sharia, there are rules and regulations on how men and women should dress. As for female covering (*ḥijāb*), I look upon it from various angles. On the first hand there is the aspect of belief. Without belief (*imān*) human beings should maybe not cover themselves, as it is the belief which creates the feeling of modesty (*ḥayā'*), in men and women alike.
>
> When I have said that, we can turn to other aspects of covering. I want to talk about covering from four different perspectives, on the level of ideas, on the psychological level, on the social level and from the perspective of economy. Firstly, on the level of ideas I believe that covering makes human beings look upon a woman not in the first hand as the female sex (*jins*) but as a human being. Whether a woman is beautiful or ugly does not matter as long as she covers her hair (*tughaṭī sha'rahā*). What matters is her intellect, her personality or her character.

He continues:

> Secondly, from the psychological perspective of women's covering and men's decency in dress, Islam teaches human beings to have a system of sexual life. In official life and also during daily life human beings are preoccupied with work, and they should not be distracted by the arousal of sexual desire. The sexual instinct is like the instinct of hunger, one should eat, but not all the time; and one should have sexual relations, but not all the time. If there is no order in one's sexual life and sex becomes part of daily life, as is one of the consequences of lightly dressed women and men in society, the result might be that human beings get bored with sexual relations with one and the same partner. There is then a danger of sexual perversion, such

> as paedophilia or sexual obsession. What might come out of this is sexual chaos (*fawḍā jinsīya*).
>
> Thirdly, on the social level, decent dressing leads to a system of social relations where the idea of sex is eliminated between members of society. The elimination of temptation (*ighrā*), such as beautiful secretaries etc., leads to a sound society with stable family relations.
>
> Fourthly, on the economic level, the female covering hinders excess in changes of fashion. As a woman puts on a big coat every time she goes out there is not such a great need for always buying new clothes according to changes of fashion. Is it not that women usually buy clothes to go out in, not for dressing up at home? [translation mine].

Khālid is a natural scientist working as a Muslim preacher (*dāʿi*) in Scandinavia, and he offers an argument building on scientific categories. Although he stresses belief as the most important, his argument is marked by the idea of a universe of order and system. His argument is based on ideas common in the western debate, such as the idea of women as human beings instead of sex objects, and the idea of sexual deviation as a result of the over-emphasis on sexuality in daily life. These are common arguments in the Islamist debate on veiling, and the same way of arguing is often found in general Islamist debate. The idea of Islam as 'the natural religion' (Hedin 1988), the religion which is in accordance with human nature, is emphasised in the contemporary debate. The concept of Islam as the natural religion seems to be a result of the influence of the 'western cultural base pattern'. The 'rationalistic' trend within Islam in modern times became prominent in the *salafīya* trend of the nineteenth century with its explicit aim of reforming Islam to make it compatible with the modern world. Khālid's position indicates a 'rationalistic' trend. His argument is built on western scientific premises with an emphasis on psychological and social factors. It also points to the difference between drive, motivation or apologetics in the discussion of veiling, as after giving the religious motivation as the first rationale he turns to the level of apologetics by identifying social, psychological and economic reasons for veiling.

It is important to note how all informants and interviewees use the term *ḥijāb* for head-scarf and this points out the difficulties in terminology as *ḥijāb* in the Koran has another meaning.

Reflections

Three of the law schools, the Shāfiʿī, the Mālikī and the Ḥanbalī, are in favour of covering the face and the hands. In the Ḥanafī school, however, covering the face is optional. In the classical debate there were also differences of opinion with regard to female veiling. In the contemporary debate the *salafī* trend tends to favour the face-veil whereas other Islamist movements tend to see the covering of the body and the hair as sufficient according to Islamic standards. What is worth drawing attention to in the contemporary Islamist debate is that in the difference of scholarly opinion in this matter, there is a tendency for scholars to refer to authorities which favour their own point of view, leaving out of the discussion those who oppose their particular position. The only scholar who emphasises the differences of opinion in this matter is al-Qaraḍāwī, who cites a variety of opinions but expresses his preference for certain points of view. However, even al-Qaraḍāwī tends not to stress his opponents' position, thus making it more difficult for the reader to judge which evidence is the strongest. The tendency to refer to views which one agrees with is not particular to the Islamist debate, as this is also a factor within scientific debate in western countries. As no scientific field is free of value and most arguments are value-laden, the researcher, whether on a verbalised or a non-verbalised level, selects those views he or she finds acceptable in order to promote certain arguments. This might be described in terms of the 'normative field' in which each researcher has a field of tension within certain base patterns which influence the individual's outlook on various issues.

With regard to Islamic female covering, the argument seems to be rather similar among the various groups, with the *salafī* movement being the only group which differs. Although many *salafīs* accept al-Albānī's view that proper Islamic dress according to the sources is the covering of the body and the hair only, the argument that at certain times the state of society demands that women cover their faces is prominent. Such an argument might be difficult to react against as most societies are haunted by violence and the sexual abuse of women in various forms. The *salafī* trend's stand on this particular matter shows the obvious influence of the 'Arab cultural base pattern' as many *salafī* scholars are linked to Saudi Arabia, either as citizens or as students at the various Islamic universities in the country. Prominent examples of this trend are Jārullāh, Hilālī and Khān.

Scholars such as Muḥammad al-Ghazzālī, Abū Shaqqa and al-Qaraḍāwī are to a great extent influenced by the 'western cultural base pattern' although they have not lived outside the Arab world. Their extensive travels to various parts of the Muslim world might have created an awareness of the necessity for change. They can be regarded within the wider framework of globalisation, where ideas and notions travel from one cultural sphere to another. The approach of these scholars might further be seen in the framework of antagonistic feelings against Islam on the issue of women. The reinterpretation or reselection of Islamic social injunctions from 'the basket' is part of a process whereby Islam is conformed to the modern world.

Like these three scholars, Islamist scholars living in western countries such as Badawi and Darsh have taken a stand against the covering of the face and hands. As indicated in their books, they even reject the face-veil, seeing it as a cultural and time-specific phenomenon. Darsh is the one whose analysis is the most thorough. He explains that the successive revelation of the various verses pertaining to veiling indicates that the Islamic standard is the covering of the body and the hair only. It is apparent that the 'western cultural base pattern' has influenced Islamic scholars living in Europe, primarily because if the head-cover alone has created hostility towards Islam in European society, how much more is this the case with the face-veil?

As for ideas on why women should cover in one way or another, these seem to coincide between the various groups and scholars. In the first place, the significance of belief is stated as a primary reason. Thereafter, the explanations include various topics such as that a woman should be accepted for her character and behaviour rather than for her outer appearance, that women need protection from being molested and the importance of a stable social family system. These arguments might be controversial in a western context where rape, for instance, is explained not as a result of lightly dressed women but as a result of men's need to exercise power due to their own experiences of abuse. The forms of explanation for such serious crimes as rape and violence against women thus seem to vary from one cultural sphere to another depending on which aspect of human life one chooses to stress in the process of interpretation. Social phenomena can be explained at different levels: drive, motivation and apologetics. An individual's drive might be difficult to evaluate, while the motivation in this particular issue might be seen as the belief that veiling is an Islamic obligation. On the apologetic level, various arguments are put forward such as those mentioned above – that veiling ensures the stability of the family in society, that it allows a Muslim woman to be accepted for her behaviour and intellect instead of her appearance, etc. The responses offered by the interviewees depend to a great extent on the affiliation of the researcher. A Muslim researcher might be given the motivational answer that veiling is an Islamic injunction, whereas a non-Muslim researcher might be offered apologetic answers since the interviewee would attempt to convince the researcher from a 'rational' point of view.

Terminology is a stumbling block in the discussion of veiling in both Muslim and non-Muslim contexts. As long as there is no established terminology for the various forms of veiling, the debate will continue to be confused. Since the term *ḥijāb*, which originally meant something different from the wearing of a head-scarf or a face-veil, continues to be the main term used in the debate as shown in the interviews with Islamists in Europe, and given that there is disagreement over the 'real' meaning of the three main terms – *ḥijāb*, *jilbāb* and *khimār* – the confusion between Muslims of various persuasions will probably persist.

13 Conclusion

Since Islam has entered the European cultural scene, the encounter between Islam and 'the West' seems to have affected both Muslims and non-Muslims. On the one hand, the increasing number of Muslims becoming European citizens and the growing conversion of Europeans to Islam tend to be regarded in terms of 'the Islamic threat'. Hostile reactions by non-Muslims to the growing Islamic presence in Europe foster antagonistic relations between Muslims and non-Muslims. On the other hand, Muslims are affected by European ways of living and thought patterns. As I have indicated above, the cultural encounter between Islam and 'the West' has caused a change in attitudes which might produce changes in actual Islamic legislation. As the source material is vast, not all aspects can possibly be represented at all times and the selection process is dependent on actual perceptions and attitudes. Moreover, Islamic legal discourse, in which underlying attitudes are decisive for the solutions proposed by Islamic scholars, also offers alternative interpretations of social issues in the Islamic sources.

In the present study I have applied a model of two oppositional cultural patterns: the 'Arab cultural base pattern' and the 'western cultural base pattern'. I broadly defined these two cultural patterns as the *patriarchal* versus the *equality* pattern respectively. Within these cultural ideals there are local variations which I have taken into account when necessary. The 'normative field' in which the process of interpretation of social issues in the Islamic sources takes place lies between these two poles.

The European Islamists' responses to various Islamic ideas show that although the trend towards change greatly depends on the length of time spent in a European country, this factor is not the only significant influence on the process of change. Since some respondents who had been in Europe for more than twenty years came up with responses which I had not expected, I came to understand that the degree of contact with the majority society is just as important for change. Those who remain within the Muslim community and have little contact with non-Muslims tend to reproduce cultural interpretations from their native lands. The Swedish suburbs in which most of the inhabitants are Muslims are good examples of how traditional attitudes towards women and family life are reproduced in a 'ghettoised' world within a new cultural context. Many Islamists with primary or secondary contact with the majority society, on the other hand, show attitudes more compatible with majority society. With their integration into European society, their change of attitude seems to be more rapid than with Muslims working exclusively within Muslim communities.

The third factor which I discovered to be an important influence on the process of change after length of stay and degree of contact, was that of group affiliation. I believe that this might be the most significant factor for well-educated Arab Islamists in Europe. In this respect I have applied Barth's concept of 'social organisation', which I defined in terms of belonging to a movement. In Barth's view 'social organisation' might be an obstruction to change, as confirmed by my observation that men and women belonging to various movements such as the Islamic Liberation Party, the Muslim Brotherhood and the *salafī* trend tended to answer in terms of these movements' ideologies. Independent Islamists, particularly those of the *post-ikhwān* trend, were more receptive of alternative views than other Islamists. The issue of female leadership is a good indicator of this, since most independent Islamists, as opposed to Islamists belonging to the various Islamic trends, answered in the affirmative on the question of whether a woman could be the leader of Muslims. The response to this question may have varied according to whether the respondent considered a woman leader to be the head of a nation-state or an Islamic empire.

As I observed in the interviews with Islamists in Europe, customs (*ʿurf*) on a non-verbalised level seem to have played a part in the creation of perceptions and attitudes. As *ʿurf* is an acceptable legal concept in the broader Islamic law (since it is a legal means both in the Mālikī and the Ḥanafī law schools), I believe that European *ʿurf* which are compatible with Islamic principles might, in the creation of a 'minority *fiqh*' in European society, be accorded a strong position on a conscious level as well. The cultural background or what the Danish anthropologist, Kirsten Hastrup, has called *biography*, might also be regarded as an important factor in the interpretation of the sources. As scholars look into the Islamic sources or into texts of Islamic law, their personal backgrounds and characteristics tend to be decisive in the selection and interpretation of texts.

Attitudes towards women tend to change in the cultural encounter between Islam and 'the West'. As in Christianity, where interpretations of biblical verses pertaining to women have been undergoing a process of change recently, in Islam a similar movement seems to be in progress. By relating Koranic passages and hadiths to their contexts, many traditional attitudes towards women might change. Another aspect of the contemporary debate is to investigate certain concepts in order to see how these have been understood. An example is the concept of *fitna* (temptation or trial). In traditional Islamic understanding, women have been regarded as temptresses. According to my findings it seems that Arab Islamists in general do not regard women as active agents of temptation, and this is in contrast to the more traditional understanding of *fitna*. One informant pointed to the difference between the active participle 'tempting' and the passive participle of 'being a temptation'; according to her this difference could actually indicate passivity on the part of women rather than signifying that women play an active role in the temptation. Thus the Islamic warning of resisting temptation pertains to men rather than being a warning to women not to be temptresses. The example of *fitna* illustrates a problem regarding the translation of Arabic terms into other languages. As terms and concepts are often value-laden, these values tend to change in the process of translation from one language to another. An example of this is the concept of 'a wife's obedience to the husband' which in Arabic conveys different values to its equivalent expression in particular European languages, where 'obedience' is linked to hierarchical systems rejected by many Europeans.

Islamists and Muslims in general have discussed the concept of *qiwāma*, which refers to the belief either that men are in charge of women or that men are responsible for women. It seems obvious that in the cultural encounter, the understanding of the concept *qiwāma* tends to be that of 'having responsibility for' rather than 'being in charge of'. This is a consequence of Islamic legal discourse. With the influence of the 'western cultural base pattern' with its attitudes towards women in general and gender relations in particular, Arab-speaking Islamists are changing their understanding of the relationship between men and women. In the case of the Sudanese Islamist Ḥasan at-Turābī, the 'African cultural base pattern' also contributes to his conceptualisation of male and female roles.

The new selection from the Islamic source material might turn many traditional perceptions of women upside-down. In the 1940s, as-Sayyid Sābiq maintained a traditional view of the female role in society as that of a domestic worker, whereas in the 1970s at-Turābī demonstrated that this traditional view of women was not necessarily the only true interpretation. By pointing to the variety of the source material, at-Turābī and other Islamists such as Muḥammad al-Ghazzālī and Yūsuf al-Qaraḍāwī have paved the way for alternative interpretations of Islamic social matters. This leads to the conclusion that there are no specific, limited roles for women in society, but rather there is flexibility such that various roles are open to a woman according to what is appropriate for her life cycle and what the needs of particular societies are in particular times. The various cultural base patterns together with the scholar's personal background and characteristics seem to play a role in the selection from the sources and the texts of Islamic law ('the basket') and subsequent interpretation of them. The basket metaphor is not a metaphor pertaining specifically to the Islamic sphere, since in Hjärpe's explanation 'the basket' pertains to all socio-political or religious spheres of ideas. The selection from 'the basket' is often a non-deliberate process, whereby in the act of interpretation one selects only those particular texts which are compatible with the present situation, or one interprets them according to one's own personal background and characteristics. This selection from 'the basket' might also be a deliberate process, so that one selects and interprets texts with an awareness of what one is doing. This is particularly true for the Muslim feminists such as Fatima Mernissi, as has been indicated in the discussion on Islamic veiling.

The matter of polygyny is another issue about which various views have been promoted. Islamists tend to disagree as to whether Islamic law prefers polygynous or monogamous marriages. Whereas *salafīs* tend to see polygyny as the norm for marriage in Islam, other Islamists take monogamy to be the norm with polygyny as an exception which is permissible under certain circumstances. Jamal Badawi who lives in Canada and Sheikh Darsh who lived in Britain, are both examples of how the 'western cultural base pattern' influences the understanding of Islam. They both regard polygyny as the exception and monogamy as the norm, thus following in the steps of Muḥammad ʿAbduh who made a similar statement in his commentary on the Koran at the turn of the nineteenth century. The latter stand reflects the actual situation in the Arab world in general, with the Muslim Gulf as a possible exception.

The male perspective is prominent in traditional interpretations of social issues in the sources. The issue of divorce indicates how, although according to the sources it is possible for women to ask for a divorce, they have to a great extent been denied this right, not only in Islamic law but also in contemporary sharia courts in Muslim countries. In matters of divorce the concept of 'turning back to the Koran and the Sunna' has given Muslim women rights which have been denied them in the development of Islamic law. By 'reproducing the past in the present', hadiths which are in favour of the female quest for divorce have come to the forefront as such a quest corresponds to contemporary attitudes, particularly in western countries. It is, however, important to draw attention to the findings of the Swedish anthropologist, Eva Evers Rosander, that women in that part of Morocco where she conducted her fieldwork were more concerned with how to keep their husbands within the bond of marriage than trying to find ways of getting rid of them. This points to a variation in perspective, whereby women within a 'western cultural base pattern' stress the 'right' to divorce, whereas women within an 'Arab cultural base pattern' stress the 'right' to remain married.

The influence of the various 'cultural base patterns' on Islamic rules and regulations is prominent in the example of Sheikh Darsh. In the 1980s he approached the question of child custody in divorce cases from a traditional Islamic perspective. Although he pointed out the importance of 'the interests (*maṣlaḥa*) of the child', he stressed that if a woman remarries, she cannot possibly have custody of her children. In the 1990s, however, he sees 'the interests of the children' as the most important principle, arguing that even if a woman remarries, she can still have custody of the children if it is to their benefit. This change in attitude must be understood in terms of Sheikh Darsh's exposure to the attitudes of western society and his continuous interaction with Muslims and their specific problems in a new cultural context. The 'western cultural base pattern' seems to have been prominent in Sheikh Darsh's selection of sources and the texts of Islamic law.

Female circumcision is the most obvious example of cultural bias in the interpretation of Islamic texts. As has been shown above, there is no indication in the Koran or in hadiths that women *should* be circumcised. There is a slight possibility that some women were circumcised at the time of the Prophet, but there is no proof that the Prophet explicitly ordered this practice to be maintained; rather, his utterances as found in hadiths suggest that he actually sought an end to the practice rather than encouraged it. In spite of this, female circumcision or rather female genital cutting has been an issue of the utmost importance in those areas where this practice was common, even in pre-Islamic times. As a consequence of the prevailing practice and acceptance of female circumcision, Islamic scholars coming from these particular areas have interpreted the Islamic sources in favour of the maintenance even of infibulation, the most drastic and cruel form of female genital mutilation, whereas scholars in areas where this practice has been unknown tend to disregard the practice. This becomes clear when one realises that, although the Shāfiʿī law school renders female circumcision obligatory, in many areas where this law school has gained influence there is no practice of female circumcision. The issue of female circumcision thus proves to be a prominent example of how cultural base patterns influence the rules and regulations within certain areas, as well as the actual practice. The selection from the 'basket', which consists of Islamic rituals, narratives, historiography, categorisations, terminology and observances, depends on the one hand on cultural expressions in the various Muslim regions and, on the other, on the various scholars' personal backgrounds and characteristics. The example of female circumcision is also prominent when it comes to 'reproducing the past in the present' where contemporary Islamists tend to come to other conclusions than scholars of the formative period of Islam. Thus ancient issues are given new answers.

Western researchers, as well as Muslim feminists and Islamists, have been active in the debate about veiling. Muslim feminists and western researchers see the Islamic veil in terms of oppression and male domination, but Islamist men and women view the veil as a symbol of dignity, honour and distinction. These different points of view are in opposition to each other, and as the debate takes place on various levels there is no contact between the different arguments. Muslim feminists see the veil as a pre-Islamic phenomenon and reject it entirely. This is an example of a deliberate selection from 'the basket'. Mernissi's discussion of the veil indicates that she selects Koranic paragraphs with a predisposition towards a certain point of view. Thus she disregards those Koranic passages which more obviously advocate a form of veiling. While Muslim feminists discuss whether Muslim women should use a head covering at all, the Islamist discussion deals with which parts of the body should be covered. Many *salafī* scholars, particularly from the Gulf states, tend to prefer the covering of the whole female body, although the *salafī* scholar, al-Albānī who lives in Jordan, has concluded that it is sufficient to cover the hair and that the covering of the face is not obligatory. This distinction between the various *salafī* scholars indicates the importance of the local cultural base patterns, since the preference for face-veiling is consistent with the long-term practice of Gulf women who cover their faces, while the preference against is consistent with the Jordanian custom of not wearing a face-veil. The difference in view between the *salafī* scholars and scholars belonging to the Muslim Brotherhood, the Islamic Liberation Party, or the *post-ikhwān* trend indicates further the importance of the scholars' personal background and characteristics in the selection of texts and the interpretation of these texts.

As the view-points expressed in the present study show, various positions are represented in the contemporary debate. I could sense in my interviews that attitudes from the 'western cultural base pattern', with its emphasis on equality between the sexes, are gaining ground in the debate. In the cultural encounter between Islam and 'the West', non-Muslims' main accusations against Muslims are within the field of women's issues, so it is likely that attitudes will be modified as a reaction to these accusations. Furthermore, with the increase in educated second- and third-generation Muslims who have absorbed western attitudes through educational institutions, western perspectives will probably have a greater impact on the expression of Islam in Europe.

Change is an inevitable feature within all systems of life, which always promotes adaptation, survival and growth. Thus religion nurtured in one cultural context and transplanted into another is bound to be subject to different forms of expression in the new environment. There is the prospect of change in attitudes towards women held by Muslims, while for non-Muslims the realisation that such changes are occurring might improve their perceptions of Islam and increase their acceptance of Islam within European society. For Muslims, these changes may strengthen women's roles within Muslim society, in Muslim communities and in the majority societies in western countries.

Future prospects

The trend I see developing from my empirical study is that Islamic attitudes towards women are about to change in European society. These changes can be understood both in the context of the challenges posed by the majority society and in terms of the integration of second-, third- and fourth-generation Muslims into European society. While the first generation of Muslim immigrants often went through the educational system in their countries of origin, following generations were educated in European countries. The stress laid on memorisation and rote-learning in many Muslim countries contrasts with western educational methods which are based upon problem-solving and open enquiry. The difference in educational approach makes the 'new' Muslims ask different questions which require different answers than those of previous generations.

Furthermore, with globalisation, particularly in terms of the media, I believe that Islamic attitudes towards women will change on an international level as well. The debate about Islamic issues in general and women's issues in particular is increasingly conducted through television programmes on Arabic satellite channels with the participation of Arabic-speaking Islamists living in Europe or in the United States. Islamic discussions on the Internet with participants from all over the world further indicate a change of perspective. The issue at stake is whether the development towards a pattern of equality between the sexes will cause a rift between European and Arab approaches to Islam. My personal opinion is that although there will not be a rapprochement between the various perspectives, there might be an approximation. Given the differences between cultural patterns which are decisive in the process of interpreting and understanding Islamic sources, a total fusion between the two would hardly be possible. My experience of Islam in the Arab world is that although the development toward a pattern of equality takes longer than it does in Europe and the United States, there is still a movement in the same direction. An example of this is the way in which women in the Gulf states have been denied the right of official political participation in general and women's suffrage in particular, yet suddenly at the end of the 1990s, in Qatar women were allowed to vote as well as to be elected in the political process. Moreover, Sheikha Fāṭima, the First Lady in the United Arab Emirates, expressed her support in the *Khaleej Times*, not only for women's work outside the home but also for women's participation in political life (*Khaleej Times*, 8 March 1999). This new approach in a region of the Arab world which has been one of the most traditional in matters concerning women's role in society, opens up a way for new understanding and new perspectives in the reformulation of the Islamic message in the modern world.

There are many manifestations of Islam in various western countries, since Muslim communities in Europe and the United States consist of Muslims from different cultural backgrounds. Each country is dominated by a certain majority Muslim group which influences the Muslim community as a whole. However, I believe that many of the same tendencies which I observed among Arab-speaking Muslims in Europe are also true of non-Arabic-speaking communities. Changes will probably occur at the level of the group, as well as on a personal level, according to the length of stay in Europe, the degree of contact with major societies, educational standards, class affiliation and personal disposition. A future research project might be to investigate cross-cultural relations within Muslim communities in European countries.

The greatest challenge Muslims face in a changing world is, in my view, to find ways of dealing with the vast hadith literature. How should hadiths be understood? Which hadiths should be applied as a foundation for Islamic legislation and which should be regarded only as offering general guidance or direction in social life? Is the social structure which implicitly informs the scenario of the hadiths, as in the hadith where Fāṭima and ʿAli's ask the Prophet for a servant, meant to be a divine pattern valid for all times and places, or should Muslims exclusively follow the explicit injunctions of the Prophet and his Companions? Furthermore, to what degree should the Companions' acts and practices be followed by contemporary Muslims? Islam in modern times is in need of profound discussion about these issues, in order to address the complicated situations faced by Muslims living in a changing world.

The contact of Muslims with the western world has been a source of awakening and renewal – not necessarily of westernisation. The vigorous Islamic legal discourse which is a consequence of social change on various levels indicates that Muslims are well prepared to meet the challenges of the modern world. Muslims are entering a new age that is dawning first in 'new lands', but that might spread to 'old lands' as well. The new age of Muslims, I predict, promises a new vision with regard to many aspects of its creed – especially with respect to women.

Notes

Preface

1 See for instance Otterbeck 1997.
2 For further reading, see Fiorenzia 1983; Hampson 1990; King 1995.
3 Many converts prefer to call themselves 'reverts' to Islam. I choose the term 'convert', however, to keep to the universal terminology of changing from one religion or world-view to another. See for instance Rambo 1993.
4 'Muslim' is used to denote anyone who confessionally belongs to Islam. Thus, for instance, a 'Muslim feminist' is a 'cultural' Muslim, who is concerned with feminist issues. I would place Fatima Mernissi, Leila Ahmad and Nawal El Saadawi in this category. 'Islamic' indicates any phenomena which have to do with Islam such as 'Islamic education', 'Islamic teachings' or 'Islamic feminism'. I would define Amina Wadud-Muhsin and Riffat Hassan as Islamic feminists. It is important to be aware that the distinction between 'Muslim feminist' and 'Islamic feminist' is not obvious, since Fatima Mernissi, in her book *Women and Islam* (1987), is concerned with Islamic issues and might thus be classified as 'Islamic feminist'. However, taking into account her other publications I believe she fits better into the category of being a 'Muslim feminist'.
5 In this context I use the concept of culture in a broader sense as in Gordon's definition of culture as 'the social heritage of man – the ways of acting and the ways of doing things which are passed down from one generation to the next, not through genetic inheritance but by formal and informal methods of teaching and demonstrating' (Gordon 1964: 32).
6 During the fieldwork I have met individuals with whom I have been in frequent contact. I name these individuals 'informants'. I have also conducted interviews with some people only once or twice, and I call these individuals 'interviewees'.

1 Research on Muslims

1 Ritzén is a frequent lecturer on multi-culturalism in Sweden.
2 It is interesting that in Scandinavia as in many other countries, in the aftermath of 'the Rushdie affair', *fatwa*, which means 'a formal legal opinion by an Islamic scholar', has become synonymous with 'death sentence'.
3 Said has been criticised, for instance for having disregarded the variety in oriental traditions. Bryan Turner points out how Said has lumped many diverse traditions into one single Orientalist tradition (Turner 1994: 5).
4 As Dumont's field of study is India and the hierarchical caste system, his criticism is mainly directed towards social scientists from western countries who

tend to regard Indian social structures in terms of the social structures of their own societies.

5 With regard to undergraduate studies, I have observed that at universities in Scandinavia there are students who write their graduate theses about Muslim immigrant women with little acknowledgement of the variety within this group.

6 Discussions during the seminars on Islamology at Lund University.

7 This might be compared with the Christian tradition of 'bridal mysticism'.

8 This argument might have its parallel in what Erving Goffman calls 'stigma' (Goffman 1963). He explores various ways in which 'stigmatised' persons behave towards 'mainstream' society. See also Berger and Luckman's work on the 'construction of social reality' (Berger and Luckman 1967).

9 Differences between Shīʿī and Sunnī Muslims are to a great extent also ethnic, as ethnic and intra-Islamic differences are often two sides of the same coin.

10 Muslims within certain trends in Islam, such as the *salafī* trend in particular, have stricter definitions of who qualifies as Muslim.

11 The *etic* level is the level of the researcher, whereas the *emic* level pertains to the level of the research objects.

12 This hadith is also found in Muslim, Book of Faith, no. 116; 117 (with a slightly different text).

13 It is important to be aware that the exclusion or inclusion of people is due to the practical consequences of defining those who were Muslims and those who were not in ancient times.

14 It is important to note that this particular hadith is understood in a different way by Muslims belonging to a Sufi tradition. See N. Keller 1991: 815; 924–7.

15 Discussions with Sufi Muslims in Jordan.

16 As for the concepts of *imān* (faith) and *kufr* (non-faith), Mawdūdī has drawn attention to the fact that the term *kufr* is not related to the concept of *atheism* meaning rejection of the existence of God. *Kufr* or non-faith in an Islamic sense of the word refers in his view rather to the rejection of *worshipping* God *with* the 'knowledge of the existence of God'. Cf. al-Mawdūdī 1965.

17 It is important to bear in mind that this movement is not the same as the *salafiya* reform movement of Jamāl ad-Din al-Afghānī and Muḥammad ʿAbduh in the nineteenth century (see Chapter 2).

18 For further explanation, see N. Keller 1991: 753.

19 I have observed such discussions particularly within the *salafī* trend.

2 Arab Muslims in Europe

1 There are also active Muslims who regard themselves as independent of any organisation, but usually they cooperate with one or more organisations or trends.

2 As for the hadith literature, there is an intra-Islamic debate on its relevance. However, I regard the discussion on 'fundamentalism' in the first case to be a debate on the primary sources, such as the Bible or the Koran.

3 Johan Fornäs has discussed the three terms 'modernization', 'modernity' and 'modernism'. He claims that 'modernization is the process, modernity the state, and modernisms are movements of response to that state' (Fornäs 1995: 39). He further regards the 'processes of modernization' as 'a combination of several conjunctional processes (commodification, industrialization, secularization, etc.)' (Fornäs 1995: 39). I believe that in the Islamist view, modernisation is associated particularly with commodification, industrialisation and technologification.

4 The globalisation process operates on various levels. As many people, particularly in the non-industrial world, regard the overarching globalisation process

to be a process of 'westernisation', it is important to note that on a lower level various ideologies undergo processes of globalisation. This is particularly true with regard to ideas associated with Arab Islamism. Through Arabic satellite television channels Islamic ideas are disseminated around the world, from western countries to Arab countries and vice versa. Thus, for instance, the thoughts of the well-known Arab Islamist, Yusūf al-Qaradāwī, are broadcast to a worldwide audience in his weekly television programme, *ash-sharīʿa wa l-ḥayā* (The Islamic Law and Life), transmitted by the Qatarian satellite television station al-Jazeera (The [Arab] Peninsula).

5 The sociologist Muhammad Anwar has recorded that there are about 10,000 Muslim doctors working in the British National Health Service, between 15,000 and 17,000 Muslims working as teachers, and about 20,000 Muslims working as engineers and scientists. His source is a document entitled *Some Aspects of Islam in Britain* published by COI, London, in 1981 (Anwar 1987: 111). It is important to be aware that the majority of British Muslims are South Asian. Moreover, Anwar points at *Muslim* intellectuals who work in Britain. Although he does not give any numbers of Islamists, I believe the numbers referred to are an indicator that within this group of employed Muslim professionals there are many Islamists.

6 Accusing Muslims of being non-Muslims is regarded by many Muslims as being contrary to the etiquette (*adab*) of Islam with reference to the hadith:

> The Prophet said: Any person who called his brother: O unbeliever! [has in fact done an act by which this unbelief] would return to one of them. If it were so, as he asserts [then the unbelief of man was confirmed but if it was not true], then it returned to him [to the man who labelled it on his brother Muslim].
>
> al-Bukhārī, Book of Manners, no. 5639; Muslim, Book of Belief, no. 92; Musnad Aḥmad, *musnad al-mukthirīn*, no. 4458)

7 An example is the *ḥabashī* movement's view of Sayyid Quṭb's commentary of the Koran, *fī ẓilāl al-qurʾān* (In the Shade of the Koran) where Quṭb explains the attributes of God as abstractions of human attributes. The *ḥabashī* movement regards this explanation as anthropomorphism and thus *kufr* (non-faith) as God is transcendentally above any of His creatures.

8 Personal communication with Amina Lombard, February 1999.

9 With regard to the *tablīgh* movement's activities in Europe, see Dasseto 1988: 159–73.

10 Khān writes in his book, *Tabligh Movement*:

> It greatly stressed him [Mawlāna Ilyās] to learn that only the less educated have surrendered themselves to his fold. On his death-bed, he writes with great pain: 'Would that the religious scholars were to take up the cause before I passed away.'
>
> (Khān 1986: 14)

11 This is an obvious Indo-Pakistani influence. In India and Pakistan few mosques are open for women. Followers of the *tablīgh* movement state that according to hadith women are encouraged to pray in their homes, not in the mosques.

12 Morocco is a country with a high illiteracy rate. From a 1982 statistic, 72 per cent of the Moroccan population were illiterate (cf. Björkegren 1985). Moroccan immigrants have permeated the West European countries. They have often lived side by side with Indo-Pakistani communities in European towns, and as a result have been influenced by their practices. Thus, the *tablīgh* movement has secured

a foothold among Moroccans. Inside Morocco, there is a long tradition of sufism, as well as the more recent popularity of the *tablīgh* movement.

13 My information about this group is based on discussions with group members and with members of other Islamist movements. See also Kepel 1985.

14 *Jāhilīya*, in the Koranic sense of the word, denotes the time before the Koranic message, i.e. pre-Islamic time, as a time of ignorance. Quṭb extends the usage of the term to mean all non-Islamic phenomena. In his view, Islam stands for the divine message of submission to God, and *jāhilīya* is its opposite in which man is forced to serve other human beings (S. Quṭb 1983: 52–4). See also Roald 1994: 179–82.

15 The following is partly taken from Roald 1994: 97–213.

16 For a more detailed historical and ideological survey of the growth and development of the Muslim Brothers, see al-Ḥusainī 1956; Mitchell 1969.

17 The *ikhwān* have a saying '*sirrīyat at-tanẓım wa ʿalanīyat ad-daʿwa*' (secrecy of the organisation and openness in *daʿwa*).

18 Muslim intellectuals such as Jamāl ad-Din al-Afghānī and Muḥammad ʿAbduh from the nineteenth century are usually categorised as the *salafīya.*

19 The main discussion of gender relations in the Muslim Brotherhood in Jordan is taken from my book, *Tarbiya: Education and Politics in Islamic Movements in Jordan and Malaysia* (1994).

20 The issue of Muslim women has been much discussed in recent decades. According to Soraya Duval, a researcher on women in rural Egypt, the discussion has suffered from 'biases and shortcomings, such as generalisations, reductionism, textualism and elitism'. In her view, female solidarity in the form of 'sub-societies', which is very strong among Middle Eastern women, can counteract the male domination of women (Duval 1993: 4). It is important to point out that urban and rural traditions often differ in their patterns of social interaction, even though traditional networks tend to some extent to continue to function when rural populations move to larger towns (cf. Wikan 1983). In addition, the Jordanian reality does not always match that of other Middle Eastern countries. The organisation of the Muslim Brothers is mainly an urban phenomenon where female bonds are not as strong as in rural and traditional areas. However, Duval's observations about Egypt can be partially applied to the Jordanian setting as well.

21 All information on the sisters' branch of the Muslim Brothers is based upon discussions and personal conversations with female members and sympathisers.

22 The 1993 student election is indicative of a major victory for the Islamists. Seventy-one out of eighty elected male representatives were Islamists.

23 *Tahwā* translated as 'she desires', from the root *h-w-ā*, conveys the meaning of an inclination which comes from the 'lower self' of human nature, according to Koranic verses such as: 'Therefore, let not him turn you aside from [the thought of] it who believe not therein but follow his own desire, lest you perish' (K.20: 16), and

> If We had willed We could have elevated him with it [the revelation], but he inclined to the earth and followed his desire. His likeness is that of the likeness of the dog; if you burden him he will breathe heavily, and if you leave him he will breathe heavily. Such is the likeness of the people who deny our revelation.
>
> (K.7: 176)

24 In recent literature about early twentieth century feminist movements in the Arab world, there is a tendency to interpret the activities of Arab feminists' activities in terms of the western feminist movement. For instance, when the

incident involving Hūdā Shaʿrāwī's throwing away the veil is referred to, it is rarely clarified that she did not remove the head-scarf but rather the face-veil. When I asked Zainab al-Ghazzālī about Shaʿrāwi and her organisation's commitment to Islam she replied that Shaʿrāwi and most women in the organisation were committed to the Islamic message. They were praying and fasting and even wearing the head-scarf. The reason why she herself had left Shaʿrāwi's organisation was that she saw this organisation as more directed towards female matters in general, whereas her own organisation was devoted to the case of Islam. She further told me that when she wanted to leave the organisation, Shaʿrāwi took her in her arms and said: 'I wanted to make you my successor (*khalīfatī*).'

25 Interview with Z. al-Ghazzālī, March 1997, in Cairo, Egypt.

26 Personal discussion with ʿAṭā Abū ar-Rashta, the official spokesman of the Islamic Liberation Party, 9 September 1991, in Amman, Jordan.

27 Personal discussions with members of the party.

28 Taji-Farouki gives no reference for this quotation.

29 Taji-Farouki gives no reference for this quotation.

30 The original Constitution was published in 1953 and the 1979 version is a revised version. Taji-Farouki translated the 1979 version and published it as an appendix in her book *A Fundamental Quest* from 1996.

31 In early Muslim history there was a conflict between those who relied on hadiths for Islamic rules (*ahl al-ḥadīth*) as was mainly done within the *Ḥanbalī madhhab*, and those who relied on scholars' views or interpretations of the body of hadith literature with reference to the Koran for developing Islamic rules (*ahl ar-raʾ*), mainly the jurists of the *Ḥanafī madhhab.*

32 Another example is that when Muslims meet they should shake hands only, as there is no authentic hadith, according to the *salafīs*, which records the Prophet kissing his friends' cheeks.

33 For example, television is regarded as *al-biḍʿa ad-dunyawīya* and acceptable, while the rosary is regarded as *al-biḍʿa ad-dīnīya* and not acceptable.

34 Eyerman and Jamison see the *movement intellectuals* as those individuals or actors in social movements who make the ideology of the movements visible.

3 Defining the area of research

1 There is a distinction between 'participant observation' and 'participant description'. I use the former to indicate an active participating role for the researcher, whereas the latter indicates a more objective approach towards the research-object.

2 Larsen has observed in her study on converts that the focus for the Islamists' *daʿwa* activities in Europe is to support the Islamic movements in the Muslim world, rather than to spread Islam among non-Muslims. It is interesting to note that the Muslim *daʿwa* as a rule is a 'domestic mission', i.e. a mission within the Muslim community (Larsen 1995: 163; Vogt 1995).

3 For a definition of *ikhwān* see Chapter 2. Briefly, I define the *ikhwān* trend to refer to those who adhere to the ideology of the Muslim Brotherhood, whether members of the organisation or not.

4 The *ʿAshārī* creed is opposed to the *salaf* creed in that it interprets physical appearances attributed to God in the Koran in a transfigural sense, i.e. 'the hand of God' is understood as the power of God. The adherents to the *salaf* creed, on the other hand, claim that 'the hand of God' should be understood in a figurative sense, i.e. as God's hand only. It is important to observe that the *salaf* creed denies any resemblance between God's features and human features. The *salaf* idea is thus to avoid interpreting or explaining the physical appearances attributed to God.

4 Theoretical reflections on change and changing processes

1 In a paper presented at the seminar of Islamology at Lund University 1997, Torsten Janson, a Ph.D. student at Lund University, dealt at length with the effects of religious norms on various organisational levels. In his paper he presented a model illustrating the inter-dependency of the individual and the organisational function of religious norms. See also Berger's and Luckman's (1967) discussion on the individual's construction of social reality and values.
2 See Chapter 7 on gender relations.
3 It is of interest to note that the idea that western colonialism is responsible for many traits which are regarded as oppressive towards women, is a common argument in the Muslim world by secular feminists and Islamists alike.
4 An example is Sheikh Muḥammad Naṣir ad-Dīn al-Albānī's book *The Prophet's Prayer*. al-Albānī searches for the strongest hadiths in every matter concerning prayer, and he refuses the various law schools' rules (al-Albānī 1993).
5 During my many fieldwork visits to Amman in Jordan I observed increased female participation in society. On my first visit there in 1985, females working outside the home were mainly teachers or domestic helpers, whereas in 1995 many women were also working as shop assistants or as clerical workers. If we turn to Saudi Arabia, many females work outside the home. There women are required in various jobs in order to keep up the strict segregation of society. Oman is another country where women are employed at all levels of society, even in high positions. During my fieldwork in Malaysia, I noticed many women working outside the home, and a high percentage of Malay students who pursue their postgraduate studies are women.
6 For further information on educational systems in Muslim countries, see Roald 1994.
7 The following is taken from Christensen 1996: 526–32.
8 For further reading of how Muslims tend to regard the Declaration of Human Rights as a product of 'the West' rather than as being built upon universal ideas, see Hjärpe 1988.
9 By using these categories, I do not attempt to describe reality; rather they are heuristic classifications. See Weber 1977.
10 By biography I mean previous experiences, gender, age, class, state of mind, etc.
11 Lawrence sees modernity as the new technological means, whereas he looks at modernism in terms of the ideological message of the modern age (Lawrence 1989).
12 This quotation is taken from Jonathan Friedman's discussion on how construction of history might be linked to formation of identity (Friedman 1994). Although Friedman's discussion is different from the discussion in the present study, this quotation is suitable in the above context.

5 Reflections on sharia

1 *Taqlīd* is often translated as *imitation* and it denotes imitating former scholars' judgements in Islamic law.
2 The historical discussion (in the eleventh/twelfth century) was less a discussion about whether one could conduct *ijtihād* or not, than about whether or not there existed qualified *mujtahids*. This is the same discussion which contemporary scholars have today.
3 The Zaidī law school which is prevalent in Yemen is less known to common Muslims.

4 Discussion with Jan Hjärpe, Lund University.
5 Ṣāliḥ builds his arguments on hadiths from among others, al-Bukhārī and Sunan Abī Dāwud.
6 Cf. also al-Bukhārī in *The Book of the Virtues of the Koran*, Chapter 2; Chapter 3.
7 This subject is called 'reasons for origin' (*asbāb an-nuzūl*), and it has a clear parallel to the Christian historical-critical concept of 'Sitz im Leben'.
8 There are various views on the number of narrator chains. Some put four as the limit for *multiplied* narrator chains, whereas others put ten.
9 For a hadith to be considered authentic (*ṣaḥīḥ*), it must have been rigorously authenticated by a hadith master who has studied the hadith's various texts and chains of transmission to confirm that both are sound. Traditional scholars assert that Muslims are obligated to believe *ṣaḥīḥ* (authentic) hadiths. See N. Keller 1991.
10 I have already referred to this in Chapter 2. This classification is probably the traditional classification of the Islamic scholars as Abū Zahra has his Islamic education from al-Azhar in Egypt.
11 See also my discussion of Christensen's theory in Chapter 4.
12 It is important to be aware that in history there exists a *fiqh al-aqallīyāt*, particularly in the Mālikī law school in Andalusia and in the Ḥanafī law school in India. See also N. Keller 1995; Abou el Fadl 1994.

6 Perceptions of women

1 The issue at stake is *how* to understand such passages. As traditionally this particular passage has been understood as a general prohibition against women's religious leadership, the modern tendency is to interpret the passage as being directed exclusively towards the women in Corinth. Instead of generalising a Pauline statement, one tends to regard it in a local context only (*sitz im leben*). It is important to be aware that it is in Lutheran Christianity that the Corinthian passage has been used in the argument against female priests. This has to do with the preaching function of the priestly office in Lutheranism, whereas in Catholicism for instance, the priest has a sacrificial function. The opposition against female priests within the two Christian traditions is thus built on different foundations.
2 The Koranic verse where *shūrā* is interpreted in a political context is 42: 38.
3 Although this hadith is obviously to be understood in context as there is a continuation of the hadith, I have heard this hadith referred to in discussions with common Muslims.
4 Mernissi refers to a follow-up of this hadith. She quotes from az-Zarkashī:

> They told ʿĀ'isha that Abū Hurayra was asserting that the Messenger of God said: 'Three things bring bad luck: the house, the woman, and the horse.' ʿĀ'isha responded: 'Abū Hurayra learned his lessons very badly. He came into our house when the Prophet was in the middle of a sentence. He only heard the end of it. What the Prophet said was: "May God refute the Jews. They say three things bring bad luck: the house, the woman, and the horse."'
>
> (Mernissi 1987: 76)

This quotation is taken from az-Zarkashī 1970: 114. Mernissi does not mention, however, that az-Zarkashī points out that this hadith referring back to ʿĀ'isha has a weak narrator chain as the link between ʿĀ'isha and the person who claimed to hear her say these words is not established (az-Zarkashī 1970: 114–15).

5 One of the Sudanese female judges is Farīda Ibrahīm Ḥussaīn who is also chief of the Judicial Bureau of Khartoum State.

7 Gender relations

1 The six authentic hadith-collections (*aṣ-ṣiḥāḥ as-sitta*) are the collections by al-Bukhārī, Muslim, Sunan at-Tirmidhī, Sunan Ibn Mājah, Sunan an-Nisā'ī and Sunan Abī Dāwud. In addition Musnad Aḥmad is held in high esteem among Muslims.
2 It is interesting to note that Abū Huraira is the only first narrator to this hadith in all versions.
3 In both al-Bukhārī's and Muslim's versions Abū Huraira is the first narrator.
4 This hadith has two first narrators, namely ʿĀ'isha and Ibn ʿAbbās.
5 This hadith is related from ʿĀ'isha by ʿUrwa bin Zubair.
6 Ibn Kathīr's original work was in four volumes. aṣ-Ṣābūnī, the Syrian scholar, investigated his work, and removed parts of Ibn Kathīr's work. Ibn Kathīr relies heavily on biblical stories taken mainly from Talmud, and he had also used weak hadiths in his commentary. aṣ-Ṣābūnī left only those hadiths which he regards as authentic and removed biblical stories which he did not find any trace of in the Islamic sources.
7 It is important to bear in mind the distinction between prophethood and messengerhood. Whereas prophethood implies revelations from God to certain persons, messengerhood implies that the person in question has received a divine message to deliver to his/her people.
8 The yearly student exam in Jordan is given great significance, and names of those who top the results list are given in the media.
9 Wehr, in his Arabic–English dictionary, translates *tataṣaraf* as 'to act independently', 'to dispose freely', 'to act without restriction', 'to administer (freely)' or 'to act', 'to behave' and 'to conduct'. In this context the term conveys an act of no restriction.
10 According to at-Tirmidhī this is a good, strange (*ḥasan, gharīb*) hadith from Abu Huraira. Ibn Mājah's version is related by ʿĀ'isha.
11 This hadith has one narrator chain with ʿAbdallāh bin Abī Dhubāb as the first narrator.
12 The term *fāḥisha* is often linked to sexual offences. For instance a prostitute or a woman with many sexual partners is often called *fāḥisha*.
13 Abū Shaqqa remarks that: 'I want to draw attention to the fact that the mention of hitting the slaves in this context means that which was usual in pre-Islamic times. As for the slave in Islam, he has respect and rights in many things.'
14 Taken from *aḥkām al-qurān li l-jaṣṣās* (vol. II).
15 It is interesting to note that Sheikh Aḥmad ʿAli al-Imām from the Sudan referred to this particular piece of legislation, saying that in previous times this law of *bait aṭ-ṭāʿa* was a protection for women. 'Earlier' he said,

> women did not have the power in society that they enjoy nowadays. Fathers could easily use their daughters to show their power, and they could deny their daughters permission to return to their husbands' houses after a marital twist. The *bait aṭ-ṭāʿa* was then a guarantee for women who wanted to return to their husbands.

Sheikh al-Imām further expressed the opinion that in contemporary times this law is no longer necessary as women, due to among other things education, are strong enough to protect their own interests. (From an interview with Sheikh Aḥmad ʿAli al-Imām in Sudan in May 1998.)

16 According to at-Tirmidhī this is a good, strange (*ḥasan*, *gharīb*) hadith from Abu Huraira. Ibn Mājah's version is related by ʿĀ'isha.
17 According to at-Tirmidhī this is a good, strange (*ḥasan*, *gharīb*) hadith. This hadith is related from Umm Salama.
18 Personal communication with Sara Johnsdotter 1998.
19 This hadith is *ḥadīth aḥad*, which means that the story goes back to only one (or a few) narrator(s). Ibn Abī Lailā heard the story from ʿAlī in all versions related above.
20 Many Muslims would see a *daʿwa* worker as a more conscientious Muslim, and therefore more inclined to follow the 'true Islam' and not the homeland's traditional practices.

8 Women's political participation in Islam

1 Discussions with Jama'at-i-Islami's members.
2 It is interesting to note that this book was republished in 1991 with the same layout but with a different title: *The Veil and the Male Elite: A Feminist Interpretation of Women's Rights in Islam*.
3 at-Tirmidhī has rendered this hadith as good, authentic (*ḥasan*, *ṣaḥīḥ*).
4 In sharia, there have to be four witnesses in cases of adultery. If there are three or less, those who witness are subject to punishment as the matter becomes an accusation with not enough evidence.
5 For further analysis on Badawi's ideas, see Roald and Ouis 1997.
6 Badawi does not refer to any written work by Darwazah.
7 In Article 67 of the Islamic Liberation Party's proposed Constitution for an Islamic state it asserts that 'the Caliph appoints a supreme judge from among those free Muslim *men* . . .' [italics mine]. However in Article 67 where the characteristics of a judge are listed, the sex of the judge is not mentioned. The Islamic Liberation Party thus implicitly rather than explicitly states that women cannot be judges. The possibility of female attorneys, however, is explicitly stated in Article 84.

9 Polygyny

1 I have chosen the term polygyny on the basis of Badawi's observation that *polygamy* means either *polygyny* (more than one wife of the same husband) or *polyandry* (more than one husband of the same wife). Only *polygyny* is permissible in the Islamic law.
2 Asad does not actually refer to Ibn ʿAbbās but quotes the same point of view and refers it back to another of the Prophet's Companions, Saʿīd ibn Jubair.
3 An example is the legal concept of *bait aṭ-ṭāʿa* which, although it might have originated in order to protect women's rights, was often used as a form of female oppression since women who wanted a divorce were forced back to their husbands due to this legal concept. Muḥammad al-Ghazzālī regards this legal concept as a 'wrong' *ijtihād* (M. al-Ghazzālī 1990: 178). See also note 15 in Chapter 7.
4 at-Tirmidhī has rendered this hadith good, authentic (*ḥasan*, *ṣaḥīḥ*). Aḥmad has a slightly different version where the reason for denying ʿAlī permission to marry is that the Prophet says that he cannot accept Fāṭima being married to the same man as the daughter of the great enemy of Islam. Musnad Aḥmad, *musnad kūfiīn*, no. 18155.
5 There are five degrees of permissibility ascribed by Muslim scholars. They are: *wājib* (obligatory), *mubāḥ* (permissible), *mandūb* (recommended), *makrūh* (reprehensible), and *ḥarām* (prohibited).

10 Divorce and child custody

1 During my fieldwork in Malaysia in 1991–2 I observed that many couples divorced and that women easily remarried after divorce.
2 I made these observation during fieldwork in Jordan from the mid-1980s onwards.
3 For further information in English, see Esposito 1982.
4 This hadith is found in at-Tirmidhī, no. 1192 (n.d., n.p.).
5 It is important to note that, according to Engineer, Ibn Taimīya opposed ʿUmar's ruling in this matter and claimed that this form of divorce counted for one divorce declaration and not three as ʿUmar had declared.
6 at-Tirmidhī claims this hadith to be *ḥasan.*
7 The system *al-ʿālamī* claims the narrator chain of this hadith as not sound.
8 In this context, traditional means the adherence to the legislation of the law schools. Cf. Roald 1994.
9 In many Muslim countries, kindergarten is also labelled *ḥaḍāna.*

11 Female circumcision

1 Wilkista Onsando from the premier women's organisation of Kenya quoted in Kassamali 1998: 50.
2 It is important to be aware that, for instance in the Sudan, there is a tendency to reject infibulation in favour of clitoridectomy, identifying clitoridectomy as the Sunna form of circumcision in order to legitimate the practice in Islamic terms. These were my impressions formed during my visits to the Sudan when I discussed female circumcision with Sudanese women, and they are reinforced by the experience of Haifaa A. Jawad (Jawad 1998: 54).
3 This is also based on personal discussions with intellectual Islamists in the Muslim world and in Europe.
4 az-Zuhairī, who is himself a staunch supporter of female circumcision, claims that although there are people who assert that al-Ghazzālī supported female circumcision, this is refuted by Dr Maḥmūd Ḥamdī Zaqzūq, the Minister of Religious Affairs in Egypt who says:

> There are some who assume that the late Islamic scholar, Sheikh Muḥammad al-Ghazzālī's view was that female circumcision is Sunna of the Prophet (p.b.u.h.), but he never said that. . . . Rather his view was, in all Islamic research meetings, that it is necessary to put an end to this evil custom. And al-Ghazzālī added that 'there is no evidence that the Noble Messenger let his daughters be circumcised'.
>
> (az-Zuhairī 1996: 16)

5 The book I have in my possession is the seventh edition and is printed in 1985. As Ḥasan al-Bannāʾ wrote a preface to the first edition, one can deduce that it was written sometime in the 1940s.
6 Sābiq does not, however, mention how the hadith is not authentic.
7 The Arabic term is *shamm* which means smell. In this context, however, it is explained to mean 'a little' or as one of my informants states, 'just like a light touch, as a smell'.
8 The Arabic word *asrā* means 'to rid someone of worries' or 'to be cheered up' etc. I have chosen to translate it with the word 'better' and in brackets 'more beautiful' as this was explained to me by many Islamists.
9 Abū Dāwud states that this hadith is weak.
10 During my fieldwork in Malaysia in 1991–2 I investigated this matter and

had deep discussions with women about sexuality and the influence of circumcision on women's sex lives. As confirmed by the Minority Rights Group Report, I also gained the impression that the tradition in Malaysia is to remove the prepuce and not the clitoris.

11 It is interesting to note that in the English women's magazine, *Cosmopolitan* (December 1996), various operations labelled 'genital surgery' are described and recommended at a very high price. These include clitoplastry (part of the clitoral hood is nipped away), liposuction to the pubic mound (fat is removed from the pubic mound), labioplastry (excess skin from the inner vaginal lips is trimmed and the remaining tissue is stitched with dissolvable sutures), and perineorrhaphy (any tears in the perineal wall and pelvic floor are repaired and the muscles of the vagina are strengthened).

12 It is important to note that in the actual hadith, al-Bukhārī, in contrast to the other hadith collections where this hadith is found, does not mention the expression 'the two circumcised'. However, the subchapter where this hadith is found is called 'The chapter of the two circumcised'.

13 For further elaboration, see Roald 1994.

14 The informant distinguished between sex and sexuality in a way which is difficult to translate into English. I have tried to convey her meaning by using 'sex' to refer to the commodification and exploitation of sex in terms of consumerism and entertainment, and 'sexuality' to refer to the biological and social realities of human sexual embodiment and relationships.

12 Islamic female dress

1 During my many lectures in Sweden to people from various parts of society, I have met this expression in various forms.

2 A hadith (with a weak narrator chain) narrated both in Sunan Abī Dāwud and Mālik tells that a woman came to Umm Salama, asking her how a woman should be dressed during prayer. Umm Salama answered that she would wear a *khimār* and a loose coat which should hide the upper part (*ẓuhūr*) of her feet (Sunan Abī Dāwud, Chapter on Prayer, no. 544; Mālik, Chapter on Call to Prayer, no. 295). Another hadith (with weak narrator chain) tells that when Umm Kulthūm died the Prophet came to the women who washed her and gave them first her loincloth, then her loose coat (*dirʿ*), then her *khimār* (Sunan Abī Dāwud, Chapter on Funerals, no. 2745; Musnad Aḥmad, *bāqi musnad al-anṣār*, no. 25884).

3 According to the system *al-ʿālamī*, this hadith is *mursal*, here: the second narrator could not possibly have been in contact with ʿĀ'isha, who is the first narrator.

4 According to al-Albānī, this hadith has an authentic (*ṣaḥīḥ*) narrator chain (al-Albānī 1994: 83).

5 Ibn Kathīr relates this hadith from Sunan Abī Dāwud, Chapter on Dressing, no. 3585 [the narrator chain is not authentic according to system *al-ʿālamī*]; at-Tirmidhī, Chapter on Manners, no. 2702. Ibn Kathīr relates that at-Tirmidhī renders this hadith *ḥasan ṣaḥīḥ* (well authentic) Ibn Kathīr 1981 vol. II: 599.

6 According to the system *al-ʿālamī*, this hadith is *ḥasan* (good) according to its narrator chain.

7 These ideas are a result of my ongoing discussions with Pernilla Ouis, a human ecologist at the University of Lund.

8 Some researchers on Islam have claimed that because Muslim feminists such as Fatima Mernissi and Riffat Hassan have questioned the use of the veil as an Islamic custom, there is no longer an Islamic consensus on female covering in Islam. I strongly refute this allegation as in Islamic law there are certain criteria (concerning education and proficiency in Islamic knowledge) with

regard to being an Islamic scholar, which obviously the Muslim feminists in question do not fulfil.

9 For further explanation of Madhhabists, cf. Roald 1994.

10 I believe that this hadith has an implication which al-Albānī has not mentioned, namely, that it refers to the female covering as a *privilege* for free believing women.

11 This hadith is found in Imām Muslim, Chapter on the Prayer of the Two ʿĪds, no. 1926.

12 This hadith is found in al-Bukhārī, Chapter on Pilgrimage, no. 589.

13 I have tried without success to find this hadith in the 'Six Authentic' hadith collections in addition to Musnad Aḥmad and Sunan ad-Dārimī.

14 Darsh refers to Jābir Ibn Zayd's arrangement of the revelations of the Koranic Suras as evidence that Sura *an-nūr* was revealed after the Sura *al-aḥzāb*.

15 For a discussion on abrogation of Koranic verses see Asad 1984: 22–3.

List of scholars

Ancient scholars

Ābādī, Fīrūz (d. 1416), Persia.
ʿAbduh, Muḥammad (d. 1905), Egypt.
Abū Hanīfa, al-Nuʿmān (d. 767), Iraq.
al-Afghānī, Jamāl ad-Dīn (d. 1897) Afghanistan (perhaps Persia).
al-Asqalānī, Ibn Ḥajar (d. 1449), Asqalān in Palestine.
al-Baihaqī, Aḥmad (d. 1066), Khurasan in Persia.
al-Baṣrī, Ḥasan (d. 782), Iraq.
al-Ghazzālī, Abū Ḥāmid Muḥammad (d. 1111), Iraq/Syria.
Ibn ʿAbbās, ʿAbdullāh (687), Arabian Peninsula.
Ibn ʿAbd al-Wahhāb, Muḥammad (d. 1787), Arabian Peninsula.
Ibn al-Athīr, ʿIzz ad-Dīn (d. 1233), Iraq.
Ibn Ḥanbal, Aḥmad (d. 855), Mecca/Medina.
Ibn Ḥazm, ʿAlī Ibn Aḥmad (d. 1064), Cordoba in Andalus.
Ibn Jawzī, ʿAbd ar-Raḥmān (d. 1201), Iraq.
Ibn Kathīr, ʿImād ad-Dīn (d. 1373), Iraq/Syria.
Ibn Khallikān, Aḥmad (d. 1282), Iraq/Syria.
Ibn Manẓūr, Jamāl ad-Dīn Muḥammad (d. 1311), Egypt/Libya.
Ibn Sīrīn, Muḥammad (d. 729), Iraq.
Ibn Taimīya, Taqī ad-Dīn (d. 1328), Iraq/Syria.
al-Jaṣṣāṣ, Aḥmad ibn ʿAlī (d. 981), Iraq.
al-Jawzīya, Ibn Qayyim (d. 1351), Syria.
al-Juwainī, ʿAbd al-Mālik (d. 1085), Persia.
Mālik ibn Anas (d. 795), Medina.
al-Miṣrī, Aḥmad ibn Naqīb (d. 1368), Eqypt.
an-Nawawī, Muḥyī ad-Dīn (d. 1277), Syria.
al-Qurṭubī, Muḥammad Ibn Aḥmad (d. 1273), Cordoba in Andalus.
Riḍā, Rashīd (d. 1935), Syria/Egypt.
ash-Shāfiʿī, Muḥammad Ibn Idrīs (d. 820), Mecca/Medina/Iraq/Egypt.
ash-Shahrastānī, Abū l-Fatḥ, Muḥammad (d. 1153), Persia/Iraq.
Shāh Walīullāh (d. 1763), the Indian subcontinent.
ash-Shawkānī, Muḥammad Ibn ʿAlī (d. 1834), Yemen.
aṣ-Suyūṭī, Jalāl ad-Dīn (d. 1505), Eqypt.
aṭ-Ṭabārī, Abū Jaʿfar Muḥammad ibn Jarīr (d. 923), Persia/Iraq.
az-Zarkashī, Badr ad-Dīn (d. 1392), Egypt/Syria.
az-Zubaidī, Muḥammad (d. 1791), the Indian subcontinent/Iraq/Egypt.

Contemporary scholars

Abū Shaqqa, ʿAbd al-Ḥalīm (d. 1996), Egypt.
al-Albānī, Muḥammad Nāṣir ad-Dīn (d. 1999), Syria/Jordan.
Asad, Muhammad (d. 1992), Poland/Germany.
Badawi, Jamal, Egypt/Canada.
al-Bannā', Ḥasan (d. 1949), Egypt.
al-Barāzī, Muḥammad Fu'ād, Syria/Denmark.
Darsh, Muḥammad (d. 1997), Egypt/Britain.
al-Ghannūshī, Rāshid, Tunis/Britain.
al-Ghazzālī, Muḥammad (d. 1966), Egypt.
al-Ghazzālī, Zainab, Egypt.
al-Imām, Aḥmad ʿAlī, Sudan.
Iqbāl, Muḥammad (d. 1938), the Indian subcontinent.
Keller, Nuah Ha Mim, USA/Jordan.
al-Mawdūdī, Abū al-ʿAlā (d. 1979), the Indian subcontinent.
an-Nabhānī, Taqī ad-Dīn (d. 1977), Palestine.
al-Qaraḍāwī, Yūsuf, Egypt/Qatar.
Quṭb, Muḥammad, Egypt/Saudi Arabia/Qatar.
Quṭb, Sayyid (d. 1966), Egypt.
Rahman, Fazlur (d. 1988), the Indian subcontinent/USA.
Sābiq, as-Sayyid, Egypt/Saudi Arabia.
aṣ-Ṣabūnī, Muḥammad ʿAlī, Syria/Saudi Arabia.
ash-Shaʿrāwī, Muḥammad Mutawalī (d. 1998), Egypt.
at-Turābī, Ḥasan, Sudan.
Wadud-Muhsin, Amina, USA.
al-Zuḥailī, Wahba, Syria.

Glossary

ʿadāt Customs.
ad-dīn al-fiṭra The natural religion.
aḥad (hadith) Hadith with less than four narrator chains.
ahl al-kitāb People of the Book (Christians and Jews).
ʿaqīda The Islamic creed.
ʿaql 'Reason'.
ʿaqlānī 'Rational'.
arkān Pillars (i.e. the five pillars of Islam).
ʿāṣī Disobedient (against God).
aṣl Origin.
ʿāṭifī Emotional.
awliyā Protectors, also saints.
ʿawra Nakedness (i.e. that which should not be exposed).
ʿazīz (hadith) Hadith with two narrator chains.
biḍʿa Innovation (i.e. in religion).
daʿīf (hadith) Hadith with weak narrator chain.
dalīl (pl. adīlla) Evidence (legal).
ḍaraba Hit.
daʿwa Call to Islam.
dhikr Remembrance of God.
dhīl (pl. dhuyūl) Skirt.
dīn Religion.
fāḥisha Monstrosity (also a female prostitute).
farḍ Obligatory.
fāsiq Trespasser.
fatwā Legal decision.
fawḍā Chaos.
fiqh Jurisprudence.
fī sabīl allāh In the path of God.
fitna Temptation or trial.
gharīb (hadith) Hadith with one narrator chain.
hadith Narrative relating deeds and utterances of the Prophet.
ḥalāl Permissible.

ḥarām Prohibited.
ḥasan (hadith) Hadith with a good narrator chain (not authentic).
ḥayāʾ Modesty
hiḍāna Caretaking of children after a divorce (also nursery).
ḥijāb Curtain (used as female covering in various forms).
ḥimāya Protection.
ḥudūd (sing. ḥadd) Bounds (in sharia: capital punishment).
ḥukm Power or rule.
ʿibādāt God worship.
iʿḍār Male circumcision.
ʿidda Women's waiting period after divorce.
iḥsān Perfection.
ijmāʿ Consensus (of Islamic scholars).
ijtihād Individual legal reasoning.
ikhtilāf Differences of opinions.
ikhwān Members (or the movement) of the Muslim Brotherhood. Used also for the Muslim Brotherhood's ideas.
imān Faith.
isnād Narrator chain of a hadith.
isrāʾīlīyāt Stories taken from the Jewish Scriptures.
istiḥsān Legal preference.
istiṣḥāb Continuity or permanence.
istiṣlāḥ Public interest.
jāhilīya Pre-Islamic time/ time of ignorance.
jilbāb (pl. jalābīb) Female covering in various forms.
jins Sexuality.
kāfir Non-believer.
khafaḍ Female circumcision.
khayr Good.
khimār (pl. khumur) Female covering in various forms.
khitān Circumcision.
khulʿ Female divorce.
kufr Non-belief.
liʿān Oath of condemnation (in adultery cases).
madhhab Law school.
madhāhib Law schools.
maḥārim Prohibitions.
mahr Dowry.
maḥram A woman's husband or an unmarriageable relative.
majlis ash-shūrā The general council.
makrama Noble.
makrūh Detestable.
marfūʿ (hadith) Hadith whose narrator chain goes back to the Prophet.
maʿrūf Good (morally acceptable).
mashhūr (hadith) Hadith with three narrator chains.

maṣlaḥa Beneficent.
matn Hadiths' content.
mawadda Love.
mawḍūʿ (hadith) Hadith with false narrator chains.
minhaj Method/way.
mirṭ (plur. murūt) Sheet/cover.
muʿāmalāt Inter-human relationship.
mubāḥ Acceptable (not necessary).
mufti Islamic jurist.
muḥaddith Scholar of hadiths.
muḥsin A person of perfection.
mujāhid One who fights for the sake of God.
mujtahid One who performs ijtihād.
mu'min A believer.
munāfiq A hypocrite.
munkar Evil or that which is not acceptable.
mursal (hadith) A hadith where a second generation Muslim is the first narrator.
mustaḥabb Preferable.
mutawātir (hadith) A hadith with more than four (some claim ten) narrator chains.
nafs Self (entity).
naṣṣ Text.
nifāq Hypocrisy.
niqāb Face-veil (most common understanding).
nushūz Ill-will.
qādī Islamic judge.
qanūn Canonised law (different in various Muslim countries).
qawwamūn ʿalā In charge of/responsible for.
qināʿ Mask (common use in contemporary time).
qiwāma In charge of/responsible for.
qiyās Analogy.
raḥma Mercy.
sabab an-nuzūl Reasons for revelation (of Koranic verses).
ṣabr Patience.
ṣaḥīḥ (hadith) Hadith with an authentic (strong) narrator chain.
salaf (pl. aslāf) Ancestor.
salafī Movement with stress on Koran and Sunna as normative.
salafīya Intellectual movement in the nineteenth century.
shahādatayn The two testimonies of faith.
sharīʿa (Sharia) The Islamic Law (basic principles).
shu'm Bad omen.
shūrā Counselling.
siwāk A small stick used to clean the teeth.
sulṭa Power.

Sunna The Prophet's example.
ṭāʿat az-zawj Obedience to the husband.
tabarruj Display of beauty.
tafsīr Interpretation (of the Koran).
ṭahāra Purity.
tajdīd Reform.
ṭalāq Male divorce.
taqwa God-consciousness.
tarbiya Upbringing, education.
taṭlīq Divorce made by a judge.
thawb A sheet to wrap around the body.
ʿulamāʾ Islamic scholars.
Umma Nation.
ʿurf Customs (verbalised and non-verbalised).
uṣūl Roots.
uṣūl al-fiqh Roots of jurisprudence.
uṣūlī 'Fundamentalist'.
waḥy Revelation
wājib Obligation.
wilāya Sovereignty.
zawj Mate.
zīna Beauty.

Bibliography

Aalund (Ålund), Aleksandra. (1991) 'Etnisk Bricolage och nya gemenskaper' in A. Sjögren (ed.) *Ungdom & Tradition: En etnologisk syn på mångkulturell uppväxt*, Stockholm: Mångkulturellt centrum.

Ābādī, Fīrūz. (1988) *tanwīr al-miqbās mn tafsīr ibn ʿabbās*, Duha, Qatar: Dār al-Ishrāq.

ʿAbd al-ʿĀṭī, Hammūd. (1977) *The Family Structure in Islam*, Indianapolis: American Trust Publications.

Abramson, Harold J. (1979) 'Migrants and cultural diversity: on ethnicity and religion in society' in *Social Compass* XXVI, 1979/1, pp. 5–29.

al-ʿAbdālāt, Marwān, A. S. (1992) *kharīṭa li l-aḥzāb as-siāsīya al-urdunīya*, Amman: Qurṭāsīya al-ʿIbra.

ʿAbduh, Muḥammad. (n.d.) *tafsīr al-manār* (vols I–XI), Cairo: Dār al-Fikr.

Abou el Fadl, Khaled. (1994) 'Islamic law and Muslim minorities: the juristic discourse on Muslim minorities from the second/eighth to the eleventh/seventeenth centuries' in *Islamic Law and Society* 1, pp. 141–87.

Abū Dāwud. (n.d.) *sunan abī dāwud*, system *al-ʿālamī*, CD-ROM, Jeddah: Company Sakhr al-ʿĀlamī.

Abū Shaqqa, ʿAbd al-Ḥalīm. (1990) *taḥrīr al-marʾa fī ʿaṣr ar-risāla*, Kuwait: Dār al-Qalam li n-Nashr wa t-Tawzīʿ.

Abū Zahra, Muhammad. (n.d.) *uṣūl al-fiqh*, Cairo: Dār al-Fikr al-ʿArabī.

Afkhami, Mahnaz (ed.) (1995) *Faith and Freedom: Women's Human Rights in the Muslim World*, London: I. B. Tauris Publishers.

Ahmad, Leila. (1992) *Women and Gender in Islam*, New Haven and London: Yale University Press.

al-Albānī, Muḥammad Nāṣir ad-Dīn. (1972) *silsila al-aḥādīth aṣ-ṣaḥīḥa* vols. I–IV, Beirut: Maktab al-Islāmī.

—— (1975) *silsila al-aḥādīth aḍ-ḍaʿīfa* vol. I, Beirut: Maktab al-Islāmī.

—— (1987) *silsila al-aḥādīth aḍ-ḍaʿīfa* vol. III, Beirut: Maktab al-Islāmī.

—— (1993) *The Prophet's Prayer*, Suffolk: al-Hanīf Publications.

—— (1994) (1370 AH, *c*. 1950 CE) *jilbāb al-marʾa l-muslima* (*The Muslim Woman's Dress*) Amman: Dār Ibn Ḥazm.

Alexander, Jeffrey C. and Seidman, Steven (eds) (1990) *Culture and Society: Contemporary Debates*, Cambridge: Cambridge University Press.

ʿAlī, Muḥammad. (1996) 'Collection and preservation of Ḥadīth' in P. K. Koya (ed.) *Ḥadīth and Sunna: Ideals and Realities*, Kuala Lumpur: Islamic Book Trust, pp. 23–57.

ʿAlī, Yūsuf. (1989) *The Holy Qurān: Text, Translation and Commentary*, Brentwood, Maryland: Amana Corporation.

Ally, Muhammad Mashuq. (1994) *The Impact of Islamic Revivalists on Muslim Religious Education in Britain*, unpublished Ph.D. thesis, University of Wales.

Altorki, S. and El-Solh, C. F. (eds) (1988) *Arab Women in the Field*, New York: Syracuse University Press.

Amīn, Sādiq. (1982) *ad-daʿwa al-islāmiyya*, Amman: Jamaʿīya ʿUmmāl al- Maṭābiʿ at-Taʿāwunīya.

Anwar, Muhammad. (1985) *Pakistanis in Britain: A Sociological Study*, London: New Century Publishers.

—— (1987) 'Religious identity in plural societies: the case of Britain' in *Journal of the Institute of Muslim Minorities Affairs* 2.2/3.1, pp. 110–21.

Appleby, R. S. and Marty, M. E. (eds) (1995) *Fundamentalism Observed*, Chicago: Chicago University Press.

Arcana, Judith. (1983) *Every Mother's Son: The Role of Mothers in the Making of Men*, London: The Women's Press.

Archer, John and Lloyd, Barbara. (1982) *Sex and Gender*, Cambridge: Cambridge University Press.

Asad, Muhammad. (1956) *Vägen till Mecka* (*The Road to Mecca*), Stockholm: Bonniers.

—— (1984) *The Message of the Qurʾān*, Gibraltar: Dar al-Andalus.

al-Ashqar, ʿUmar Sulaymān. (1982) *tarīkh al-fiqh al-islāmī*, Kuwait: Maktabat al Falāḥ.

—— (1983) *al-ʿaqīda fī allāh*, Kuwait: Maktabat al-Falāḥ.

al-Atas, Syed Farid. (1986) 'Notes on various theories regarding the Islamization of the Malay archipelago' in *The Muslim World*.

al-Attas, Syed Muhammad al-Naquib. (1978) *Islam and Secularism*, Kuala Lumpur: ABIM, A-1 Jalan Pantai Baru.

al-ʿAẓamī, Muḥammad. (1978) *Studies in Early Ḥadīth Literature*, Indianapolis: American Trust Publications.

—— (1985) *On Schacht's 'Origins of Muhammadan Jurisprudence'*, Chichester: Wiley.

—— (1996) '*Isnād* and its significance' in P. K. Koya, (ed.) *Ḥadīth and Sunna: Ideals and Realities*, Kuala Lumpur: Islamic Book Trust, pp. 58–71.

Badawi, Jamal. (1995) *Gender Equity in Islam: Basic Principles*, Indianapolis: American Trust Publications.

al-Bannāʾ, Ḥasan. (1984) *majmūʿa rasāʾil al-imām ash-shahīd ḥasan al- bannāʾ*, Beirut: al-Muʾassasa l-Islāmīya.

al-Barāzī, Muḥammad Fuʾād. (1995) *ḥijāb al-muslima*, Riadh: Maktaba Aḍwāʾ s-Salaf.

Barber, Benjamin. (1996) *Jihad vs. Mcworld*, New York: Ballantine Books.

Barnes, Virginia Lee and Boddy, Janice. (eds) (1995) *Aman: The Story of a Somali Girl*, New York: Vintage Books.

Barth, Fredrik. (1989) 'The analysis of culture in complex societies' in *Ethnos* 3–4, pp. 120–42.

—— (1995) 'Ethnicity and the concept of culture' in D. R. Imig and P. Slavsky, (eds) *Nonviolent Sanctions and Cultural Survival Seminars*, Center for International Affairs, Harvard University.

Beckford, J. (1989) *Religion and Advanced Industrial Society*, London: Unwin Hyman.
Berger, Peter and Luckman, Thomas. (1967) *The Social Construction of Reality*, New York: Anchor Books.
Bernström, Muḥammad Knut. (1998) *Koranens Budskap*, Stockholm: Proprius.
Beyer, Peter. (1994) *Religion and Globalisation*, London: Sage.
Bird, Phyllis A. (1991) 'Sexual differentiation and divine image in the Genesis creation texts' in *Image of God and Gender Models*, Oslo: Solums Forlag.
Björkegren, Hans (ed.) (1985) *Hela världen i fakta*, Stockholm: Bonnier Fakta.
Blake, Christopher. (1959) 'Can history be objective?' in Patrick Gardner (ed.) *Theories of History*, New York: The Free Press of Glence.
Bowie, Fiona. (1989) *Beguine Spirituality*, London: SPCK.
Branté, Thomas. (1984) *Vetenskapens Sociala Grunder: En studie av konflikter i forskarvärlden*, Stockholm: Rabén & Sjögren.
Broch-Due, Vigdis, Rudie, Ingrid and Bleie, Tone (eds) (1993) *Carved Flesh/Cast Selves: Gendered Symbols and Social Practices*, Oxford: Berg Publishers.
Brod, Harry (ed.) (1987) *The Making of Masculinities: The New Men's Studies*, Boston: Allen & Unwin.
Brown, Daniel W. (1996) *Rethinking Tradition in Modern Islamic Thought*, Cambridge: Cambridge University Press.
al-Bukhārī. (n.d.) *ṣaḥīḥ al-bukhārī*, system *al-ʿālamī*, CD-ROM, Jeddah: Company Sakhr al-ʿĀlamī.
Burton, John. (1977) *The Collection of the Qu'ran*, Cambridge: Cambridge University Press.
Carlbom, Aje. (1998) 'Allahs tårar: Islam som integrerande kraft i stadsdelen Rosengård', presented at the SAND-conference at Lund University.
Christensen, Anna. (1996) 'Skydd för etablerad position – ett normativt grundmönster' in *Tidskrift for Rettsvitenskap 4*, Oslo/Copenhagen/Stockholm/Boston: Scandinavian University Press.
Cohen, A. (1982) *Political Parties in the West Bank under the Jordanian Regime 1949–1967*, Ithaca, New York: Cornell University Press.
Collingwood, R. G. (1976) (1936) *Human Nature and Human History*, New York: Haskell House Publishers Ltd.
Connell, R. W. (1987) *Gender and Power: Society, the Person and Sexual Politics*, Cambridge: Polity Press.
Coulson, N. J. (1964) *A History of Islamic Law*, Edinburgh: Edinburgh University Press.
Crapanzano, Vincent. (1980) *Tuhami – Portrait of a Moroccan*, Chicago: University of Chicago Press.
Crecelius, Daniel. (1983) 'Nonideological responses of the Egyptian Ulama to modernization' in *The Ulama in the Modern Muslim Nation-State*, Kuala Lumpur: Muslim Youth Movement in Malaysia, pp. 97–140.
Daly, Mary. (1986) *Beyond God the Father: Towards a Philosophy of Women's Liberation*, Boston: Beacon Press.
ad-Dārimī. (n.d.) *sunan ad-dārimī*, system *al-ʿālamī*, CD-ROM, Jeddah, Company Sakhr al-ʿĀlamī.
Darsh, S. M. (1984) *An Outline of Islamic Family Law*, London: Ta Ha Publishers.
—— (1995) *Hijab or Niqab*, London: Dar al Dawa Bookshop.

Dasseto, Felice. (1988) 'The Tabligh organisation in Belgium' in Tomas Gerholm and Yngve Lithman (eds) *The New Islamic Presence in Western Europe*, London: Mansell.

Dirks, Nicholas B. (1993) *The Hollow Crown: Ethnohistory of an Indian Kingdom*, Michigan: University of Michigan Press.

Doi, ʿAbd ar-Raḥmān I. (1984) *Sharīʿah: The Islamic Law*, London: Ta Ha Publishers.

Dumont, Louis. (1977) 'Caste, racism, and "Stratifications": reflections of a social anthropologist' in *Symbolic Anthropology: A Reader in the Study of Symbols and Meanings*, New York: Columbia University Press.

—— (1980) *Homo Hierarchicus: The Caste System and Its Implications*, Chicago: University of Chicago Press.

—— (1986) *Essays on Individualism: Modern Ideology in Anthropological Perspective*, Chicago and London: University of Chicago Press.

Duval, Soraya. (1993) 'Absent husbands and remaining wives: women's changing roles in rural Egypt', paper presented at the Development Sociology Workshop at the Swedish Sociological Conference 28–31 January 1993, University of Lund, Lund.

Elias, Norbert and Scotson, J. L. (eds) (1994) *The Established and the Outsiders*, London: Sage.

El Saadawi, Nawal. (1980) *The Hidden Face of Eve: Women in the Arab World*, Boston: Beacon Press.

El-Solh, C. F. and Mabro, J. (eds) (1994) *Muslim Women's Choices*, London: Berg Publishers.

Engineer, Asghar Ali. (1992) *The Rights of Women in Islam*, London: C. Hurts & Company.

Eriksson, Anders. (1998) *Traditions and Rhetorical Proof: Pauline Argumentation in 1 Corinthians*, CB New Testament Series 29, Stockholm: Almqvist & Wiksell International.

Esposito, John L. (1982) *Women in Muslim Family Law*, New York: Syracuse University Press.

Eyerman, Ron and Jamison, Andrew. (1991) *Social Movements*, London: Polity Press.

Fayyāḍ, Samīra. (1992) 'Future opportunities and prospects for women in Islam', paper submitted to a seminar on Muslim–Christian dialogue at the Vatican in Rome, June.

Fiorenzia, E. S. (1983) *In Memory of Her: A Feminist Theological Reconstruction of Christian Origins*, New York: SCM Press Ltd.

Foucault, Michel. (1993) *Diskursens Ordning*, Stockholm: Symposium, Stehag B. Östlings Bokförlag.

Fornäs, Johan. (1995) *Cultural Theory and Late Modernity*, London: Sage.

Friedl, Ernestine (1967) 'The position of women: appearance and reality' in *Anthropological Quarterly* 40(3) pp. 98–105.

Friedman, Jonathan. (1994) *Cultural Identity and Global Process*, London: Sage.

Geertz, Clifford. (1973) *Interpretation of Cultures*, New York: Basic Books.

—— (1980) 'Blurred genres' in *American Scholar* 49, pp. 165–79.

—— (1984) 'Anti-anti relativism' in *American Anthropologist* 86(2), pp. 263–77.

Gerholm, L. and Gerholm, T. (1992) *Doktorhatten: En studie av forskarutbildningen inom sex discipliner vid Stockholms universitet*, Stockholm: Carlsson.

al-Ghazzālī Muḥammad. (1989) *as-sunna an-nabawīya bayna ahl al-fiqh wa ahl al-ḥadīth*, Cairo: Dār ash-Shurūq.
—— (1990) *qaḍāyā l-marʾa*, Cairo: Dār ash-Shurūq.
—— (1991) *kayfa nataʿāmal maʿ al-qurʾān*, Herndon: International Institute for Islamic Thought.
al-Ghazzālī, Zainab. (1987) *ayām min ḥayātī*, Cairo: Dār ash-Shurūq.
—— (1994a) *naẓarāt fī kitāb allāh* vols. I and II, Cairo: Dār ash-Shurūq.
—— (1994b) *Return of the Pharaoh*, Leicester: The Islamic Foundation.
Gibb, H. A. R. and Kramers, J. H. (eds) (1974) (1953) *Shorter Encyclopaedia of Islam*, Leiden: E. J. Brill.
Göçek, Fatme Muge and Balaghi, Shiva (eds) (1994) *Reconstructing Gender in the Middle East*, New York: Columbia University Press.
Goffman, Erving. (1963) *Stigma*, London: Penguin Books.
Goldenberg, Naomi R. (1979) *Changing of the Gods*, Boston: Beacon Press.
Gordon, Milton, M. (1964) *Assimilation in American Life: The Role of Race, Religions and National Origins*, New York: Oxford University Press.
Greenberg, Blu. (1981) *On Women and Judaism: A View from Tradition*, Philadelphia: The Jewish Publication Society of America.
Guillaume, A. (1990) (1955) *The Life of Muhammad: A Translation of Ibn Ishaq's SIRAT RASUL ALLAH*, Karachi: Oxford University Press.
Habbe, Peter. (1997) 'The significance of definition in the study of religions', graduate dissertation thesis, The Institute of History of Religion, Lund University.
Hale, S. (1989) 'The politics of gender in the Middle East' in S. Morgan (ed.) *Gender and Anthropology: Critical Reviews for Research and Teaching*, Washington, DC: American Anthropological Association.
Hamadeh, Najla. (1996) 'Islamic family legislation: the authoritarian discourse of silence' in M. Yamani (ed.) *Feminism and Islam*, London: Ithaca Press.
Hampson, D. (1990) *Theology and Feminism*, Oxford: Blackwell.
Ḥasan, Aḥmad. (1984) (1978) *The Doctrine of ijmāʾ in Islam*, Islamabad: Islamic Research Institute Press.
Hassan, Riffat. (1990) 'An Islamic perspective' in J. Becher (ed.) *Women, Religion and Sexuality*, Geneva: World Council of Churches Publication.
Hastrup, Kirsten. (1992) 'Writing ethnography: state of art' in J. Okely and H. Callaway (eds) *Anthropology and Autobiography*, London: Routledge.
Hearn, Jeff. (1987) *The Gender of Oppression: Men, Masculinity, and the Critique of Marxism*, Brighton: Wheatsheaf.
Hedin, Christer. (1988) *Alla är födda Muslimer*, Uppsala: Verbum.
al-Hibri, Aziza (1982) 'A study of Islamic herstory: or how did we get into this mess?' in A. al-Hibri (ed.) *Women and Islam*, Oxford: Pergamon Press.
Hilāli, M. and Khān, M. M. (1993) *Interpretation of the Meaning of the Noble Qurʾan in the English Language*, Riadh: Maktaba Dār as-Salām.
Hitti, Philip. (1961) *History of the Arabs*, London: The Macmillan Press Ltd.
ḥizb at-taḥrīr. (1953) *ḥizb at-taḥrīr*.
—— (1963) *muqaddima ad-dustūr*.
—— (1985) *at-takātul al-ḥizbī*.
Hjärpe, Jan. (1983) *Politisk Islam*, Stockholm: Skeab Förlag.
—— (1988) 'The contemporary debate in the Muslim world on the definition of human rights' in *Islam, State, and Society*, London: Curzon Press, pp. 26–38.

—— (1993) 'Islamisk Rätt och diskussionen om Mänskliga Rättigheter' in *Retfærd* 60(16) Årgang, pp. 3–14.
—— (1994) *Araber och Arabism*, Stockholm: Rabén Prisma.
—— (1997) 'What will be chosen from the Islamic basket?' *European Review* 5(3), July, pp. 267–74.
—— (1998) 'Religionens 2 ansikten' *Forskning och Framsteg* 3, April, pp. 32–6.
Hofstadter, Douglas. (1985) *Metamagical Themas: Questing for the Essence of Mind and Pattern*, New York: Basic Books.
Horowitz, I. L. (1982) 'The new fundamentalism' in *Trans Action* 20(1), pp. 40–7.
Hourani, Albert. (1962) *Arabic Thought in the Liberal Age 1798–1939*, Cambridge: Cambridge University Press.
Huntington, Samuel P. (1996) *The Clash of Civilizations and the Remaking of World Order*, New York: Simon & Schuster.
al-Ḥusainī, Musa Isḥāq. (1956) *The Muslim Brethren: The Greatest of Modern Islamic Movements*, Beirut.
Hylland Eriksen, Thomas. (1994) 'Vad är norskt' in *Sydsvenska Dagbladet*, 27 February.
Ibn Ḥanbal, Aḥmad. (n.d.) *musnad aḥmad*, system *al-ʿālamī* CD-ROM, Jeddah: Company Sakhr al-ʿĀlamī.
Ibn Isḥāq. (1983) *The Life of Muhammad*, translated by A. Guillaume, Karachi: Oxford University Press.
Ibn Jawzī, Jamāl ad-Dīn. (1988) *kitāb aḥkām an-nisāʾ*, Beirut: Mu'assasa al-Maktab ath-Thaqāfīya.
Ibn Kathīr, ʿImād ad-Dīn. (1981) *mukhtasir tafsīr ibn kathīr* vols I–III, Beirut: Dār al-Qurʾān al-Karīm.
—— (1989) *tafsīr al-qurʾān al-ʿāẓīm* vols I–IV, Beirut: Dār al-Maʿrifa.
Ibn Majah. (n.d.) *sunan ibn majah*, system *al-ʿālamī*, CD-ROM, Jeddah: Company Sakhr al-ʿĀlamī.
Ibn Manẓūr, Jamāl ad-Dīn Muḥammad. (1955) (1882–90) *lisān al-ʿarab* vols I–XX, Cairo: Bulaq Misr.
Ibn Taimīya, Taqī ad-Dīn. (1972) (1391 AH) *kitāb al-imān*, Beirut: Maktab al-Islām.
Ibrahim, Sa'ad Eddin. (1984) *Palestine, Fundamentalism, and Liberalism*, Amman: Arab Thought Forum.
Imām Muslim. (1971) *Ṣaḥīḥ Muslim*, Beirut: Dar al-Arabia.
Inden, Ronald. (1990) *Imagining India*, Oxford and Cambridge, Mass.: Blackwell.
Jackson, Michael. (1989) *Path toward a Clearing: Radical Empiricism and Ethnographic Inquiry*, Indiana: Indiana University Press.
Jalbani, G. N. (1979) (1967) *Teachings of Shah Waliyullah of Delhi*, Lahore: Sh. Muhammad Ashraf, Kashmiri Bazar.
Jansson, Torsten. (1997) 'Den disciplinära religiösa organisationens metamorfologi', unpublished manuscript presented at a seminar at Lund University.
Jārullāh, ʿAbdullāh. (1983) (1404 AH) *masʾūlīya l-marʾa al-muslima*, Saudi Arabia: Ministry of Information.
Jawad, Haifaa A. (1998) *The Rights of Women in Islam: An Authentic Approach*, London: Macmillan Press Ltd.
Johnsdotter, S., Carlbom, A., Geesdiir, A. and Almi, A. (2000) *Som Gud Skapade Oss: Förhållningssätt till kvinnlig omskärelse bland Somalier: Malmö*, Malmö: Malmö Stads Program för Sexuell Hälsa.

Jones, Kenneth. (1978) 'Paradigm shifts and identity theory' in Hans Mol (ed.) *Identity and Religion*, London: Sage Studies in International Sociology 16.

Joseph, Suad. (1988) 'Feminization, familism, self, and politics: research as a Mughtaribi' in S. Altorki and C. F. El-Solh (eds) *Arab Women in the Field*, New York: Syracuse University Press.

al-Juwainī, ʿAbd al-Mālik. (n.d.) *al-burḥān fī ʾuṣūl al-fiqh*, Ms. 714, Cairo: Dār al-Kutub al-Miṣrīya.

Juynboll, G. H. A. (1983) *Muslim Tradition*, Cambridge: Cambridge University Press.

Kandiyoti, D. (1991) 'Islam and patriarchy' in N. R. Keddie and B. Baron (eds) *Women in Middle Eastern History: Shifting Boundaries in Sex and Gender*, New Haven and London: Yale University Press.

Karim, Wazir Jahan. (1992) *Women and Culture: Between Malay Adat and Islam*, Westview: Boulder.

—— (1995) (ed.) *'Male' and 'Female' in Developing Southeast Asia*, London: Berg Publishers.

Karmi, Ghada. (1996) 'Women, Islam and patriarchalism' in M. Yamani (ed.) *Feminism and Islam*, London: Ithaca Press.

Kassamali, Noor J. (1998) 'When modernity confronts traditional practices: female genital cutting in Northeast Africa' in *Women in Muslim Societies: Diversity within Unity*, London: Lynne Rienner Publishers.

Keller, Evelyn Fox. (1978) 'Gender and science' in *Psychoanalysis and Contemporary Thought* 1(3), pp. 409–33.

Keller, Noah. (1991) *The Reliance of the Traveller*, UAE: Modern Printing Press.

—— (1995) 'Which of the four orthodox madhhabs has the most developed fiqh for Muslims living as minorities' http://sunna.org/fiqh4htm.

Kepel, Gilles. (1985) *The Prophet and the Pharaoh*, London: Saqi Books.

—— (1993) *The Revenge of God: The Resurgence of Islam, Christendom and Judaism in the Modern World*, University Park, Pennsylvania: Pennsylvania State University Press and Oxford: Polity Press.

Khān, M. M. (1985) *The Translation of the Meanings of Sahih Al-Bukhari*, Medina: Islamic University.

Khān, Mawlāna Waḥīd ad-Dīn. (1986) *Tabligh Movement*, New Delhi: Ruskin House.

King, Ursula. (1995) *Religion and Gender*, Oxford and Cambridge, Mass.: Blackwell.

Knott, Kim. (1986) 'Religion and identity, and the study of ethnic minorities in Britain' in *Identity Issues and World Religions*, Australian Association for the Study of Religions at the South Australian College of Advanced Education.

Koya, Abd ar-Rahman (ed.) (1996) *Ḥadīth and Sunna: Ideals and Realities*, Kuala Lumpur: Islamic Book Trust.

Kucukcan, Talip. (1991) 'The nature of Islamic resurgences in Near and Middle Eastern Muslim societies' in *Hamdard*, Karachi.

Kuhn, Thomas. (1962) *The Structure of Scientific Revolutions*, Chicago: University of Chicago Press.

Laderman, Carol. (1991) *Taming the Wind of Desire*, Berkeley: University of California Press.

Larsen, Lena. (1995) *Velkommen til en Stor Familie: Islam: Konversjon i norsk kontekst*, unpublished theses in history of religion, University of Oslo.

Lawrence, Bruce. (1989) *Defenders of God: the Fundamentalist Revolt against the Modern Age*, San Francisco: Harper & Row.
Lewis, Bernard. (1984) *The Jews of Islam*, London: Routledge & Kegan Paul.
Liedman, Sven-Eric. (1997) *I Skuggan av Framtiden*, Stockholm: Bonnier Alba.
Lukes, Steven (ed.) (1986) *Power*, Oxford and Cambridge, Mass.: Blackwell.
Makdisi, Jean Said. (1996) 'The mythology of modernity: women and democracy in Lebanon' in Mai Yamani (ed.) *Feminism and Islam*, London: Ithaca Press.
Marcus, George E. and Fischer, Michael M. J. (1986) *Anthropology as Cultural Critique*, Chicago and London: University of Chicago Press.
al-Mawdūdī, A. A. (1965) *Tarjuman al-Qur'an* 62(5), January, Lahore: Islamic Publications (Pvt) Ltd.
—— (1972) *Purdah and the Status of Women in Islam*, Lahore: Islamic Publications (Pvt) Ltd.
Merchant, Carolyn. (1994) *The Death of Nature: Women, Ecology and the Scientific Revolution*, Stockholm: Symposion.
Mernissi, Fatima. (1975) *Beyond the Veil*, Cambridge: Schenkman.
—— (1987) *Women and Islam: An Historical and Theological Enquiry*, Oxford: Blackwell.
—— (1988) *Doing Daily Battle*, London: The Women's Press.
—— (1991) *The Veil and the Male Elite: A Feminist Interpretation of Women's Rights in Islam*, Reading, Mass.: Addison-Wesley.
The Minority Rights Group. (1985) report no. 47, London.
Mir-Hosseini, Ziba. (1993) *Marriage on Trial: A Study of Islamic Law, Iran and Morocco Compared*, London: Taurus.
Mitchell, Richard. (1969) *The Society of the Muslim Brothers*, Oxford: Oxford University Press.
Moghadam, V. M. (1990) *Gender, Development, and Policy: Toward Equity and Empowerment*, Helsinki: World Institute for Development Economics Research of the United Nations University.
Moir, Anne and Jessel, David. (1989) *Brain Sex: The Real Difference Between Men and Women*, London: Joseph.
Motzki, H. (1991) 'The *musannaf* of ʿAbd ar-Razzāq as-Sanʿānī as a source of authentic *aḥādīth* of the first century AH' in *Journal of Near East Studies* 50, pp. 1–21.
Muslim. (n.d.) *ṣaḥīḥ muslim*, system *al-ʿālamī* CD-ROM, Jeddah: Company Sakhr al-ʿĀlamī.
The Muslim Brotherhood. (1994) *The Role of Women in Islamic Society According to the Muslim Brotherhood*, London: International Islamic Forum.
The Muslim Brothers. (1989) '*an-niẓām al-ʿāmm lil-ikhwān al-muslimin*' in ʿAbdullāh Fahd (ed.) *al-ḥaraka al-islāmīya ruʾyat mustaqbalīya*, Cairo: Maktabat Madbūlī.
Mutalib, Hussin. (1990) *Islam and Ethnicity in Malay Politics*, Singapore: Oxford University Press.
Muzaffar, Chandra. (1987) *Islamic Resurgence in Malaysia*, Petaling Jaya.
Nagata, Judith. (1984) *Reflowering of Malaysian Islam*, Vancouver: University of British Columbia.
—— (1995) 'Modern Malay women and the message of the "veil"' in W. J. Karim (ed.) *'Male' and 'Female' in Developing Southeast Asia*, London: Berg Publishers.

an-Nafīsī, ʿAbdullāh Fahd (ed.) (1989) '*an-niẓām al-ʿāmm lil-ikhwān al-muslimin*' in *al-ḥaraka al-islāmīya: ruʾyat mustaqbalīya*, Cairo: Maktaba Madbūlī.

an-Nawawī, Muḥyī ad-Dīn (1976) *Forty Hadith*, Damascus: The Holy Koran Publishing House.

—— (1983) *Riyāḍ aṣ-Ṣāliḥīn*, Damascus: Dār ath-Thaqāfa al-ʿArabīya.

Nazlee, Sajda. (1996) *Feminism and Muslim Women*, London: Ta-Ha Publishers.

an-Nisāʾī. (n.d.) *sunan an-nisāʾī*, system *al-ʿālamī*, CD-ROM, Jeddah: Company Sakhr al-ʿĀlamī.

O'Connor, June. (1989) 'Rereading, reconceiving and reconstructing traditions: feminist research in religion' in *Women's Studies* 17(1), pp. 101–23.

Otterbeck, Jonas. (1997) 'Bilden av islam är mångfacetterad' in *Pedagogiska Magasinet* 3, Stockholm.

Ouis, Pernilla. (1997) 'McDonalds in Mecca', paper presented at a seminar at Lund University.

Philips, Abū Amīna Bilāl. (1988) *The Evolution of Fiqh*, Riadh: International Islamic Publishing House.

Plaskow, Judith. (1990) *Standing again at Sinai: Judaism from a Feminist Perspective*, San Francisco: Harper.

Pomeroy, Sarah B. (1975) *Goddesses, Whores, Wives, and Slaves: Women in Classical Antiquity*, New York: Schocken.

Price C. A. (1969) 'A study of assimilation' in J. A. Jackson (ed.) *Migration*, Cambridge: Cambridge University Press.

Pryce-Jones, David. (1992) *At War with Modernity: Islam's Challenge to the West*, London: Institute for European Defence and Strategic Studies.

Pye, E. M. (1979) 'On comparing Buddhism and Christianity' in *Studies 5*, University of Tsukuba, pp. 1–20.

al-Qaraḍāwī, Yūsuf. (1980) *at-tarbiya al-islāmīya wa madrasa ḥasan al-bannāʾ*, Beirut: Maktabat al-Falāḥ.

—— (1990) *kayfa nataʿāmal maʿ as-sunna an-nabawīya*, Herdnon: International Institute for Islamic Thought.

—— (1995) *Introduction to Know Islam*, Cairo: Islamic Inc.

—— (1996) *fatāwā muʿāṣira* (Contemporary Legal Decisions), Kuwait: Dār al-Qalam.

al-Qāsimī, Z. N. (1974) *al-hukm fīash-sharīʿa wa at-tarīkh*, Dār an-Nafāʾis, Beirut.

Quṭb, Muḥammad. (1985) *shubuhāt ḥawla al-islām*, Kuwait: Dār al-Qalam.

Quṭb, Sayyid. (1983) *maʿālim fī ṭ-ṭarīq*, Beirut: Maktabat al-Falāḥ.

—— (1986) *fī ḍalīl al-qurʾān* vols I–VII, Cairo: Dār ash-Shurūq.

Rabo, Annika. (1993) *Beyond the Veil: Gender, State and Development in Jordan and Syria*, unpublished paper, Linköping.

Raḥman, Fazlur. (1970) 'Revival and reform in Islam' in Ann Lambton and Bernard Lewis (eds) *The Cambridge History of Islam* vol. II, Cambridge: Cambridge University Press.

—— (1996) 'The Living Sunnah and *al-ṣunnah wa'l-jamāʿah*' in P. K. Koya (ed.) *Ḥadīth and Sunna: Ideals and Realities*, Kuala Lumpur: Islamic Book Trust.

Rambo, Lewis. (1993) *Understanding Religious Conversion*, New Haven and London: Yale University Press.

Rapoport, Amos. (1981) *Housing and Identity: Cross-cultural Perspectives*, ed. James S. Duncan, London: Croom Helm.

Ridd, Rosemary. (1994) 'Separate but more than equal' in C. F. El-Solh and J. Mabro (eds) *Muslim Women's Choices*, London: Berg Publishers.
Rippin, Andrew. (1990) *Muslims: Their Religious Beliefs and Practices*, vol. 1: *The Formative Period*, London: Routledge.
—— (1993) *Muslims: Their Religious Beliefs and Practices*, vol. II: *The Contemporary Period*, London: Routledge.
Roald, Anne Sofie. (1994) *Tarbiya: Education and Politics in Islamic Movements in Jordan and Malaysia*, Stockholm: Almqvist & Wiksell International.
—— (1998) 'Feminist reinterpretation of Islamic sources: Muslim feminist theology in the light of the Christian tradition of feminist thought' in Karin Ask and Marit Tjomsland (eds) *Women and Islamisation*, London: Berg Publishers pp. 17–44.
Roald, Anne Sofie and Ouis, Pernilla. (1997) 'Lyssna på männen: att leva i en patriarkalisk muslimsk kontext' in *Kvinnovetenskaplig Tidskrift*, pp. 91–108.
Rodinson, Maxime. (1991) *Europe and the Mystique of Islam*, London: University of Washington Press.
Rosaldo, Michelle Z. and Lamphere, Louise (eds) (1974) *Woman, Culture and Society*, Stanford: Stanford University Press.
Rosaldo, Renato. (1989) *Culture and Truth*, London: Routledge.
Rosander, Eva Evers. (1991) *Women in a Borderland: Managing Muslim Identity Where Morocco Meets Spain*, Stockholm: Stockholm Studies in Social Anthropology.
Ruether, R. R. (1983) (4th edition) *Sexism and God-Talk: Towards a Feminist Theology*, Boston: Beacon Press.
Sābiq, as-Sayyid. (1985) *fiqh as-sunna* vols I–III, Beirut: Dār al-Kitāb al-ʿArabī.
aṣ-Ṣabūnī, Muḥammad ʿAlī. (1981) *ṣafwa t-tafāsīr*, Beirut: Dār al-Qurʾān al-Karīm.
Said, Edward. (1979) *Orientalism*, London: Routledge & Kegan Paul.
—— (1981) *Covering Islam*, New York: Pantheon Books.
—— (1990) 'Reflections on exile' in Russell Ferguson, Martha Gever, Trinh T. Minh-ha and Cornel West (eds) *Out There, Marginalization and Contemporary Cultures*, Cambridge, Mass.: MIT Press.
Ṣāliḥ, Ṣubḥī. (1979) *mabāḥith fī ʿulūm al-qurʾān*, Beirut: Dār al-ʿIlm li l-Malāiīn.
Sanders, Åke. (1997) 'To what extent is the Swedish Muslim religious?' in Steven Vertovec and Ceri Peach (eds) *Islam in Europe: The Politics of Religion and Community*, Warwick: Centre for Research in Ethnic Relations, University of Warwick.
Saulat, Sarwat. (1979) *Maulana Maududi*, Karachi: International Islamic Publishers.
Schacht, Joseph. (1950) *The Origins of Muhammedan Jurisprudence*, Oxford: Claredon.
Schüssler Fiorenza, Elizabeth. (1983) *In Memory of Her*, London: SCM Press Ltd.
—— (ed.) (1994) *Searching the Scripture*, London: SCM Press Ltd.
Shaaban, Bouthana. (1995) 'The muted voices of women interpreters' in M. Afkhami (ed.) *Faith and Freedom: Women's Human Rights in the Muslim World*, London: I. B. Tauris Publishers, pp. 61–77.
Shalabī, Muḥammad Muṣṭafā. (1969) *al-madkhal fī t-taʿrīf bi l-fiqh al-islāmī*, Beirut: Dār an-Nahḍa al-ʿArabīya.
al-Sharastānī. (1910) *kitāb al-milāl wa n-niḥāl*, Cairo: Maktaba al-Azhar.

ash-Shaʿrāwī, Mutawallā Muḥammad. (n.d.) *al-marʾa fī l-qurān al-karīm.*
Sivan, E. (1992) 'Radical Islam' in A. Giddens (ed.) *Human Societies – An Introductory Reader in Sociology*, Cambridge: Polity Press, pp. 237–49.
Spellberg, Denise A. (1994) *Politics, Gender and the Islamic Past: The Legacy of ʿĀʾisha bint Abī Bakr*, New York: Columbia University Press.
Steedman, Carolyn. (1991) 'Living historically now?' in *Arena 97.*
Stoller, Paul and Olkes, Cheryl. (1987) *In Sorcery's Shadow*, Chicago: University of Chicago Press.
Stowasser, Barbara. (1994) *Women in the Qur'an, Traditions and Interpretation*, Oxford: Oxford University Press.
aṣ-Ṣuyūtī, Jalāl ad-Dīn. (n.d.) *al-itqān fī ʿulūm al-qurʾān* vols I and II, Beirut: Dār al-Fikr.
Svensson, Jonas. (1996) *Muslimsk Feminism*, Religio 46, Lund: Department of Theology.
aṭ-Ṭābarī, Abū Jaʿfar Muḥammad ibn Jarīr. (1994) *tafsīr aṭ-ṭabarī*, Beirut: al-Muʾassasa r-Risāla.
Taji-Farouki, Suha. (1996) *A Fundamental Quest: Hizb al-Tahrir and the Search for the Islamic Caliphate*, London: Grey Seal.
Thesiger, Wilfred. (1959) *Arabian Sands*, London: Longmans.
Tillion, Germaine. (1983) *The Republic of Cousins: Women's Oppression in Mediterranean Society*, London: Al Saqi Books (first edition in French 1966).
at-Tirmidhī. (n.d.) *sunan at-tirmidhī*, system *al-ʿālamī*, CD-ROM, Jeddah: Company Sakhr al-ʿĀlamī.
Tong, Rosemarie. (1992) *Feminist Thought: A Comprehensive Introduction*, London: Routledge.
at-Turābī, Ḥasan. (n.d.) *al-marʾa bayna taʿālīm ad-dīn wa taqālīd al-mujtamaʿ*, Jamaʿīya ar-Raʿāya wa l-Iṣlāḥ al-Ijtimāʿī.
—— (1990) *manhaj at-tashrīʿ al-islāmī*, Tunis: Dār aṣ-Ṣahwa li n-Nashr wa at-Tawzīʿ.
—— (1993) *Women in Islam and Muslim Society*, Nigeria: Islamic Education Trust.
Turner, Bryan. (1994) *Orientalism, Postmodernism and Globalism*, London: Routledge.
Turner, John C. and Giles, Howard (eds). (1981) *Intergroup Behaviour*, Oxford: Blackwell.
Tylor, Sir Edward. (1871) *Primitive Culture*, London: John Murray.
al-ʿUbaidī, A. J. (1991) *jamāʿat al-ikhwān al-muslimīn fī l-urdun wa falasṭīn 1945–1970*, Amman: Dār al-Furqān.
Vogt, Kari. (1995) *Kommet for å bli: Muslimer i Europa*, Oslo: J. W. Cappelens Forlag A.S.
Wadud-Muhsin, Amina. (1992) *Qur'an and Woman*, Kuala Lumpur: Penerbit Fajar Bakti SDN. BHD.
Waines, David. (1995) *An Introduction to Islam*, Cambridge: Cambridge University Press.
Wansbrough, John. (1977) *Quranic Studies: Sources and Methods of Scriptural Interpretation*, Oxford: Oxford University Press.
—— (1978) *The Sectarian Milieu: Content and Composition of Islamic Salvation History*, Oxford: Oxford University Press.
Weber, Max. (1977) *Vetenskap och Politik*, selected and translated by Aino and Sten Andersson, Göteborg: Korpen.

Weedon, Chris. (1987) *Feminist Practice and Poststructuralist Theory*, Oxford: Blackwell.
Wehr, Hans. (1980) *A Dictionary of Modern Written Arabic*, Beirut: Libraire du Liban.
Werbner, Pnina. (1990) (1961) *The Migration Process*, New York and Oxford: Berg Publishers.
Westerlund, D. and Hallencreutz, C. F. (eds) (1996) *Questioning the Secular State: The Worldwide Resurgence of Religion in Politics*, London: Hurts and Company.
Wikan, Unni. (1983) *I morgen, hvis Gud vil: Kvinneliv i Kairos Bakgater*, Oslo.
Winkel, Eric. (1995) 'A Muslim perspective on female circumcision' in *Women and Health*, 23(1), pp. 1–7.
Wright, W. (1981) *A Grammar of the Arabic Language*, Beirut:Libraire du Liban.
Yakan, Fatḥī. (1992) *mādha ya'nī intimā' li l-islām*, Beirut: Mu'assasa r-Risālā.
Yamani, Mai. (1996) *Feminism and Islam*. London: Ithaca Press.
az-Zarkashī, Badr ad-Dīn. (1970) (1939) *al-ijāba*, Beirut: al-Maktab al-Islāmī.
Zetterstéen, K.V. (1979) (1917) *Koranen*, Stockholm: Wahlström & Widstrand.
Zubaida, Sami. (1989) *Islam, the People, and the State*, London: Routledge.
az-Zuḥailī, Wahba. (1989) (1984) *al-fiqh al-islāmī wa adillatuhu* (*Islamic Jurisprudence and its Evidences*) vols I–VIII, Damascus: Dār al-Fikr.
az-Zuhairī, Abī al-Ashbāl. (1996) *mashrūīya al-khitān li banāt wa l-banīn*.
Zuhur, Sherifa. (1992) *Revealing Reveiling*, New York: State University of New York Press.

Newspapers

Guardian Weekly, 16 November 1997.
Khaleej Times, 8 March 1999.
Sydsvenska Dagbladet, 27 February 1994.

Interviews

Abū ar-Rashta, 'Aṭā, September 1991, Jordan.
al-Barāzī, Muḥammad Fu'ād, November 1998, Denmark/Sweden.
Darsh, Muḥammad, December 1995, London, UK.
al-Ghannūshī, Rāshid, December 1995, Manchester, UK.
al-Ghazzālī al-Jubailī, Zainab, March 1997, Cairo.
Ḥussain, Fu'ād, December 1995, Manchester, UK.
al-Imām, Aḥmad 'Alī, May 1998, Khartoum, Sudan.
al-Mahdī, Wiṣāl, December 1997, Sana'a, Yemen.
al-Qaraḍāwī, Yūsuf, December 1998, Duha, Qatar.
at-Turābī, Ḥasan, August 1996, Khartoum, Sudan.

Index

g indicates a glossary definition